LIFE IS A DREAM

Paul Durcan

Life is a Dream

40 Years Reading Poems
1967–2007

Harvill *Secker*
LONDON

Published by Harvill Secker 2009

2 4 6 8 10 9 7 5 3 1

Copyright © Paul Durcan 2009

Paul Durcan has asserted his right under the Copyright,
Designs and Patents Act 1988 to be identified as the author of this work

First published in Great Britain in 2009 by
HARVILL SECKER
Random House, 20 Vauxhall Bridge Road
London SW1V 2SA

www.rbooks.co.uk

Addresses for companies within The Random House Group Limited can be found at:
www.randomhouse.co.uk/offices.htm

The Random House Group Limited Reg. No. 954009

A CIP catalogue record for this book is available from the British Library

ISBN 9781846550249

The Random House Group Limited supports The Forest Stewardship
Council (FSC), the leading international forest certification organisation. All our titles
that are printed on Greenpeace approved FSC certified paper carry the FSC logo. Our
paper procurement policy can be found at www.rbooks.co.uk/environment

Mixed Sources
Product group from well-managed
forests and other controlled sources
www.fsc.org Cert no. TT-COC-2139
© 1996 Forest Stewardship Council
FSC

Typeset by Palimpsest Book Production Limited,
Grangemouth, Stirlingshire
Printed and bound in Great Britain by
Clay, Ltd, St Ives plc

Contents

TERESA'S BAR (1976)

SAM'S CROSS (1978)

JESUS, BREAK HIS FALL (1980)

JUMPING THE TRAIN TRACKS WITH ANGELA (1983)

THE BERLIN WALL CAFÉ (1985)

*

GOING HOME TO RUSSIA (1987)

*

*

DADDY, DADDY (1990)

*

*

CRAZY ABOUT WOMEN (1991)

THE LAUGHTER OF MOTHERS (2007)

*

Foreword

This book is a retrospective. For as long as I can remember I have regarded the publication of each volume of my verse as being akin to an exhibition. That is to say, I no more imagined that every poem was of equal value, much less worthy of preservation, than an artist would look upon every artwork as being of equal value and worthy of preservation.

When T. S. Eliot made an LP recording of *Four Quartets* for EMI in 1957, he wrote his own liner notes in which he stated that if a reader wishes to know the "exact notation of the author's metric", the reader must hear the poet's own recitation; punctuation, metre, enjambment, he wrote, are not enough. "The chief value of the author's recording, then, is as a guide to the rhythms."

So it is that I have spent forty years giving readings of my poetry; sometimes in pleasant places, sometimes in not so pleasant places, mostly in my native country but occasionally in other countries and other continents. I dread the act of reading and its circumstance, but I know, as Eliot asserted, that public reading is the life blood of the art of poetry.

I have given many hundreds, perhaps thousands of readings over forty years, but there has been no LP. In this, as in so much else, my hero T. S. Eliot has left me standing.

This book is the first collection of my work, and I have made it knowing that it is unlikely there will be another in my lifetime.

PAUL DURCAN
Dublin / Mayo
February–March 2009

Acknowledgements

I wish to thank Michael Coady and Harry Clifton for their advice. I would like also to thank Pádraic Carr, without whose gratuitous kindness, when the author fell ill, this book could not have been assembled.

To Monika and Cyril Murray, Catriona Crowe, Michael Murphy, Boyan Georgiev and Ivor Browne, who came to my aid during the preparation of the book when my roof collapsed in heavy rain, I owe debts that cannot be repaid.

I am, I think, perhaps the most perfect stranger present.
ARTHUR HUGH CLOUGH, *The Bothie of Tober-na-Vuolich*

ENDSVILLE (1967)

The White Window

Of my love's body I think
That it is a white window.
Her clothes are curtains:
By day drawn over
To conceal the light;
By night drawn back
To reveal the dark.

O WESTPORT IN THE LIGHT OF ASIA MINOR (1975)

Nessa

I met her on the first of August
In the Shangri-La Hotel,
She took me by the index finger
And dropped me in her well.
And that was a whirlpool, that was a whirlpool,
And I very nearly drowned.

Take off your pants, she said to me,
And I very nearly didn't;
Would you care to swim? she said to me,
And I hopped into the Irish Sea.
And that was a whirlpool, that was a whirlpool,
And I very nearly drowned.

On the way back I fell in the field
And she fell down beside me,
I'd have lain in the grass with her all my life
With Nessa:
She was a whirlpool, she was a whirlpool,
And I very nearly drowned.

O Nessa my dear, Nessa my dear,
Will you stay with me on the rocks?
Will you come for me into the Irish Sea
And for me let your red hair down?
And then we will ride into Dublin City
In a taxi-cab wrapped up in dust.
Oh you are a whirlpool, you are a whirlpool,
And I am very nearly drowned.

Gate 8

for Nessa

Lean your behind on the departure gate
For to clown out of the wound of separation
With Ali smile and Ali shuffle:
Such was the advice and such was how
We kept each other from feeling low.

What do you make of the Bunny Beds I mean
The Bunny Clubs? Tails
I love you, heads I don't. The dead
Are pure was what my father said
The night he swapped his wife for lead.

I am afraid to ask if they are the shoes
Bought you by your mother yesterday.
FLIGHT 118 TO LONDON: BOARDING NOW.
Come to London: I will, I will.
And the poet's stone fell up the hill.

Is there no end to corridors?
Thank God you did not turn to wave.
They would not allow me on the roof
So right then I took a return coach
Into the darkening city.

Rain and the streets emptied
Of people and you.
What am I to think?
Of the man inside the TV man
Propped on the seat behind

Tell-telling the outside man
To produce *The Playboy of the Western World*
On an ice rink with an all-negro cast?
Yes and of no and the sky
That holds you now. I doubt

If you love me and . . . you know
My footwork's not good and my eyes cut bad.

On a BEA Trident Jet

The shadows of the Pyrenees on the clouds,
Husbands awake about sleeping wives,
These are the regions beyond calculation,
Your wife is sleeping because she is your wife.

A marriage is a March overture to superstition
And then when you lose it – your life –
And pieces of it are washed up on some foreign shore
People will know it was yours.

Hymn to Nessa

Climbing back over to zero
I nearly fell over the sea;
Climbing back over to zero
The sea fell over me.

Behind me on the sea shore Nessa lay;
She is the red sun at nightfall.
Behind me on the sea shore Nessa lay;
Watching me walk out to sea.

I looked back and saw her wave towards me;
She burned through her eyes.
I looked back and saw her wave towards me;
Her face burning in coals.

Behind her a cliff stood with grass on it;
She lay at the base of the cliff.
Behind her a cliff stood with grass on it;
She waved from the base of the cliff.

She waved and she waved and she waved;
She lay down and shuttered her eyes.
She waved and she waved and she waved;
Shuttering her eyes in the sun.

When I looked back again she was not gone;
She was sleeping under the sun.
When I looked back again she was not gone;
She was sleeping under the sun.

Le Bal

And around John Keats and around
Life the Ballerina spun
And faster
Until she was no more than her spinning:
A delirious circumference, a freezing absence,
Inside of which – not even *he* could breathe.

O Westport in the Light of Asia Minor

I

Feet crossed, arms behind his head,
God lay below the skyline hidden from sight;
And Gauloise smoke trailed up the sky.

British frocks and dresses lay draped on the rocks,
Grey flashing windows of a nineteenth-century boutique,
While on the sands the girls lay lazily on their sides
All moon in the daylight
Musing "What is he like?" but at the back of their minds
The heart raged on:
Flame seamed with all the scorn of a soldier
Saying "After the battle."

II

But often the Reek would stand with a cloud round its head;
Behind the sky stood God with a cleaver raised;
Yet when cocky men peered round the curtain of sky
There was no god and the mists came,

Lay down on the west coast,
Fur off the back of a graveyard,
As if an ape had got the tedium of a thousand years between his
    maulers
And shoved it across the world onto our land:
The mists put the fear of our mother into us:
I am what I am for fear of hiding in the action
And yet –

If this world is not simply atmosphere pierced through and
    through
With the good doubt,
Then here it was Red Riding Hood who was laid up in bed;
It was Red-Eared Black Tongue who crouched at the bedside;
And she did the child no harm but good.

But there were some who had guts, took action and stayed;
And standing on the mountains of their dread saw
The islands come up through the mists –
Seductive garments that a man might dream of –
And with the islands finally the sun;
Black at the edges, pure red at the centre.

They came at a run down the mountain
Landing with such falls that even the few small hard gold
    pieces in their pockets
Smashed into pieces so infinitesimal that not even a Shylock
    ever would find them;
They came starting out of their breeches out onto the stony
    shore,
The sea was a great unnamed flower whose leaves they stood
    under
And danced to ring upon ring;
Thin prickly bearded men casting ridiculousness to the multitude,
Casting it in great armfuls made bountiful by the slow and
    graceful whirling of their arms,
And they sang: As if a rock were naked.

Phoenix Park Vespers

I

A man hiking the roads or tramping the streets
Has elegies for hills and epitaphs for houses
But his wife, while she has thought only for the ultimate
    destination
And is much more strict about weekly attendance at church,
Has much less belief in an afterlife or in heaven –
Thus under the conifers of the Phoenix Park,
Under the exceedingly lonely conifers of the Phoenix Park,
Under their blunt cones and amidst their piercing needles,
I squatted down and wept;
I who have but rarely shed a tear in sorrow.

The hurriedly-emptying October evening skies neither
    affirmed nor denied
A metaphysics of sex
But reflected themselves merely in the fields below
As flocks of kindred groups, courting couples, and footballers,
Old men, and babes, and loving friends,
And youths and maidens gay,
Scattered for homes.

The floor where I crouched was lit up by litters
Of the terracotta cones
And in the darkness at the heart of the wood
Kids played at giants and gnomes.
A woman (of whom I was so fond I actually told her so),
Not as a query but as a rebuke
Said to me: "What are you thinking?"
And I knew that whatever I said she would add
Half-coyly, mockingly, coaxingly:
"O my dear little *buachaillín*, but it is all one;
Enough of Baudelaire, there *is* no connection."

II

I think now of her face as of a clock
With the long hand passing over her eyes
But passing over backwards as well as forwards,
To and fro – like a speedometer needle.
And this long hand, where once was her hound-like nose,
At once tells the time and points a warning finger;
Warning me to bear in mind that while the cradle is but a grave
The grave is not a cradle but is for ever.
And while her iron voice clanks tonelessly away
Her face grows blacker under her heaped-over hair;
And I see that all church architecture is but coiffure
And all mystical entrances are through women's faces.
She opens her mouth and I step out onto her ice-pink tongue
To be swallowed up for ever in the womb of time.

In the Springtime of Her Life My Love Cut Off Her Hair

She rat-tat-tatted on the glass-paned door of our flat-roofed
    suburban home
And I unlatched it with much faith as ever and before;
But when I saw what she had done I knew pain to the marrow
    bone
And saw that all I had written and worked for was no more.
For what Keats said of his long poem was true of my love's
Auburn hair – smoke in autumn but redder
Than down-goings of carrot suns on summer's eves –
"A place to wander in" in figures-of-eight along somnambulent
    rivers.
From that day on – in April cruel as ever –
A figure-of-eight was severed and I am sleepless
In a Chinese prison of all-human loneliness
In which I cannot sleep but think, think of her
As she was and – cut off from the Tree of Life – ignobly pine.
I loved her for her auburn hair and not herself alone.

The Daughters Singing to Their Father

Now he will grope back into the abode and crouch down;
Another dry holocaust in the suburban complex over;
Over another stagger home along the semi-detached gauntlet;
Another day done. It has never not been,
Not even on worse days when only grave-dark was craved for.
He will crouch down and whether the night
Be starry or not
He will behold no stillness take shape upon his knees;
Nor rainbow book nor snow-white cat;
Nor will that woman of women, fire of fires – the one of the old
    smile
Breaking out in sheet gold in her cave-red hair –
Hover near, nor turn the page over
For her votary in the broken chair.
No matter what bedlam or vacuum the night may rear
He will hear only his daughters singing to him
From behind the arabic numerals of the clock:
"There is no going back, boy, there is no going back."
Long will he gaze into the clock, and to that last spouse
Under the skyline – for his daughters give thanks.

The Nun's Bath

I drink to the middle of it all.
Between the sandhills,
The sandhills between the hayfields and the sea,
There stood a tub and in it
A buxom nun who scrubbed herself as if
The early morning air was itself the water –
A water dance that was being wound
Round her by a yellow duck.

Now here in this gruesome London pub
I make myself the middle of it all.
I know that when I stand to get my beer
Another nomad may well steal my stool;

And let the barmaid be mournful if she will.
My job is to be present which I am.
There is the day ahead with more or less agony
Than to suffer all day in the Convent of Mercy.

Combe Florey

to Laura Waugh

Wilderness that not always would deliver:
But to us come from the hot clink of London
It was Tel Aviv, the Hill of Spring and Garden of the Sea
To wake in the morning and to hear the stillness –
And that in spite or because of
The racket of birds – more than one
Woodpecker inhabited the oak outside my window
And at six each morning wound up their clocks in a loud manner
Not to speak of the woodpigeon, the cuckoo, the others
Whose names I do not know.
I said to the woman of the house in my own painful and
    boulder fashion:
It is a crying shame to be a creature of this earth
And not know the names of the birds in the trees
And yet I know the names of fifty motor cars.
She said: Lord, I do not think I know the name of even one of
    the little creatures.
And so saying, she gave tiny feet back to my boulder and pain.

Please Stay in the Family, Clovis

Please stay in the family, Clovis:
The tawny curtains in the front parlour –
Though we do not use that room –
Would somehow not look quite the same
Without you – when you get married
We could put the presents in the front parlour –
Blankets pillowcases teaspoons carvers –
All in a row on the sideboard:

No better or more thoughtful present
Than a quality set of carvers, Clovis:
Why – you and Olive and (DV) your children
Could live here with us:
All it would mean would be a bit more cleaning
And do not snap back that I am only just dreaming:
I'm talking about reality Clovis:
And we still would not have to use the front parlour:
Love Mother.

Black Sister

Black sister with an afro halo round your head
And a handbag by your side and a string of beads,
Watching for news from a newsreel in the dark
Of the television lounge of a country hotel,
You are lean, tall and fruitful as a young beech
And seductive as the tree of knowledge
But – forgive me, this *is* the millennium to enquire –
Is that not you yourself stepping across the screen
Out of missionary fields into a country courthouse
Machine gun firing from your thigh, and freedom
On your dying lips?
But you are whispering to me tonight:
O Acton, let us be ambiguous tonight.

Instead you are cooped up in Ireland in a small hotel
Waiting for your boy whose magic daddy
Though no niggard to mission fields at Sunday Mass
Is not standing for his son to hitch up with a black bitch
Even if she's a Catholic virgin.
She's black and therefore a whore.
And electric mammy, than whom there is no more fiercesome
Drum-beater for black babies,
Short-circuited when she glimpsed the sun dancing halo round
    your head.
But you're a patient girl –
While over dark deep well waters lit up by huge arc lights
You are whispering to me tonight:
O Acton, let us be ambiguous tonight.

November 30, 1967

to Katherine

I awoke with a pain in my head
And my mother standing at the end of the bed;
"There's bad news in the paper," she said,
"Patrick Kavanagh is dead."

After a week which was not real
At last I settled down to a natural meal;
I was sitting over a pint and a beef sandwich
In Mooney's across the street from the Rotunda.

By accident I happened to tune in
To the conversation at the table from me;
I heard an old Northsider tell to his missus
"He was pure straight, God rest him, not like us."

They Say the Butterfly is the Hardest Stroke

to Richard Riordan

From coves below the cliffs of the years
I have dipped into *Ulysses*,
A Vagrant, Tarry Flynn –
But for no more than ten minutes or a page;
For no more than to keep in touch
With minds kindred in their romance with silence.
I have not "met" God, I have not "read"
David Gascoyne, James Joyce, or Patrick Kavanagh:
I believe in them.
Of the song of him with the world in his care
I am content to know the air.

La Terre des Hommes

Fancy meeting *you* out here in the desert:
Hallo Clockface.

Aughawall Graveyard

Lonely lonely lonely lonely:
The story with a middle only.

Ireland 1972

Next to the fresh grave of my belovèd grandmother
The grave of my first love murdered by my brother.

The Girl with the Keys to Pearse's Cottage

to John and Judith Meagher

When I was sixteen I met a dark girl;
Her dark hair was darker because her smile was so bright;
She was the girl with the keys to Pearse's Cottage;
And her name was Cáit Killann.

The cottage was built into the side of a hill;
I recall two windows and cosmic peace
Of bare brown rooms and on whitewashed walls
Photographs of the passionate and pale Pearse.

I recall wet thatch and peeling jambs
And how all was best seen from below in the field;
I used sit in the rushes with ledger-book and pencil
Compiling poems of passion for Cáit Killann.

Often she used linger on the sill of a window;
Hands by her side and brown legs akimbo;
In sun-red skirt and moon-black blazer;
Looking toward our strange world wide-eyed.

Our world was strange because it had no future;
She was America-bound at summer's end.
She had no choice but to leave her home –
The girl with the keys to Pearse's Cottage.

O Cáit Killann, O Cáit Killann,
You have gone with your keys from your own native place.
Yet here in this dark – El Greco eyes blaze back
From your Connemara postman's daughter's proudly mortal face.

Dún Chaoin

for Bob, Angela, and Rachel, in Nigeria

I was standing at the counter
In a bar at the world's end.
The large weathered man behind it
Was more native to the place than the place itself.
His father's fathers . . .
A big blue man like that, I thought, could not be strange
With a stranger
So when he did not speak
An old fear whistled through me:
I am not welcome in this place.
I kept a grip on my pint glass
And my eyes to the left of me
Gripping the bay window and outside
The red sun at nightfall
In the same plane as the bar room
Descending the window pane.
Its going down took about as long
As it takes a boy or girl to climb down a tree.
Gone and not long after
I thought I could hear

A long-lost music long lost from the earth
And as I looked up from the counter, shaking my head,
The big man too was shaking his, birds and tears
Falling out of the rafters of his eyes. The both of us
Laughed and he turned up the volume
Of his openly concealed battered old wireless,
Telefunken,
And when we were going out he said: Good night
And may God bless you on the road.
I went out willing to sleep on mountainsides anywhere,
Fearing no man or beast, machine or mist.

The Day of the Starter

I have known Donal Dowd these forty years.
He may well be the biggest butcher in town
But I mind the day – and it breaks my heart
To mind it – when he was a messenger boy
Down in the abbatoir.
I may say, men, he is the same man
Today as he was forty years ago,
Except of course for the casa on the hill
His wife and six daughters.
Donal Dowd has given that woman everything – every
Conceivable gadget on this earth –
Walkie-talkie dishwasher, clothes washer, carpet washer.
No, love is love: each
Morning as he starts the Rover 2000 with the automatic gears
He revs thrice for the wife.
She, beaming from the rear, shrieks after him into the exhaust:
"Oh, he's a perfect starter, he's my beau."

The Limerickman that Went to the Bad

Well, fellas, as ye all know, I'm a Limerick stalwart
Who was chosen for the British Lions team for South Africa
And I went out there – but to play football not politics.
One night after a function in J-Burg

A Limerick exile came up to me and flung his maulers
    around me
And naturally I thought I was amongst one of our own.
But d'ye know what he said – looking funny-like out of his
    headlights –
He said: "I've just seen two young glorious African gentlemen
Playing handball in church."
And with that he deliberately poured his entire pint glass of
    lager
Over my head.
I was not surprised to find out later that he was a spoilt priest
And that no sooner had he landed in South Africa
Than he had started cohabiting with a coloured skivvy.
Like all Limerickmen that go to the bad he had a history.
But for sheer blasphemy, can you imagine anything more
    fucking blasphemous
Than two coloureds playing handball in church? Jasus.

The Night They Murdered Boyle Somerville

As I was travelling one morning in an empty carriage
On a train passing south through the west
A small old woman with her husband who was smaller
Hobbled in, shut the door and sat down.
They told me they were going home to Skibbereen,
That they were old-age pensioners and proud of it
Enjoying free travel up and down the country.
They sat down opposite me and we conversed
When it suited us
Such was the ease with which we comported our silences.
Outside, the fields in their summer, lay on their sides in the sun,
Their season of flashing over.
Nor did we evade each other's eyes
Nor pronounce solutions to the awful war-in-progress
Except by a sign-language acknowledging
That here was the scar that lay *inside* the wound,
The self-betrayal beyond all chat.
And all this ease and all this sombre wisdom came
Not from me who am not by nature wise

But from the two old-age pensioners in their seventies.
He was a king-figure from out the islands of time,
A short round-shouldered man with a globe of a skull
Whose lips were the lips of an African chieftain
Having that expression from which there is no escape,
A gaze of the lips,
Interrupted only by the ritual blowing of an ancient pipe.
His wife – being a queen – told him to put away his pipe;
Did he not see the sticker on the windowpane?
It said *"Ná Caith Tobac"* – but he did not hear her
No more than he heard the ticket inspector
Who having failed to draw attention to the warning notice
Withdrew apologetically, apologising for the intrusion.
So, while the old man blew on his walnut plug
His wife gazed out the window and so did I.
When she spoke, she spoke of the old times and the *scoraíocht*
Back in Skibbereen and of the new times and the new words.
"Ah but," he interposed, glaring out into the blue-walled sky,
"I found out what was in it, and was not in it,
The night they murdered Boyle Somerville;
I knew then that it was only the sky had a roof."
Whereupon beads of sweat trembled on his upper lip
Between the black bristles of his pouring flesh.
Here was an old man, fit to humble death.

1972

Tribute to a Reporter in Belfast, *1974*

Poets, is not this solitary man's own uniquely
Utilitarian technique of truth-telling,
This finely apparent effort of his
To split the atom of a noun and reach truth through language,
To chip-carve each word and report
As if language itself were the very conscience of reality –
A poetry more
Than poetry is.
Tonight once more he has done his work with words
And fish roots and echoes of all manner and kind
Did flower up out of an ocean-floor resonance

So rapidly but with such clarity
That you were made to look out of the eyes of another
Even as the other shot you dead in the back,
Out of the eyes of a Catholic republican
Whose grandparents were Quakers in Norwich,
But likewise out of the eyes
Of a seventeenth-century Norfolkman in Virginia
Sailing a copper knife through the soft pink air
Of an Indian's open mouth . . .

Gratias for the verbal honesty of Liam Hourican
In a country where words also have died an unnatural death
Or else have been used on all sides for unnatural ends
And by poets as much as by gunmen or churchmen.
Day and night his integrity of words has sustained us.

Letter to Ben, 1972

4 The Terrace, at the Ridge of the Two Air-Demons, Co Leitrim

It is half-past nine on a July night
The town's, and the emperor's, artillery are outside,
Are all perched up inside an ocean wave that's riding –
Along with the weed-adorned boards of sunlight, filthy jewels
    and millefiori refuse –
Sea breezes that themselves are riding into each other at right
    angles
Across this broken street we call *The Terrace*;
And there is grass growing in the sand and old Ben
Is stretched out happily in a sunny corner too – never again
Will he or I be a cause of fright to each other;
We're on the same side, just different sides of the ocean.

Come on up, Ben, take a seat in the gods,
The roof has at least three-quarters blown off,
Even the grey pools by the bridge cannot help
But be motherfathers to wildflowers
And all the wild animals too, including ourselves, the bear and
    the fox,

Whom tycoons thought to cage,
Have broke grave and cursed no one:
We know the mines will produce in their own time
Abundance:
Iron hills in the east
And gold in the north-west.

Oh such light from the east, Ben,
And it is only half-past nine on a summer's night.
Darkness has entered already the arena
Trampling the manure-larded sand and straw
With all her young splendour more bare and ebony than before;
Her ceremonial chains proclaiming no escape nor for the
    spectator.
So, in history, the ridge becomes deserted now and then:
Right now, just you and me, Ben, and the species.

TERESA'S BAR *(1976)*

The Difficulty that is Marriage

We disagree to disagree, we divide, we differ;
Yet each night as I lie in bed beside you
And you are faraway curled up in sleep
I array the moonlit ceiling with a mosaic of question marks;
How was it I was so lucky to have ever met you?
I am no brave pagan proud of my mortality
Yet gladly on this changeling earth I should live for ever
If it were with you, my sleeping friend.
I have my troubles and I shall always have them
But I should rather live with you for ever
Than exchange my troubles for a changeless kingdom.
But I do not put you on a pedestal or throne;
You must have your faults but I do not see them.
If it were with you, I should live for ever.

She Mends an Ancient Wireless

You never claimed to be someone special;
Sometimes you said you had no special talent;
Yet I have seen you rear two dancing daughters
With care and patience and love unstinted;
Reading or telling stories, knitting gansies
And all the while holding down a job
In the teeming city, morning until dusk.
And in the house when anything went wrong
You were the one who fixed it without fuss;
The electricity switch which was neither on nor off,
The TV aerial forever falling out;
And now as I watch you mend an ancient wireless
From my tiny perch I cry once more your praises
And call out your name across the great divide – Nessa.

Two in a Boat

She took one oar and I took the other
But mine had slipped from me when she pulled on hers;
And then when at last I had got a grip
She had raised hers in victory glittering over sable waters,
The sun merely accentuating victory's glitter in each pearly
    globule.
And so we pulled in opposite directions,
Drifting out of quarrels into accidents and out of accidents into
    quarrels.
I thought of our two children in another country and of their
    being free
From their parents until came a collision
With two other frail craft and later
Drifting onto a grass bank we had to be pushed out into the sun
    again.
But the sun did not alter the pattern until out of the blue
Came glorious fresh rain
And pulling in opposite directions we reached land again.

Anna Swanton

I met her on the road to Ballavary;
She asked me why do boys always hurry;
And when I told her I had the train to take
She turned and said she'd come and wave goodbye.

Along that wide road blue green and dusty
That lopes along the land to Ballavary
I listened to her words come over to me
As from over the most deserted ancient valley.

We walked along the platform at Ballavary;
I stopped to pluck daisies to make a chain;
I put it round her neck and though it parted
I did not make another for we have not.

For the train no more stopped at Ballavary;
It had stopped for the last time the week before;
Next year we got the stationmaster's cottage
And our children are growing up playing real trains.

And yet although I live in terror of the tracks
For fear that they should prove our children's grave
I live in greater terror of the thought
Of life without Anna Swanton on this earth;

Or of how I might be rich in far-off Nottingham
And married to another kind of woman.
I'd rather rain for ever in the fields with Anna Swanton
Than a car or a goddess in the sun.

Wife Who Smashed Television Gets Jail

"She came home, my Lord, and smashed in the television;
Me and the kids were peaceably watching *Kojak*
When she marched into the living room and declared
That if I didn't turn off the television immediately
She'd put her boot through the screen;
I didn't turn it off, so instead she turned it off –
I remember the moment exactly because Kojak
After shooting a dame with the same name as my wife
Snarled at the corpse – Goodnight, Queen Maeve –
And then she took off her boots and smashed in the television;
I had to bring the kids round to my mother's place;
We got there just before the finish of *Kojak*;
(My mother has a fondness for *Kojak*, my Lord);
When I returned home my wife had deposited
What was left of the television into the dustbin,
Saying – I didn't get married to a television
And I don't see why my kids or anybody else's kids
Should have a television for a father or mother,
We'd be much better off all down in the pub talking
Or playing bar-billiards –
Whereupon she disappeared off back down again to the pub."
Justice O'Brádaigh said wives who preferred bar-billiards to family
    television

Were a threat to the family which was the basic unit of society
As indeed the television itself could be said to be a basic unit of
    the family
And when as in this case wives expressed their preference in forms
    of violence
Jail was the only place for them. Leave to appeal was refused.

Teresa's Bar

We sat all day in Teresa's Bar
And talked, or did not talk, the time away;
The only danger was that we might not leave sober
But that is a price you have to pay.
Outside in the rain the powers-that-be
Chemist, draper, garda, priest
Paced up and down in unspeakable rage
That we could sit all day in Teresa's Bar
"Doing nothing."

Behind the bar it was often empty;
Teresa, like all of us,
Besides doing nothing
Had other things to do
Such as cooking meals
Or washing out underwear
For her mad father
And her madder husband,
Or enduring their screams.

But Teresa deep down had no time for time
Or for those whose business has to do with time;
She would lean against the bar and smile through her weariness
By turns being serious and light with us;
Her eyes were birds on the waves of the sea;
A mother-figure but also a sun-girl;
An image of tranquillity but of perpetual creation;
A process in which there is no contradiction
For those with guts not to be blackmailed by time.
There is no time in Teresa's Bar;
The Garda Síochána or the Guardia Civil –
The Junior Chamber or the Roman Curia –

The Poetry Society or the GAA –
The Rugby Club or the Maynooth Hierarchy –
RTE or Conor's Cabaret –
It makes no difference in Teresa's Bar
Where the air is as annotated with the tobacco smoke of
    inventiveness
As the mind of a Berkleyan philosopher.

The small town abounds with rumours
About Teresa's Bar;
A hive of drug-takers (poor bees)
A nest of fornicators (poor birds)
Homosexual not to mention heterosexual;
Poor birds and bees trapped in metaphors of malice.
The truth is that here, as along by the path
By the river that flows along by the edge of the town,
Young and old meet in a life-obtaining sequence
Of days interspersed by nights, seasons by seasons,
Deaths by deaths;
While the members of the resurrection of judgement
Growl and scowl behind arrases in drawing rooms
Here are the members of the resurrection of life
And their tutelary goddess is Teresa
Thirty-five, small, heavy, and dark,
And who would sleep with any man who was honest enough
Not to mouth the platitudes of love;
A sensual woman, brave and true,
Bringer of dry wisdom and free laughter
As well as of glasses and bowls,
And who has sent forth into the hostile world
Persons whose universal compassion is infinitesimally more
    catholic
Than that of any scion of academe
Such as James Felix Hennessy
Who has been on the dole for sixteen years
As well as making poems and reading books
And who when accused of obscenity
By the Right Rev. Fr O'Doherty
Riposted with all the humility of Melchisedech:
"You must learn the reality of the flesh, Father;
You must learn the reality of the flesh."

If there be a heaven
Heaven would be
Being with Teresa
Inside the rain;
So let's lock up the bar, Teresa,
Lay ourselves on the floor,
Put some more coal on the fire,
Pour ourselves each a large whiskey;
Let's drink to Teresa of Teresa's Bar
Reclining on the floor with one of her boys,
And big black coals burning bright,
And yellowest whiskey in a brown bottle,
And outside a downpour relentlessly pouring down.

Polycarp

Polycarp has quit the priesthood
And he is living back at home;
He wears a smile upon his lips
That blooms from the marrow bone.

It's a smile that flowers and withers
Like fruit upon a tree;
In winter he stands at corners
In the streets all nakedly.

They are waxing pretty angry –
Are Respectability's crew;
It's a crime against all decency
To be one of the very few

Who has had courage like Polycarp
To be his own sweet self;
Not to mind the small town sneers
When they call him a "fucking elf"

Or the do-it-yourself-men boors
Who despise men with feminine souls;
Boors who when they were boys
Spoke of girls as "ruddy holes"

And now who are married and proper
Living up on Respectability Hill
And in their spare time make their own coffins
Which they use first as coffee tables.

But Polycarp polkas the streets
As free and easy as he feels;
Sometimes he walks on his toes,
Sometimes on his heels.

Yet they'll put him upon his knees
In the amphitheatre soon;
But his smile will wear them down
By the blood-light of the moon;

And in summer's golden rains
He'll burst out in fruit all over;
She's here, she's here, she's here;
And it is Polycarp that knows how to love her.

Swags of red apples are his cheeks;
Swags of yellow pears are his eyes;
Foliages of dark green oaks are his torsos;
And in the cambium of his bark juice lies.

Desire under the steeples and spires,
Polycarp's back in town;
Desire under the steeples and spires,
Polycarp's back in town.

Lord Mayo

I had to go and work in officeblocks in Shepherd's Bush
    And I worked such hours that I could not write letters;
I spent my few free hours in The Railway Tavern talking
    With a Carlow-born clerk and two Belfast bricklayers;
But I came back to you, Lord Mayo.

Now you are older and angrier and I am still young and gay
    And what, my lord, are we going to do?
If you were but to smile once as once you used to
    I'd jump into bed with you for ever;
For I came back to you, Lord Mayo.

I'd go live with you in the wilds of Erris
    Rearing children despite bog and rain;
I'd row with you the dark depths of Beltra and of Conn
    If you'd but smile on me;
For I came back to you, Lord Mayo.

The Drover's Path Murder

The drover's path slopes round between the bog-edge
And the mountainside and along it on a winter's night
The beautifullest woman in West Mayo walked home.
But she was known not merely for her ebony curls
And her billowing bosom on which no man had slept
And her narrow waist and legs that blossomed into thighs –
Trees with their heads in the clouds;
She was known also for her jewellery, all pure gold,
Which she carried about with her, wherever she went.
So, on a winter's night two men lay in wait for her
Behind a moon-lit boulder on the drover's path;
Fiercely she fought them but they pinned her down
And searched her savagely but could find no gold.
They raped and murdered her because they could find no gold;
She had hidden it, as had long been her practice,
On winter's night journeys along the drover's path,
In the roots of her curls, long fabled in Mayo,
And over the tangled roots she had knotted her hair
Until all under a black mass the yellow gold lay concealed.

Now in a gale-attacked sun-lit February day
Years later, as with men I work at men's trades,
Fencing off mountains to fence in sheep,
And our hands too numb to grasp pliers and hacksaw,

34

And our lives in danger from the bog concealed in water,
Five miles to be walked over before dry land is reached,
We look over and upward at the drover's path,
Where the beautifullest woman in West Mayo was murdered;
That it is a black spot is demonstrably evident
For it gives off of itself a malodorous shadow
From which even the sheep and the goats steer clear.
As three men, thrice murderous, we bow our heads,
Yet soon we too may have to pay with our lives
And we shall have only our faces for gold,
Only our faces for gold.
I stare at the murder-spot and recall many faces
Of dead sheep floating upwards in the glittering bog
And will I ever see them again, not to speak of myself,
In the mirror of a day that would know not one murder
But only the warmth of women and of women's voices?

Before the Celtic Yoke

What was it like in Ireland before the Celtic yoke –
Before war insinuated its slime into the forests of the folk?

Elizabethan, Norman, Viking, Celt,
Conquistadores all:
Imperialists, racialists, from across the seas,
Merciless whalesback riders
Thrusting their languages down my virgin throat,
And to rape not merely but to garotte
My human voice:
To screw my soul to orthodoxy and break my neck.

But I survive, recall
That these are but Micky-come-latelies
Puritanical, totalitarian, by contrast with my primal tongue:
My vocabularies are boulders cast up on time's beaches;
Masses of sea-rolled stones reared up in mile-high ricks
Along the shores and curving coasts of all my island;
Verbs dripping fresh from geologic epochs;
Scorched, drenched, in metamorphosis, vulcanicity, ice ages.

35

No Celt
Nor Viking, Norman, Elizabethan,
Could exterminate me –
I am as palpable and inscrutable
As is a mother to her man-child;
If you would contemplate me
You will know the terror that an old man knows
As he shrinks back from the grassy womb of his chirping
    mamma.

In Ireland before the Celtic yoke I was the voice of Seeing
And my island people's Speaking was their Being;
So go now, brother – cast off all cultural shrouds
And speak like me – like the mighty sun through the clouds.

What is a Protestant, Daddy?

Gaiters were sinister
And you dared not
Glance up at the visage;
It was a long lean visage
With a crooked nose
And beaked dry lips
And streaky grey hair
And they used scurry about
In small black cars
(Unlike Catholic bishops
Stately in big cars
Or Pope Pius XII
In his gold-plated Cadillac)
And they'd make dashes for it
Across deserted streets
And disappear quickly
Into vast cathedrals
All silent and aloof,
Forlorn and leafless,
Their belfry louvres
Like dead men's lips,
And whose congregations, if any,
Were all octogenarian

With names like Iris;
More likely
There were no congregations
And these rodent-like clergymen
Were conspirators;
You could see it in their faces;
But as to what the conspiracies
Were about, as children
We were at a loss to know;
Our parents called them "parsons"
Which turned them from being rodents
Into black hooded crows
Evilly flapping their wings
About our virginal souls;
And these "parsons" had wives –
As unimaginable a state of affairs
As it would have been to imagine
A pope in a urinal;
Protestants were Martians
Light years more weird
Than zoological creatures;
But soon they would all go away
For as a species they were dying out,
Soon there would be no more Protestants . . .
Oh Yea, Oh Lord,
I was a proper little Irish Catholic boy
Way back in the 1950s.

The Weeping Headstones of the Isaac Becketts

The Protestant graveyard was a forbidden place
So naturally as children we explored its precincts:
Clambered over drystone walls under elms and chestnuts,
Parted long grasses and weeds, poked about under yews,
Reconnoitred the chapel whose oak doors were always closed,
Stared at the schist headstones of the Isaac Becketts.
And then we would depart with mortal sins in our bones
As ineradicable as an arthritis;
But we had seen enough to know what the old folks meant

When we would overhear them whisperingly at night refer to
"The headstones of the Becketts – they would make you weep".
These arthritises of sin:
But although we had only six years each on our backs
We could decipher
Brand-new roads open up through heaven's fields
And upon them – like thousands upon thousands
Of pilgrims kneeling in the desert –
The weeping headstones of the Isaac Becketts.

In Memory of Those Murdered in the Dublin Massacre, May 1974

In the grime-ridden sunlight in the downtown Wimpy bar
I think of all the crucial aeons – and of the labels
That freedom fighters stick onto the lost destinies of unborn
    children;
The early morning sunlight carries in the whole street from
    outside;
The whole wide street from outside through the plate-glass
    windows;
Wholly, sparklingly, surgingly, carried in from outside;
And the waitresses cannot help but be happy and gay
As they swipe at the tabletops with their dishcloths –
Such a moment as would provide the heroic freedom fighter
With his perfect meat.
And I think of those heroes – heroes? – heroes.

And as I stand up to walk out –
The aproned old woman who's been sweeping the floor
Has mop stuck in bucket, leaning on it;
And she's trembling all over, like a flower in the breeze.
She'd make a mighty fine explosion now, if you were to blow
    her up;
An explosion of petals, of aeons, and the waitresses too, flying
    breasts and limbs,
For a free Ireland.

Mr Newspapers

The small town lies at the end of a long valley,
A disc of light at the end of a long dark tunnel.
On one side of the valley on a peak of a ridge
Crouches a huge gothic red-brick pile
With dormer windows and campanile;
It used to be known as the county home
But now it is known as the psychiatric hospital.
Dr Ryan – Dr Alphonsus Ryan – operates a personal
    gulag
"Specialising" as he opines "in drop-outs" –
A rabbit-dropping phrase
Which drops out of his visor-visaged tight-lipped mouth
Not less than thirty-five times a day;
He opines that there should be a law whereby
"Drop-outs should be compelled to work
For a two-year period of preventive detention
To get them back into a healthy way of living."
Dr Ryan himself exemplifies the "healthy way of living"
In a mock-Tudor detached house called "Clonmacnoise"
Replete with mahogany sideboards of silverware
And bookshelves displaying the works of Len Deighton
    and Teresa of Avila.
He rides with the local hunt
And his children board at the most expensive
Fee-paying schools in Ireland.
His wife is chief witch
At coffee covens of the select elect.
Young drop-outs get special treatment from Dr Ryan;
Blitzkriegs of electric shock, and threats of leucotomy;
But the older men are not duped by Dr Ryan,
Old Mr Newspapers least of all,
Who twice weekly takes a taxi into the nearest city
And earns himself fifty pounds as a pavement artist;
He brings back cigarettes and sweets for all the boys
And they in turn keep him supplied in newspapers;
On summer's evenings he sits out on the breeze-block
    veranda
Hands crossed across his chest, hat cocked back on head,

And slow-talking as the daytime stars rolling across the
     sky,
And as majestic,
And the well-stuffed newspapers showing from beneath
     the turn-ups of his trousers;
Would you like a Bull's Eye, he roars, a Bull's Eye?

The Baker

After a night at the ovens
In the big city bakery
The baker walks home alone:
He stalks through the dawn
Gropingly
Like a man through a plate-glass door
(There have been many such –
Oh many such – years
And nights of it
And it has been so
Hot)
He feels fragile and eerily pure
Like a loaf new out of oven,
All heat through-and-through,
And he does not look sure
That the air is not a plate-glass door;
So gropingly he stalks
In his hobnailed boots
Up the steep terraced street:
Like a tiny giant walking in glue:
Like a human being about to split in two.

The Archbishop Dreams of the Harlot of Rathkeale

My dream is non-committal – it is no sin –
(Thomas, I think, would be tickled by it –
As indeed I am myself; in it is a neat point).
I am simply lying here in my double-bed
Dreaming of the harlot of Rathkeale;
I see her walking down the road at evening

Wearing a red scarf and black high-heel shoes;
She is wearing nothing else and the sun
In the western sky is a-dying slowly
In a blue sky half as old as time;
A car approaches her but from behind
Resembling palely an approaching elephant
Seen through binoculars in the bush;
It does not halt – I think the driver
Is too shocked – he looks back aghast –
A god-fearing man – and in my dream, I laugh
And say her name out aloud in my mind
"Esmé – Esmé, the harlot of Rathkeale";
She is walking towards me when the dream ends
And I wake up in the morning feeling like an old bull
Plumb to charge through my brethren in my sermon.

The Friary Golf Club

They do not like me at the local golf club
But take my green fee out of some necessity.
The green keeper is secretary because in early days
He seduced a daughter of the local gentry
And they in holy matrimony were joined
And she now tends the bar.
Faithful sheep such as the parish priest
Bleat in all climes for her
While her massive husband – she being a creature minuscule in all –
Revolves about the golf course in a farmyard tractor
Glowering at players as they seek to hit
Past monastic ruins on the seventh fairway.
Did monks who prayed here in the fourteenth century
Envisage tiny white discs in flight through the air
Being chased by human beings with clubs and sticks?
Can you, golfer, at your twentieth-century ritual
Envisage monks at prayer here in the fourteenth century?
For where now your golf ball reclines astutely
A prior sunbathed in the grass;
But the parish priest in the golf-club bar intones:
"Thou shalt not imagine anything."

The Hat Factory

Eleven o'clock and the bar is empty
Except for myself and an old man;
We sit with our backs to the street-window,
The sun in the east streaming through it;
And I think of childhood and swimming
Underwater by a famine pier;
The ashlar coursing of the stonework
Like the bar-room shelves
Seen through tidal amber seaweed
In the antique mirror;
Now myself and the old man floating
In the glow of the early morning sun
Twined round each other and our newspapers;
And our pint glasses like capstans on the pier.
We do not read our daily charters –
Charters of liberty to know what's going on –
But hold them as capes before reality's bull
And with grace of ease we make our passes;
El Cordobes might envy this old small man
For the sweet veronicas he makes in daily life.
He is the recipient of an old-age pension
While I am that low in society's scale
I do not rate the dole
But I am at peace with myself and so is he;
Although I do not know what he is thinking
His small round fragile noble mouth
Has the look of the door of Aladdin's cave
Quivering in expectation of the magic words;
Open sesame;
I suspect that like me he is thinking
Of the nothing-in-particular;
Myself, I am thinking of the local hat factory,
Of its history and the eerie fact
That in my small town I have never known
Anyone who worked in it
Or had to do with it at all;
As a child I used look through a hole in the hedge
At the hat factory down below in the valley;

I used lie flat on my face in the long grass
And put out my head through the hole;
Had the hatters looked out through their porthole windows
They would have seen high up in the hillside
A long wild hedgerow broken only
By the head of the child looking out through the hole;
I speculate;
And as to what kind of hats they make;
And do they have a range in black birettas;
And do they have a conveyor belt of toppers;
And do the workers get free hats?
And I recall the Pope's skullcap
Placed on my head when as a boy-child
In a city hospital I lay near to death
And the black homburg of the red-nosed undertaker
And the balaclavas of assassins
And the pixies of the lost children of the murdered earth
And the multicoloured yamulka of the wandering Jew
And the black kippa of my American friend
In Jerusalem in the snow
And the portly Egyptian's tiny fez
And the tragic Bedouin's kefia in the sands of sun
And the monk's cowl and the nun's wimple
And the funeral mortarboards of airborn puritans
And the megalithic coifs of the pancake women of Brittany
And the sleek fedoras of well-to-do thugs
And sadistic squires' Napoleonic tricorns
And prancing horse-cavalry in their cruel shakos
And the heroic lifeboatman's black sou'wester
And the nicotine-stained wig of the curly-haired barrister
And the black busby used as a handbag by my laughing
    brother
And the silken turban of the highbrow widow
And foreign legionaries in nullah kepis
And May Day presidiums in astrakhans
And bonnets and boaters and sombreros and stetsons
And stovepipes and steeples and mantillas and berets
And topis and sunhats and deerstalkers and pillboxes
And naughty grandmothers in toques
And bishops' mitres and soldiers' helmets;
. And in Languedoc and in Aran – cloth caps.

And what if you were a hatter
And you married a hatter
And all your sons and daughters worked as hatters
And you inhabited a hat-house all full of hats:
Hats, hats, hats, hats.
Hats: the apotheosis of an ancient craft;
And I think of all the nationalities of Israel
And of how each always clings to his native hat,
His priceless and moveable roof,
His hat which is the last and first symbol
Of a man's slender foothold on this earth.
Women and girls also work in the factory
But not many of them wear hats;
Some wear scarves, but rarely hats;
Now there'll be no more courting of maidens
In schooner hats on dangerous cliffs;
It seems part of the slavery of liberation
To empty relationships of all courtship
Of which hats were an exciting part.
Probably, I shall never wear a hat:
So thus I ask the old man
If I may look at his trilby –
Old honesty –
And graciously he hands it to me
And with surprise
I note that it was manufactured
In the local hat factory
And I hand it back to him –
A crown to its king –
And like a king he blesses me when he goes,
Wishing me a good day before he starts
His frail progress home along the streets,
Along the lanes and terraces of the hillside,
To his one up and one down.
I turn about and see
Over the windowpane's frosted hemisphere
A small black hat sail slowly past my eyes
Into the unknown ocean of the sun at noon.

The Crown of Widowhood

When the black and yellow motor car sprang around the street
    corner
– Black roof, yellow body –
And drove over her straight between the shoulderblades
She was walking up the main street deep in thought
Wearing the crown of widowhood.

Though it was a winter's day her face was sunlight
And her eyes were freshwaters alive with trout leaping
And she was a delicate creature in flight treading stepping-
    stones;
She was a walking, talking, Japanese gardens
Wearing the crown of widowhood.

But though it was a winter's day the driver wore sunglasses
And a petite homburg perched in his white fuzzy hair
And a cigarette stub in his red, blue, face;
He did not see her, and he would never see her
Wearing the crown of widowhood.

He was transporting a rocking-chair on the motor-car roof-rack
Which he had bought cheap at a small auction
And he was bringing it back home to exhibit to himself;
He was God and he had no time for man or woman
Wearing the crown of widowhood.

Protestant Old Folks' Coach Tour of the Ring of Kerry

Although it was a summer's day
It rained as though it was winter;
And I pressed my nose against the windowpane,
The zoo-like windowpane of the coach,
And I closed my eyes and dreamed,
Dreamed that I was swimming,
Swimming in the coves of Kerry
With my young man Danny

And no one else about;
Danny, Danny, dripping wet,
Laughing through his teeth;
Blown to bits at Ypres.
Behind my eyes it is sunshine still
Although he has gone;
And my mother and father pad about the farm
Like ghosts cut out of cardboard;
When they died I too looked ghostly
But I stayed alive although I don't know how;
Dreaming to put the beehives back on their feet,
Waiting for Danny to come home.
And now I'm keeping house for brother Giles
Who stayed at home today to milk the cows;
Myself, I am a great jowled cow untended
And when I die I would like to die alone.

Goodbye Tipperary

In a small town under Tipperary hills
She thought she was in Czechoslovakia,
House-fronts painted but not at the rears.
We had been through a long day's work up in high cold fields
And we had not met before and time was scarce;
The bar roof over our heads was low
And you could see night congregating outside the door.
She had been born during the war in Massachusetts
Of a Scots Protestant father and an English Catholic mother –
From birth a creature of religion's wars and exile.
But being a serious woman, she laughed, she laughed much.
We spoke each at the same time, listening hard,
So that while I was telling her about our Irish tolerance
Of everything except women and freedom of conscience,
She was saying how inside her head she could hear
The tramp-a-tramp tramp-a-tramp tramp tramp tramp
Of a Soviet paratrooper overheard on the railway carriage
As her train crossed over the border from Vienna into Bratislava.
She was not a gambler or a drinker, she said, although once
She had put a bet for her father on a horse called Wessex Gold;

"My mother said he was drunk but I paid no heed –
That was when I was young and wise." And again
She gritted her eyes so deeply bright that even yet to recall her
I can see under a mountain stream's black waters
The yellow sands staying.
Then in the dark a whistle blew and
Doors banged, and voices shrieked, and
Goodbyes got somehow wrung.
Goodbye Tipperary.

The Kilfenora Teaboy

I'm the Kilfenora teaboy
And I'm not so very young,
But though the land is going to pieces
I will not take up the gun;
I am happy making tea,
I make lots of it when I can,
And when I can't – I just make do;
And I do a small bit of sheepfarming on the side.

Oh but it's the small bit of furze between two towns
Is what makes the Kilfenora teaboy really run.

I have nine healthy daughters
And please God I will have more,
Sometimes my dear wife beats me
But on the whole she's a gentle soul;
When I'm not making her some tea
I sit out and watch them all
Ring-a-rosying in the street;
And I do a small bit of sheepfarming on the side.

Oh but it's the small bit of furze between two towns
Is what makes the Kilfenora teaboy really run.

Oh indeed my wife is handsome,
She has a fire lighting in each eye,
You can pluck laughter from her elbows
And from her knees pour money's tears;

47

I make all my tea for her,
I'm her teaboy on the hill,
And I also thatch her roof;
And I do a small bit of sheepfarming on the side.

Oh but it's the small bit of furze between two towns
Is what makes the Kilfenora teaboy really run.

And I'm not only a famous teaboy,
I'm a famous caveman too;
I paint pictures by the hundred
But you can't sell walls;
Although the people praise my pictures
As well as my turf-perfumèd blend
They rarely fling a fiver in my face;
Oh don't we do an awful lot of dying on the side?

But oh it's the small bit of furze between two towns
Is what makes the Kilfenora teaboy really run.

SAM'S CROSS (1978)

Birth of a Coachman

His father and grandfather before him were coachmen:
How strange, then, to think that this small, bloody, lump
    of flesh,
This tiny moneybags of brains, veins, and intestines,
This zipped-up purse of most peculiar coin,
Will one day be coachman of the Cork to Dublin route,
In a great black greatcoat and white gauntlets,
In full command of one of our famous coaches
– *Wonder, Perseverance, Diligence,* or *Lightning* –
In charge of all our lives on foul winter nights,
Crackling his whip, whirling it, lashing it,
Driving on the hapless horses across the moors
Of the Kilworth hills, beating them on
Across rivers in spate, rounding sharp bends
On only two wheels, shriekings of axle-trees,
Rock-scrapes, rut-squeals, quagmire-squelches,
For ever in dread of the pitiless highwayman
Lurking in ambush with a brace of pistols;
Then cantering carefully in the lee of the Galtees,
Bowing his head to the stone gods of Cashel;
Then again thrusting through Urlingford;
Doing his bit, and his nut, past the Devilsbit;
Praising the breasts of the hills round Port Laoise;
Sailing full furrow through the Curragh of Kildare,
Through the thousand sea-daisies of a thousand white
    sheep;
Thrashing gaily the air at first glimpse of the Liffey;
Until stepping down from his high perch in Dublin
Into the sanctuary of a cobbled courtyard,
Into the arms of a crowd like a triumphant toreador
All sweat and tears: the man of the moment
Who now is but a small body of but some fleeting seconds
    old.

The Brother

On St John's night
I went out for a walk
At 9 p.m.;
When I returned from my walk
At 3 a.m.
And saw the corpse of my brother
Spattered with blood
I stepped over it
And went to bed.

The next day I met my other brother
In the courtyard:
He said he had killed our brother
And I asked him why;
He said he thought he was a werewolf.

Well, I inherited the farm,
And that's the long and the short of it:
One brother murdered;
The other in jail for life;
And myself alone on the farm.

I am known locally as
"The brother".

Fermoy Calling Moscow

Gunmen terrorise the tribe;
Parliamentarians dissemble and bribe;
Churchmice and churchmen scratch heaven;
But they'll not knock Mrs Crotty down.

She sells her sweetmeats and she makes her tea
And when things get bad on RTE
She tunes in to Radio Moscow while she irons:
O they'll not knock Mrs Crotty down.

Although the noise in Fermoy would make you brown
And the river floods houses in the rainy season
It's still not a bad old town:
O they'll not knock Mrs Crotty down.

On the wall of her lively room there's a sepia portrait
Of de Valera at a graveside and around her head his
    arm
When she was seven: through sorrow's smile he is about
    to state:
O they will never knock Mrs Crotty down.

Memoirs of a Fallen Blackbird

They liked me when I was on the wing
And I could whistle and I could sing;
But now that I am in my bed of clay
They come no more to be with me.

It was on the main road half way between
Newcastle West and Abbeyfeale;
A juggernaut glanced me as it passed me by
And that was the end of the road for me.

Later that day, as I lay on the verge,
A thin rake of a young man picked me up
Into his trembling hands, and he stared
At me full quarter of an hour, he stared

At me and then he laid me down
And with his hands scooped me a shallow grave;
His soul passed into me as he covered me o'er;
I fear for him now where'er he be.

They liked me when I was on the wing
And I could whistle and I could sing;
But now that I am in my bed of clay
They come no more to be with me.

The Lovely Old Pair of Kilmallock

She thinks he's a strange, old, lonely, poor creature
– Much the same as what he thinks of himself –
While he thinks she's a flower from another planet
Which she is but she does not know it;
Before she goes out to eight-o-clock Mass every morning
She brings him up a cup of tea and a cigarette;
Yea – a flower of immortality in the mortal world.
He thinks of himself also as a matchstick in an empty
    landscape
And each night she strikes fire out of him and blows him out
– Phew – Just like that –
So that he sleeps the sleep of the faithful departed;
No man has died more times more peacefully than he
And when his time for the graveyard comes, he will have been
    there before,
She following at an angel's stately pace.

The Pregnant Proprietress of the Fish and Chipper

The pregnant proprietress of the fish and chipper
Is not the mother of God: but she is the mother of life
In the city of death: she has shed all beauty
And huge with child she plods in the sawdust
Wrapping the fishes, and scooping the chips.
She talks with her back to you; tiny but huge
In her stained blue coat and her frayed black slippers
And all the boys and the girls, the strays and the runaways,
Catching the fraction in the mathematics of talk.
She deals them out fivepences to play her favourite song
On the jukebox; "Play me *One-Man Band* by Leo Sayer."
But her own conversation is music – a one-woman symphony
In whose congenial forests boys and girls can rediscover
Their true monkey natures, their gibbon greatness.

54

Parents

A child's face is a drowned face:
Her parents stare down at her asleep
Estranged from her by a sea:
She is under the sea
And they are above the sea:
If she looked up she would see them
As if locked out of their own home,
Their mouths open,
Their foreheads furrowed –
Pursed-up orifices of fearful fish –
Their big ears are fins behind glass
And in her sleep she is calling out to them
    Father, Father
    Mother, Mother
But they cannot hear her:
She is inside the sea
And they are outside the sea.
Through the night, stranded, they stare
At the drowned, drowned face of their child.

She Transforms the Ruins into a Winter Palace

This morning, early, I received a shock: for marriage
Is a hard life and each new winter marks
A darker degree of dark, a darker image,
Another tree-ring added to the soul's thick bark.
And as the happy homeland of childhood recedes
And the unknown land of death pronounces warning
Nerves fray and two people's different needs
And fears diverge. So, when this morning
I awoke to snowfall and rainmurk
I felt guilty at her going out to work;
But she, before she left, came back into the room
And, as though she stood in the archway of a ruin,
Spoke sincerely with a smile and said:
"It is snowing, freezing, you should stay in bed."

Mícheál Mac Liammóir

"Dear boy, what a superlative day for a funeral:
It seems St Stephen's Green put on the appareil
Of early springtime especially for me.
That is no vanity: but – dare I say it – humility
In the fell face of those nay-neighers who say we die
At dying-time. Die? Why, I must needs cry
No, no, no, no,
Now I am living whereas before – no –
'Twas but breathing, choking, croaking, singing,
Superb sometimes but nevertheless but breathing:
You should have seen the scene in University Church:
Packed to the hammer-beams with me left in the lurch
All on my ownio up-front centrestage;
People of every nationality in Ireland and of every age;
Old age and youth – Oh, everpresent, oldest, wished-for youth;
And old Dublin ladies telling their beads for old me; forsooth.
'Twould have fired the cockles of John Henry's heart
And his mussels too: only Sarah Bernhardt
Was missing but I was so glad to see Marie Conmee
Fresh, as always, as the morning sea.
We paid a last farewell to dear Harcourt Terrace,
Dear old, bedraggled, doomed Harcourt Terrace
Where I enjoyed, amongst the crocuses, a Continual Glimpse
     of Heaven
By having, for a living partner, Hilton.
Around the corner the canal waters from Athy gleamed
Engaged in their neverending courtship of Ringsend.
Then onward to the Gate – and to the rose-cheeked ghost
     of Lord Edward Longford;
I could not bear to look at Patrick Bedford.
Oh tears there were, there and everywhere,
But especially there; there outside the Gate where
For fifty years we wooed the goddess of our art;
How many, many nights she pierced my heart.
Ach, níl aon tinteán mar do thinteán féin:
The Gate and the *Taibhdhearc* – each was our name;
I dreamed a dream of Jean Cocteau
Leaning against a wall in Killnamoe;

And so I voyaged through all the nations of Ireland with
   McMaster
And played in Cinderella an ugly, but oh so ugly, sister.
Ah but we could not tarry forever outside the Gate;
Life, as always, must go on or we'd be late
For my rendezvous with my brave gravediggers
Who were as shy but snappy as my best of dressers.
We sped past the vast suburb of Clontarf – all those lives
Full of hardworking Brian Borús with their busy wives.
In St Fintan's Cemetery there was spray from the sea
As well as from the noonday sun, and clay on me:
And a green carnation on my lonely oaken coffin.
Lonely in heaven? Yes, I must not soften
The deep pain I feel at even a momentary separation
From my dear, sweet friends. A green carnation
For you all, dear boy. If you must weep, ba(w)ll;
Slán agus Beannacht, Mícheál."

March 1978

Lament for Cearbhall Ó Dálaigh

Into a simple grave six feet deep,
Next grave to a Kerry sheepfarmer,
Your plain oak coffin was laid
In a hail of hail:
The gods in the Macgillycuddy's Reeks
(Snow on their summits)
Were in a white, dancing rage
Together with the two don-
Keys who would not budge
From the graveyard,
And the poets and the painters,
The actors and the actresses,
The etchers and the sculptors,
The child-singers – those multiplying few
Who, despite the ever-darkening night,
Believe with their hearts' might
As did you
In a spoken music of the utter earth:

You who, for a brief hour,
Were Chieftain of a Rising People;
Who brought back into Tara's Halls
The blind poets and the blinder harpists;
Who, the brief hour barely ended,
Were insulted massively,
Betrayed
By a sanctimonious bourgeoisie;
And, worse by far,
By *la trahaison des clercs*;
Where were those talented men
In the government of the talents
When the jackbooted
Bourgeois crackled the whip?
The talented men kept their silence,
Their souls committed to finance;
Now hear their mouth-traps snap shut:
"No comment, no comment, no comment, no comment."
Ah, Cearbhall, but in your death
You led them all a merry dance:
Hauling them all out of their soft Dublin haunts,
Out of their Slickness and Glickness,
Out of their Snugvilles and Smugtowns,
You had them travel all the long,
Long way down to Sneem:
Sneem of the Beautiful Knot:
By God, and by Dana,
Cearbhall, forgive me
But it was a joy to watch them
With their wind-flayed faces
Getting all knotted up
In the knot of your funeral;
Wind, rain, hail and sleet,
Were on your side;
And spears of sunlight
Who, like yourself, did not lie;
Blue Lightning,
Gold Thunder.

In all our memories, Cearbhall,
You will remain as fresh

As the green rock jutting up
In mid-stream
Where fresh and salt waters meet
Under the bridge at Sneem.

How the respectability squirmed
In the church when beside your coffin
The Ó Riada choir sang pagan laments
For their dead chieftain:
"O he is my hero, my brave loved one."
Papal Nuncio, bishops, monsignori,
Passed wind in their misericords,
Their stony faces expressionless.
A Gaelic Chinaman whose birthplace
At 85 Main Street, Bray,
Is today a Chinese restaurant
(The Jasmine, owned by Chi Leung Nam);
O tan-man smiling on the mountain,
You are gone from us now, O Yellow Sun:
Small laughing man,
Cearbhall of the merry eyes,
A Gaelic Charlie Chaplin who became
Chief Justice and President,
Hear our mute confessions now:
We were afraid of the man that licks
Life with such relish;
We were not up to your tricks,
Did not deserve you, Cearbhall
Of the City Centre and the Mountain Pool:
Príomh Breitheamh, Uachtarán: Slán.

March 1978

The Butterfly Collector of Corofin

The Butterfly Collector of Corofin
Is himself a butterfly: in a red cardigan
And skintight pants striped bluegreen
And white cravat stippled with yellow

He flutters about the back-garden
Completely at home amongst the "speckled woods" and the
    "red admirals":
A thirty-five-year-old male creature of shyness.
And he flutters about in the living room also
Crying out: "Would you?" or "Shall I?" or "Oh dear, no"
And should a female enter into the room
He hovers about her before swooping downstairs
Out into the flowery street of the village.
Spinning, he spins into a pub
Whose darkness yields him respite
And after a few pints and a couple of large whiskeys
He confides to the squirrel of a boy-barman:
"If only I could go back to being a caterpillar again
But there is no going back:
No going back for an old butterfly like me;
My life is a process of being crushed gradually to death.
Then, I will be collected by the Great Collector Himself:
He, the Invisible One, in the Country of the Long Grass
Casting wide his vast sieve-mesh net.
But what then? Does he put us all under glass
For ever – for the benefit of the keen-eyed arch-angels
Labelling us by our names and addresses:
E.g. Eamon de Valera, Áras an Uactaráin,
Or Molly Malone, The Coombe, Dublin?
No, the idea does not bear thinking about:
To be transfixed for ever in a cruel unrest.
I want only to be a caterpillar again"
Cries out the Butterfly Collector of Corofin:
But Black Time, like his Mother, is beckoning him home
For now he must hibernate in the cell of his bedroom
And survive the tragic winter of his innate contradiction.

The Death of Constance Purfield

When Constance Purfield was in her eighty-fourth year
She requested me to drive her out to a country graveyard
Thirteen miles outside Dublin: it was Autumn
And in her shrill, biscuit-tin voice

She waxed grandiloquent on the new estates,
Chirping: "But I prefer trees."

At the graveyard everything was prepared
(She had made all the arrangements herself –
A singular, single lady to the last)
And, the suave surgeon with the toothbrush moustache
Having injected her,
And the small priest having stuttered Last Prayers
While she, like a conductor, conducted him
She wished me well in the war-riven world
And tweaking the surgeon on the cheek
She chuckled
"I eat surgeon for breakfast, you know"
And bidding me Adieu
(She reminded me of a Wild Goose Earl
Climbing into a currach at nightfall
In a hidden cove on the western coast)
She clambered into the coffin
Which was immediately lidded
And by four ropes
Lowered down into the deep grave:
Speedily the gravediggers filled it in,
Their spades plashing like oars,
And as I drove back into the Hole of Light
– Into the City of Dublin –
I could hear her shrill, biscuit-tin voice come over the seas
Chirping: "But I prefer trees."

The Head Transplant

The doctor said to me: Your father needs a *new* head.
So I said to the doctor: You can give him *my* head.

My days were numbered – broken marriage, cancer,
False teeth, bad dreams – so "Yes" was his answer.

Now I lie in my bed wondering away in my head
What will my father look like with his new head?

Will he look like a bull with the head of a daffodil
Or like a nonagenarian pontiff with the head of a harlot?

Or like a heavyweight weightlifter with the head of a fox
Or like a withered, agèd, tree with the sun in its branches?

My dreams and memories will percolate down his legs and arms;
My ideas will seep down his spine like the roots of a tree.

And my eyes will swivel in obeisance to their new rotator.
His friends will say: "Quite remarkable the change in Old Johnny –

His new head seems to be doing him the world of good.
Jolly lucky that blackguard son of his snuffed it when he did."

And I, when I'm dead, will walk alone in the graveyard,
A ghost with no head, an authentic hobgoblin.

A truly real Irishman, a *giolla gan ceann*.

Poetry, a Natural Thing

Basking salmon under the salmon bridge at Galway
or deer at a windowsill of Magdalen College
being fed breadcrumbs by my friend Michael Lurgan –
It was October and he was reading Proust
and I was an inmate of a London hostel for homeless boys

Where I shared a room with a boy from Blackpool
whose silence was the silence of a bear in a cave
and who had a passion for looking at himself in the looking-glass:
I had the feeling that he had the makings of a policeman
and that one day he would truncheon somebody to death.

But basking salmon of self-sufficiency or, supplicant deer,
or, answers to questions, always remain:
It is not I who am hiding in the trees from my father:
it is he who is hiding in the trees, and he is waiting to ambush me
as I step out the bright forest path to the spring.

That's poetry, a natural thing.

The Bus Driver

As our two double-decker buses
Glided past each other slowly
Travelling in opposite directions,
The other driver slid his window across
And yelled out: "How's Lara?"

Now, my wife Lara had been dead
Nearly a year of a heart attack
And I thought I had learned
To live without her with courage;
But "How's Lara?" he yelled out again

As if I had not heard him the first time:
O my God:
I nearly knocked an old woman down:
With one hand on my heart, the other on my head,
One or the other is about to flake out.

My solitary, black windscreen wiper
Wipes the rain away but not my tears:
Gone are the days when I cajoled my passengers
With "If you come on my bus, you'll have to dance":
Gone are the days of singing at the wheel.

Playing Croquet with Fionnuala on the Alpine Lawn

Playing croquet with Fionnuala on the Alpine Lawn
I could never concentrate on the hoops:
When I swung the mallet to and fro between my legs,
Knocking the balls,
I was always aiming at your eyes Fionnuala
But I always missed.

Playing Chinese Chequers with Fionnuala on the Cliffs
I could never concentrate on the board:
I was forever puzzling through a China exploring for you,
Or for a route that would find you,
Your black mandarin hair tied up in a pig tail,
But I could never find you.

Swimming with Fionnuala off the Steps of the Pier
I strove to impress her with my crawl:
I performed daring dives but all to no avail
For she was not even looking, preoccupied as she was
In perfecting her breaststroke: and desire stormed in my head
When she tripped dripping up the steps, glittering nakedness.

I gave her "Love-Hearts" from which I expected much
But girls see boys through the wrong end of the telescope
And, laughing, she ran from me
Down the brief, steep hill of youth:
I wrote love letters to her boarding school
But she wrote back saying "Don't be a fool".

Twenty years later I meet you on a city street
Underneath high black palings upon which centuries are
    impaled
And through which we perceive a hospice for the dying;
And you are a shy woman with a prayer book in your hands;
Now you are the searching one, the wholly desperate soul,
And, when we part, we part twins, in love's death toll.

Backside to the Wind

A fourteen-year-old boy is out rambling alone
By the scimitar shores of Killala Bay
And he is dreaming of a French Ireland,
Backside to the wind.

What kind of village would I now be living in?
French vocabularies intertwined with Gaelic
And Irish women with French fathers,
Backsides to the wind.

The Ballina Road would become the Rue Humbert
And wine would be the staple drink of the people;
A staple diet of potatoes and wine,
Backsides to the wind.

Monsieur Duffy might be the harbourmaster
And Madame Duffy the mother of thirteen
Tiny philosophers to overthrow Maynooth,
Backsides to the wind.

Father Molloy might be a worker-priest
Up to his knees in manure at the cattle-mart;
And dancing and loving on the streets at evening
Backsides to the wind.

Jean Arthur Rimbaud might have grown up here
In a hillside terrace under the round tower;
Would he, like me, have dreamed of an Arabian Dublin,
Backside to the wind?

Garda Ned MacHale might now be a gendarme
Having hysterics at the crossroads;
Excommunicating male motorists, ogling females,
Backside to the wind.

I walk on, facing the village ahead of me,
A small concrete oasis in the wild countryside;
Not the embodiment of the dream of a boy,
Backside to the wind.

Seagulls and crows, priests and nuns,
Perch on the rooftops and steeples,
And their Anglo-American mores asphyxiate me,
Backside to the wind.

Not to mention the Japanese invasion:
Blunt people as solemn as ourselves
And as humourless; money is our God,
Backside to the wind.

The medieval Franciscan Friary of Moyne
Stands house-high, roofless, by;
Past it rolls a vast asphalt pipe,
Backside to the wind,

Ferrying chemical waste out to sea
From the Asahi synthetic-fibre plant;
Where once monks sang, wage-earners slave,
Backside to the wind.

Run on, sweet River Moy,
Although I end my song; you are
The scales of a salmon of a boy,
Backside to the wind.

Yet I have no choice but to leave, to leave,
And yet there is nowhere I more yearn to live
Than in my own wild countryside,
Backside to the wind.

1976

Going Home to Mayo, Winter, 1949

Leaving behind us the alien, foreign city of Dublin,
My father drove through the night in an old Ford Anglia,
His five-year-old son in the seat beside him,
The rexine seat of red leatherette,
And a yellow moon peered in through the windscreen.
"Daddy, Daddy," I cried, "pass out the moon,"
But no matter how hard he drove he could not pass out the
    moon.
Each town we passed through was another milestone
And their names were magic passwords into eternity:
Kilcock, Kinnegad, Strokestown, Elphin,
Tarmonbarry, Tulsk, Ballaghaderreen, Ballavary;
Now we were in Mayo and the next stop was Turlough,
The village of Turlough in the heartland of Mayo,
And my father's mother's house, all oil lamps and women,
And my bedroom over the public bar below,
And in the morning cattle-cries and cock-crows:
Life's seemingly seamless garment gorgeously rent
By their screeches and bellowings. And in the evenings
I walked with my father in the high grass down by the river
Talking with him – an unheard-of thing in the city.

But home was not home and the moon could be no more
    outflanked
Than the daylight nightmare of Dublin City:
Back down along the canal we chugged into the city
And each lock-gate tolled our mutual doom;
And railings and palings and asphalt and traffic lights,
And blocks after blocks of so-called "new" tenements –
Thousands of crosses of loneliness planted
In the narrowing grave of the life of the father;
In the wide, wide cemetery of the boy's childhood.

Fat Molly

I was fostered out to a woman called Fat Molly:
It was in the year 744
On the other side of the forest from the monk-fort at Kells
Where the bird-men were scribing their magnificent comic
The Book of Kells.
I'd say Molly was about thirty when I went to her
And she taught me the art of passionate kissing:
From minuscule kisses to majuscule
On lips, breasts, neck, shoulders, lips,
And the enwrapping of tongue around tongue.
I was about fourteen
And she used make me kiss her for hours non-stop
And I'd sit in her lap with my hands
Around her waist gulping her down
And eating her green apples
That hung in bunches from her thighs
And the clusters of hot grapes between her breasts
Until from the backs of my ears down to my toes
All of me tingled
And in the backs of her eyes I saw that her glass had no
    bottom;
Nothing in life afterwards ever tasted quite so luscious
As Fat Molly's kisses;
                        O spirals of animals,
Interlaces of birds;
Sweet, warm, wet, were the kisses she kissed;

Juicy oranges on a naked platter.
She lived all alone in a crannóg
Which had an underwater zigzag causeway
And people said – and it was not altogether a fiction –
That only a completely drunk man
Could successfully negotiate Fat Molly's entrance;
Completely drunk, I used stagger home
And fall asleep in the arms of her laughter:
Oh sweet crucifixion, crucified on each other.

Well, that was half a century ago
And now the Vikings are here –
Bloody foreigners –
And there's nothing but blood in the air:
But thank you Fat Molly for a grand education;
Like all great education it was perfectly useless.

Making Love Outside Áras an Uachtaráin

When I was a boy, myself and my girl
Used bicycle up to the Phoenix Park;
Outside the gates we used lie in the grass
Making love outside Áras an Uachtaráin.

Often I wondered what de Valera would have thought
Inside in his ivory tower
If he knew that we were in his green, green grass
Making love outside Áras an Uachtaráin.

Because the odd thing was – oh how odd it was –
We both revered Irish patriots
And we dreamed our dreams of a green, green flag
Making love outside Áras an Uachtaráin.

But even had our names been Diarmaid and Gráinne
We doubted de Valera's approval
For a poet's son and a judge's daughter
Making love outside Áras an Uachtaráin.

I see him now in the heat-haze of the day
Blindly stalking us down;
And, levelling an ancient rifle, he says "Stop
Making love outside Áras an Uachtaráin."

The County Engineer

A tall heavy man with a short curly beard
He is a dragon on the site: bureaucrats quail
Before him, and gangers wince.
But in bed at night with his wife
She whispers to him
"Oh my little engineer."
And she is tiny as a bird
And her black, sleek stilettos
Make her tiny legs bird-like
And her pointed breasts
Behind her red silk blouses
Are also bird-like
And her curled-up tongues
(Lizards in leaves)
And her pouncing eyes
(Tigers in cages)
Are veiled under wings
Of her long black tresses
Combed down to her thighs.
Her children think of her
As their favourite rag doll
And few of her neighbours
Consider her real;
But at night in bed with her spouse
Grasping him between her knees
She whispers to him
"Oh my little engineer";
And being a practical creature
She has had an extra-large bath
Installed in the bathroom
For the bath is her favourite haunt

For the love-act
And immersed with her spouse
She whispers to him
"Oh my little engineer."

The Ballet Dancer

For thirty years he has come home like this
In the late afternoons after rehearsals,
Pitter-patter up the street,
In his belted raincoat and his peaked cap;
And still his neighbours look askance at him.

His two eldest sons are engine drivers
With CIE – the national railways –
And his wife is a local battleaxe
On church committees of all kinds;
But still his neighbours look askance at him.

Only his only daughter and his youngest son
Took after him and, when the three of them
Come home together, they link arms in the street,
Pirouetting, miming, all three together;
But still his neighbours look askance at him.
Oh how they dread the woman in the man.

Sister Agnes Writes to Her Belovèd Mother

Dear Mother, thank you for the egg cosy;
Sister Alberta (from near Clonakilty)
Said it was the nicest, positively the nicest,
Egg cosy she had ever seen. Here
The big news is that Rev. Mother is pregnant;
The whole convent is simply delighted;
We don't know who the lucky father is
But we have a shrewd idea who it might be:
Do you remember that Retreat Director
I wrote to you about? – The lovely old Jesuit

70

With a rosy nose – We think it was he –
So shy and retiring, just the type;
Fr P. J. Pegasus SJ.
Of course, it's all hush-hush,
Nobody is supposed to know anything
In case the Bishop – that young hypocrite –
Might get to hear about it.
When her time comes Rev. Mother officially
Will go away on retreat
And the cherub will be reared in another convent.
But, considering the general decline in vocations,
We are all pleased as pea-shooters
That God has blessed the Order of the Little Tree
With another new sapling, all of our own making,
And of Jesuit pedigree, too.
Nevertheless – not a word.
Myself, I am crocheting a cradle shawl;
Hope you're doing your novenas. Love, Aggie.

Ireland 1977

"I've become so lonely, I could die" – he writes,
The native who is an exile in his native land:
"Do you hear me whispering to you across the Golden Vale?
Do you hear me bawling to you across the hearthrug?"

Irish Hierarchy Bans Colour Photography

After a spring meeting in their nineteenth-century fastness at
    Maynooth
The Irish Hierarchy has issued a total ban on the practice of
    colour photography:
A spokesman added that while in accordance with tradition
No logical explanation would be provided
There were a number of illogical explanations which he
    would discuss;
He stated that it was not true that the ban was the result

Of the Hierarchy's tacit endorsement of racial discrimination;
(And, here, the spokesman, Fr Marksman, smiled to himself
But when asked to elaborate on his smile, he would not elaborate
Except to growl some categorical expletives which included the
    word "liberal")
He stated that if the press corps would countenance an unhappy
    pun
He would say that negative thinking lay at the root of the ban;
Colour pictures produced in the minds of people,
Especially in the minds (if any) of young people,
A serious distortion of reality;
Colour pictures showed reality to be rich and various
Whereas reality in point of fact was the opposite;
The innate black-and-white nature of reality would have to be
    safeguarded
At all costs and, talking of costs, said Fr Marksman,
It ought to be borne in mind, as indeed the Hierarchy had borne
    in its collective mind,
That colour photography was far costlier than black-and-white
    photography
And, as a consequence, more immoral;
The Hierarchy, stated Fr Marksman, was once again smiting two
    birds with one boulder;
And the joint hegemony of Morality and Economics was being
    upheld.

The total ban came as a total surprise to the accumulated press
    corps
And Irish Roman Catholic pressmen and presswomen present
Had to be helped away as they wept copiously in their cups:
"No more oranges and lemons in Maynooth," sobbed one camera
    boy.
The general public, however, is expected to pay no heed to the
    ban;
Only politicians and time-servers are likely to pay the required lip
    service;
But the operative noun is lip: there will be no hand or foot service.
And next year Ireland is expected to become
The EEC's largest moneyspender in colour photography.

This is Claudia Conway, RTE News (Colour), Maynooth.

The Married Man Who Fell in Love with a Semi-State Body

Ted Rice was that abnormal creature – a normal man:
Merrily married, he was a good husband to his wife,
A good father to his children, and a friendly neighbour:
Until in the winter of 1964 he resigned his job
As manager of a centre-city pub to become
An executive with a Semi-State Body, Bord Ól,
In charge of the promotion of the Alcohol Industry.
So much did Ted Rice grow to love the Semi-State Body,
So hard he worked for her,
So heroically he hullaballoo'd for her,
So hopefully he hopped for her,
So heartily he hooted for her,
So hoity-toitily he hocked for her,
So harshly he harped for her,
So headlong he hunted for her,
That he began to think of her as The Woman in his Life
And one day as the train shot slowly down the line towards Cork
He had a vision of her as an American negress in a state of
    semi-undress
And, as such, he introduced her to the Cork Chamber of
    Commerce:
Even the most drunken members of his audience blinked
As Mr Rice introduced the invisible woman standing beside him;
And when, in the peroration of his speech, he fondled her breasts
Temperance men broke their pledges and ordered double-
    brandies:
When Mr Rice departed for the railway station on the arm of his
    queen
He left behind him the Metropole Hotel strewn with bodies;
And halfway up the line he pulled the excommunication cord
And, introducing his Semi-State Body to the medieval ruins of a
    friary, declared:
"Let us sleep here together until the advertising boys arrive . . ."
Since then he has eked out the years in a mental hospital ward,
Tramping up and down the aisle of gloom in a shower of tears,
Repeating over and over: "O my Semi-State Body, O my
    Semi-State Body!"

Two History Professors Found Guilty of Murder

This morning in the Central Criminal Court in Dublin
Two Professors of History at the University of Mullingar,
Columba A. Cantwell and Columba B. Cantwell,
Were found guilty of the murder of Jesus Trinidad,
A thirty-year-old West Indian tutor in history at Mullingar.

Justice Columba C. Cantwell sentenced both accused to life
    imprisonment
Suspended on condition that they never get caught again.
The jury, who took a record thirty seconds to reach their verdict,
Were recommended for full-time jury service.

Earlier, evidence had been given by Mrs Jesus Trinidad
That the two professors had called to her mud-hut
In the backwoods of Mullingar
On the night of the 12th of July with a carpet-bag
Which they handed to her: it contained
Chopped-up segments of her husband's head.
However, she continued, this had come as no surprise
As for the last three years her husband had come home each day
    crying
"They are using a bacon-slicer on my mind – I cannot survive."

After having handed over the carpet-bag to her
The two professors had said: Apart from the fact that your
    husband
Was a disgustingly intelligent West Indian, a Witty Wog,
He had consistently encouraged his students to ascertain the true
    facts
Of the history of Ulster, despite constant warnings not to do so.
Finally, the two professors had themselves attended Trinidad's
    tutorials
In the hope of browbeating him: as a last resort
They took it in turns to excrete on the floor throughout his
    tutorials
But not even this esoteric ploy changed Trinidad's attitude:
Therefore, they said, they had no choice but to apply a final solution.
Justice Cantwell said that Trinidad was both a foreigner and a fool

And no tears whatsoever should be shed on behalf of his wife.
The court expressed sympathy with the two murderers
And wished them continued, further success in the green fields
– In the green, green, green fields – of their academic endeavours.

1978

In Memory: The Miami Showband –
Massacred 31 July 1975

Beautiful are the feet of them that preach the gospel of peace,
Of them that bring glad tidings of good things

In a public house, darkly lit, a patriotic (sic)
Versifier whines into my face: "You must take one side
Or the other, or you're but a fucking romantic."
His eyes glitter hate and vanity, porter and whiskey,
And I realise that he is blind to the braille connection
Between a music and a music-maker.
"You must take one side or the other
Or you're but a fucking romantic":
The whine is icy
And his eyes hang loose like sheets from poles
On a bare wet hillside in winter
And his mouth gapes like a cave in ice;
It is a whine in the crotch of whose fear
Is fondled a dream gun blood-smeared;
It is in war – not poetry or music –
That men find their niche, their glory hole;
Like most of his fellows
He will abide no contradiction in the mind.
He whines: "If there is birth, there cannot be death"
And – jabbing a hysterical forefinger into my nose and eyes –
"If there is death, there cannot be birth."
Peace to the souls of those who unlike my fellow poet
Were true to their trade
Despite death-dealing blackmail by racists:
You made music, and that was all: You were realists
And beautiful were your feet.

75

National Day of Mourning for Twelve Protestants

Throughout the Republic of Ireland yesterday
A National Day of Mourning was observed
For the 12 Protestant dog-lovers and junior motorcyclists
Who were burnt to death last Friday night
At the La Mon House Restaurant in Comber, Co. Down,
By a gang of Republican Assassins.
In Dublin the Taoiseach, Mr Jack Lynch,
Together with the Roman Catholic Archbishop of Armagh,
    Dr Ó Fíaich
Led a Vigil of Mourning
Outside the Kevin Street headquarters of the Republican
    Terrorists.
A symbolic fire was lit
And both the Taoiseach and the Archbishop
Joined together as one man
And blew it out with one breath.
The Vigil concluded with the momentous announcement
That Mrs Mairín Lynch, wife of the Taoiseach,
Was to forgo a crucial week of fête-openings
In order to make the twelve-hour train journey to Belfast
At the invitation of the Peace People.
Later the GIS (the Government Information Services)
Denied rumours that the principals at the Vigil of Mourning
Were impostors and that the real Dr Ó Fíaich,
Together with the real Mr and Mrs Lynch,
Were attending a Gaelic football match somewhere in
    Corkery.
Government officials stated that reality did not enter into the
    matter.

February 1978

Margaret Thatcher Joins IRA

At a ritual ceremony in a fairy ring fort
Near Bodenstown Graveyard, Co. Kildare
(Burial place of Theobald Wolfe Tone)
Margaret Thatcher joined the IRA
And the IRA joined Margaret Thatcher.

Black dresses were worn by all for the occasion
In which a historical union was consummated.

On the circular bank of the rath
Gunmen and High Tories crawled on all fours
Jangling their testicles;
While the sun gleamed off their buttocks.

At the navel of the rath
Waltzed Ruarí Ó Brádaigh,
His arms round Mrs Thatcher
In a sweet embrace.
Behind them Messrs
Airey Neave & Daithí O'Connell
Shared a seat on a pig.

Proceedings concluded
With Sir Ó Brádaigh, an Thatcher, an Neave, agus Sir
    O'Connell
Playing cops and robbers in souterrains.

Meanwhile in his leaba (his grave)
In nearby Bodenstown
Theobald Wolfe Tone was to be observed
Revolving sixty revolutions per minute;
This came as no surprise to observers
Since Tone was a thoroughgoing dissenter
And never would have had truck
With the likes of Margaret Thatcher or the IRA.

February 1978

JESUS, BREAK HIS FALL (1980)

Spitting the Pips Out – with the College Lecturer
in Philosophy

When I took up my new appointment as college lecturer in
    philosophy
And I was allotted the subject of epistemology,
I arranged for a svelte Swedish girl
To act as a model for my inaugural lecture.
The males in the auditorium chortled
And the females let off titters – titters.

But – sizing up the situation –
I produced a box of Hamlet cigars
And, having lit up one, I handed it to my model
So that she could relax the more
On the *chaise-longue*, which with great difficulty,
I must say, I had procured from the chaplaincy.

"Epistemology," I began, "is the science of knowing!
Do we know, or do we not know, that this young woman
Is reclining beside me on a *chaise-longue*?
And if we know, how do we know?"
I placed my hand on her left breast but before
I could make my point clear, my words were drowned
In such a porridge of pandemonium as I have not anywhere else
    experienced
In all my peregrinations from Ballyferriter to Düsseldorf and back.

There was nothing for it but to take drastic action.
Drastic, Philip, drastic.
I snatched up my files and flung them all at the class,
Jarring them into muteness. And I let the muteness
Evolve until all that was audible was her puffing of the cigar –
Puff . . . Puff . . . Puff . . . Puff . . . Puff . . .
And then I trumpeted: "Write an essay for next week
On whether or not I am right in saying – nay, asseverating –
That this beautiful girl here is all in the mind."
When the riff-raff dispersed she smiled and whispered to me:
"Let's go back to my horrid little flat and make love in the mind."

Making love in the mind – making love in the mind:
I am so ugly and she is so kind.
"Pour me out a caress from your teapot," she sighed.
And I did just that while she poured a hot whiskey down my
     throat.

Ah yes, the intellectual life. There's nothing to beat it.
Nothing to beat it, Philip, nothing to beat it –
Except perhaps my mother
With a couple of eggs and one very long, very memorable,
     wooden spoon.

The Hole, Spring, 1980

i. m. Jean-Paul Sartre

Darling, the great conundrum is the conundrum of the
     hole.
The hole must be concealed at all costs
And at all times. That's why I drink – I mean think –

That, now and at once, you should make up your mind
(If you have a mind – no insult intended –
What's a mind between bodies?) you should make up your
     mind

To enroll in that university correspondence course in law
And tort. I have always thought that tort is the sort of sport
To interest a girl like you – and it would conceal the hole.

Take *me*: as you recline there in bed this filthy April
     morning
What do you see? (That's assuming you can see anything
Through all that cigarette smoke – really, Darling,

I wish you would give up the old fags
If only for my teeny-weeny sake.) Well, what do you see?
You see a man, don't you, a man who is starkers

82

Except for a purple tie and purple socks.
Concealing the hole, you see; and with style;
To match one's socks with one's necktie

While at the same time concealing the hole
Is no mean feat. Darling, are you receiving me?
It's not the soul that's the crux of the matter, it's the hole:

It's not the soul that's the crux of the matter, it's the hole.

April 1980

Little Old Ladies Also Can Write Poems Such as This Poem Written in Widow's Blood in a Rented Top-Storey Room in Downtown Cork

The light in the window went out last night.
For four years I had grown used to that light
In the window on the opposite side of the street.
All night, every night, for four total years

It glowed in the china-shop dark while I read
Autobiography after autobiography, waiting for daybreak.
Daybreak when at last I could shut
My eye flaps and grope my way

Into a coal cellar of half-sleep. The light
In the opposite window had a shredded saffron face.
But to whom it belonged I never knew.
That it glowed was enough, dedicatedly,

Punctually, courteously, over the innumerable,
Serrated, darkening years.
"Kind saffron light" – I used chirp when I'd
Peer out my window at the window on the opposite

Side of the street. I'd say there are at least
Fifteen, maybe twenty, alive in that house,
Men and women, but because – in a manner of speaking –
I sleep by day – I never see these people.

Or if I do, it is only their overcoated spines that I see
As they teeter in the porch, foostering with key rings.
In any case, they all wear hats and raincoats
And sometimes they have suitcases in their hands.

Light that was gold fruit in an amber tea towel
And I was a moth in the penumbra of its core;
No one swiped at me with yesterday's newspapers
Or slapped at my mouth with the soles of slippers.

This morning I did not go to sleep.
I waited for the coffin to come – and it did.
Two men carried it in and four men carried it out.
Such is the Weight of Light.

In the city cemetery now, under earth,
The Light of my Mind glows downward alone.
I can feel the transvestite worms massaging
My cheeks, my eyes screeching to stay alive.

I want to live: O God, to whom I have prayed
Every day of my life – will you never comprehend
That *to live* was my one continual and desperate dream?
Help me a little now; either in, or out, of my death.

The Death by Heroin of Sid Vicious

There – but for the clutch of luck – go I.

At daybreak – in the arctic fog of a February daybreak –
Shoulder-length helmets in the watchtowers of the
	concentration camp
Caught me out in the intersecting arcs of the swirling
	searchlights.

There were at least a zillion of us caught out there –
Like ladybirds under a boulder –
But under the microscope each of us was unique,

84

Unique and we broke for cover, crazily breasting
The barbed wire and some of us made it
To the forest edge, but many of us did not

Make it, although their unborn children did –
Such as you whom the camp commandant branded
Sid Vicious of the Sex Pistols. Jesus, break his fall:

There – but for the clutch of luck – go we all.

February 1979

The Boy Who Was Conceived in the Leithreas

My Lord, and ladies & gentlemen of the jury,
I beg leave to opine that you think that you know your man
– A young middle-class pup who needs teaching a lesson –
However, you do not know that that wild boy
– That ignorant, curly-haired, forked catastrophe
Of a nineteen-year-old boy stooped there in the dock –
Was conceived in the *leithreas*
While the Dublin-to-Cork train was stationary at Limerick
    Junction:
Swaying, I grant you, but nevertheless, stationary.

And but barely in time too – for the train leapt
Into motion only seconds after the crucial coupling
And the coaches slid to and fro,
Severing their links, or nearly:
And the Madame collapsed halfway off the lavatory lid,
That ignoble dome of black plastic
On which she was spreadeagled so,
And the Monsieur – as Monsieurs will –
Explored for a space to stare at and he found it
Where the soaped-glass window was slid down a millimetre to
    reveal
A thigh of horse-racing track:
And horses pounded through his cranium
Out the coiled horns of his brain to their doom.

85

And what hath this wretched nineteen-year-old forked *misérable*
    done?
Forged a few cheques and dreamt himself a billionaire.
Not a ha'p'orth more.
And now his pater and mater do not even share the same bed,
Never mind the same *leithreas*.

My Lord, and Ladies & Gentlemen of the Jury,
I beg that you show clemency to
The boy who was conceived in the *leithreas*
While the Dublin-to-Cork train was stationary at Limerick
    Junction.
I have done.

The Drimoleague Blues

to Sarah and Síabhra

Oh I know this mean town is not always mean
And I know that you do not always mean what you mean
And the meaning of meaning can both mean and not
    mean:
But I mean to say, I mean to say,
I've got the Drimoleague Blues, I've got the Drimoleague
    Blues,
I've got the Drimoleague Blues so bad I can't move:
Even if you were to plug in Drimoleague to every oil well in
    Arabia –
I'd still have the Drimoleague Blues.

Oh this town is so mean that it's got its own mean
And that's to be as mean as green, as mean as green:
Shoot a girl dead and win yourself a bride,
Shoot a horse dead and win yourself a car.
Oh I've got the Drimoleague Blues, I've got the Drimoleague
    Blues,
I've got the Drimoleague Blues so bad I can't move:
Even if you were to plug in Drimoleague to every oil well in
    Arabia –
I'd still have the Drimoleague Blues.

86

And so on right down to the end of the line
Mean with Mean will always rhyme
And Man with Man: Oh where is the Woman
With the Plough, where is her Daughter with the Stars?
Oh I've got the Drimoleague Blues, I've got the Drimoleague
    Blues,
I've got the Drimoleague Blues so bad I can't move:
Even if you were to plug in Drimoleague to every oil well in
    Arabia –
I'd still have the Drimoleague Blues.

The Anatomy of Divorce *by Joe Commonwealth*

My dearest and most hateful Deirdre:
I am reading a new book over breakfast.
(Remember how you used loathe to see me
Reading at meal times and you were quite right;
I much preferred reading to listening to *you*,
Especially at that hour of the early afternoon
When I had had but one chilled bottle of lager
To poultice the parched desert of my palate.)
It's an Albatross Special, ninety-five pence,
Called *The Anatomy of Divorce* by Joe Commonwealth:
Do you know something, Deirdre? If you and I
Had read this book before we got our divorce
It would have made absolutely no difference:
Hope things in the haberdashery are going dashingly;
I'm binding away in my bindery, humph-humph:
Wishing you lots & lots of odium: Seán.

That Propeller I Left in Bilbao

Would you like a whiskey? Good.
That's my girl: how I do like to see
You with a glass of whiskey in your hand,
And that gleam of a smile beneath your hat:

And that gleam of a smile beneath your hat:
But that propeller I left in Bilbao –
I ought to tell you about it now –
But blast it, I won't: let's have a row:

Ow: ow: ow: let's have a row:
Let's pink the pink floor pinker than pink:
I am a pink place in which a pink pig plashes:
You are a pink peach in which a pink babe perishes –

Perishes to be born! Put in a new cassette!
And let the cherry blossom blossom till it fall
Asunder – O my Pink Thunder – asunder
And that propeller I left in Bilbao

Is still that propeller I left in Bilbao:
But you have sheared off all your robes
And you would like, if it please me, a second whiskey:
Why of course, my Big Pink Thunderbird –

My Big Pink Thunderbird – why of course –
Do you know how many telephone calls I had today?
The flaming phone never stopped flaming ringing
And all about that propeller I left in Bilbao:

All about that propeller I left in Bilbao:
I said: "Telex" to them all: "Telex":
And now to you, love, Telex For Ever and For Ever Telex,
And may that propeller I left in Bilbao,

Well – may that propeller I left in Bilbao –
That propeller I left in Bilbao –
Propeller I left in Bilbao –
I left in Bilbao.

On Buying a New Pair of Chains for Her Husband

No, young man, I do not want Guaranteed Irish Chains.
I want Chains period, Chains for my husband.
Have you got anything in the way of French chains?
He has a hankering for French chains.

Oh alright, a lavatory chain will do
Provided you can give it to me without a loo:
Although, mind you, it would be nice to see him strutting about
In a lavatory chain with a cistern on his head
And a bowl in his hand; rather Ethiopian, don't you think?
The coming thing. Yes, I tell you what –
I'll take 14 lavatory chains and 9 sets of smelly
Out-of-date telephone directories
Bound in whatever-you-call-it by Adrians of Kilkenny:
He'd like that – poor, dear, rat.

The Man Whose Name Was Tom-and-Ann

When you enter a room where there is a party in progress
Normally you ignore the introductions:
This is Tom; and Jerry; and Micky; and Mouse –
They are all much the same – male mouths
Malevolent with magnanimity or females
Grinning gratuitously: but tonight
I paid attention when I was introduced to a man
Whose name was Tom-and-Ann:
All night I looked hard at him from all angles,
Even going so far as to look down his brass neck,
But all I could see was a young middle-aged man
With coal-black hair cut in a crew cut such
As would make you freeze, or faint, of electric shock:
Nobody had noticed that his wife was not with him:
She was at another party being introduced to *my* wife
Who, when she came home, started humming,
"Tonight I met a woman whose name was Ann-and-Tom."

Well, next time I throw a party for all the Foleys in Ireland,
God help us, I will do the introductions myself:
'Darling Donal – this is Tom-and-Ann
And his beautiful wife Ann-and-Tom.'

Tullynoe: Tête-à-Tête in the Parish Priest's Parlour

"Ah, he was a grand man."
"He was: he fell out of the train going to Sligo."
"He did: he thought he was going to the lavatory."
"He did: in fact he stepped out the rear door of the train."
"He did: God, he must have got an awful fright."
"He did: he saw that it wasn't the lavatory at all."
"He did: he saw that it was the railway tracks going away from
    him."
"He did: I wonder if . . . but he was a grand man."
"He was: he had the most expensive Toyota you can buy."
"He had: well, it was only beautiful."
"It was: he used to have an Audi."
"He had: as a matter of fact he used to have two Audis."
"He had: and then he had an Avenger."
"He had: and then he had a Volvo."
"He had: in the beginning he had a lot of Volkses."
"He had: he was a great man for the Volkses."
"He was: did he once have an Escort?"
"He had not: he had a son a doctor."
"He had: and he had a Morris Minor too."
"He had: he had a sister a hairdresser in Kilmallock."
"He had: he had another sister a hairdresser in Ballybunion."
"He had: he was put in a coffin which was put in his father's cart."
"He was: his lady wife sat on top of the coffin driving the donkey."
"She did: Ah, but he was a grand man."
"He was: he was a grand man . . ."
"Good night, Father."
"Good night, Mary."

En Famille, 1979

Bring me back to the dark school – to the dark school of
   childhood:
To where tiny is tiny, and massive is massive.

Madman

Every child has a madman on their street:
The only trouble about *our* madman is that he's our father.

Sally

Sally, I was happy with *you*.

Yet a dirty cafeteria in a railway station –
In the hour before dawn over a Formica table
Confettied with cigarette ash and coffee stains –
Was all we ever knew of a home together.

"Give me a child and let me go":
"Give me a child and let me stay":
She to him and he to her:
Which said *which* and *who* was *who?*

Sally, I was happy with *you*.

The Daughter Finds Her Father Dead

to A. D.

The day that Father died
I went up to wake him at 8.30 a.m.
Before I left home for school:
The night before he had said
Before I went up to bed:
"Remember to wake me at 8.30 a.m.
Remember to wake me at 8.30 a.m."

The day that Father died
At 8.30 a.m. I went up to wake him
And I thought at first he was dead:
He did not move when I shook him,
But then he said, then he said:
"Rider Haggard, Rider Haggard:
Storm Jameson, Storm Jameson."

The day that Father died
Those were the last words he said:
"Rider Haggard, Rider Haggard:
Storm Jameson, Storm Jameson."
I thought then he was alive
But he was dead, he was dead;
When I came home from school he was dead.

The day that Father died
I glimpsed him telescopically:
Inside in his eyes inside in his head
A small voice in a faraway world
Spinning like a tiny coin:
"Rider Haggard, Rider Haggard:
Storm Jameson, Storm Jameson."

Apparently – I suppose I should say
"It seems" – Father was a man
Who thought God was a woman
And that was why he was always sad,
Bad at being glad:
"Rider Haggard, Rider Haggard:
Storm Jameson, Storm Jameson."

He cries and he cries, over and over,
In the empty nights that are emptier
And the dark days that are darker:
"Rider Haggard, Rider Haggard:
Storm Jameson, Storm Jameson":
And I take a look out from my bunk bed
As if all the world were a black silhouette

Or an infinite series of black silhouettes
Brokenly riding the white skyline:
"Rider Haggard, Rider Haggard:
Storm Jameson, Storm Jameson":
And just as my father thought God was a woman,
I think God is a man: are both of us wrong?
Oh if only a horse could write a song:

Oh if only a horse could write a song.

This Week the Court is Sleeping in Loughrea

The perplexed defendants stand upright in the dock
While round about their spiked and barred forecastle,
Like corpses of mutinous sailors strewn about the deck
Of a ghost schooner becalmed in summer heat,
Recline solicitors in suits and barristers in wigs and gowns,
Snoring in their sleeves.
On high, upon the judge's bench,
His Lordship also snores,
Dreaming of the good old days as a drunken devil
Dozing in Doneraile.
From a hook in the ceiling the Court Crier hangs,
His eyes dangling out of their sockets.
Below him the Registrar is smoothing the breasts of his spectacles.
In the varnished witness box crouches Reverend Father Perjury
With a knife through his back.
Behind him in the dark aisles, like coshed dummies, lurk
Policemen stupefied by *poitín*.
Up in the amphitheatre of the public gallery
An invisible mob are chewing the cud.
An open window lets in the thudding sounds of blows
As, on the green, tinker men brawl,
As they have done so there down the centuries –
The Sweeneys and the Maughans.
Such slender justice as may be said to subsist in Loughrea
Is to be discerned
In the form of a streamlet behind the house-backs of the town,
Which carries water out to the parched fields
Where cleg-ridden cattle wait thirsty in the shadowy lees,

Their domain far away from the sleeping courtroom of human
    battle.
Is it any surprise that there are children who would rather be
    cattle?

Charlie's Mother

Brendan, does *your* mother have a hold over *you?*
Mine does over *me.* I keep beseeching her
To take her purple-veined hand out of my head
But do you know what she says, the old cabbage?
Stirring and churning her hand round inside in my head
She crows: "Charlie m'boy, you've got a lot of neck."

Mind you, when I think about it, she has a point:
My neck *is* thick and there *is* rather a lot of it;
And look at all the *mun* I have made
Without having to do a flick of work for it.
I rub my neck wryly when Mother crows:
"That's m'boy, Charlie, lots of *mun* for *mum.*"

And you know, Brendan – would you like another drink?
Double brandy there, please – I often think, Brendan,
When I look at myself in the mirror each morning –
And I must admit that that's my favourite moment of each day –
Even on black bloody days like today – I always see
Somewhere behind my fat neck my tiny little mother winking up
    at me.

Another drink? Certainly Brendan. Double brandy there, please.
Down, Bismarck, down. Down, Bismarck, down.
Damned Alsatian bitch but a friendly bitch at heart;
Mother gave her to me as a Christian – I mean Christmas –
    present.
Another drink? Certainly Brendan, quadruple brandy there, please.
Down, Bismarck, down. Down, Bismarck, down.

But Brendan, you were saying about Micky Finn of Castlepollard
That his mother has run away and left him for another man?

94

Another case, I'm afraid, of not keeping the hand in the till;
Not enough neck at all at all. Can you hear me, Brendan?
Come on, *a mhic*, straighten up for Christ's sake – or at least for
    Ireland's sake.
Down, Bismarck, down. Down, Bismarck, down.

Brendan, do you realise, you pixillated, feckless sot,
That if my mother came in here just now, as she might very
    well do.
(Mothers tend to eavesdrop in the footsteps of their favourite
    offspring),
She might think that I am to blame for the condition you're in?
You're not just drunk – you're in a coma:
She might even decide to turn Bismarck against me.

Eat him, Bismarck, eat him.
    Eat him, Bismarck, eat him.

Nyum: nyum, nyum, nyum, nyum, nyum; *nyum.*

For My Lord Tennyson I Shall Lay Down My Life

to Anthony Cronin

Here at the Mont Saint-Michel of my master,
At the horn of beaches outside Locksley Hall,
On the farthest and coldest shore
In the June day under pain of night,
I keep at my mind to make it say,
Make it say, make it say,
As his assassins make for me,
The pair of them revolving nearer and nearer
(And yet, between breaths, farther and farther),
Make it say:
"For my Lord Tennyson I shall lay down my life."

I say that – as nearer and nearer they goose-step –
Vanity, and *Gloom* not far behind.
"For my Lord Tennyson I shall lay down my life."

95

Hopping Round Knock Shrine in the Falling Rain, 1958

to Karol Wojtyla

When I was thirteen I broke my leg.

Being the sensible, superstitious old lady that she was,
My Aunt Sarah knew that while to know God was good,
To get the ear of his mother was a more practical step:
Kneeling on the flagstone floor of her kitchen, all teaspoons
    and whins,
Outspoken as Moses, she called out litanies to Our Lady:
The trick was to circumambulate the shrine fifteen times
Repeating the rosary, telling your beads.
And so: that is how I came to be
Hopping round Knock Shrine in the falling rain.

In the heel of that spiritual hunt
I became a falling figure clinging to the shrine wall
While Mayo rain pelleted down, jamming and jetting:
And while all the stalls – of relics, and phials of holy water,
And souvenir grottoes, and souvenir postcards,
And spheres which, when shaken, shook with fairy snow,
And sticks of Knock rock –
Were being folded up for the day, I veered on,
Falling round Knock Shrine in the hopping rain.

Gable, O Gable, is there no Respite to thy Mercy?

The trick did not work
But that is scarcely the point:
That day was a crucial day
In my hedge school of belief,
In the potential of miracle,
In the actuality of vision:
And, therefore, I am grateful
For my plateful
Of hopping round Knock Shrine in the falling rain.

Mr Goldsmith, My Father's Friend

My father who was stern and staid
Had a most peculiar friend,
The uproarious Mr Goldsmith,
Who stammered so much at the hall door,
One night he fell flat on the floor,
And who did not use the upstairs toilet
But relieved himself in the garden.

My father indeed was a legal man
– Cut off, therefore, from the rest of man –
Except for Mr Goldsmith, who
Returned from London with a stolen
Police helmet for us children,
And who did not use the upstairs toilet
But relieved himself in the garden.

Yes, my father who was so saturnine
Had a most delightful friend,
The uproarious Mr Goldsmith,
Who laughed so much at supper time,
He spattered the tablecloth with wine,
And who did not use the upstairs toilet
But relieved himself in the garden.

But my father who was stern and staid
Cherished his most peculiar friend
For being verbally delirious,
When people said it was not right
That a grown-up man should talk all night,
And who did not use the upstairs toilet
But relieved himself in the garden.

My father, extremely vehemently,
Defended his most peculiar friend,
The uproarious Mr Goldsmith,
Who was expelled from boarding school
Because he broke the golden rule,
And who did not use the upstairs toilet
But relieved himself in the garden.

Perhaps my very serious father
Was the hand that helped to shove the arm
Of the needle when it stuck in the groove;
Shoved the wheel stuck in the rut
When Mr Goldsmith could not utt –
Who di-did not use the upstairs toi-toilet
But re-relieved himself in the ga-garden.

Oh Mr Goldsmith, Mr Goldsmith,
That you were a black man red as veal
Engulfed me but did not threaten.
I was at an age when books were real
And all the world was full of colour.
And I was proud of my father's friend,
Who did not use the upstairs toilet
But relieved himself in the garden.

JUMPING THE TRAIN TRACKS
WITH ANGELA (1983)

The Woman Who Keeps Her Breasts in the Back Garden

Why do you keep your breasts in the back garden?
Well – it's a male-dominated society, isn't it?
Yes, I know it is, but could you explain . . . ?
Certainly I'll explain, certainly:
Seeing as how it's a male-dominated society
And there is all this ballyhoo about breasts,
I decided to keep my pair of breasts in the back garden
And once or twice a day I take them out for a walk –
Usually on a leash but sometimes I unleash them –
And they jump up and down and prance a bit
And in that way the males can get their bosom-gaping done with
And I can get on with my other activities.
I used to leave them out at night under the glorious stars
But then little men started coming in over the walls.
I have other things on my mind besides my breasts:
Australia – for example – Australia.
To tell you the truth, I think a great deal about Australia.
Thank you very much for talking to us, Miss Delia Fair.

Interview for a Job

   – I had a nervous breakdown when I was seventeen.
   – You had not?
   – I had.
   – But how could a beautiful girl like you
      Have had such a thing as a nervous breakdown?
   – I don't know, sir.
   – But you have such luscious hair!
   – They said I had some kind of depression.
   – With long black curls like yours? Depression?
   – Erogenous depression.
   – Erogenous depression?
   – It's a new kind of depression, sir.
   – You're wearing clothes, do you know that?
   – Am I?
   – You are: I like your lips too.

– My lips?

– Your lips: they're kissable.

– Kissable?

– And your hips: I would say they handle well.

– I beg your pardon, sir?

– Tell me, what kind of man is your father?

– He stays in bed every second week.

– Your mother?

– She stays in bed every second week as well.

– A happy Irish marriage.

– Why do you say that, sir?

– Well, it's not every husband and wife who go to bed together
  For a whole week, every second week.

– You misunderstand, sir; they take it in turns.

– OK: so you want a job?

– Yes, sir.

– Well you can't have one.

– I beg your pardon, sir?

– You had one hell of a nerve applying for a job.
  You have no right to have a job here or anywhere.
  Get out of my office before I bellow for my Little Willie
  To kick you in the buck teeth and whack you on the bottom.

– Thank you verra much, sir.

– Don't mention it, girrul.

– Well then, sir, d'ye mind if I sit on in your office for five minutes:
  It is terrible cold outside and I have no overcoat.

– Bloody woman, shag off; vamoose; make yourself scarce.

– But sir, I *am* scarce; my name on the form . . . *Scarcity*.

– Now *Scarcity*, don't act the smart ass with me: beat it.

Going Home to Meet Sylvia

I

I am going down the road with Sylvia;
And I will not be going home;
I am going down the road with Sylvia;
And I will not be going home.

II

I will be going to the Carnival with Sylvia;
I hope to meet nobody there;
I will be going to the Carnival with Sylvia;
I hope to meet nobody there.

III

I am going down the road to meet Sylvia;
Sylvia is not going to meet me;
I will be coming back down the road from Sylvia;
And I will not be going home.

IV

I am going down the road with Sylvia;
And I will not be going home;
I am going down the road with Sylvia;
And I will not be going home.

Papua, New Guinea

On discovering that his girlfriend had done a bunk to Papua, New
    Guinea,
Micky MacCarthy phoned CIE
And requested permission to prostrate himself on the Tralee-to-
    Dublin line,
So that he could behead himself by means of the afternoon train.
'Certainly – *Ná Caith Tobac*,' replied CIE:
'Certainly – Prostrate Yourself – Do Not Smoke.'

However, as happens with CIE,
The afternoon train was delayed for eight or nine hours
(Only the previous week it had been delayed for two or three days)
And as Night in the Western Hemisphere
Commenced to spread o'er earth with starry and sable mantle
Micky MacCarthy felt rather cold
And in the end, after making trebly sure that nobody was looking

And that his pants were properly buttoned up,
He repaired to Cissy Buckley's pub
At Lemass Cross
Where right now he is filtering his cranium with whiskey
And beginning to see the world, including Papua, New Guinea,
In a slightly different light.

Michelangelo Road

What? A little old Jewish couple in their seventies
In their little old house on Michelangelo Road.
"Would you like a book? Would you like a cup of tea?
We are children, and unto children we shalt return."
The old lady does the talking, and the old man does the smiling:
"He has been cogitating a book on the passage of time:
But that naughty old river outside the window
Is proving to be an almost libidinous distraction.
He says that it has the same effect on him as I did
When I was a girl. Whereas for other men
I was stationary, for Benjamin I was moving:
And now he is having an affair with the River Ladle
Darkly curling in the sunlight outside our window
Instead of writing his tome on the passage of time.
But I am not jealous of the river – I do not flap
My ears at it, for I am happy that Benjamin is happy" –
She laughed like a prehistoric rabbit, unperturbed by the firing
    squad.

Old Lady, Middle Parish

When the small old lady introduced the small old man to me –
"This is my gunman" –
I found it awkward to keep my composure.
"Your husband?" – I corrected her, for I considered myself
Well versed in the culverts of colloquial confusion.
"No, sir, my gunman," she smiled a tiny quiet smile.
"We have been married forty-eight years

And he is the best gunman a woman could have ever had.
If I was to live my life over again,
I would marry the very same gunman."
I peeped at the gentleman
But he only peeped back at me, his eyes wet with merriment,
His toothless mouth like a knotted-up silk handkerchief,
Orange silk with clusters of black stains on it.
I formed the impression that he was hard of hearing
But in any case she chattered on like a lark's party in Mozart.
"He was a faithful gunman all his life
And now we live in a gunman's flat
In North Main Street,
Just enough room for the pair of us,
Just enough to make do
When you add his gunman's pension
To what I scrape myself – I do for Mrs Dunne –
The Mrs Dunne – Number 3 Winston Churchill Villas –
Just opposite the back gates of UCC –
Two and a half hours, Monday, Wednesday and Friday –
Two pounds fifty an hour.
I like it but it is a queer rake of a house – the Dunne house.
Makes you curious, doesn't it? Curious to know like.
Oh I am always glad to get home to my own gunman
And after we have had tea and watched telly
– *Coronation Street* or *Fame* or the *News* –
We climb into bed – we have got a huge double bed –
From the Coal Quay – old black brass.
It is so high that I have to give my gunman a leg up
When he does not feel strong enough to take a run at it.
That is when I am at my sprightliest – at my most serenest –
Then, and when I am at First Mass on Weekdays & Last Mass on
    Sundays –
Then, when I am there all alone in the dark night
In the rooftops of my native city –
The hills of Cork city all around me
And the moonlight leaping in the window
And my gunman tucked in beside me,
The pair of us back to back;
O my dearly belovèd gunman,
Once RIC & IRA; shortly to be RIP.
And out there on the rooftops – the future – like a rooster cock

In the wide-awake silence . . . Valentia 1017 millibars rising slowly . . .
God bless him beside me – oh & the poor world too –
The Lebanon – the Lebanon that I used think was Heaven –
And Belfast too and Derry and Portrush –
My gunman used irritate me but he also used delight me
And now I am – yes I am – I am rising slowly into sleep:
If only the whole world could learn to sleep:
You never know but we might wake up in the morning
And cotton on to ourselves: cotton on to ourselves:
Lord, will we ever cotton on to ourselves? . . . Bog cotton."

The Rose of Blackpool

He was a goalkeeper and I am a postmistress
And the pair of us believed – I say "believed" – in Valentine's Day.
What chance had we?
(I speak in hindsight, of course:
I would not have spoken like that in front of the Great Irish Elk
Or, for that matter, in front of a twenty-two-inch colour TV.)
What chance had we?
Every chance – and at the same time not a chance in the world.

You see, I had my own little post office at the very top of the hill
And I kept it completely and absolutely empty except for the counter.
One day he had said: "You are the Rose of Blackpool";
And that night in bed on my own with my head in the pillow
(*Feathers*, I may say – I cannot abide *foam* –
Nor could *he*)
I whispered to myself: "All right, that's what I'll be,
I'll be – the Rose of Blackpool."

Many's the Valentine's Day that went by
Before I got my hands on a PO of my own
But got it I did – and right on top of the hill!
And in that bare, spic-and-span, unfurnished shop,
With its solitary counter at the very far end,
I stood like a flower in a flowerpot
All the day long – drips and leaves and what-have-ye:
All the year round – "*Number 365, are you still alive?*"

106

And when the door of my PO opened
(And as the years went by, it opened less and less and less, I can tell
    you that)
The doorbell gave out such a ring – such a peal –
That the customer leapt – stood dead – and I smiled
Until my cheeks were redder than even
A Portadown Rose in a Sam McGredy Dream.
And I had my black hair tied up in a bun
And my teeth – well this is what my goalkeeper used say –
Were whiter than the snow in Greece when he played a
Game there in nineteen hundred and fifty-three.
The trouble with my goalkeeper was that he was too good of a
    goalkeeper:
He simply would not let the ball in – not even when you got a penalty
    against him.
Now it sounds Funny Peculiar – and it is –
(But then so is Valentine's Day
And all who steer by the star)
But to be a successful goalkeeper in this world
You simply have to let the odd ball in.
Benny would *not* – and so one night the inevitable happened.
We were up in Dublin and the game was being played under lights
And he hit his head off the crossbar making a save
And the two uprights fell across him
And the removals were the next night and the burial was the day after.

Of course some people say that he's living in Argentina with a white
    woman.
(I'm brown, by the way, and my name is Conchita.)
But *that's* what *they* say – *what* do *they* know?
I stand alone in my little old lofty and lonely PO,
The Rose of Blackpool,
And I do not believe that there was ever another man in the world
Who could court a woman like my goalkeeper courted *me*,
Especially at away matches at nights under lights.
Benny courted Conchita like a fella in a story;
And no matter how many shots he had stopped in the foregoing year
He always – oh he always – and he always –
Posted *me* his Valentine.

O Rose of Blackpool, let Mine be always Thine.

The Night They Put John Lennon Down

The night they put John Lennon down,
    Off came my record dealer's lid:
"A pity the bugger did not die
    Three weeks before he did."
Oh John, in the era of record crap
    It was always good to hear you;
To hear behind your steel voice,
    Your smile a-breaking through.

My record dealer was sad because
    He was almost out of stock,
And all the money that could be made
    With Christmas on the clock!
In death, in life, you beat them all,
    The dealers you would not woo:
And we glimpse behind your granny specs,
    Your smile a-breaking through.

The night they put John Lennon down,
    The night flew out John Lennon's head:
In light John Lennon to the night said:
    "O what is your name, Poor Night?"
"M'name's Chapman," twanged the night,
    "An' Chapman's a code name, Mark *you*."
"Imagine!" – wept John Lennon,
    His smile a-breaking through.

The night they put John Lennon down,
    Pat stepped out with Bríd;
And on General Hackett Esplanade
    To John Lennon they paid heed.
The waters bid the ships be still:
    "I will freeze fridges, I will love *you*,
Like walls like bridges" – Bríd sang to Pat,
    Her smile a-breaking through.

The night they put John Lennon down,
    I heard an old man cry:
"O where is the boy? O where is the boy?"
    And he gave the sky a black eye.
An old woman came out of a house
    And John, she was the image of *you*:
"Old man, the boy is not yet born" –
    Her smile a-breaking through.

The night they put John Lennon down,
    A girl clung to a street corner,
Crooning an old oriental number:
    "O My Accidental One".
The affrighted river whispered to her:
    "You threw me five pounds, did you?"
She replied – "Here's ten pounds' change" –
    Her smile a-breaking through.

The night they put John Lennon down,
    I heard a third woman call
That the only truth a leaf knows
    Is that it's going to fall.
Oh John, it was a moving thing
    That a lonely heart like you
Should perceive behind a woman's tears –
    Her smile a-breaking through.

Change, Changer, Change. Fall, Faller, Fall.

The Crucifixion Circus, Good Friday, Paris, 1981

At the sixth station there was a soft explosion,
And it was not the frantic swish of Veronica's towel
Scouring the face of the gory Christ
Like a pulped prizefighter slumped in his corner.
Perhaps, I thought, it is the man in the porch
With the pistol in his right hand clasped by his left,
Held high above his head pointed into space;
(I had wondered about him on my way in).

It was like the air precipitately being let out of a balloon,
Or the rapid deflation of the bladder of a football.
A tall, saffron-faced lady in long grey skirts,
Barely able to stand on account of her age
Had urinated into her massive black silk drawers –
"My stage curtains," she used to call them to her great-
    grandchildren.
The gold urine trickled slowly, as if patiently, across the stone
    flags,
Delineating a map of Europe on the floor as it trickled –
Trickled until it had become a series of migrations
From Smolensk to Paris;
A urine sample for Doctor God to hold up to the light,
Or to be microscopic about –
A clue to the secret biology of the Universe –
Or for his wastrel son to muck about in.

Her husband gripped her trembling hand
And with his other hand he adjusted the lilac bonnet on her
    head
To make her look more pretty.
That he should think of that at a time like this,
That he should treat his wife with the exact same courtesy
As he did when he was a young man courting a princess,
And that she should crawl forth from her bed
To topple like this,
To bear witness in a public church,
To risk all or nearly,
In order to stand by the side of the subversive Christ,
These are things that do not make me laugh;
These are things that make me weep stone tears.
In spite of the living scandal of the warring churches,
On the map of Europe there is a country of the heart.

Fellow catechumens looked down askance at the floor,
Then up at the radiant, tormented faces of the agèd couple.
Why do people of their age and station
Behave like this – they ought to know better –
At the Stations of the Cross and on – of all days – Good
    Friday?
We had not yet even arrived at Golgotha Hill:

The old pair did not look as if they intended to budge from the
    pool
In which they stood – out of whose banana-yellow ooze
They flowered and towered like agèd tropical trees,
All wizened and green, all grey and fruity.

The wife kept her eyes fixed on the Cross of Jesus.
Her husband kept his eyes both on her and on the Cross.
Urine or no urine
They were going to bear witness to today's Via Dolorosa
Right out to the end;
If the fellow under the Cross – a dark-skinned young Jew,
Extraordinarily long-haired, even if it is the fashion –
Could himself keep it up to the end. With blood in both eyes
And on his hands and on his feet, he too was in difficulties –
Difficulties with his bodily functions.
Behind the Jew traipsed the priests and the acolytes
In linen albs and lamb's wool surplices:
Voices taunted from the planets: "And where are your assets?"

When at the eleventh station they crucified Christ
The old man held high his head with glittering eyes,
Like a man in the stands at a racecourse
Watching a 20-to-1 winner come home,
His wife holding on to the hem of his raincoat,
Not unused to her husband's gambling coups – a loser in
    society,
A winner in life. If at night she had a blackout
And forgot to say her prayers (ever since the war she'd been
    having blackouts)
She could always be sure that he would say them for her.
Such things were unspoken of between them
As now they poked their way
In and out the archipelagos and the peninsulas and the lagoons
    of urine,
The rivulets and the puddles,
Until they found the centre aisle
From which they gazed up at the stalagmite organ in the far-off
    loft
Famed for its harpies carved in oak.
During the Stations of the Cross

A family of Germans had been snapping photographs of the
     organ,
With tripod and flash,
Turning their backs on the ludicrous procession-in-progress.

The old man knew that his wife knew what he knew:
That at the end of the war a German soldier
Had hid in the organ loft
In a nest made for him by the sacristy charwoman.
For three weeks he had got away with it until the parish priest –
An armchair general in the French Resistance –
Had flushed him out. The pair of them –
The young German soldier and the young French charwoman –
Were shot in the back of the head – collaborators –
No Jesus Christ to make it a trio, or was there?
The parish priest murmured over his bread and wine
That such things happen, and have to happen, in war.
Just so, just so – murmured a Communist intellectual,
Blood-red wine seeping out of the stained corners of his mouth,
Le Monde for a napkin on his knee.

By now the Crime of the Urine had been doctrinally detected
And the sacristan followed the trail up the centre aisle,
Up and under the organ loft, round by the holy-water font,
Out onto the steps overlooking the Place de la Concorde.
He thought: the guillotine would not be good enough
For people who urinate in churches.
But he consoled himself with the observation that Bonaparte
Had good taste in Egyptian obelisks – painted penises, I should think.

In their crusty old rooms
In the mansards overlooking the Madeleine
The two quaking spouses helped each other to undress.
Having laid their two windowsills
With breadcrumbs for the pigeons,
They climbed into bed into one another's arms,
In an exhaustion beyond even their own contemplation –
Beyond the trees and the water, beyond youth and childhood.
He was the first to fall asleep, his eyelids like forest streams,
And the sun – high in the west over the Eiffel Tower and
     St-Cloud –

Framed his golden white-haired face like a face in a shrine,
A gaunt embryo in a monstrance.
As sleep came over her she heard him say in his sleep:
"To keep one another warm – warm as urine."
And in Byzantium she saw the gold urine
Mosaicise in her sleep-fog like breath:
A diptych of Madonna and Child – at birth and at death.

THE BERLIN WALL CAFÉ (1985)

The Haulier's Wife Meets Jesus on the Road Near Moone

I live in the town of Cahir,
In the Glen of Aherlow,
Not far from Peekaun
In the townland of Toureen,
At the foot of Galtee Mór
In the County of Tipperary.
I am thirty-three years old,
In the prime of my womanhood:
The mountain stream of my sex
In spate and darkly foaming;
The white hills of my breasts
Brimful and breathing;
The tall trees of my eyes
Screening blue skies;
Yet in each palm of my hand
A sheaf of fallen headstones.
When I stand in profile
Before my bedroom mirror
With my hands on my hips in my slip,
Proud of my body,
Unashamed of my pride,
I appear to myself a naked stranger,
A woman whom I do not know
Except fictionally in the looking-glass,
Quite dramatically beautiful.
Yet in my soul I yearn for affection,
My soul is empty for the want of affection.
I am married to a haulier,
A popular and a wealthy man,
An alcoholic and a county councillor,
Father with me of four sons,
By repute a sensitive man and he is
Except when he makes love to me:
He takes leave of his senses,
Handling me as if I were a sack of gravel
Or a carnival dummy,
A fruit machine or a dodgem.
He makes love to me about twice a year;

Thereafter he does not speak to me for weeks,
Sometimes not for months.
One night in Cruise's Hotel in Limerick
I whispered to him: Please *take* me.
(We had been married five years
And we had two children.)
Christ, do you know what he said?
Where? Where do you want me to take you?
And he rolled over and fell asleep,
Tanked up with seventeen pints of beer.
We live in a Georgian, Tudor, Classical Greek,
Moorish, Spanish Hacienda, Regency Period,
Ranch House, Three-Storey Bungalow
On the edge of the edge of town:
"Poor Joe's Row"
The townspeople call it,
But our real address is "Ronald Reagan Hill" –
That vulturous-looking man in the States.
We're about twelve miles from Ballyporeen
Or, as the vulture flies, about eight miles.
After a month or two of silence
He says to me: Wife, I'm sorry;
I know that we should be separated,
Annulled or whatever,
But on account of the clients and the neighbours,
Not to mention the children, it is plain
As a pikestaff we are glued to one another
Until death do us part.
Why don't you treat yourself
To a weekend up in Dublin,
A night out at the theatre:
I'll pay for the whole shagging lot.

There was a play on at the time
In the Abbey Theatre in Dublin
Called *The Gigli Concert*,
And, because I liked the name –
But also because it starred
My favourite actor, Tom Hickey –
I telephoned the Abbey from Cahir.
They had but one vacant seat left!

I was so thrilled with myself,
And at the prospect of Tom Hickey
In a play called *The Gigli Concert*
(Such a euphonious name for a play, I thought),
That one wet day I drove over to Clonmel
And I went wild, and I bought a whole new outfit.
I am not one bit afraid to say
That I spent all of £200 on it
(Not, of course, that Tom Hickey would see me
But I'd be seeing myself seeing Tom Hickey
Which would be almost, if not quite,
The very next best thing):
A long, tight-fitting, black skirt
Of Chinese silk,
With matching black jacket
And lace-frilled, pearl-white blouse;
Black fishnet stockings with sequins;
Black stiletto high-heeled shoes
Of pure ostrich leather.
I thought to myself – subconsciously, of course –
If I don't transpose to be somebody's *femme fatale*
It won't anyhow be for the want of trying.

Driving up to Dublin I began to daydream
And either at Horse & Jockey or Abbeyleix
I took a wrong turn and within a quarter of an hour
I knew I was lost. I stopped the car
And I asked the first man I saw on the road
For directions:
"Follow me" – he said – "my name is Jesus:
Have no fear of me – I am a travelling actor.
We'll have a drink together in the nearby inn."
It turned out we were on the road near Moone.
(Have you ever been to the Cross at Moone?
Once my children and I had a picnic at Moone
When they were little and we were on one
Of our Flight into Egypt jaunts to Dublin.
They ran round the High Cross round and round
As if it were a maypole, which maybe it is:
Figure carvings of loaves and fishes, lions and dolphins.
I drank black coffee from a Thermos flask

And the children drank red lemonade
And they were wearing blue duffle coats with red scarves
And their small, round, laughing, freckled faces
Looked pointedly like the faces of the twelve apostles
Gazing out at us from the plinth of the Cross
Across a thousand years.
Only, of course, their father was not with us:
He was busy – busy being our family euphemism.
(Every family in Ireland has its own family euphemism
Like a heraldic device or a coat of arms.)
Jesus turned out to be a lovely man,
All that a woman could ever possibly dream of:
Gentle, wild, soft-spoken, courteous, sad;
Angular, awkward, candid, methodical;
Humorous, passionate, angry, kind;
Entirely sensitive to a woman's world.
Discreetly I invited Jesus to spend the night with me –
Stay with me, the day is almost over and it is getting dark –
But he waved me aside with one wave of his hand,
Not contemptuously, but compassionately.
"Our night will come," he smiled,
And he resumed chatting about my children,
All curiosity for their welfare and well-being.
It was like a fire burning in me when he talked to me.
There was only one matter I felt guilty about
And that was my empty vacant seat in the Abbey.
At closing time he kissed me on both cheeks
And we bade one another goodbye and then –
Just as I had all but given up hope –
He kissed me full on the mouth,
My mouth wet with alizarin lipstick
(A tube of Guerlain 4 which I've had for twelve years).
As I drove on into Dublin to the Shelbourne Hotel
I kept hearing his Midlands voice
Saying to me over and over, across the Garden of Gethsemane –
Our night will come.

Back in the town of Cahir,
In the Glen of Aherlow,
Not far from Peekaun
In the townland of Toureen,

At the foot of Galtee Mór
In the County of Tipperary,
For the sake of something to say
In front of our four sons
My husband said to me:
Well, what was Benjamino Gigli like?
Oh, 'twas a phenomenal concert!
And what was Tom Hickey like?
Miraculous – I whispered – miraculous.
Our night will come – he had smiled – our night will come.

10.30 a.m. Mass, 16 June 1985

When the priest made his entrance on the altar on the stroke of
    10.30,
He looked like a film star at an international airport
After having flown in from the other side of the world;
As if the other side of the world was the other side of the
    street;
Only, instead of an overnight bag slung over his shoulder,
He was carrying the chalice in its triangular green veil –
The way a dapper comedian cloaks a dove in a silk
    handkerchief.
Having kissed the altar, he strode over to the microphone:
I'd like to say how glad I am to be here with you this morning.

Oddly, you could see quite well that he was genuinely glad –
As if, in fact, he had been actually looking forward to this
    Sunday service,
Much the way I had been looking forward to it myself;
As if, in fact, this was the big moment of his day – of his week,
Not merely another ritual to be sanctimoniously performed.
He was a small, stocky, handsome man in his forties
With a big mop of curly grey hair
And black, horn-rimmed, tinted spectacles.
I am sure that more than half the women in the church
Fell in love with him on the spot –
Not to mention the men.
The reading from the prophet Ezekiel (17: 22–24)

Was a piece about cedar trees in Israel.
The epistle was St Paul.
With the Gospel, however, things began to look up –
The parable of the mustard seed as being the kingdom of
    heaven;
Now, then, the homily, at best probably inoffensively boring.

It's Father's Day – this small, solid, serious, sexy priest began –
And I want to tell you about my own father
Because none of you knew him.
If there was one thing he liked, it was a pint of Guinness;
If there was one thing he liked more than a pint of Guinness
It was two pints of Guinness.
But then when he was fifty-five he gave up drink.
I never knew why, but I had my suspicions.
Long after he had died my mother told me why:
He was so proud of me when I entered the seminary
That he gave up drinking as his way of thanking God.
But he himself never said a word about it to me –
He kept his secret to the end. He died from cancer
A few weeks before I was ordained a priest.
I'd like to go to Confession – he said to me:
OK – I'll go and get a priest – I said to him:
No – don't do that – I'd prefer to talk to *you.*
Dying, he confessed to me the story of his life.
How many of you here at Mass today are fathers?
I want all of you who are fathers to stand up.

Not one male in transept or aisle or nave stood up –
It was as if all the fathers in the church had been caught out
In the profanity of their sanctity,
In the bodily nakedness of their fatherhood,
In the carnal deed of their fathering;
Then, in ones and twos and threes, fifty or sixty of us
    clambered to our feet
And blushed to the roots of our being.
Now – declared the priest – let the rest of us
Praise these men our fathers.
He began to clap hands.
Gradually the congregation began to clap hands,
Until the entire church was ablaze with clapping hands –

Wives vying with daughters, sons with sons,
Clapping clapping clapping clapping clapping,
While I stood there in a trance, tears streaming down my
    cheeks:
Jesus!
I want to tell you about my own father
Because none of you knew him!

High-Speed Car Wash

We were making love in the high-speed car wash
When a peculiar thing occurred:
When I chanced to glance around
As we were readjusting our seat belts,
I saw two nuns
Peering in the back window of my new Peugeot!
They were not aware that I could see them.
Their faces were suffused in a golden red
Sanctuary light as they stared in at us entranced:
The plush, emerald, furry rollers of the car wash
Plied, wheeled, shuddered, backwards – forwards,
Crawling all over the body of the car.
We let ourselves be clawed in it, and by it,
Surrendering ourselves to it;
Immersed, and yet not immersed, in its floods and suds,
Flowing into one another like Christ flowing into the Cross,
In one another's throats soaking together.

As we drove off, the car was dripping wet;
The two nuns in black gleaming in the sun,
Each with, in her hands behind her back,
A rolled-up red umbrella twirling to and fro,
Snatches of converse floating on the air:
– It's a lovely-looking car, really, isn't it, the new Peugeot?
– Oh it is . . . I thought it looked lovely in the car wash.
And I said to Maeve Smith: Maria Callas –
    didn't she really have a truly divine voice?
And Maeve Smith said to me: Yes, but do you know that her real
    name was Maria Anna Kalageropoulos?

The Day Kerry Became Dublin

I was reading gas meters in Rialto –
In and out the keeled-over, weeping dustbins –
When, through the open doorway of the woman in the green
    tracksuit
Who's six feet tall and who has nine kids,
I heard a newsreader on the radio announcing
That the Bishop of Kerry had been appointed Archbishop of Dublin.
I couldn't help thinking that her bottom
Seemed to be independent of the rest of her body,
And how nice it would be to shake a leg with her
In a ballroom on a Sunday afternoon
Or to waltz with her soul at the bottom of the sea.
"Isn't that gas?" – she sizzles –
"Making the Bishop of Kerry the Archbishop of Dublin!"
Under her gas meter I get down on my knees
And say a prayer to the side-altars of her thighs,
And the three-light window of her breasts.
Excuse me, may I beam my torch in your crypt?
I go to Mass every morning, but I know no more
About the Archbishop of Dublin than I do about the Pope of Rome.
Still, I often think it would be
Uplifting to meet the Dalai Lama,
And to go to bed forever with the woman of my dreams,
And scatter the world with my children.

The Man with Five Penises

My father was a man with five penises.
I caught a glimpse of him in the bath one morning,
A Sunday morning after Mass and Holy Communion
(Normally he went to Golf after Mass and Holy Communion
But owing probably to weather conditions –
Sand-bunkers flooded and greens waterlogged –
There was no Golf on the Sunday morning in question).
I stepped into the bathroom, thinking it empty:
There he was, immobile as a crocodile,

In communion with waters that looked immensely fishy.
He peered at me out of his amphibious eyes;
I stepped back out, as out of a jungle comic.
"I am having a bath," he growled fretfully.
I could have sworn I saw, as I say,
At least four or five penises floating about,
Possibly six or seven.
For a long time after that, I used to feel sorry for him,
Concerned as well as sorry:
He must have a right old job on his hands every morning
Stuffing that lot into his pants.
And imagine what he must feel
When he has to use the public toilets,
Holding himself together for fear
All that lot might spill out –
What would the blokes in the next stalls say to him?
But also I began to worry about myself:
Maybe it was me who was all missing,
Me with my solitary member.
Over the next years I watched anxiously
For signs of new members
But membership remained steadfastly at one.
Now that I know the score –
Or at least now that I think I know the score –
I am inclined to think
One penis is more than enough.
Although I will always cherish the notion
Of my father as the man with five penises,
Initially I interpreted it as a sinister spectacle
And frankly it comes as a relief to discover
That there was in fact only one of them.
Unquestionably, one penis is more than enough.

Bewley's Oriental Café, Westmoreland Street

When she asked me to keep an eye on her things
I told her I'd be glad to keep an eye on her things.
While she breakdanced off to the ladies' loo
I concentrated on keeping an eye on her things.

What are you doing? a Security Guard growled,
His moustache gnawing at the beak of his peaked cap.
When I told him that a young woman whom I did not know
Had asked me to keep an eye on her things, he barked:
Instead of keeping an eye on the things
Of a young woman whom you do not know,
Keep an eye on your own things.
I put my two hands on his hips and squeezed him:
Look – for me the equivalent of the Easter Rising
Is to be accosted by a woman whom I do not know
And asked by her to keep an eye on her things;
On her medieval backpack and on her space-age Walkman;
Calm down and cast aside your peaked cap
And take down your trousers and take off your shoes
And I will keep an eye on your things also.
Do we not cherish all the children of the nation equally?
That young woman does not know the joy she has given me
By asking me if I would keep an eye on her things;
I feel as if I am on a Dart to Bray,
Keeping an eye on her things;
More radical than being on the pig's back,
Keeping an eye on nothing.
The Security Guard made a heap on the floor
Of his pants and shoes,
Sailing his peaked cap across the café like a frisbee.
His moustache sipped at a glass of milk.
It is as chivalrous as it is transcendental
To be sitting in Bewley's Oriental Café
With a naked Security Guard,
Keeping an eye on his things
And on old ladies
With, under their palaeolithic oxters, thousands of loaves of coarse
    brown bread.

The National Gallery Restaurant

One of the snags about the National Gallery Restaurant
Is that in order to gain access to it
One has to pass through the National Gallery.
I don't mind saying that at half-past twelve in the day,

In my handmade pigskin brogues and my pinstripe double-vent,
I don't feel like being looked at by persons in pictures
Or, worse, having to wax eloquent to a client's wife
About why it is that St Joseph is a black man
In Poussin's picture of *The Holy Family*:
The historical fact is that St Joseph was a white man.
I'd prefer to converse about her BMW – or my BMW –
Or the pros and cons of open-plan in office-block architecture.
I clench the handle of my briefcase
Wishing to Jesus Christ that I could strangle Homan Potterton –
The new young dynamic whizz-kid Director.
Oh but he's a flash in the pan –
Otherwise he'd have the savvy to close the National Gallery
When the National Gallery Restaurant is open.
Who does Homan Potterton think he is – Homan Potterton?

Man Smoking a Cigarette in the Barcelona Metro

I was standing in the Metro in the Plaza de Cataluña
Waiting for the rush-hour train to take me home to Tibidabo
When, gazing and staring – as one does gaze and stare –
At the passengers on the opposite platform,
I saw a naked man smoking a cigarette.
I cannot tell you how shocked I was.
He was by no means the only passenger smoking a cigarette
But he was the only naked passenger smoking a cigarette.
It was like seeing a horse in the rush hour smoking in the crowd.
Although I was in a hurry to get home to Tibidabo
I was so shocked that I ran back down the stairs,
Past the buskers and the jasmine-sellers and the Guardia Civil,
And crossed the tunnel to the other side of the tracks.
I went straight up to him and with no beating about the bush
I expressed to him my indignation and my ideological position:
"I happen to regard the naked human body as sacred –
If you want to profane it by smoking a cigarette
Have the decency to put on some clothes
And go about your smoking like everyone else
In shame and concealment, in jeans and ponchos.
What do you think clothes are for but to provide an alibi

For perversity, a cover-up for unnatural practices?"
He snatched the cigarette from his mouth and threw it down into
    the tracks,
And immediately he looked like a human being metamorphosed –
He began to quake with laughter, whinnying, neighing –
As if he were the first horse on earth,
Sauntering up and down the platform of the Metro
All knees and neck,
The bells of his genitals tolling in the groin of time.
As he rode up and down the platform,
In ones and twos and threes the women passengers
Began to fling their smoking cigarettes down into the tracks
And, as they did,
Their garments fell away from them
And they stepped out into themselves cigaretteless,
As with a newborn sense of pride and attraction.
In the end only all the men were left –
Fuming aliens –
Chain-smoking in their clobber,
Glaring with clumsy envy
At the naked man, cigaretteless,
Circled round by all of his newly equipped fans
Fanning him with nothing but the fans of their bodies
Riding high on thigh-bone and wrist:
No longer hooked on trains, or appearances, or loss.

Bob Dylan Concert at Slane, 1984

"I saw close up the make-up on Bob Dylan's face!"
She confides into the dressing-table looking glass in our bedroom,
Randy to report the felicity of what's morbid:
Mock-shock, sex-scandal, night-delight.

I glimpse the drenched pair of hips –
The drenched denimed pair of hips
Of the boy who, swimming across the river to get in,
Drowned. And while Bob Dylan and his band –
And a hundred thousand fans –
Made noise that out-Táined the Táin,

The St John of Malta Ambulance Women
Fished out a corpse –
Cradled it in a stretcher and wrapped it round
In grey swaddling – prison issue.

They offloaded him into the White Ambulance,
As into a Black Maria, then off and away – with him –
To begin a life sentence
For which there is no parole – no parole at all.
Not for nothing do men wear make-up
And poets earrings: not for nothing
Was Bob Dylan's noise noise, his music music.

The Cabinet Table

Alice Gunn is a cleaner woman
Down at Government Buildings,
And after seven o'clock Mass last night
(Isn't it a treat to be able to go to Sunday Mass
On a Saturday! To sit down to Saturday Night TV
Knowing you've fulfilled your Sunday obligation!)
She came back over to The Flats for a cup of tea
(I offered her sherry but she declined –
Oh, I never touch sherry on a Saturday night –
Whatever she meant by that, I don't know).
She had us in stitches, telling us
How one afternoon after a Cabinet Meeting
She got one of the security men
To lie down on the Cabinet Table,
And what she didn't do to him –
And what she did do to him –
She didn't half tell us;
But she told us enough to be going on with.
"Do you know what it is?" she says to me:
"No," says I, "what is it?"
"It's mahogany," she says, "pure mahogany."

The Feast of St Brigid, Friday the First of February 1985

Don't suppose Derrylin will ever be prestigious as Auschwitz:
So what?

Funny to think that we're here living in Derrylin:
So what?

Doubt if anybody has ever heard of Derrylin:
Maybe so.

In Enniskillen and Armagh they'd know about Derrylin:
Maybe so.

But in Belfast or Dublin they'd not know about Derrylin:
Maybe so.

Conceivable that somebody in Mexico might know about Derrylin:
Maybe so.

A thirty-nine-year-old father of two in Derrylin:
So what?

What's a thirty-nine-year-old father of two?
In all my years in Mexico I never heard of such a thing.

Waiting to drive a busload of Derrylin schoolkids to swimming pool:
So what?

Shot at the wheel, staggered up the aisle of the bus, shot dead:
So what?

Killers cheered as they climbed out of bus into getaway car:
Maybe so.

Drove off across the Border into the Republic of Ireland:
Maybe so.

Children had to wait for three hours before removal of corpse:
So what?

Children had to step over pool of blood and broken glass:
So what?

But you know what children are like:
So what?

On the First Day of Spring, on the Feast Day of Saint Brigid.
Maybe so.

* * *

Hymn to a Broken Marriage

Dear Nessa – Now that our marriage is over
I would like you to know that, if I could put back the clock
Fifteen years to the cold March day of our wedding,
I would wed you again and, if that marriage also broke,
I would wed you yet again and, if it a third time broke,
Wed you again, and again, and again, and again, and again:
If you would have me which, of course, you would not.
For, even you – in spite of your patience and your innocence
(Strange characteristics in an age such as our own) –
Even you require to shake off the addiction of romantic love
And seek, instead, the herbal remedy of a sane affection
In which are mixed in profuse and fair proportion
Loverliness, brotherliness, fatherliness:
A sane man could not espouse a more intimate friend than you.

"Windfall", 8 Parnell Hill, Cork

But, then, at the end of day I could always say –
Well, now, I am going home.
I felt elected, steeped, sovereign to be able to say –
I am going home.
When I was at home I liked to stay at home;
At home I stayed at home for weeks;
At home I used sit in a winged chair by the window
Overlooking the river and the factory chimneys,
The electricity power station and the car assembly works,
The fleets of trawlers and the pilot tugs,
Dreaming that life is a dream which is real,
The river a reflection of itself in its own waters,
Goya sketching Goya among the smoky mirrors.
The industrial vista was my Mont Sainte-Victoire.
While my children sat on my knees watching TV
Their mother, my wife, reclined on the couch
Knitting a bright-coloured scarf, drinking a cup of black coffee,
Smoking a cigarette – one of her own roll-ups.
I closed my eyes and breathed in and breathed out.

It is ecstasy to breathe if you are at home in the world.
What a windfall! A home of our own!
Our neighbours' houses had names like "Con Amore",
"Sans Souci", "Pacelli", "Montini", "Homesville".
But we called our home "Windfall".
"Windfall", 8 Parnell Hill, Cork.
In the gut of my head coursed the leaf of tranquillity
Which I dreamed was known only to Buddhist Monks
In lotus monasteries high up in the Hindu Kush.
Down here in the dark depths of Ireland,
Below sea level in the city of Cork,
In a city as intimate and homicidal as a Little Marseilles,
In a country where all the children of the nation
Are not cherished equally
And where the best go homeless, while the worst
Erect block-house palaces – self-regardingly ugly –
Having a home of your own can give to a family
A chance in a lifetime to transcend death.

At the high window, shipping from all over the world
Being borne up and down the busy, yet contemplative, river;
Skylines drifting in and out of skylines in the cloudy valley;
Firelight at dusk, and city lights;
Beyond them the control tower of the airport on the hill –
A lighthouse in the sky flashing green to white to green;
Our black-and-white cat snoozing in the corner of a chair;
Pastels and etchings on the four walls, and over the mantelpiece
"Van Gogh's Grave" and "Lovers in Water";
A room wallpapered in books and family photograph albums
Chronicling the adventures and metamorphoses of family life:
In swaddling clothes in Mammy's arms on baptism day;
Being a baby of nine months and not remembering it;
Face-down in a pram, incarcerated in a high chair;
Everybody, including strangers, wearing shop-window smiles;
With Granny in Felixstowe, with Granny in Ballymaloe;
In a group photo in First Infants, on a bike at thirteen;
In the back garden in London, in the back garden in Cork;
Performing a headstand after First Holy Communion;
Getting a kiss from the Bishop on Confirmation Day;
Straw hats in the Bois de Boulogne, wearing wings at the
     seaside;

Mammy and Daddy holding hands on the Normandy Beaches;
Mammy and Daddy at the wedding of Jeremiah and Margot;
Mammy and Daddy queueing up for *Last Tango in Paris*;
Boating on the Shannon, climbing mountains in Kerry;
Building sandcastles in Killala, camping in Barley Cove;
Picnicking in Moone, hide-and-go-seek in Clonmacnoise;
Riding horses, cantering, jumping fences;
Pushing out toy yachts in the pond in the Tuileries;
The Irish College revisited in the Rue des Irlandais;
Sipping an *orange pressé* through a straw on the roof of the
    Beaubourg;
Dancing in Père Lachaise, weeping at Auvers.
Year in, year out, I pored over these albums accumulating,
My children looking over my shoulder, exhilarated as I was,
Their mother presiding at our ritual from a distance –
The far side of the hearthrug, diffidently, proudly.
Schoolbooks on the floor and pyjamas on the couch –
Whose turn is it tonight to put the children to bed?

Our children swam about our home
As if it was their private sea,
Their own unique, symbiotic fluid
Of which their parents also partook.
Such is home – a sea of your own –
In which you hang upside down from the ceiling
With equanimity, while postcards from Thailand on the
    mantelpiece
Are raising their eyebrow markings benignly:
Your hands dangling their prayers to the floorboards of your
    home,
Sifting the sands underneath the surfaces of conversations,
The marine insect life of the family psyche.
A home of your own – or a sea of your own –
In which climbing the walls is as natural
As making love on the stairs;
In which when the telephone rings
Husband and wife are metamorphosed into smiling accomplices,
Both declining to answer it;
Initiating, instead, a yet more subversive kiss –
A kiss they have perhaps never attempted before –
And might never have dreamed of attempting

Were it not for the telephone belling.
Through the bannisters or along the bannister rails
The pyjama-clad children solemnly watching
Their parents at play, jumping up and down in support,
Race back to bed, gesticulating wordlessly:
The most subversive unit in society is the human family.

We're almost home, pet, almost home . . .
Our home is at . . .
I'll be home . . .
I have to go home now . . .
I want to go home now . . .
Are you feeling homesick?
Are you anxious to get home? . . .
I can't wait to get home . . .
Let's stay at home tonight and . . .
What time will you be coming home at? . . .
If I'm not home by six at the latest, I'll phone . . .
We're nearly home, don't worry, we're nearly home . . .

But then with good reason
I was put out of my home:
By a keen wind felled.
I find myself now without a home
Having to live homeless in the alien, foreign city of Dublin.
It is an eerie enough feeling to be homesick
Yet knowing you will be going home next week;
It is an eerie feeling beyond all ornithological analysis
To be homesick knowing that there is no home to go home to:
Day by day, creeping, crawling,
Moonlighting, escaping,
Bed-and-breakfast to bed-and-breakfast;
Hostels, centres, one-night hotels.

Homeless in Ðublin,
Blown about the suburban streets at evening,
Peering in the windows of other people's homes,
Wondering what it must feel like
To be sitting around a fire –
Apache or Cherokee or Bourgeoisie –
Beholding the firelit faces of your family,

Beholding their starry or their TV gaze:
Windfall to Windfall – can you hear me?
Windfall to Windfall . . .
We're almost home, pet, don't worry anymore, we're almost home.

The Jewish Bride

after Rembrandt

At the black canvas of estrangement,
As the smoke empties from the ruins under a gold winter sky,
Death-trains clattering across the back gardens of Amsterdam –
Sheds, buckets, wire, concrete,
Manholes, pumps, pliers, scaffolding –
I see, as if for the first time,
The person you were, and are, and always will be
Despite the evil that men do:
The teenage girl on the brink of womanhood
Who, when I met you, was on the brink of everything –
Composing fairytales and making drawings
That used remind your friends of Anderson and Thurber –
Living your hidden life that promised everything
Despite all the maimed, unreliable men and women
Who were at that moment congregating all around you:
Including, of course, most of all, myself.
You made of your bedroom a flowing stream
Into which, daily, you threw proofs of your dreams;
Pinned to your bedroom wall with brass-studded drawing pins
Newspaper and magazine photographs of your heroes and
     heroines.
People who met you breathed the air of freedom,
And sensuality fragile as it was wild:
"Nessa's air makes free," people used say,
Like in the dark ages, "Town air makes free."
The miracle is that you survived me.
You stroll about the malls and alleyways of Amsterdam,
About its islands and bridges, its archways and jetties,
With spring in your heels, although it is winter;
Privately, publicly, along the Grand Parade;

A Jewish Bride who has survived the death camp,
Free at last of my swastika eyes
Staring at you from across spiked dinner plates
Or from out of the bunker of a TV armchair;
Free of the glare off my jackboot silence;
Free of the hysteria of my gestapo voice;
Now your shyness replenished with all your old cheeky confidence –
That grassy well at which red horses used rear up and sip
With young men naked riding bareback calling your name.
Dog-muzzle of tension torn down from your face;
Black polythene of asphyxiation peeled away from your soul;
Your green eyes quivering with dark, sunny laughter
And – all spreadeagled and supple again – your loving, freckled
    hands.

Around the Corner from Francis Bacon

Around the corner from Francis Bacon
Was where we made our first nest together
On the waters of the flood;
Where we first lived in sin:
The sunniest, most virtuous days of our life.
Not even the pastoral squalor of Clapham Common,
Nor the ghetto life of Notting Hill Gate,
Nor the racial drama of Barcelona,
Nor the cliffhanging bourgeois life of Cork City
Could ever equal those initial, primeval times together
Living in sin
In the halcyon ambience of South Kensington,
A haven for peaceful revolutionaries such as Harriet Waugh
Or Francis Bacon, or ourselves.
I slept on an ironing board in the kitchen
And you slept in the attic:
Late at night when all the other flat-dwellers
Were abed and – we thought wishfully – asleep,
You crept down the attic ladder
To make love with me on the ironing board,
As if we had known each other in a previous life
So waterily did our two body-phones attune,

Underwater swimming face to face in the dark,
Francis Bacon-Cimabue style.
My body-phone was made in Dublin
But your body-phone was made in Japan.
Standing up naked on the kitchen floor,
In the smog-filtered moonlight,
You placed your hand on my little folly, murmuring:
I have come to iron you, Sir Board.
Far from the tyrant liberties of Dublin, Ireland,
Where the comedy of freedom was by law forbidden
And truth, since the freedom of the State, gone underground.
When you had finished ironing me
I felt like hot silk queueing up to be bathèd
Under a waterfall in Samarkand
Or a mountain stream in Enniskerry.
Every evening I waited for you to come home,
Nipping out only in the rush hour to the delicatessen
Where Francis Bacon, basket under arm,
Surfacing like Mr Mole from his mews around the corner,
Used be stocking up in tomato purée and curry powder
Before heading off into the night and The Colony Room Club
Into whose green dark you and I sometimes also tiptoed.
In your own way you were equally Beatrix Potter-like,
Coming home to me laden with fish fingers and baked beans.
While I read to you from Dahlberg, you taught me about the
    psyche
Of the female orang-outang caged in the zoo:
Coronation Street ... Z Cars ... The World in Action ...
Then Z Cars to beat all Z Cars – our own world in action –
The baskets of your eyes chock-a-block with your unique
    brands
Of tomato purée and curry powder;
Or, *That Was The Week That Was*, and then, my sleeping friend,
In the sandhills of whose shoulders sloping secretly down
Into small, hot havens of pure unscathèd sands
Where the only sounds are the sounds of the sea's tidal waters
Flooding backwards and forwards,
Tonight is the night that always is forever –
Ten or twenty minutes in the dark,
And in four million years or so
My stomach will swarm again suddenly with butterflies,

As with your bowl of water and your towel,
Your candle and your attic ladder,
Your taut high wire and your balancing pole,
A green minidress over your arm, a Penguin paperback in
    your hand,
I watch you coming towards me in the twilight of rush hour
On your hands and knees
And on the wet, mauve tip of your extended tongue
The two multicoloured birds of your plumed eyes ablaze
Around the corner from Francis Bacon.

Raymond of the Rooftops

The morning after the night
The roof flew off the house
And our sleeping children narrowly missed
Being decapitated by falling slates,
I asked my husband if he would
Help me put back the roof:
But no – he was too busy at his work
Writing for a women's magazine in London
An Irish fairytale called *Raymond of the Rooftops*.
Will you have a heart, woman – he bellowed –
Can't you see I am up to my eyes and ears in work,
Breaking my neck to finish *Raymond of the Rooftops*,
Fighting against time to finish *Raymond of the Rooftops*,
Putting everything I have got into *Raymond of the Rooftops*?

Isn't is well for him? *Everything he has got!*

All I wanted him to do was to stand
For an hour, maybe two hours, three at the most,
At the bottom of the stepladder
And hand me up slates while I slated the roof:
But no – once again I was proving to be the insensitive,
Thoughtless, feckless even, wife of the artist.
There was I up to my fat, raw knees in rainwater
Worrying him about the hole in our roof
While he was up to his neck in *Raymond of the Rooftops*.

Will you have a heart, woman – he bellowed –
Can't you see I am up to my eyes and ears in work,
Breaking my neck to finish *Raymond of the Rooftops*,
Fighting against time to finish *Raymond of the Rooftops*,
Putting everything I have got into *Raymond of the Rooftops*?

Isn't it well for him? *Everything he has got*!

The Pièta's Over

The Pièta's over – and, now, my dear, droll husband,
As middle age tolls its bell along the via dolorosa of life,
It is time for you to get down off my knees
And learn to walk on your own two feet.
I will admit it is difficult for a man of forty
Who has spent all his life reclining in his wife's lap,
Being given birth to by her again and again, year in, year out.
To stand on his own two feet, but it has to be done –
Even if at the end of the day he commits hari-kari.
A man cannot be a messiah for ever,
Messiahing about in his wife's lap,
Suffering fluently in her arms,
Flowing up and down in the lee of her bosom,
Forever being mourned for by the eternal feminine,
Being keened over every night of the week for sixty mortal
     years.

The Pièta's over – it is Easter over all our lives:
The revelation of our broken marriage, and its resurrection;
The breaking open of the tomb, and the setting free.
Painful as it was for me, I put you down off my knee
And I showed you the door.
Although you pleaded with me to keep you on my knee
And to mollycoddle you, humour you, within the family circle
("Don't put me out into the cold world," you cried),
I did not take the easy way out and yield to you.
Instead I took down the door off its hinges
So that the sunlight shone all the more squarely
Upon the pure, original brokenness of our marriage;

I whispered to you, quietly, yet audibly,
For all the diaspora of your soul to hear:
The Pièta's over.

Yet even now, one year later, you keep looking back
From one side of Europe to the other,
Gaping at my knees as if my knees
Were the source of all that you have been, are, or will be.
By all means look around you, but stop looking back.
I would not give you shelter if you were homeless in the streets
For you must make your home in yourself, not in a woman.
Keep going out the road for it is only out there –
Out there where the river achieves its riverlessness –
That you and I can become at last strangers to one another,
Ready to join up again on Resurrection Day.
Therefore, I must keep whispering to you, over and over:
My dear loved one, I have to tell you,
You have run the gamut of piety –
The Pièta's over.

Wives May Be Coveted But Not by Their Husbands

We lived in a remote dower house in Cork
Leaving the doors and windows always unlocked.
When herds of deer came streaming through the kitchen
At first we laughed, but then we quarrelled –
As the years went by, we quarrelled more than laughed:
"You seem to care more about deer than about me" –
"I am weary of subsisting in an eyrie of antlers" –
"Be a man and erect a fence" –
"Be a woman and put venison in the pot."
When an old gold stag dawdled by her rocking chair
And she caressed his warm hide with smiling hands,
I locked myself in the attic and sulked for weeks.
Stags, does, and fauns, grew thick around her bed
As in her bloom of life she evolved, alone.

The Turkish Carpet

No man could have been more unfaithful
To his wife than me;
Scarcely a day passed
That I was not unfaithful to her.
I would be in the living room ostensibly reading or writing
When she'd come home from work unexpectedly early
And, popping her head round the door, find me wrapped round
A figure of despair.
It would not have been too bad if I'd been wrapped round
Another woman – that would have been infidelity of a kind
With which my wife could have coped.
What she could not cope with, try as she did,
Was the infidelity of unhope,
The personal betrayal of universal despair.
When my wife called to me from the living-room door
Tremblingly ajar, with her head peering round it –
The paintwork studded with headwounds and knuckleprints –
Called to me across the red, red grass of home –
The Turkish Carpet –
Which her gay mother had given us as a wedding present
(And on which our children had so often played
Dolls' houses on their hands and knees
And headstands and cartwheels and dances,
And on which we ourselves had so often made love),
I clutched my despair to my breast
And with brutality kissed it – Sweet Despair –
Staring red-eyed down at *The Turkish Carpet*.
O my dear husband, will you not be faithful to me?
Have I not given you hope all the days of my life?

The Berlin Wall Café

Once we were Berlin – you and I . . .
Until an agèd priest,
As shepherdlike a pastor as one could hope to meet
In the neon forest –

Father Boniface –
Married us with a gun.
Tears of joy were in his eyes as, with a flick of his wrist
(All mottled and bluey),
He waved his pistol in the air, firing gaily:
A long white wall unfurled from it,
Trailing its roll-top and its graffiti.

Thus it was we pitched our tent in the continuing city:
Ecstatically lonely together in a two-room flat
In Bernauer Strasse beside the Berlin Wall,
Around the corner from the open-air table tennis tables
In Swinemünder Strasse,
Handy for the *U-Bahn* in Volta Strasse.
I counted myself the luckiest man alive in Berlin
To be marooned with you:
You – incarnate coincidence of the beautiful and the true –
All risk and give –
Reticent woman whose eyes were caves
Concealed in cascades of red hair.
Yet all I could talk about was the Berlin Wall,
As if the Berlin Wall was more important than you!
On the night you gave birth to our child
I was too busy to attend – addressing a meeting
On the Berlin Wall!
When I should have been cooking your supper
After your long day's work in the office in Spandau,
I was manning the Observation Platforms –
Making faces at the *Volkspolizei*!

At the end of 1980,
When I should have been minding our marriage
And concentrating on loving you,
All I could consider was whether or not
I should become Editor of the *Berlin Wall Gazette*:
I was a most proper Charlie!
No wonder that your friends could not abide me!
Whenever they saw me approaching they scattered:
"Watch out – here he comes – Checkpoint Charlie."
In 1984 you could stand it no more:
You escaped from West Berlin

Into East Berlin – where you are free of me
And of the Show Biz of the Free Democracies
Advertising Unemployment and All That Jazz.
Purple with envy, I hear you have teamed up
With an all-woman jazz combo in Unter den Linden.
They say there's no more exciting woman in Berlin
Than when you're alone on the high-hat cymbals
To beat the band in the Berlin Wall Café:
Once we were Berlin – you and I . . .

The Marriage Contract

She is the kind of person
(The kind of person I like)
Who never reads the small print in contracts:
Eg – where it says "he's a xenophobic psychopath",
She took no notice, taking me at face value.

Today – our broken marriage broken –
Busybodies are quick to tell her
What a noble, handsome soul she is
And what a bowsy her ex-husband was:
But she has no time for these
Soothsayers of the marriage contract,
She being an anarchist herself –
With always, at the worst of times,
Dreams of good times;
And with always, at the best of times,
Memories of bad times.
Besides, it is of no piquancy to her now
To be told that her husband
Was a retarded third-degree necrophiliac:
She remembers him as he was,
Pimples and all,
The man she loved and the man she married.
The pimples bloomed in swarms
Quite naturally over the years
Until there were simply too many of them.
She took a second glance at the contract,

And realized that it had run out.
Afterwards, she gave it to him as a souvenir
Knowing his passion for such memorabilia:
By the light of a TV programme he was not watching –
A black-and-white film of *King Lear* with the sound turned down –
He sunk it into the frontal lobes of his brain,
Like a blank cheque from God sunk into stone.

At the Funeral of the Marriage

At the funeral of the marriage
My wife and I paced
On either side of the hearse,
Our children racing behind it . . .
As the coffin was emptied
Down into the bottomless grave,
Our children stood in a half-circle,
Playing on flutes and recorders.
My wife and I held hands.
While the mourners wept and the gravediggers
Unfurled shovelfuls of clay
Down on top of the coffin,
We slowly walked away,
Accomplices beneath the yew trees.
We had a cup of tea in the graveyard café
Across the street from the gates:
We discussed the texture of the undertaker's face,
Its beetroot quality.
As I gazed at my wife
I wondered who on earth she was –
I saw that she was a green-eyed stranger.
I said to her: Would you like to go to a film?
She said: I would love to go to a film.
In the back seats of the cinema,
As we slid up and down in our seats
In a frenzy of hooks and clasps,
The manager courteously asked us not to take off our clothes.
We walked off urgently through the rain-strewn streets
Into a leaf-sodden cul-de-sac

And as, from the tropic isle of our bed,
Chock-a-block with sighs and cries,
We threw our funeral garments on the floor,
We could hear laughter outside the door.
There is no noise children love more to hear
Than the noise of their parents making love:
O my darling, who on earth are you?

On Falling in Love with a Salesman in a Shoe Shop

I live in a room with no windows:
Weeks go by with but a memory of daylight
Trickling under the door.
After one such week under a naked light bulb,
Crouched by a gas fire in a torn-up armchair
Whose springs have all gasped their last gasp,
I emerged into daylight in order to purchase
A new pair of shoes.
There was no need for me to purchase a new pair of shoes,
But I felt that if I did purchase a new pair of shoes
I would somehow feel better
About the world, for in my experience
The world is not the sort of place
I would choose to inhabit
If I had had any choice in the matter.
I am so cold I have to sleep in my overcoat.
There are three inches of water on the kitchen floor.
There was a young man in the shop,
Not my type at all,
A brisk, athletic, TV advertisement sort of chap:
But his matter-of-fact gentleness,
His courtesy,
Shocked me.
After I had picked out a pair of watertight shoes,
He invited me to sit down beside him on a bench
And to talk with him about the new situation:
There we sat alone in the shoe shop
While the world marched up and down outside
Like the Grand Old Duke of York

(For whom, I may say, I have an old affection
From the days when I used discuss him with my baby daughters);
There we sat alone in the shoe shop
Discussing shoes – discussing watertight shoes.
When I came out of the shop
I could not stand still;
When I got back to my bedsit
I put my feet in a basin of hot water,
A red plastic basin of hot water,
And I closed my eyes and dreamed
Of what it would be like
To love and be loved –
To die of it.
I wish that my wife,
Instead of leaving me,
Had taken my head in her hands
And put it into a basin of water
And kept it deep down there until dead.
On the other hand, if the shoe salesman were to marry me,
I suppose that he would also probably leave me.

The Vision of St Hubert

after Breughel

I decided to hunt down my wife:
Gauleiters of Revenge revved up in my veins
Egged on by Storm-Troopers of Greed;
I gathered round me all my Dogs of Self-Pity,
Long, lean, Bloodhounds of Self-Pity,
Black-and-white fellows with pointed wet snouts,
And into the city we plunged –
Where I knew she had been hidden away
By her friends in a Jewish ghetto.
Tonight I would hunt down my wife –
She who had taken from me
My home and my children,
She who had taken from me herself!
What right had she who belonged to me
To take from me herself?

If, with tears and fears, she has the neck
To exhibit herself as the hapless doe with her fauns,
I will prove myself to be more than a stag for her:
I will put the fear of God the Führer into her
And smear the walls of her bedroom with the blood of her children;
I will prove myself to be a true male savage, three-leggèd and
    merciless.

It was not difficult to hunt her down:
I rode around the rooftops of the city
Until I unearthed her, with her children,
In a bedroom on a cliff overlooking the city.
Go away from me, Hubert! – she cried
And, as she cried it out again and again,
Go away from me, Hubert, go away from me!
I heard in her cry her voice:
Her voice that last I'd heard when first we'd met –
Seventeen odd years ago.
In the seventeen odd years
Since we'd first met and married
I had never listened to her voice,
Listening out only for the voice of my wife.

World, I'd like to introduce you to my wife –
O Hubert, don't talk like a jumped-up pimp.

But now as I heard her voice in her voice
I fell in love with her, as it was in the beginning:
I got down off my high horse and knelt at her feet
In the bedroom doorway, and while all my murderous
Drunken accomplices of the night melted away,
Dawn lit up the chimney-stack skyline of Cork City;
And while our two sleeping children clasped in their hands
Close up to their foreheads a frog and a lizard,
Calmly I pledged her my prayer and affection,
Promising her never again to seek her out,
Never again in this city to darken her doorway,
To woo her only and always in the eternity of my loss:
Let us now praise famous women – and their children.

GOING HOME TO RUSSIA (1987)

The Rape of Europa

after Titian

to Seamus and Marie

"Is life a dream?" – my sleeping daughter beseeches me,
Gaping up at me anxiously out of the ashes of her sleep
As I bend down low over her to kiss her goodnight –
"I was playing on the shore with the other girls,
Under the cliff where the Car Assembly Works is,
When the man who works in Mr Conway's field,
The big fellow who lives alone and who always says hallo,
Casually came striding towards us through the barbed wire,
The muscles in his arms bubbling in the sun
As if the empty sandhills were packed stadia,
And his body – he had left off all his clothes –
Was a nude of crimson triangles of blood,
Where the barbs had pierced his snow-white flesh;
The other girls began to cry –
I do not know why I did not also begin to cry,
Only I thought he looked quite beautiful the way he was.
The more I gazed into his grassy eyes
The more his wounds from the barbed wire appeared to teem,
Until curly hair sprouted from each wound, and big floppy ears,
And his mouth and nostrils became one large, wet, slithery snout,
And when he leaned over towards me, putting his two hands
On the yellow sand, they changed into hooves,
And two legs fell down slowly out of his backside
With a thin, smiling tail the length of a clothesline.
He curled up on the sand and he looked so forlorn
I thought of how I would like to go to sleep on his back
And caress his hide with my hand round his horn
And pillow my face in his shoulderblades
And float off across the ocean to the Island of Bulls
In whose blue and red skies
I could see astronaut babies cascading in embryos.
And when I asked him if he would give me a ride
He lowed as if the dusk was a towel on his brow
And I put flowers on his head,

151

Flowers which I had been gathering with the other girls
In the seaside meadows among the hills of fern –
Wild rose, yellow crocus, narcissus, violet, hyacinth –
And just then as I mounted him you came into my bedroom
And I looked up and I saw you
Bending down low over me to kiss me goodnight.
"Life is a dream, Papa, isn't it? Life is a dream?"

"Life is a dream, Phoenix, life is a dream.
Go back to sleep now and have a wild ride on your bull
For there's only noise to lose when quietude is on the rampage.
Dream is life's element and symbol – as the sea's the eel's;
We expire if we're deprived of our element and symbol.
Smeared, daubed, licked, bloodied in entrails of dream.
If the bull has loosed the paddock of his flesh it means
That boys might once more again be boys and girls girls,
Not entrepreneurs and shareholders in the Car Assembly Works,
To be assessed and calculated in the files of newspapers.
When you wake up in the morning
Before you brush your teeth, before even you say your prayers,
Turn over on your back and count
The big fellow who works in Mr Conway's field
As you count sheep when you're going to sleep;
Count all the babies who have never been born
As well as all the babies who have been born.
If you're late for school, I'll write a note for teacher.
Sleep, Phoenix, sleep."

The Poetry Reading Last Night in the Royal Hibernian Hotel

The main thing – the first and last thing – to say
About the poetry reading last night in the Royal Hibernian Hotel
Is that the Royal Hibernian Hotel does not exist;
It was demolished last year to make way for an office block.
If, therefore, anyone was to ask me what a poetry reading is,
I should have the utmost difficulty in enlightening them,
All the more so after having attended last night's poetry reading
In the Royal Hibernian Hotel which does not exist.
A poetry reading appears to be a type of esoteric social ritual

Peculiar to the cities of northern Europe and North America.
What happens is that for one reason or another,
Connected usually with moods in adolescence
To do with Family and School and Sexuality,
A chap – or a dame – begins writing things
Which he – she – calls "Poetry"
And over the years – especially between the ages of fourteen and
    sixty-four –
What with one kind of wangling or another,
He – she – publishes seventeen or nineteen slim volumes
Entitled *Stones* or *Bricks* or *Pebbles* or *Gravel*;
Or *History Notes* or *Digs* or *French Class*.
He – she – is hellbent on boring the pants off people
And that's where the poetry-reading trick comes in.
The best poets are the poets who can bore you the most,
Such as the fellow last night who was so adept at boring us
That for the entire hour that he stood there mumbling and whining
My mind was altogether elsewhere with the reindeer
In Auden's Cemetery for the Silently and Very Fast.
A poetry reading is a ritual in communal schizophrenia
In which the minds of the audience are altogether elsewhere
While their bodies are kept sitting upright or in position.
Afterwards it is the custom to clap as feebly as you can –
A subtle exercise appropriate to the overall scheme.
To clap feebly – or to feebly clap – is as tricky as it sounds.
It is the custom then to invite the poet to autograph the slim
    volume
And while the queue forms like the queue outside a confessional,
The poet cringing archly on an upright chair,
You say to your neighbour "A fine reading, wasn't it?"
To which he must riposte
"Indeed – nice to see you lying through your teeth."
The fully clothèd audience departs, leaving the poet
Who bored the pants off them
Laughing all the way to the toilet
Of a hotel that does not exist,
Thence to the car park that *does* exist
Where he has left his Peugeot with the broken exhaust pipe.
"Night-night" – he mews to the automatic carpark attendant
Who replies with one bright, emphatic, onomatopoeic monosyllable:
"Creep."

Cardinal Dies of Heart Attack in Dublin Brothel

Edifying, edifying – you cry – edifying –
As in silence we sit listening to the six o'clock TV news
That our belovèd cardinal has died
In the arms of his favourite prostitute.
At last – I think to myself in the solitude of my soul –
A sign that the Church of God is moving into the light.

I put on my overcoat and, as there are rainclouds,
I take the precaution of bringing along my umbrella.
I have to walk the long way round to the church
Whose candlelit darkness proves always consoling.
I insert a 50p piece in the moneybox and light three candles:
One for the Cardinal, one for the Lady,
And one for the Unknown Soldier in all of us.
I kneel down in a pew to pray
But I quickly translate myself into a sitting position.
The sitting position is my natural position.
My soul is borne up on wings of flame
In which I think again of the agèd cardinal's submission
To that lovely, ephemeral woman
And of her compassion which, by all accounts,
Was as tender as it was fiery.
I depart the church, feeling restored in body and soul.
As you say, my dear wife, with your characteristic wit
And solicitude – our belovèd cardinal who has died in a brothel
Was, in the very last analysis, "a broth of a cardinal".

What Shall I Wear, Darling, to The Great Hunger?

"What shall I wear, darling, to *The Great Hunger?*"
She shrieked at me helplessly from the east bedroom
Where the west wind does be blowing betimes.
I did not hesitate to hazard a spontaneous response:
"Your green evening gown –
Your see-through, sleeveless, backless, green evening gown."
We arrived at the Peacock

In good time for everybody to have a good gawk at her
Before the curtain went up on *The Great Hunger*.
At the interval everybody was clucking about, cooing
That it was simply stunning – her dress –
"Darling, you look like Mother Divinity in your see-through,
Sleeveless, backless, green evening gown – it's so visual!"
At the party after the show – simply everybody was there –
Winston Lenihan, Consolata O'Carroll-Riviera, Yves St Kiekegaard –
She was so busy being admired that she forgot to get drunk.
But the next morning it was business as usual –
Grey serge pants, blue donkey jacket – driving around Dolphin's
    Barn
In her Opel Kadett hatchback
Checking up on the rents. "All these unmarried young mothers
And their frogspawn, living on the welfare –
You would think that it never occurs to them
That it's their rents that pay for the outfits I have to wear
Whenever *The Great Hunger* is playing at the Peacock.
No, it never occurs to them that in Ireland today
It is not easy to be a landlord and a patron of the arts.
It is not for nothing that we in Fail Gael have a social conscience:
Either you pay the shagging rent or you get out on the street.
Next week I have to attend three-and-a-half *Great Hungers*,
Not to mention a half-dozen *Juno and the Paycocks*."

The Late Mr Charles Lynch Digresses

to Síabhra

Having sat all morning at the bay window
Of the run-down boarding house on the bitch-bedecked hill
Overlooking the drowned city of Cork
With a long-stemmed wine-glass balancing on the fulcrum
Of his ladylike, crossed knees – the deceased piano virtuoso
In the threadbare black greatcoat and frayed white shirt
Tiptoes through the urban heat
And scrupulously digresses into the Cork School of Music
When, from next door's crucial radio studios,
A production technician, Evie, comes skittering –

"Mr Lynch, they necessitate you urgently next door."
Without altering the adagio of his gait, or its cantabile,
The ghostly pianist, the master digresser,
Perilously whispers:
"I'm sorry, Evie – but I'm *dashing*."

The Anglo-Irish Agreement, 1986

to Constance Short

I

The British Army barracks in Crossmaglen
Has the air of an exclusive suburb in Dublin:
All silent and inimical, aloof and airy.
Except for the toings and froings of helicopters and crickets
You could hear a pin drop – or a bomb.
Strolling across the village square in Crossmaglen
You might be in Ailesbury Road in Ballsbridge
Where each detached and fortress-visaged residence
Has the air of a habitat inhabited by no one.
There are two hundred troops inside the British Army barracks
But you would never know it – no more than you would know
That there is a solicitor on £130,000 a year
Inside that mansion with his wife and two children.
All armies
Are armies of occupation.
The exclusive suburbs of Dublin city
Are necklaces of Crossmaglens
In which armies of occupation fester
Behind fortified walls and electronically controlled gates.

II

Let the armies exchange uniforms.
Let the British Army in Crossmaglen
Patrol the village square in Nissan Bluebirds
Or in chauffeur-driven Datsun Laurels
And wear Celtic pinstripe suits on duty

Or Laura Ashley frocks,
While in Ailesbury Road and Clyde Road,
Elgin, Raglan and Shrewsbury,
Let the residents disport
In British Army uniform,
Mothers-in-law and newly marrieds
Darting in and out of gateways with bayonets at the ready,
Walkie-talkies and backpacks.
The Anglo-Irish Agreement
Which has been in force
For longer than we can remember –
For at least sixty-four years and more likely
Eleven thousand years –
Should make it mandatory for residents of Ballsbridge
– Killiney and Rathgar, Foxrock and Howth –
To do a tour of duty
In the British Army barracks in Crossmaglen.
The rest of us can pretend to be natives –
What we have always been,
Working-class people in our place.

The Divorce Referendum, Ireland, 1986

By the time the priest started into his sermon
I was adrift on a leaf of tranquillity,
Feeling only the need and desire to praise,
To feed praise to the tiger of life.
Hosanna, Hosanna, Hosanna.
He was a gentle-voiced, middle-aged man,
Slightly stooped under a gulf of grey hair,
Slightly tormented by an excess of humility.
He talked felicitously of the Holy Spirit –
As if he really believed in what he was preaching –
Not as if he was aiming to annotate a diagram
Or to sub-edit the Gospel,
But as if the Holy Spirit was real as rainwater.
Then his voice changed colour –
You could see it change from pink into white.
He rasped: "It is the wish of the Hierarchy

That today the clergy of Ireland put before you
Christ's teaching on the indissolubility of marriage
And to remind you that when you vote in the Divorce Referendum
The Church's teaching and Christ's teaching are one and the
    same."
Stunned, I stared up at him from my pew
As he stood there supported by candles and gladioli,
Vestments, and altarboys at his feet;
I could feel my breastplate tighten and my shoulderblades quiver;
I knew the anger that Jesus Christ felt
When he drove from the temple the traders and stockbrokers.
I have come into this temple today to pray
And be healed by, and joined with, the Spirit of Life,
Not to be invaded by ideology.
I say unto you, preacher and orators of the Hierarchy,
Do not bring ideology into my house of prayer.

I closed my eyes
And I did not open them again until I could hear
The priest murmuring the prayers of the Consecration.
At Holy Communion I kept my eyes on a small girl
To whom the priest had to bend low to give her the host.
Curtseying, she smiled eagerly, and flew back down the aisle,
Carrying in her breast the Eucharist of her innocence:
May she have children of her own
And as many husbands as will praise her –
For what are husbands for, but to praise their wives?

EI Flight 106: New York–Dublin

After J. M. W. Turner

There was an empty seat between us as the jumbo began to taxi
And she – a craggy girl of about seventy-five years of age –
Leaned over and whispered conspiratorially, huskily:
"We've got an empty seat to ourselves – between ourselves."
She winked, all her wing-flaps trembling,
Slashes of eyeshadow, daubs of rouge,
Her eyes roving around in their sockets as they scoured me

For what pusillanimous portions of manhood I might possess.
She exuded femininity as an elephant exudes hide:
Wearing all of her seventy-five years as ethereally
As an adolescent girl wearing earrings.
"We've got an empty seat to ourselves," she rasped
As I gazed at her pink, silk, sleeveless dress with turquoise triskeles
And at her moist, fiery eyes rearing up in her skull.
"Ladies and gentlemen, our feature film tonight is *The Flamingo Kid*.
We'll be commencing our take-off in approximately five minutes."
As we continued to taxi she showed me her bottle of Drambuie –
      "Duty-free!"
High over Kennedy, as we turned tail on Manhattan,
Heading out over Long Island for the North Atlantic,
She had a member of the cabin crew fetch her a baby scotch
And a tumbler chock-a-block with ice cubes.
She sighed: "I don't drink myself,"
As I stared down at the Cape Cod coastline,
"Except, of course, when I'm flying.
Rusty Nails is what I like – Drambuie and scotch."
I could not keep my eyes off her as she guzzled it down,
And the urban necklaces far below on the breast of the coastline.
"Do you know," she remarked, "you are a truly handsome little
      man.
I feel proud to be sitting beside you – with an empty seat between
      us."
Before I could begin to make my puny reply, she added:
"Cheer up – the worst that could happen would be if we crashed.
Imagine floating about in the midst of all this debris and
      wreckage."
I glanced around at my 350 fellow passengers,
All sunset and chains.
She disembarked at Shannon at dawn in the mist
And I flew on to Dublin, not worried whether I lived to tell the tale
Of how I had had the great good fortune
To fly from New York to Dublin with *The Flamingo Kid*
Clutching a glass of Rusty Nails in her freckled claws,
Her beaked eyes playing on the floodwaters of her smile:
"Cheer up – the worst that could happen would be if we crashed.
Imagine floating about in the midst of all this debris and
      wreckage."

A Vision of Africa on the Coast of Kerry

On the coast at Meenogahane,
Near Causeway,
Nellie presides in the kitchen of her cottage,
At eighty-five, exchanging the time of day
With tourists, educating us:
Nellie who has never in her life
Been out of her townland
Except "the wanst".
Five years ago at eighty,
When she had a stroke,
She was transported
By county ambulance
To the Regional Hospital in Cork.
Do you know what I saw there?
No, Nellie, what did you see?
I saw a black man.
A black man?
A black man – you should have seen his neck!
His neck?
Oh the neck of him – the lovely neck of him!
The lovely, wet, shiny, rubbery neck of him!
I asked him if he would let me put my hand on it
And he did, he let me –
And it was all black, do you know?
Oh it was lovely, I tell you, lovely!

Martha's Wall

Her pleasure – what gave her pleasure – was to be walked
Down her wall, the South Wall, a skinny, crinkly, golden-stemmed
    wall
That contracts and expands, worms and unworms, in and out of
    Dublin Bay,
Across the sea's thighs pillowing in, besotted, under daisy-gartered
    skies.
She'd curl her finger around my finger and I'd lead her out on to it.

160

She liked it when the flowering sea was shedding spray across it.
She'd tense up with delight to see me get wet
And wetter still, and wetter – the wetter it was
The better she liked it, and me – and she wanted always
To get down, away down, to the very end of it
Where there is a deep-red lighthouse, and the deep-red lighthouse
Was hers also, hers, and we'd sit down on a bench under it
And she'd put her arm around my neck and we'd stop needing to
    speak
And we'd sit there, breathless, in silence, for a long time.

Doris Fashions

to Sarah

On the instructions of the parole officer, I telephoned the prison
At 1 p.m. from the main post office in town.
They said they'd send a prison van in to collect me.
While I was waiting – I had to wait about an hour –
Leaning up against the post-office wall in the noonday sun
I caught a glimpse of myself in the display window
Of a shop across the street – Doris Fashions.
I glimpsed a strange man whom I do not know
And whom, when on the odd occasion I have glimpsed him before,
I have not warmed to – his over-intense visage,
Hurted, hurtful,
All that ice, and all that eyebrow.
I averted my eyes from the mirror-image in Doris Fashions,
Yet thinking that it is good that Doris Fashions –
That there is that much
To be salvaged from the wreckage of the moment –
That Doris Fashions.

If you had a daughter called Doris, and after you had spent years
Rearing her and schooling her and enjoying her and loving her,
She left home and set up shop in a country town
And called it Doris Fashions – how would you feel?
You would be proud of her, wouldn't you?
Or if you fell in love with a girl called Doris

And it turned out that she had a little shop of her own
Called Doris Fashions – you'd be tickled pink, wouldn't you?

All my life I've dreamed of having a motto of my own –
My own logo – my own signature tune.
Waiting for the prison van to collect me,
In the window of Doris Fashions I see into myself
And I adopt as my own logo, my own signature tune,
Doris Fashions –
Trying it out to myself on the road out to the prison:
Doris Fashions Paul Durcan – Paul Durcan Doris Fashions.
For who made the world?
Doris made the world –
And I believe in Doris, and in Doris only,
And never – never – never – never – never – never – never
In John O'Donoghue.

The Hay-Carrier

after Veronica Bolay

Have you ever saved hay in Mayo in the rain?
Have you ever made hay in Mayo in the sun?
Have you ever carried above your head a haycock on a pitchfork?
Have you ever slept in a haybarn on the road from Mayo into
    Egypt?
I am a hay-carrier.
My father was a hay-carrier.
My mother was a hay-carrier.
My brother were hay-carriers.
My sisters were hay-carriers.
My wife is a hay-carrier.
My son is a hay-carrier.
His sons are hay-carriers.
His daughters are hay-carriers.
We were always all hay-carriers.
We will always be hay-carriers.
For the great gate of night stands painted red –
And all of heaven lies waiting to be fed.

Six Nuns Die in Convent Inferno

To the
happy memory of six Loreto nuns
who died
between midnight and morning of
2 June 1986

I

We resided in a Loreto convent in the centre of Dublin city
On the east side of a public gardens, St Stephen's Green.
Grafton Street – the *paseo*
Where everybody *paseo*'d, including even ourselves –
Debouched on the north side, and at the top of Grafton Street,
Or round the base of the great patriotic pebble of O'Donovan Rossa,
Knelt tableaus of punk girls and punk boys.
When I used pass them – scurrying as I went –
Often as not to catch a mass in Clarendon Street,
The Carmelite Church in Clarendon Street
(Myself, I never used the Clarendon Street entrance,
I always slipped in by way of Johnson's Court,
Opposite the side entrance to Bewley's Oriental Café),
I could not help but smile, as I sucked on a Fox's mint,
That for all the half-shaven heads and the martial garb
And the dyed hair-dos and the nappy pins
They looked so conventional, really, and vulnerable,
Clinging to warpaint and to uniforms and to one another.
I knew it was myself who was the ultimate drop-out,
The delinquent, the recidivist, the vagabond,
The wild woman, the subversive, the original punk.
Yet, although I confess I was smiling, I was also afraid,
Appalled by my own nerve, my own fervour,
My apocalyptic enthusiasm, my other-worldly hubris:
To opt out of the world and to
Choose such exotic loneliness,
Such terrestrial abandonment,
A lifetime of bicycle lamps and bicycle pumps,
A lifetime of galoshes stowed under the stairs,
A lifetime of umbrellas drying out in the kitchens.

I was an old nun – an agèd beadswoman –
But I was no daw.
I knew what a weird bird I was, I knew that when we
Went to bed we were as eerie an aviary as you'd find
In all the blown-off rooftops of the city:
Scuttling about our dorm, wheezing, shrieking, croaking,
In our yellowy corsets, wonky suspenders, strung-out garters,
A bony crew in the gods of the sleeping city.
Many's the night I lay awake in bed
Dreaming what would befall us if there were a fire:
No fire-escapes outside, no fire-extinguishers inside;
To coin a Dublin saying,
We'd not stand a snowball's chance in hell. Fancy that!
It seemed too good to be true:
Happy death vouchsafed only to the few.
Sleeping up there was like sleeping at the top of the mast
Of a nineteenth-century schooner, and in the daytime
We old nuns were the ones who crawled out on the yardarms
To stitch and sew the rigging and the canvas.
To be sure we were weird birds, oddballs, Christniks,
For we had done the weirdest thing a woman can do –
Surrendered the marvellous passions of girlhood,
The innocent dreams of childhood,
Not for a night or a weekend or even a Lent or a season,
But for a lifetime.
Never to know the love of a man or a woman;
Never to have children of our own;
Never to have a home of our own;
All for why and for what?
To follow a young man – would you believe it –
Who lived two thousand years ago in Palestine
And who died a common criminal strung up on a tree.

As we stood there in the disintegrating dormitory
Burning to death in the arms of Christ –
O Christ, Christ, come quickly, quickly –
Fluttering about in our tight, gold bodices,
Beating our wings in vain,
It reminded me of the snaps one of the sisters took
When we took a seaside holiday in 1956
(The year Cardinal Mindszenty went into hiding

In the US legation in Budapest.
He was a great hero of ours, Cardinal Mindszenty,
Any of us would have given our right arm
To have been his nun – darning his socks, cooking his meals,
Making his bed, doing his washing and ironing.)
Somebody – an affluent buddy of the bishop's repenting his
     affluence –
Loaned Mother Superior a secluded beach in Co. Waterford –
Ardmore, along the coast from Tramore –
A cove with palm trees, no less, well off the main road.
There we were, fluttering up and down the beach,
Scampering hither and thither in our starched bathing-costumes.
Tonight, expiring in the fire, was quite much like that,
Only instead of scampering into the waves of the sea,
Now we were scampering into the flames of the fire.

That was one of the gayest days of my life,
The day the sisters went swimming.
Often in the silent darkness of the chapel after Benediction,
During the Exposition of the Blessed Sacrament,
I glimpsed the sea again as it was that day.
Praying – daydreaming really –
I became aware that Christ is the ocean
Forever rising and falling on the world's shore.
Now tonight in the convent Christ is the fire in whose waves
We are doomed but delighted to drown.
And, darting in and out of the flames of the dormitory,
Gabriel, with that extraordinary message of his on his boyish lips,
Frenetically pedalling his skybike.
He whispers into my ear what I must do
And I do it – and die.
Each of us in our own tiny, frail, furtive way
Was a Mother of God, mothering forth illegitimate Christs
In the street life of Dublin city.
God have mercy on our whirring souls –
Wild women were we all –
And on the misfortunate, poor fire-brigade men
Whose task it will be to shovel up our ashes and shovel
What is left of us into black plastic refuse sacks.
Fire-brigade men are the salt of the earth.

Isn't it a marvellous thing how your hour comes
When you least expect it? When you lose a thing,
Not to know about it until it actually happens?
How, in so many ways, losing things is such a refreshing
     experience,
Giving you a sense of freedom you've not often experienced?
How lucky I was to lose – I say, lose – lose my life.
It was a Sunday night, and after vespers
I skipped bathroom so that I could hop straight into bed
And get in a bit of a read before lights out:
Conor Cruise O'Brien's new book *The Siege*,
All about Israel and superlatively insightful
For a man who they say is reputedly an agnostic –
I got a loan of it from the brother-in-law's married niece –
But I was tired out and I fell asleep with the book open
Face down across my breast and I woke
To the racket of bellowing flame and snarling glass.
The first thing I thought was that the brother-in-law's married niece
Would never again get her Conor Cruise O'Brien back
And I had seen on the price-tag that it cost £23.00:
Small wonder that the custom of snipping off the price
As an exercise in social deportment has simply died out;
Indeed a book today is almost worth buying for its price,
Its price frequently being more remarkable than its contents.

The strange Eucharist of my death –
To be eaten alive by fire and smoke.
I clapsed the dragon to my breast
And stroked his red-hot ears.
Strange! There we were, all sleeping molecules,
Suddenly all giving birth to our deaths,
All frantically in labour.
Doctors and midwives weaved in and out
In gowns of smoke and gloves of fire.
Christ, like an Orthodox patriarch in his dressing gown,
Flew up and down the dormitory, splashing water on our souls:
Sister Eucharia; Sister Seraphia; Sister Rosario;
Sister Gonzaga; Sister Margaret; Sister Edith.
If you will remember us – six nuns burnt to death –
Remember us for the frisky girls that we were,
Now more than ever kittens in the sun.

II

When Jesus heard these words at the top of Grafton Street
Uttered by a small, agèd, emaciated, female punk
Clad all in mourning black, and grieving like an alley cat,
He was annulled with astonishment, and turning round
He declared to the gangs of teenagers and dicemen following him:
"I tell you, not even in New York City
Have I found faith like this."

That night in St Stephen's Green,
After the keepers had locked the gates,
And the courting couples had found cinemas themselves to die in,
The six nuns who had died in the convent inferno,
From the bandstand they'd been hiding under, crept out
And knelt together by the Fountain of the Three Fates,
Reciting the Agnus Dei: reciting it as if it were the torch song
Of all aid – Live Aid, Self Aid, Aids, and All Aid –
Lord, I am not worthy
That thou should'st enter under my roof;
Say but the word and my soul shall be healed.

* * *

The Beckett at the Gate

to Derek Mahon

That spring in Dublin
You could not go anywhere
Without people barking at you,
Buttonholing you in the street and barking at you,
Accosting you and barking at you:
"Have you not seen Barry McGovern's Beckett?"
Or else, which was worse,
"Have you not been to the Beckett at the Gate?"
I was fed up with people barking at me:
"Have you not seen Barry McGovern's Beckett?
Have you not been to the Beckett at the Gate?"

"No, I have not seen Barry McGovern's Beckett –
No, I have not been to the Beckett at the Gate –"
I'd mutter, affecting
To look under my legs
As if it was I
Who was the weary, put-upon virtuoso of bathos,
My limp tail of ejection.
In any case, I am not mad
About going to the theatre,
Going alone to the theatre
Upon a gloomy night in May.
It was, therefore, in spite of myself,
Quite against the grain,
That I took the initiative
By booking a ticket
For a Tuesday night at the Gate
In the third week of May
For Barry McGovern's Beckett,
The Beckett at the Gate.
C9 was the number of my ticket,
Centre, third row from the front.
I got there in good time.
I like to get to a thing in good time
Whatever it is – the bus into town,
Or the bus back out of town –

With at least a quarter of an hour to spare,
Preferably half an hour, ample time
In which to work up an adequate steam of anxiety.
When I stepped into the auditorium
I was relieved to see it was near empty,
I was heartened to see
That it was near empty,
Four or five patrons
Scattered about the theatre.

Consoled, a little less disconcerted
By the general regatta,
A little less addled
By the whole regrettable adventure,
A little less regretful
That I had not stayed put
In my bedsit,
I made my way to my seat,
Only to discover that one
Of the four or five patrons
Scattered about the near-empty theatre
Transpired to be ensconced
In the adjacent tip-up seat
Right next to my own.
In silence we sat, side by side,
All the house-lights on,
For the entire fifteen minutes before curtain-up.
I felt a right, roaring idiot,
Crouched there in all that silence
In row C of the Gate
Shoulder to shoulder with that –
That other human being
A woman to boot,
A young woman to boot.

To make matters worse
She was more sprawled than seated,
More dispersed than disposed,
More horizontal than vertical,
Engrossed in a paperback book
The name of which by dint
Of craning of the neck

I did manage to pick out.
It was a Picador paperback
Entitled *One Hundred Years of Solitude*.
As if that was not bad enough
There was not enough leg-room;
So that I had to scrunch up my legs,
Thereby having to sit closer to her.
A minute before the performance began
Someone (obviously some kind of friend,
Some ilk of accomplice)
Hailed her from five rows back:
"Michelle, Michelle!"
I said to myself
If only Michelle's friends
Would invite Michelle to sit with them
Then I'd have all of row C
To myself which at least
Would make the next hour and a half
If not less of a cauchemar
At least a bearable cauchemar.
But no – Michelle stayed put
And the lights went out,
And the curtain up,
And I knew I was for it.
Why had I let myself
Be bothered and browbeaten
By all those cultural groupies
Going on, and on, and on,
"Have you not seen Barry McGovern's Beckett?
Have you not been to the Beckett at the Gate?"

Well, it was out of the top drawer,
As Joseph Holloway would have put it,
Or would not have put it.
Not since the Depression of the 1950s
And the clowns in Duffy's Circus
Have I laughed myself so sorry,
So sorry that I was ready to shout,
If anyone else had shouted:
"Stop Beckett! Stop McGovern!"

And Michelle? Well, Michelle –
I mean talk about Susannah,
Or Judith and Holofernes,
Or any or all of those females
In the Old Testament,
Sarah or Rachel or even Eve;
Not to mention the New Testament,
Martha or Mary or Magdalen –
Michelle was – well, Michelle.
All right, I ought to have said
She was exceptionally petite –
But it's a small point
And to dwell on it
Would detract from her own performance.
She gave herself over to her own laughter
To such an exuberant extent
That she was wholly inside it – within the orbit
Of her own transparent laughter,
All rouge and polythene.
Every time she laughed
She kicked me in the legs,
In the backs of my legs,
Or nudged me in the kneecaps –
Unintentionally, of course.
Abruptly, she sat up in her seat
Tucking her legs in under her bottom –
Crimson red booties, blue skin-tight jeans,
Airy black blouse.
She leaned her head on my shoulder,
As if we had been espoused for years,
Donkeys' years, camels' years, elephants' years.
Occasionally, at a particularly
Outrageous piece of malarkey
By Beckett-McGovern,
She'd grip my arm tight
And howl – luminously howl.
Well, obviously, things
Had got quite out of hand
And I wanted to say to her
"Please please please please
Go on doing what you're doing."

But I did not say anything.
A mum's-the-word man
Is what I am;
Not a word to the Reverend Mother,
Not a smoke-signal to Chief Sitting Mountain.
If there was an interval – and it said
In the programme that there was
An interval of fifteen minutes –
I do not remember any interval.
All I remember is Michelle's head
On my shoulder, and the kick
Of her hair brushing against my cheekbone.
Many years had elapsed since last
I had been made aware of my cheekbone –
Her mousy hair brushing against it,
Scented, and wet, and calamitous.

When the curtain came down
And the applause had drained away
I turned around to gaze
In rapture at Michelle
But she had slipped away.
Mother of God
Chosen by the Eternal Council!
I walked back down along O'Connell Street,
Muttering to myself,
"Have you not seen Barry McGovern's Beckett?
Have you not been to the Beckett at the Gate?"
Every few steps, covertly,
I gave a kick in the air:
"Have you not seen Barry McGovern's Beckett?
Have you not been to the Beckett at the Gate?"
It was dusk – lucid,
Warm, limpid,
On O'Connell Street Bridge.
Spilling over with self-pity
And lasciviously gazing down
At the bicycle-filled waters
Of the River Liffey running on, on,
I elected to walk on
Back to my bedsit in Ringsend

(Instead of taking the bus)
Through the East European parts of Dublin City,
Past the gasometer and Grand Canal Dock,
Misery Hill, The Gut, The Drain,
The Three Locks, Camden, Buckingham, Westmoreland.
At Ringsend there was a full moon over
The Sugar Loaf and the Wicklow Hills,
And the crimson lights of the telecommunications aerial
On the Three Rock Mountain were trembling
And on the television transmitter in Donnybrook;
And the hand-painted signs of the local public houses,
FitzHarris's and The Oarsman,
Looked childmade in the lamplight, homely
By the River Dodder,
As I balanced in a trance on the humpbacked bridge,
On a fulcrum of poignancy,
And I felt like a stranger in a new city,
An urchin in a New Jerusalem,
A bareheaded protagonist
In a vision of reality,
All caught up in a huge romance,
In a hot erotic cold tumult.
On the street corner in Ringsend village
Not at, but close to, a bus stop,
A tiny young woman was standing,
Hovering, twirling, stamping,
And when I saw that it was Michelle –
As I passed her by
She scrutinized me serenely
As if she had never seen me before –
As if she had never seen me before.
I keep on walking;
I'll go on, I think, I'll go on.
Next year in Carrickmines
I'll play tennis with whatever
Woman will play tennis with me
And I'll never be never again.
Next year in Carrickmines.
On grass. Love all.
Fifteen Love. Thirty Love. Forty Love.
Deuce. Advantage Miss Always.

Game, Set and Match.
Why you, Michelle? why you?
Will you join me? Join me?
If you're the joining kind, please join me.
Next year in Carrickmines,
Greystones, Delgany, Killiney, Bray, Dalkey, Shankill, Kilmacud,
Galloping Green, Stillorgan – perhaps even Dublin.

There's a beckett at the gate, there's a beckett
at the gate, Michelle;
There's a Beckett at the gate, there's a Beckett
at the gate, Michelle;
There's a beckett at the Gate, there's a beckett
at the Gate, Michelle;
There's a Beckett at the Gate, there's a Beckett
at the Gate, Michelle.

* * *

Peredelkino: at the Grave of Pasternak

to A. K. Avelichev

I

After all these years, Boris Leonidovich Pasternak,
I have found you.
How self-engrossed and paranoid I must appear to you
Lurking at the foot of your grave,

A blue corduroy cap on my head
That I purchased in a West-of-Ireland village;
A green scarf tied around my throat,
A Japanese automatic camera in my hand.

But you are not vexed by my foibles –
If anything you rejoice in and applaud me –
A middle-aged gear-laden telephone engineer
Frantic to grapple with your trinity of pines.

Be still, my strapped-up and harnessed soul.
I begin at last to stand at ease.
Instead of grappling with them, I overhear myself
Conversing with the Father, the Son and the Holy Spirit.

But it is they who do most of the conversing.
I am amazed by their point of view.
Although the enemy once again is almost
At the gates of Moscow and Borodino,

They egg me to pay no heed:
Instead of darkening my energy
With bombast and humbug
I should daub my soul with leaves of mud.

While warplanes fly to and fro overhead
And cars race up and down the Kiev Highway,
Pay heed to the housewife on the skyline,
On whose head God has put a price.

175

At the heart of atheism God is at home;
Man locked into history opening the door.
Closer to God is the atheist opening the door
Than the churchman closing the door in your face.

II

Strange that anybody can visit your grave,
    Even a naïf like me;
Surely the dead are entitled to privacy,
    If not also the living.

Your grave out here in the Vineyard of Peredelkino
    Is open to all comers:
I gaze through the railings at your headstone,
    Let myself in by the gate.

I am borne back to another railing'd grave
    In Kilcrea in West Cork:
"Lo Arthur Leary, generous, handsome, brave,
    Slain in his bloom lies in this humble grave."

Slain in his bloom like you,
    Lo Boris Leonidovich;
Who died for the right to ride a white horse;
    You – generous, handsome, brave.

Sitting down on the wooden bench, I note
    That it is I who am trapped in life
Whilst in death you are free,
    Golden eagle on a black leaf.

Over the grave of Art O'Leary at midnight
    On a summer's evening,
Your young priest-like friend from Zima, Yevtushenko,
    Broke – broke a bottle of red wine.

Somewhere in the petals of the crowd in the metro
    My dead mother is peering out at me;
My mother who went to Russia when I was three
    And who died in Moscow.

Somewhere in the trees of the hand-painted forest
    Ivinskaya is peering out at me;
A man without his woman is a right hand without a left;
    I kiss the back of her wrought-bone hand.

Voices of a man and a woman through the foliage,
    A father and mother
At the fresh grave next to yours of a nineteen-year-old boy
    Slain in the Afghanistan wars.

I have not read the novel of *Doctor Zhivago*,
    Yet I lack the courage to say so;
Isn't it heartbreakingly funny how relentlessly
    Pretentious men are.

How often I myself have met intellectuals
    Who have read Bulgakov
They say – whose faces go blank if you talk
    To them about Titian Tabidze.

All alone at your grave, I have a two-hour conversation
    With myself and the trees;
My blue corduroy cap perched all alone
    On the damp bench watching us.

A babushka is propelling herself like a pram
    Across the road with three goats;
In the car returning to Moscow, the driver remarks
    "Your blue cap looks Jewish – is it German?"

That night we make love in an apartment beside
    The Cultural Palace of the Ball-Bearing Plant;
Next morning under Shevchenko's statue by the Moskva River
    I set fire to my cap.

Oh Song of the Blue Cap, for Boris Leonidovich,
    From the West of Ireland.
It makes a soft explosion (two books of matches inside it),
    An orgasm of gentleness.

In the leaf-strewn post-coital smoke-pall,
    The cars do not stop reiterating your name
As they race down Kalinin Prospekt to Red Square –
    Pasternak! Pasternak!

Moskviches, Zhigulis, Volgas, Chaikas,
    And the odd, conspicuous Zil:
Pasternak, Pasternak! Pasternak, Pasternak!
    Victory to the Blue Cap Boy.

Diarrhoea Attack at Party Headquarters in Leningrad

An attack of diarrhoea at Party Headquarters in Leningrad
Was not something I imagined ever happening to me
Which is perhaps partly why it did happen to me.
The presidium had barely taken its place
Under the iconic portraits of V. I. Lenin and M. S. Gorbachev
When I could feel the initial missiles
Firing down the sky of my stomach
Setting in motion something that was irreversible –
The *realpolitik* of the irreversible.
The only consolation was that I was wearing underpants.
The fact is that sometimes I do not wear underpants.
Oddly enough I was wearing red underpants
Which I had originally purchased in Marks & Spencer's.
The first explosion resulted in immediate devastation –
The ensuing explosions serving only to define
The innately irreversible dialectic of catastrophe.
I whispered magnanimously into the earhole of my interpreter.
He reciprocated that since he also had "a trauma of the
    intestine"
We should both take our leave *immédiatement* and he showed me
Such fraternal solicitude that in my mind's eye
I can still see Lenin peering down at me
As if he were peering down at nobody else in the hall.
A black Volga whisked us back to our hotel and ignominy –
My ignominy – not anybody else's ignominy – and that night
Over cups of tea we discussed the war in Afghanistan,

178

Agreeing that realistically it appeared an insoluble problem,
Yet hoping against hope that somehow it would be solved
And that – as you put it, Slava – "Russian boys come home."
There is nothing necessarily ignominious about anything.

The Red Arrow

In the history of transport – is there any other history? –
The highest form of transport is the Red Arrow,
The night train from Leningrad to Moscow.
With whom will I be sharing my compartment tonight?
The editor of the *Jazz Front Gazette*, it transpires.
But, affable, polite, as she is, how can she compare
With Svetka with whom I shared in 1981?
We sat up half the night chin-wagging, colloguing,
And when awkwardly I began to undress and she said:
"Ah yes, it is all right – would you like to?"
Naturally I liked to,
And the train was about halfway between Leningrad and Moscow
When I fell out of her bunk on to the floor
And the wagon-lady put her head in the door
To check what was the matter
And Svetka said in Russian: "These foreigners
They cannot even keep from falling out of bed –
Always needing to be treated like babies."
The wagon-lady grunted and slid the door shut
And I climbed back into the bunk with Svetka.
Each time we made love she groaned:
"I am the little horse in your snow."
I let up the window blind and, as we made love again –
A blizzard upside down at the windowpane –
When she opened her eyes, she murmured
"You are snowing on my tail, my dear man."
As the Red Arrow flew into Moscow, Svetka said:
"My dear man, you must meet me tomorrow.
Tell them you have a problem with your business.
Meet me in the Melodiya Music Store on Kalinin.
I will be in the Classical Russian Music section.
Look me up under Rachmaninov."

179

It was a grey Moscow afternoon – not a bead of sunlight –
But we traipsed up and down the Arbat in seventh heaven.
"My dear, dear man," she keeps murmuring over and over.
Although that was all of seven years ago –
She who shot the Red Arrow through my heart.

Bringing Home the Watermelon from Samarkand

to E. Shepilova

I loved Papa – even though he was an old bollox.
But my patience – and Mama's patience –
Ran out the day he made a hames
Of bringing home the watermelon from Samarkand.

All he had to do was to carry them back on the plane,
Carry them back in his arms on the plane,
A pair of enormous, oval, tubular, golden
Watermelon from Samarkand,
Each of them tied up erotically in a string bag –
Metaphysical brassières, perchance, Andrushka –
But he was embarrassed – he complained – embarrassed,
Holding in his arms a pair of melons.
It made him look – he shushshushed – like a woman with bosoms.
Askance my mother glared at him across the tip-up table
At 29,000 feet over the Caspian Sea,
Trembling her own great pair of bosoms at him:
She swore silently – "These are mine, my melons."

But Papa combined to act the dog in the manger
And the hurt, injured, sad son of a bitch
At 29,000 feet over the Caspian Sea.
To evade the issue, he barked at me
What he has been barking at me for forty-two years:
"The Caspian – Sturgeon's Roe – Caviar – Beluga – *Huso huso!*"
Mama leaned across and took hold of one melon
And planted it between her buoyant, floating bosoms,
Resting her double chin in the cup of her hand,
Gazing out of a porthole from her seat on the outside aisle,

Thinly smiling to herself.
Men are not capable even of being women
And the burden of life goes on,
Goes on being a woman's burden, burden,
Bringing home the watermelon from Samarkand.

Zina in Murmansk

As a schoolgirl, Zina
Was all that a Pioneer instructor
Could dream of, and her parents –
Druzhniki, gribniki,
Peace-keepers, mushroom-hunters –
Were proud of her as a mushroom,
Their own miniscule red mushroom.
She was droll, elegant, gay,
Her company always a pleasure.
It was expected that after schooldays
She would attend the Literary Institute
In Moscow, or the Leningrad Art College.
Instead, she became a grade-A typist
And applied for a resident's permit
In Murmansk, in the arctic region
Of the Far North.
Zina – diminutive of Zinaida –
Had always been a dreamer
With her feet on the ground.
She was certain that Murmansk
Was the kind of town she would find
The old-fashioned man she yearned for,
A specimen of manhood whose ancestors
Had been living the same sort of life
For thousands and thousands and thousands of –
A Mesolithic Man of the twentieth century
Who would fish for shark in the White Sea
And hunt polar bear in the tundra,
Who would live with her in a log cabin
And at night read to her from Tolstoy,
Valentin Rasputin and Chingitz Aitmatov,

While she darned his mighty socks,
Or applied her awl to his boots,
Boring tunnels for thong piping.
But such men are no more extant
In Murmansk than in Moscow.
She could not find even one man
Who had a drop of Mesolithic sexuality
Left in his pasteurised blood.
To this day Zina remains
A single girl in Murmansk,
Typing out the correspondence of the chairman
Of the White Sea Shipping Company,
At 18 Komintern Street,
While he attends to his fourth wife
And the nightly routine of television and fornication.
It is the same the wide world over
From Murmansk to Batumi,
From Novosibirsk to Shamaka:
A question of whether or not there is *time*
– Time, I said, time, time and time again –
To squeeze in a quick fornication
Between the 9 p.m. newscast
And the 9.30 p.m. current affairs, musical chairs programme.
Soon shark and bear will be extinct –
And women too:
Soon there will be no more women.
Zina goes nightly to her bunk
As to her belovèd grave.
Reading in bed late at night in Murmansk,
Am I the last woman left alive in the world?

Estonian Farewell, 1983

to Arvo

Midwinter in the snowed-up port of Tallinn,
Midnight on the platform of Tallinn railway station,
Leaning out the window of the midnight train
As it begins to pull out for Leningrad and fever,

And Arvo rooted to the platform waving farewell to us,
Clutching in his hands
A little book in blue-and-gold wrappers –
Teach Yourself Irish by Myles Dillon.

Arvo, I have been to the moon and found you;
I wave and you wave; you wave and I wave;
As you squat there in your furry nimbus,
And my mother – a ghost with a knife through her halo –
Is stumbling through the birch trees to keep up with the train,
The birch trees between the tracks and the fields,
And she is crying, crying, crying, crying, crying, crying:
"My son, my son, why hast thou forsaken me?"

The Return of Solzhenitsyn

Alexander Isayevich, for how much longer
Will we have to wait for you to come home?
It has been twelve years now since last you clapped
Your mittens in Gorki Street and marvelled at the fumes
Of your own breath writhing in the Russian air.
For twelve years now we have waited –
Don't you think it is time for you to think of us
Who require and implore you to come home?
Prodigal son whom we revere and cherish,
Not least a party man such as myself
Who was only an apparatchik of twenty-two
When Queen Brezhnev kicked you out.
Alexander Isayevich, we have served our sentence:
Have mercy on us and, if you please, come home.

The Fairy Tale of 1937

i. m. A. Tarkovsky

Once upon a time there was a czar called S
Who was afeard of a wanderer called M
Because M, who was a stubble-faced and wispy fellow
With thick red lips and soft white teeth,

Had the peculiar habit of what we call
"Giving ourselves back to ourselves" –
Like Bulat Okudzhava, in our own era.
That is to say, whenever M met you on the golden boulevard,
And you were not in the best of sorts, even out of sorts,
He'd kiss you on both cheeks and put his arms around you,
All very quietly, undemonstratively, and he'd say –
Like Bruce Springsteen –
With a quick burst of a laugh, with but a quick burst of a
    laugh –
"Jesus, let me give you back to yourself."
He'd look you straight in the face –
His blue, granny eyes grinning out at you.

The Czar S became so afeard of M
That he issued a ukase
That every telephone in Russia was to be shot dead.
By the end of 1936 every telephone in Russia and Georgia
Had been shot dead.
But still M was wandering about Moscow and Leningrad and
    Tbilisi
Giving people back to themselves . . .
So that in 1937 the Czar S had M interned
And committed to an empty psychiatric hospital
In a derelict cul-de-sac on the docks,
Sentencing him to total and solitary confinement forever.
To this day nobody has ever set foot in that house
And it is known to us all as House 1937:
Operator, please get me One-Nine-Three-Seven . . .

One day someone – a red woman –
Will step through a wall into the House of 1937
And what will she find there?
On his back wandering in the rain?
Sitting in the chair by the window?
With his feet in a milkpail of rainwater?
Stretched out on the iron bed in the corner?
With his head on a bolster of rainwater?
She will find one-and-a-half million people
Pressed between the pages of poetry books,
Not even their tongues or their toes curled up at the edges,

Not even their clitorises or penises curled up at the edges,
Not even the serrated peripheries of their brains curled up at
    the edges.

O my Red Jesus,
Let me be the harlot who will step back into 1937,
The House on the Docks,
To heap up my elbows around your smiling knees,
And to kiss-with-my-tongue, kiss-with-my-tongue, kiss-with-my-
    tongue
Your big-eared, wide-eyed feet.

Trauma Junction

The answer to your question is that I am not your mother;
Your mother was another mother and she died in Russia.

Hymn to My Father

Dear Daddy, on your last legs now,
Can you hear me
In your bedroom in the treetops,
Chained to your footwarmer and your pills,
Death notices in newspapers your exclusive reading?
We had no life together – or almost none.
Yet you made me what I am –
A man in search of his Russia.
After schooldays I became a poet –
A metamorphosis you could no more fathom
Than I could fathom your own osmosis –
Lawyer with a secret life,
As secret as the life of a poet.
You had a history for every milestone,
A saga for every place name –
The Bovril Sign, the Ballast Office Clock, the Broadstone –
And so, at your knee, at your elbow, I became you.
Estranged as we are,
I am glad that it was in this life

I loved you,
Not the next.
O Russian Knight at the Crossroads!
If you turn to the right, you will lose your horse;
To the left, your head;
If you go straight on, your life.
If you were me – which you are –
Knight at the Crossroads,
You would go home to Russia this very night.

The Woman with the Keys to Stalin's House

You would imagine – would you not –
That the town of Gori,
The town of Joseph Vissarionovich Dzhugashvili,
By virtue of being just that –
Stalin's home town –
Would be a self-centred, uninhabited, pock-marked crater,
"The town that gave birth to . . ."

Galya has lived all her life in the town of Gori
Under the statue of Stalin,
A buxom, humorous, lugubrious woman,
Her ash-blond nail varnish matching her ash-blond hair
Corbelled in a ponytail.
After traipsing about the Stalin Museum
And the house where Stalin was born,
Which Stalin personally had preserved as a monument to himself –
Sentimental Soso –
We had a meal together in the local hotel
Around the corner in Stalin Square.
"I am the saddest woman in all Georgia,"
She remarked to me with a smile
That played on her mauve-painted lips
Long after her words had died,
Spreadeagling her arms
So that her breasts could breathe
In the asphyxiating atmosphere,
Black rain knifing the windowpane.

While we ate and drank in silence
She opened the buttons of her blouse,
Beckoning me to follow suit.
She motioned to me to open my mouth
And swilling her own mouth with champagne,
She put her lips to mine,
Letting the champagne swill
Into my mouth from her mouth.
The mountains askew above the town
Leaned slightly across the sky
As we lurched around the room
Making big love and little love.
We bathèd one another
With jug and basin.
As I towelled her down
She shut her eyes, tightly.
Stalin Street was deserted
As we embraced goodbye.
She remarked:
"I like you a little because you have mixed feelings."
In the car returning to Tbilisi,
Riding down the Georgian Military Highway,
I considered that if Eve had been even half as affectionate
As Galya in Gori,
Well, how lucky I was to have been her Adam;
And Jahweh – that old Stalin on his plinth –
Had failed to cow us. Galya,
Can there be anyone in the world who has not got mixed feelings?
Should there be anyone in the world who has not got mixed feelings?

Going Home to Russia

to A. Voznesensky

Hanging about the duty-free in Shannon Airport,
Waiting for the flight to Moscow to be called;
Waiting for the Havana–Moscow Illushin 62
To come in for refuelling, and to pick me up.

I am the solitary passenger joining the flight at Shannon;
The Irish immigration officer eyes me mournfully;
"Good luck," he mutters as if to say "you will need it";
He does not know that I am versed in luck.

"Good luck," he mutters as if to a hostage or convict,
Not knowing that he is speaking to an Irish dissident
Who knows that in Ireland scarcely anybody is free
To work or to have a home or to read or write.

We Irish have had our bellyful of *blat*
And *blarney*, more than our share
Of the *nomenklatura* of Church and Party,
The *nachalstvo* of the legal and medical mafia.

Going down the airbridge, I slow my step,
Savouring the moment of liberation;
As soon as I step aboard the Aeroflot airliner
I will have stepped from godlessness into faith:

Into a winter of shoe-swapping;
Into a springtime of prams;
Into a summer of riverbanks and mountain huts;
Into an autumn of mushroom-hunting.

It is not until I am aboard the carrier
That I realise I am going home;
I have been ill at ease – on tenterhooks –
Because I have not realised I am going home.

Yet the doorway of the aircraft is still open;
The airbridge has not yet been disconnected;
At the last moment I might be taken off –
Not until we are airborne will I be free.

At the entrance to the cabin the pilot looms,
Shirtsleeves rolled up to his elbows;
He has the look of the long-distance bus driver
On the Galway–Limerick–Cork route:

A man much loved by his wife and friends;
The shape of his mind is the shape of the route;
Smoking his Cosmos, what is he thinking of?
He knows every bend in the road, every skyline,

And that the world, despite obstinate man, is round.
He will bend over the Baltic;
He will turn a corner at Riga, and at Moscow
He will let Asia run her fingers through our hair.

Take-off – the hips of the Shannon Estuary:
The pores of the gooseflesh of Ireland;
Wet, unrequited yearnings by the prickly inch;
The River Shannon lying crumpled on the mudflats of Foynes.

Copenhagen – the Baltic – Riga – Smolensk –
If there be a heaven, then this is what
It must feel like to be going down into heaven –
To be going home to Russia.

Beyond Smolensk the long approach begins,
The long approach into Moscow;
From far out at an angle of forty-five degrees,
The long descent into Sheremetyeva.

By his engine-murmurs, the pilot sounds like a man
Who has chosen to make love instead of to rape;
He caresses the Russian plains
With a long, slow descent – a prolonged kiss.

With the night down below us, with Russia
Under her mantle of snow and forest;
A block of flats lights up out of nowhere –
The shock in a lover's eyes at the impact of ecstasy.

O Svetka, Svetka! Don't, don't!
Say my name! Oh say my name!
O God O Russia! Don't, don't!
Say my name! Oh say my name!

In the aftermath of touchdown, gently we taxi;
We do not immediately put on our clothes;
In the jubilation of silence we taste our arrival –
The survival of sex.

The nose of the jet interlocks with the doorway;
At the top of the airbridge a militiaman stands smiling;
Outside the arrivals building I get lost in the snow;
I meet a woman who is also lost in the snow.

Going home to Russia to be with you –
Dark secret of life;
Going home to Russia to be with you –
Svetka in the snow.

Block after block after block after block –
You are squeaky-sick with laughter that I've come home;
Your neighbour, Madame Noses, sneaks a peep at me –
Dear, dear Svetka.

For sure I have no TV, and my radio
I use only for these weather reports:
This way we do it – it is good, no?
There are so many of us, so many.

I have come home to you to greet you
To watch with you the trains for Yaroslavl;
Train after train from your fifth-storey window –
What contentment! It is Moscow, and we are alone.

I have come home to you to greet you
In your own tiny kitchen – a kitchen lit for lovers;
To press red maple leaves between the pages of books,
To take off my tin hat and put on your shoes;

To sleep with you on the settee and to become with you
Creatures of the new forest, crushed deer;
Never again to have to endure the persecution
Of landlords, the humiliation of advertisers;

To live again with nature as before I lived
In Ireland before all the trees were felled;
Bouquets of leaves in Moscow in October,
Closer to you than I am to myself.

My dear loved one, let me lick your nose;
Nine months in your belly, I can smell your soul;
Your two heads are smiling – not one but both of them –
Isn't it good, Svetka, good, that I have come home?

O Svetka, Svetka! Don't, don't!
Say my name! Oh say my name!
O God O Russia! Don't, don't!
Say my name! Oh say my name.

1986

John Field's Dressing Gown with Onion Domes and Spires

"Take a right turn at the Sputnik Cinema" –
These were the street directions from an abrupt,
Voluptuous passerby, in black high-heel boots
And rabbit-skin fur hat,
On how to find the Vedenskoye Cemetery
In which the nineteenth-century Irish pianist
And composer, John Field, lies buried.

Behind the Sputnik Cinema on the side of a hill
Overlooking the Yauza River
Across the road from the deserted tennis courts
– High wire netting melancholy against the sky –
A pastoral red kremlin I had never seen before:
A long, high, crenellated redbrick wall
And behind it a forest of birch and pine
In among the mausolea and the tombs.

Madame Nina, the caretaker, was reluctant
To guide me to your grave
For fear that as your fellow-countryman
I would be mortified by its delapidated,

Untended condition – I assured Madame Nina
I would not be mortified, and she believed me.
What was aggravating her was that a week had elapsed
Since she had last had time to polish you –
A half-dozen or so mussels of bird-droppings
Adorned your green marble quilt.

As we strolled down the aisles of tombstones and trees
It struck me as curious that while travellers
Correctly pay homage to the cemeteries of Paris
– Père-Lachaise, Montparnasse, Montmartre, Passy –
Nobody sings the praises of the cemeteries of Moscow
– Novodevichy, Vagankovskoye, Pyatnitskoye –
And now, the most stately cemetery in Russia,
The Vedenskoye.

Madame Nina bustled ahead of me,
Five or six paces ahead of me,
Believing, as she remarked afterwards,
That I should be left alone with my own thoughts.
But instead of piety or grief or awe
I felt that apologetic awkwardness
One feels as one tiptoes down the corridors
Of a big city hospital, down the aisles past the beds
To visit one's father whom one has never met,
The legendary, mythical, prodigal father.

You were sitting up in bed, and when you saw me
You stammered "O my poor – poor boy"
And beckoning to Madame Nina to leave us alone
You grasped my two hands and shook your head.
With my head in your breast, I stared
At your blue-and-gold, silk, fur-trimmed dressing gown
With onion domes and spires.

The old ladies of the cemetery
Gathered themselves round us
With their brooms and wheelbarrows,
Their shovels and buckets.
Madame Nina proffered me a yellow leaf

Which I placed at the foot of your grave.
It was only twelve o'clock noon,
Yet already the Moscow sky was darkening,
Making goldener the cupolas of golden leaves,
Goldener also the black mud,
Goldener October.
As I steadied myself to take a last photograph
You produced from under your pillow
The italicised inscription on your tomb:

Erected
To His Memory
By
Mis Grateful Friends
and
Scholars
John Field
Born in Ireland
in 1782
Dead in Moscow
in 1837.

After mulling the wine of the idiosyncratic syntax
I had behind a birch and said last prayers.
You murmured again – no need for such as you to clamour
Or to put your foot down on the pedal –
You murmured:
"I have been living in the Vedenskoye Cemetery
For one hundred and forty-nine years;
That is w'what it m'means to be *Dead in Moscow*.
And to h'have *Mis Grateful Friends in Moscow*
Is to be cherished by women whose nerve and verve
– O the diabolical shoulderblades of women! –
Would put to s'shame all the m'marshals of h'history;
Louise, Maria, Agate – and Ekaterina
Who subscribed one hundred roubles to my erection."

The photographs came back from the printers
With a tag: *Blank Film.*

Dasvidanya, John Field – Nobody of the Nocturne.
A nobody in Gorki Street,
I wrap myself, against my fate of rain,
In your blue-and-gold, silk, fur-trimmed dressing gown
With onion domes and spires.

October, 1986

John Field Visits His Seventy-Eight-Year-Old Widowed Mother

When I went round to see Mother on Sunday night
I found her dead in bed. Dead in bed.
I who am renowned for being "Dead in Moscow".
I don't know. I straightened out her pillow.
I tucked in the blankets that had come loose.
I tried to make her more comfortable.
I folded her hands across her breast
Because I thought she looked more – more herself that way.
I don't know. I lit a candle on her bedside table.
I sat down beside her like I always do –
Watching the grease coagulate and coalesce.
I crossed my knees and listened to the silence.
We often do that – Mother and I – listen to the silence:
Not spoiling everything with dialogue.
There is too much dialogue in the world.
Silence is what is wanted. *Silenzio.*
I don't know. I stood up and gazed out the window
At my vague, dissipated face, pockmarked with tears.
I sat down at the pianoforte, and played
For Mother dead in bed my Nocturne in E flat major.
It sounded much more textured than before.
The circumstance of Mother's being dead in bed
May have enriched it, I suppose – I don't know.
Her fruit cakes were always rich, all raisins and almonds.
I invented the Nocturne on the basis of her fruit cake:
Retaining the icing – dispensing with the actual cake.
Dead in bed. Mother. Dead in bed.
I who am renowned for being "Dead in Moscow".

DADDY, DADDY *(1990)*

The Centre of the Universe

I

Pushing my trolley about in the supermarket,
I am the centre of the universe;
Up and down the aisles of beans and juices,
I am the centre of the universe;
It does not matter that I live alone;
It does not matter that I am a jilted lover;
It does not matter that I am a misfit in my job;
I am the centre of the universe.

I'm always here, if you want me –
I am the centre of the universe.

II

I enjoy being the centre of the universe.
It is not easy being the centre of the universe
But I enjoy it.
I take pleasure in,
I delight in,
Being the centre of the universe.
At six o'clock a.m. this morning I had a phone call;
It was from a friend, a man in Los Angeles:
"Paul, I don't know what time it is in Dublin
But I simply had to call you:
I cannot stand LA so I thought I'd call you."
I calmed him down as best I could.

I'm always here, if you want me –
I am the centre of the universe.

III

I had barely put the phone down when it rang again,
This time from a friend in São Paulo in Brazil:
"Paul – do you know what is the population of São Paulo?
I will tell you: it is twelve million skulls.

Twelve million pairs of feet in the one footbath.
Twelve million pairs of eyes in the one fishbowl.
It is unspeakable, I tell you, unspeakable."
I calmed him down as best I could.

I'm always here, if you want me –
I am the centre of the universe.

IV

But then when the phone rang a third time and it was not yet
    6.30 a.m.,
The petals of my own hysteria began to awaken and unfurl.
This time it was a woman I know in New York City:
"Paul – New York City is a cage,"
And she began to cry a little bit over the phone,
To sob over the phone,
And from three thousand miles away I mopped up her tears,
I dabbed each tear from her cheeks
With just a word or two or three from my calm voice.

I'm always here, if you want me –
I am the centre of the universe.

V

But now tonight it is myself;
Sitting at my aluminium double-glazed window in Dublin City;
Crying just a little bit into my black T-shirt.
If only there was just one human being out there
With whom I could make a home? Share a home?
Just one creature out there in the night –
Is there not just one creature out there in the night?
In Helsinki, perhaps? Or in Reykjavik?
Or in Chapelizod? Or in Malahide?
So you see, I have to calm myself down also
If I am to remain the centre of the universe;
It's by no means an exclusively self-centred automatic thing
Being the centre of the universe.

I'm always here, if you want me –
I am the centre of the universe.

Felicity in Turin

We met in the Valentino in Turin
And travelled down through Italy by train,
Sleeping together.
I do not mean having sex.
I mean sleeping together.
Of which sexuality is,
And is not, a part.
It is this sleeping together
That is sacred to me.
This yawning together.
You can have sex with anyone
But with whom can you sleep?

I hate you
Because having slept with me
You left me.

Ho Chi Minh

My birthday today – one year to the day
She stopped speaking to me. Got a plane home this morning
To Dublin from Leeds–Bradford. On the hall floor
A packet addressed to me in her flamboyant majuscule.
Hand delivered. Franked with no stamp.
A small anthology of North Vietnamese Women's Pain
Purchased last week in Ho Chi Minh Airport
In Ho Chi Minh City. When she was a girl in New York City
She had posters of Ho Chi Minh
On the bedroom wall of her cold-water pad in the Village.
I flick through its minuscule, indecipherable pages.
Each paragraph of pain accompanied by a miniature batik,
Small women combing out their long black manes
While behind them in scurrying silence
Their small men tend to them,
Bowls of water dragged into focus.

I drag out from under the stairs an unopened brand-new suitcase
Which she gave me last year as a birthday gift
The day she stopped speaking to me.
I drop the little green book down into the depths of the suitcase,
Down into its synthetic silk drawers, and close it,
Putting it away for another year
In the cupboard under the stairs, where the mice are.
Collectively things look like what they sound like.
Ho Chi Minh.

The Deep Supermarket, Next Door to Ajay's

Traipsing the streets of Leicester city
In need of refreshment, I went into a shop
Called The Deep Supermarket.
It had a low ceiling and it was long and narrow and dark
And crammed with produce.
Behind the till, barely visible, barely audible,
Stood a small Asian woman whose beauty
Was such that I found it awkward to look at her
Straight in the eye.
"May I have two apples?" I asked her.
"I am sorry" – she replied in a low voice –
"I do not have apples,
But if you try Ajay next door
I am sure he will be able to oblige you very well."

Back out on the pavement
I glanced back up at her shop
And at its name, The Deep Supermarket,
And at the name of the shop next door,
Ajay's.
I went into Ajay's.
A small, lean, stout man with a moustache
Who stood at the till declared:
"Good Afternoon, sir,"
As if he had been waiting all afternoon
For my arrival and for the transaction
We were about to understake and enact.

Ajay's shop, by contrast with The Deep Supermarket,
Appeared to have almost no stock,
Appeared to be almost empty,
Except for being provisioned with daylight from two sides,
Being situated, as it was, on a street corner.
There were a few shelves
With piles and arrays
Of rice and tea, and cardboard boxes
Of tins of curry powder, and trays of confectionery,
And on the floor, three or four cartons of fruit.
I picked up two shiny green apples and handed them to him.
He loaded them into the pre-war weighing scales
Behind the pre-war cash register.
Having meticulously calculated their weight,
He asked me for thirty-two pence.
He dropped the two apples into a brown paper bag
Which he twirled to fold
And as he handed it over to me he declared Thank You
With such rectitude, such solicitude,
That I felt as though it was I
Who had sold him the apples.
On an impulse of need as well as of etiquette
I considered a second purchase was in order.
"May I have a small bottle of Lucozade?"
He smiled gently – "I am sorry, sir,
I do not have Lucozade
But if you go into The Deep Supermarket next door
I am sure she will be able to oblige you very well."
As I took my leave of him
He said Goodbye
With such accentuated warmth
That I glanced back over my shoulder at him
And I saw in a sepia print of my dead father,
Hayseed in his hair,
A shy young man in a field in Mayo raking hay
Or in Sind.
I went back into The Deep Supermarket
And as Ajay had promised,
She stocked Lucozade in The Deep Supermarket.
She contemplated me curiously, sympathetically,
As I pocketed the change.

I continued traipsing on towards the outskirts of Leicester
In a caravan of immigrants,
Shy of man's splendour,
His fragility,
His transhumance,
His pollen,
Hoist to his own petard by the seed of his destiny,
By retaliation,
By the relation of man to woman on this earth
Be
He or she
From Mayo or Sind
And living in Leicester city,
Estrangement or harmony;
How it might be between a man and a woman;
The Deep Supermarket, next door to Ajay's.

1989

Tullamore Poetry Recital

It was a one-man show in Tullamore,
"The Sonnets of Shakespeare."
The newspaper advertisement bubbled:
"Bring Your Own Knitting."
The audience of twenty-five
Was devout, polite, attentive,
All with their knitting,
Men and women alike with their knitting.
I shut my eyes and glimpsed
Between the tidal breakers of iambic pentameter
The knitting needles flashing like the oars of Odysseus.

But as the evening wore on, and the centuries passed,
And the meditations, and the thanksgivings,
And darkness fell, and with it a fullish moon,
Not quite full but fullish,
Putting on weight by the teaspoonful,
One was aware of a reversal advancing,

Of incoming tides being dragged backwards.
The knitting needles were no longer oars
But fiddles in orchestras sawing to halts.
One became aware of one's own silence.
One was no longer where one thought one was.
One was alone in the pit of oneself, knitting needles.

Member of the European Parliament

It was Good Friday lunchtime in the Canaries.
We were planning to attend the holy ceremonies at 4 p.m.
In the compound chapel in Puerto Rico.
I was sitting out on our balcony
Preening myself and reading biographies
Of Ernest Hemingway and Nora Barnacle.
I was reading the two of them
At the same time.
I was aware of the couple on the balcony below
Pottering about but I was so preoccupied
With Ernest Hemingway and Nora Barnacle
Changing places on my lap
That I was only aware of them.
It only dawned on me
That what they were doing
Was having intercourse
Underneath a table that had an enormous bowl
Of apricots perched on its edge.

I kept looking back down at my pair of biographies
For fear of catching myself out looking at the couple.
Although I am no paragon myself,
A bit of a gull in point of fact,
I found it difficult to believe my eyes.
I tried to pretend to myself
That I was not seeing what I was seeing.
What made it inconvenient
Was that I knew the couple,
Or rather, I knew him
And I knew that she was his research assistant in Brussels.

They were spending Holy Week in the Canaries
To refresh his Spanish.
In fact it was this couple
With whom we had arranged to attend
The Good Friday ceremonies.
While we stood in the bare stripped-down chapel,
About two hundred kilometres off north-west Africa,
With its stained-glass windows by Engels O'Hara,
Contemplating the details of the Crucifixion,
Two Irish couples,
My mind was on only one thing,
On one thing only,
The image of a member –
A purple-gummed hedgehog
Expanding –
Protracting and retracting
Underneath a table that had an enormous bowl
Of apricots perched on its edge.

Later in the wine bar, when the topic of conversation
Came round to the Holocaust, he got even more hedgehoggy,
Self-righteous and scornful, and he said to me:
"I have to say
That I am a Member of the European Parliament."
"I know you are" – I answered him.

Putney Garage

to Brian Fallon

The morning after the poetry reading
At the Poetry Society in Earl's Court Square
I decided to go to a film in Leicester Square,
Having already that auburn October day
Changed my mind five times.
I would catch the 4.35 p.m. showing
Of *Au Revoir Les Enfants* in the Première.
I strolled along the north side of Piccadilly

But the closer I came to the cinema
The more I felt like going home to Brixton,
To Bill and Pippa, Ben and Sam and Jo,
In 64 Milton Road,
Pampas grass in the front garden,
Up the lane from Electric Avenue,
The child's playground that is London in October,
Its wild mildness, its puberty,
Kick of spentoutedness in my calf muscles.

I crossed over to the south side of Piccadilly,
Retraced my steps.
At the bus stop outside the Egyptian State Tourist Office
Francis Bacon was waiting for a bus;
Those ancient, glittering eyes on black steel rods
Socketed in their Sicilian pouches;
That teenager's ageing mouth
All cheek and tongue-in-cheek.

I fell into line.
We stood in silence,
He lounging against the corner of the bus shelter
In a lounge suit,
Hands in trench-coat pockets,
Belted trench coat flapping open, loose, horny epaulettes,
Black polished shoes, one over t'other,
Idly alert,
Courtly corner boy.

Luckily I had not got with me my pocket Olympus camera.
Two Number 19s passed,
Flocks of cabs.
I did not allow advertisements for the pyramids
And for a boy Pharaoh
To distract me from the nape of Bacon's neck,
The henna-dyed hairs, gelled, spiky,
Gilded in October evening sun.
The breeze lifted the hair on the crown of his skull,
The proud, soft, blown comb of the cock.

A Number 14 bus sailed into view,
The Statue of Eros in its rear-view mirror.
He put out his hand,
His left hand – bare, ungloved.
He stepped up onto the platform.
But although he was first in the queue
He stood back to permit
A young Asian gentleman,
Lean, prematurely grey,
To cut inside him to the lower deck.
Then he, aged eighty years,
Swung up the staircase like a gibbon
In the Dublin zoo.

I stepped back out of the queue,
Mulling on Vincent's memorial in Auvers
By Osip Zadkine – man at work or
Study of a man in a landscape.
I studied him sit himself down
Halfway down the aisle of the upper deck
On the north side.
What to call it? And by whom?
Good Evening, Childhood by J. M. W. Turner?
The bus sailed out into the smog-scrapered sun
Towards Hyde Park and Kensington,
Its terminus in white on black:
Putney Garage.

Seamus Heaney's Fiftieth Birthday

I am disconcerted by all this cant of your fiftieth birthday,
Yet here I am at your sill with my tray of images,
Finding as I had hoped and half-expected
A *Please Do Not Disturb* sign on the door knob.
I put it down on the floor, glimpsing through the keyhole
A mistle thrush's nest in the font of a roofless side chapel.
What are they gossiping about? What can they mean?
As if you were a kind of superannuated dropout
In some Tahiti of the mind

Being girded up about the frothy loins
With grass skirt and a straw hat
Or a Buddha on Broadway or an anointed godfather
With sceptre and orb in a TV studio.

Do they not yet know the stations of innocence?
That you have three ceremonies to attend to on your birthday?
At the first of which there is the liturgy of your real absence;
At the second of which there is the liturgy of your immortal oblivion;
At the third of which there is the liturgy of your sublime unimportance;
One candle;
Altar girl with blue jeans showing beneath red soutane
And altar boys in Doc Martens
Hug candle snuffers with shy pride,
The cook's own sons and daughter.

She stands alone in the kitchen, watching the light on the estuary,
Waiting on the oven and the tide,
A small woman elevated on the rim of the turning world;
A Vision of Ingredients in the Twentieth Century;
Royal Baking Powder, eggs and butter, sugar and flour;
The silence coming in, and the silence going out;
Promontory, ewe, lamb; chapel, stone wall, water.
Her cookery encyclopaedia is open on a missal stand;
The poinsettia on the windowsill is chanting;
And the cat among the cruets is asleep.
Fie on your fiftieth birthday! What blasphemy!
I wish you well, married priest of the night stair,
You who, without cant, in our time
Redeemed the noun "oven" from the rubric of murder
And gave back to us a verb of our mother:
To mother and to mother and to mother –
That one day we would feel warm enough to speak.

The Death of the Ayatollah Khomeini

The day the Ayatollah Ruhollah Khomeini died
In a suburb in northern Teheran
I went to 12 noon Mass in Drogheda.

Although the temple was three-quarters empty,
The sixty-five-year-old, erect, creamy-haired pastor
Preached with passion.
He spoke deliberately, with precision and clarity;
With mercy, also, sense and charity.

"Young people of Drogheda" – he said –
"I beg you not to come to church on Sundays.
Sunday churchgoing has become a scandal.
You are young and open and sincere.
I beg you to remain young and open and sincere
To yourselves and to one another;
To live out the Gospel on weekdays
In all its idealism.
On Sundays I beg you to stay in bed
While your parents get up to go to church.
We – the older generations –
Have become a nation of Sunday churchgoers.
The Gospel means nothing to us on weekdays.
Our religion is comfort and the supermarket.
We have betrayed you.
Either we have given you bad example
Or we have given you no example.
We are insincere in word and in deed,
Most especially in word.
Not satisfied with having put doors on our emotions
Where there were no doors before,
We have closed the doors of our emotions.
Young people of Drogheda,
The roof of my church is unworthy of you.
Stay in bed on Sundays and dream
Of how life might be
When it is on earth as it is in heaven."

The silence after he had spoken
Was the silence of a newly baked cake,
To be savoured by the actual sight of it,
Fresh out of oven.
As he approached the commemoration of the Last Supper
And the metamorphosis of bread and wine
Into body and blood

The congregation looked awake, alert, apprehensive,
As if we were in danger from the priest
Or as if he were in danger from us
Or as if we were all in danger together
As the moment of truth approached.
There was that sense of the moment of truth approaching.
There was an air of drama, expectation, butterflies.

As he began to annunciate the fatal, fateful words,
An infant girl in yellow smock,
Barely able to stagger,
Pink cardigan and white sandals,
Began to waddle up the centre aisle.
She did not know
Where she was going.
She was exploring
The far end of the garden,
Risking marbled, chrysanthemum borders.
She arrived at the steps of the altar
And gazed at the priest
High up above her.
The priest looked like a young naked woman
Looking down from a height
Upon a small, frock-coated, middle-aged gentleman.
"Do this in commemoration of me,"
He was saying and she nodded her head
And cried out, "I will",
And turned around
And waddled all the way back down the aisle
Chanting
"I will".
We all turned our heads to observe her.
She did not look back.
She left the church like a young bride never to return –
The young mother-to-be
Of the Ayatollah Ruhollah Khomeini.

Loosestrife in Ballyferriter

to Brian Friel on his sixtieth birthday

I

Dear Master – Homesick for Athens
In this summer of rain, I prayed to the Mother
Of God but she did not appear to answer
And the Loosestrife in Ballyferriter near broke my heart.

II

But then I came to the Gallarus Oratory.
Its small black door-space was a Mount of Venus.
Within the womb of that miniature iconostasis
What I saw was a haven white as salt.

III

An Trá Bhán, an Trá Bhán,
Cá bhfuil m'athair, cá bhfuil mo mháthair?
An Trá Bhán, an Trá Bhán,
Cá bhfuil m'athair, cá bhfuil mo mháthair?

IV

I stood in the delivery ward outside the Gallarus Oratory,
Overtaken by coachload after coachload of tourists
From Celtic, from Medieval, from Modern times,
Expiring, only to be given birth to, in that small black door-space.

V

The embryonic majority were from the heel of Italy.
There were French, Swedish, German, Dutch.
There were siblings also from North America
To whom Ireland is an odyssey odder than Iowa.

VI

("Iowa" – she keened from behind a drystone wall –
"Iowa – I don't want to have to go to Iowa.
Iowa doesn't want me and I don't want Iowa.
Why must I forsake Ireland for Iowa?")

VII

There was a traffic snarl-up at the Gallarus Oratory,
All of the newly born vying to find parking space
In a gauntlet of fuchsia. In the small black door-space
I gave vent to my grief for my foreign mother.

VIII

What is the nature of Loosestrife in Ballyferriter?
What class of a massacre occurred on the Great Blasket?
Who burned the islanders out of their island homes?
Was it the Irish who burned us out of our island homes?

IX

What we did not know as we scurried out over the waves
In the rain-laden sunlight to feed our eyes on the corpse of the Blasket
Was that we were being observed from a small black door-space
By a small old man blacker than his own door-space.

X

Only the small old man living alone in his own black door-space,
Counting us swooping in and out of the corpse of the Blasket,
In the showdown saluted me and he whistled in the cosmos,
His eyes floating in the sheep's carcass of his skull,

XI

His larynx thinned by the white sand of his eyes:
"It was the Irish who burned us out of our island homes,"
And his smile was moist so that it stuck on the breeze:
"It was the Irish who burned us out of our island homes."

XII

An Trá Bhán, an Trá Bhán,
Cá bhfuil m'athair, cá bhfuil mo mháthair?
An Trá Bhán, an Trá Bhán,
Cá bhfuil m'athair, cá bhfuil mo mháthair?

XIII

Dear Master – Homesick for Athens
In this summer of rain, my closest grief
Lies in Tyrone dust. There is no man
Who would not murder his brother. Joy of all who grieve.

XIV

There is no God – only his Mother;
There is no God – only his Mother and;
There is no God – only his Mother and Loosestrife;
There is no God – only his Mother and Loosestrife in Ballyferriter.

The Sign of Peace

Being a middle-aged woman,
I do not often attend Mass
But when I do, the part I like
Is the bit where everybody is meant
To give one another the Sign of Peace.
The priest intones: "In the name of Christ Jesus
Let us give one another the Sign of Peace."

This morning when I found myself next
A bald small man with fiery eyes
I felt a spurt of something in my side
And when it came to the Sign of Peace
Without thinking about it
I turned around, as if in a trance,
And kissed him on both cheeks.

His eyes flapped their wings at me
And flew low across his cheeks
And he pushed out his two arms around me
And standing on tippy-toes
He kissed me one quick peck on the lips.
I could hear the gates of heaven clang open wide
And choirs of angels serenading us with raised spears.

You can imagine my surprise when at lunchtime
I got a phone call from the parish priest to say
That the annual house-to-house parish collection
Was being made this afternoon
And that envelopes were to be returned not later than Wednesday
And that by the way, my dear child of God,
The Sign of Peace is never given in the form of a kiss.
The Sign of Peace is given always in the form of a handshake.

The cheek of him.

Lord United Ireland, Christmas 1989

I

Peace
To your crackers.
Peace
To your plum pudding.

Each one of us has at least one affectation,
One convolvulus in bloom.
My father was chief of staff of the IRA
And *his* affectation was that he had *one* arm.
But I had *two* arms
And therefore grew up to believe
That a man with two arms
Was by definition inferior
To a man with one arm.

My solution
Was to insist that I had *three* arms,

As a consequence of which
I was stashed away in a psychiatric unit in Epping Forest
For three and a half years
With the help of money from my Fine Gael uncle
Who owns a chain of supermarkets in Middlesex
And his sister-in-law who is a nun in the Isle of Wight.

II

I was reborn in Epping
And since my return flight from Leeds–Bradford Airport
I have believed I have *eight* arms.
I live in a manger at the bottom of Kildare Street,
Tended to by the three wise women of Leinster House,
Carolina and Desdemona and Allanah,
With all their caravans of Camels & Opels, Gourds & Saabs.
In the word of the prophet Isaiah:
I am your local friendly Camel dealer.
I have come to prepare the way for the private motorist.

With my eight arms,
Lord United Ireland, they call me.
When I brandish my eight arms at them
They interrogate me: "Are you United, United?"
"Are you Ireland, Ireland?"

Up and down the streets
Of Dublin and Belfast I go,
Octopus in search of his octopussy,
Flailing my arms, all eight of them,
Lord United Ireland.
You cannot see my head for my arms,
My snubby head.
My eyeless, mouthless, noseless head.
My blue bag of head.

III

As I make faces at you, this Christmas evening in Erin,
I am sitting in the window of the Dublin–Belfast train,
Ticking over at Semtex Station,
While bomb buggers pause from their bomb buggery to behold me

Juggling my cup of coffee from my fifth arm to my seventh arm,
The eight-armed juggler,
Lord United Ireland.

I have a high, as well as a low, opinion of myself.
Peace
To your crackers.
Peace
To your plum pudding.

Paul

In the rush-hour traffic outside the centre-city church
I stood with my bicycle waiting for the lights to change –
A Raleigh bicycle with upright handlebars
That I had purchased for two pounds fifty pence in The Pearl –
When a priest in black soutane and white surplice
Materialised in the darkness of the porch.
He glided over to me:
"I am about to begin a funeral Mass but I have no mourners.
Would you be prepared to act as a mourner for me?"

As we paced up the aisle, the priest enlightened me:
"He was about the same age as yourself,
All we know about him is that his name was Paul."

I knelt in the front pew,
The coffin on trestles alongside me,
Its flat abdomen next to my skull.
I felt as a mother must feel
All alone in the maternity ward
With her infant in the cot at the foot of the bed,
A feeling that everything is going to be all right
But that we are all aliens in the cupboard,
All coat hangers in the universe.

The priest – a seven-foot-tall, silver-haired peasant in his eighties –
Instructed me to put my bicycle in the hearse beside the coffin.
He and I sat in front with the driver.
At a major traffic junction near the cemetery of Mount Prospect

We had to brake to avoid knocking down a small boy.
The car behind us bumped into our rear bumper,
Inducing the bicycle to bump against the coffin.
We recognised a prominent politician in the back seat blessing herself.
At the graveside as the priest said prayers
I got the feeling that the coffin was empty;
That Paul, whoever he was,
Was somewhere else.

"How do you know that his name was Paul?"
I asked the priest as we tiptoed away.
He handed me a creased sheet
Of blue vellum, unlined notepaper – Belvedere Bond:
Dear Paul – Thank you for your marriage proposal
But I am engaged to be married in Rome in June.
Best wishes always, Mary

Queen of Loneliness.

The Christies Foxhunters Chase over Three Miles and Two Furlongs

to Síabhra

I feel all saliva and go,
Applying my lipstick before the big race.
If I am going to fall,
I ask myself at which jump I will fall.
Will it be at the third ditch
Or at the second-last from home?
I anticipate the stony, mossy tones of the race commentator:
"Lonely Moorland has unseated his rider at the first."

I purse my lips and swivel my tongue.
Betimes in dreams I find myself
Putting my tongue in my stirrup.
I extend my tongue to achieve maximum moisture.
It is a pale pink lipstick which I favour.
I check my bit.
If I were a man, I'd envy myself.

I smack my lips to seal my fate.
I feel in love with myself, which is a good omen.
Self-love is the secret of love.
If I love myself, I will love you.
Win or fall
I will have given all.

Hommage à Cézanne

This morning when I am trying to get myself together for work,
Piece myself together for work,
Shaving with one hand and making coffee with the other,
There's a ring on the doorbell and it's Olympia:
"There's a horse on my staircase, Paul."
I am forty-three – Olympia is nineteen.
She stands there laconically
In a miniskirt the size of a hanky
And a black bowler hat and a white blouse
And a green suede hunting jacket:
"There's a horse on my staircase, Paul."

I do not know what I am supposed to do about it.
I procrastinate on the balls of my feet,
Trying to wipe the shaving cream from off my face
And glancing down at the brand-new coffee stain
On my turquoise cotton shirt.
She gives me the sort of cat-on-the-wall smile
That twangs its garters between tail-swishes:
"You and I have a secret
But neither of us knows what it is."

I do not know what it is.
Foggily, I do not know what it is.
Then she says that thing to me again:
"There's a horse on my staircase, Paul,"
And just as I am about to say to her "Come in,"
She steps up to me on the tips of her toes
And flicks me a kiss high on the cheekbone
And spins around and steps back into the elevator.
I step back into my apartment

And squirt some shaving cream into my coffee filter
And stir my mug with my razor:
"There's a horse on my staircase, Paul."

I am walking around in circles in my own apartment.
I am supposed to be at work one hour ago.
What am I supposed to say to my boss?
My boss is a chic fifty-seven-year-old mother of five:
"Paul, why don't you go to sleep for a week?
We can take a look at your equestrian needs
When you get to feeling a little less distracted."

Am I dreaming?
No, I am not dreaming.
I can hear the sound of my own hooves
Stamping on the marble steps of her staircase.
I go back to sleep again
To the sound of my own hooves
Stamping on the marble steps of her staircase:
"You are the horse on my staircase, Paul."

Self-Portrait, Nude with Steering Wheel

I am forty-five and do not
Know how to drive a car
– And you tell me I am cultured.

Forty-five years creeping and crawling about the earth,
Going up and down the world,
And I do not know the difference between a carburettor and a
    gasket
– And you tell me I am a Homo sapiens.

Forty-five years sitting in the back seat giving directions
– And you say that I am not an egotist.

Forty-five years sitting in the passenger seat
With my gloved hands folded primly in my lap
– And you think I am liberated.

Forty-five years getting in and out of cars
And I do not know where the dipstick is
– And you tell me that I am a superb lover.

Forty-five years grovelling behind a windscreen
– And you talk of my pride and courage and self-reliance.

Forty-five years of not caring to know the meaning of words
Like *transmission, clutch, choke, battery, leads*
– And you say that I am articulate.

Forty-five years bumming lifts off other people –
And you tell me I am an independent, solitary, romantic spirit.

> So it is that you find me tonight
> Loitering here outside your front door
> Having paid off a taxi in three ten-pound notes,
> Nude, with a steering wheel in my hands.

Phyllis Goldberg

Of all the women working in our office
Phyllis Goldberg is the quiestest, most polite, most solicitous,
Most diligent, most discreet, most generous.
She'd been with us about twenty years when she went sick
And George Webb asked me to drop in on her on the way home.
An old lady in a walking frame answered the door,
Motioned me upstairs with her eyebrows.
She was sitting up in bed naked
With a bottle of whiskey in one hand
And a half-pint tooth mug in the other.
I enquired:
"Is there anything I can do for you?"
She gazed upon me with tears in her eyes,
Owls of tears.
She blinked: "Make love to me,"
In a tone at once passionate and dispassionate.
Since boyhood I had dreamed of being seduced
By a woman in her bedroom –

Is there a man who has not? –
Yet now it was the last thing I wanted to do
Or have done to me.
I undressed,
Unbuttoning my crisp pink shirt over thin, hairy, white legs.

After we had made love –
Angry flesh –
She fell asleep
And I sat up in bed with her head in my lap,
Patting her damp brown hair.
As I came down the staircase
I felt like a minor French count
In a nineteenth-century film
After having strangled his mistress,
Putting on his top hat and white kid gloves,
Twirling his ivory-knobbed cane.
Her mother watched from her walking frame
As I crossed the hall floor to the door.
When I opened the door I was afraid to look back
In case I should find the walking frame empty.
As I picked my steps through the snow
All I could hear was an empty walking frame.
I began to hurry through the snow
For fear that the empty walking frame
Would begin to chase after me.
No one will ever believe me
That I did what I did
Because it seemed what I ought to do.

That night Phyllis Goldberg telephoned me,
The first and only time that she telephoned me in twenty years.
"Thank you for making love to me," she said.
"Not at all," I said,
"Glad to be –"
She put down the phone
And I sat down behind my desk in the dark,
At my silent word processor, with its chin in its hands,
And I waited.
I knew that it was only a matter of time
Before the door would open of its own accord

And in the half-light from the hallway
I would behold the shadow of the empty walking frame.
I would cry out for help but it would be too late.
The next day a card from Phyllis Goldberg would swoop through
   my letter box
With such a flutter that everybody in the cinema would behold
Its butterfly trajectory:
Thank you for making love to me. Love, Phyllis Goldberg.

The Dream of Life

A woman waiting for her man
In Dowth of the slow-footed consonants
Draws down the sash window of her bedroom.
A pair of house martins – the last house martins of summer –
From mud huts under eaves
Alight on the precipice
Of the top ledge of the window frame,
Testing their propellers, whirring,
The voyage to Africa,
Hawks in the cliffs of Sicily
Avid for food for their hawk chicks.

Reading Primo Levi by the Family Fireside at Evening

I turn the pages, wisdom
Dissolving into despair.
When woman and child speak to me
I do not hear them.
What am I to do?
Continue the book,
Pursue the truth,
Make sad the family?

Or close the book
And into the hole in my head
Let lamplight filter?

Little Mark wants to know
If I will play Labyrinth.
Holding the book open in my hand,
I tell him that I can't
Play Labyrinth.
"Why can't you?" he enquires.
I put down the book on the floor
And repeat: "I can't."
"Why can't you?" he enquires,
And I say, "I don't know",
And I stand up and I leave the living room
And I go downstairs into the kitchen
Where I can be alone
Beside the oven
With the dog and the cat,
Fódhla and *Ketchel*,
And press my two hands against the sides of my head,
Palms on temples,
To try and stop
This fallingdownbackwards from my chimney,
This callingbackupatme from my stairwell.
"Will you play a game of Labyrinth?"
I can't, I can't. You must, you must.

* * *

Nights in the Gardens of Clare

to Kay Sheehy

A dialogue between two lovers, Soledad and Donal: Soledad, the daughter of a ship's captain, is a survivor of the Armada wreck the *San Marcos*, which went aground at Lurga Point, County Clare, in September 1588; Donal Thornton is a local Clareman and silversmith.

SOLEDAD   Our ships fell out of the sky at Malbay.
Street gangs of reefs slit our keels from heel to throat
At Lurga Point and Doonbeg.
Fat seas flung us up onto the jet-black shore.
Oh the coasts of Clare are black, black, black.
Thousands of natives stood there inspecting us,
Their eyes gleaming at the prospect of plunder.
I picked myself up off the sand, ready to die.
They stripped me naked and hung masks of devils
From my buttocks and they painted faces on my breasts,
With marker pens they drew eyes on my breasts,
The native Irish are obsessed with heads,
The native Irish are all heads, or rather,
They see themselves as being bodiless heads,
Their men are so full of their own heads
They think they have brains in their private parts.
They tied my hands behind my back
And pointed to a tower and a gibbet on the hill.
As I staggered towards it I glimpsed your nephew
And threw myself on his mercy.
He pulled me into his breast and he put
His mantle round me, concealing me
In that instant – it all happened
Quicker than an eyeblink – and I was safe
In the nest of his breast.
Safe in the wingspan of his cloak.
Let me be clear as the skyline of Clare,
The treeless skyline of Clare.
I did not lust for nor flirt with your nephew,
I simply asked him to rescue me and he did.
It was necessity that gave birth to Adam and Eve.

It was necessity that brought me and Donal together.
We are creatures of necessity.
Necessity is the mother of Love.

DONAL   It is exactly as Soledad has said, no less, no more.
It was not her deep beauty as a Spanish Lady,
Believe it or believe it not,
That drew me to her, but her cry for help.
Early that morning I was at work in my workshop,
Hammering out silver brooches in the shapes of the plants
Of the Burren –
Irish Orchids – Pyramidal Bugles – Bear Berries –
When Miko Vaughan and Nacey Considine,
T. J. Minogue and Franky Spellissey,
Arrived in to say that there were Spanish ships
Falling out of the sky at Doolin and Doonbeg.
"Let's go over and watch the ships
Breaking up on the rocks," cried Nacey.
"It'll be surely great crack
Watching the ships breaking up on the rocks.
There's nothing like a disaster – a good shipwrecking –
To cheer the heart on a late September day.
Besides, there'd be the hangings,
And you'd meet people, like, hanging about at the
    hangings."
There were thousands of spectators at Lurga Point,
Doolin and Doonbeg,
Watching the ships breaking up;
I lay on the cliff edge munching grass,
Watching the ships breaking up.
The soldiers – the joint militias of the Irish and English –
Were hacking the heads off Spanish survivors;
The white horses of the waves were bleeding to death.
Clare's trendiest film-maker was there,
Boethius Clancy,
As famous for his wenching and boozing
As for his film-making – a big bearded lout
In dark glasses and sleeveless black leather jacket,
Parading up and down the seafront at Doolin
With a loudhailer in one hand, and a leg of a chair in the
    other.

When I asked who was the leather-clad, yellow-haired lady
    on his arm
Someone said: "That's his KitKat."
She was Swedish from Nottingham, Minnesota.
She was heard to bleat:
"Eat me, Boethius, eat me."
I got up off my face and ran down
Onto the rocks to where the survivors
Whose heads had not been hacked off
Were being rounded up, stripped,
And marched in lines to Tromra Tower.
It was then I saw Soledad fall towards me.

SOLEDAD Necessity drew us together,
Nights in the Gardens of Clare.
Day by day we grew together.
Love fell upon us like a bird of prey.
With the help of the Northern Irish
In Antrim and Scotland
We will escape to Salamanca and a new life,
Never to return to this haunted country.
I will miss only the hills of Clare,
The Burren and Mount Callan;
Above all,
The Heights of Ennis where I found a home
In front of a shop called Epicene.

DONAL Oh I will meet you *on the Height*, Soledad;
I will sit beside you *on the Height*, Soledad;
I will come to you *on the Height*, Soledad;
I will mince pies with you *on the Height*, Soledad;
On the Height we'll watch the world go waltzing by;
On the Height we'll watch the heads go marching past;
On the Height we'll read the *Clare Champion* and the *Hot Press* too;
On the Height we'll listen to the colour of the crack;
On the Height we'll listen to what they're saying
About us – even if it isn't very true:

"They had a mad one last night on the Height";
"She's got cool boots, that Spanish One";
"But he was really polluted and so was she";
"They're having a party tonight in Corrovorin."

225

"Will I see you down in Brogan's later on?"
"Will I see you in the Auburn later on?"
"Will I see you in Dillinger's later on?"
"Or will I find you later on in the Old Ground?"

I saw a Pair of Reindeer in O'Dea's.
It was you.
O Soledad.

SOLEDAD   O Donal,
Once in Ennis there was a Pair of Ears.
It was on the Height that I first saw the Pair of Ears.
As fine a Pair of Ears you've never set eyes on,
That is – until God put a Head between the Pair of Ears.
From that day on, the Head took over.
It was the Head all the way,
Head, Head, Head, nothing but Head,
And up in O'Dea's Bar on the hill
Instead of the Pair of Ears in the corner
There was the Head in the corner,
The Head with a head under his arm.
What could I do but go home to Spain,
Grieving for my lost Pair of Ears?
A Pair of Ears I first met in Ennis,
A Pair of Ears on the Height of Ennis.

DONAL   Your breasts are in my eyes, O my love,
Nights in the Gardens of Clare;
O my love, O my river-swallowing sea,
Nights in the Gardens of Clare.

SOLEDAD   *Si,*
And here is my hymn to my de Valera,
My Spanish Clareman, my Clare Spaniard.
There is no reason why you, de Valera,
Should not shed your puritanical plumage
And become, as once you were with Sinéad,
Gay and festive, carefree and frisky –
All that is most truly Spain, most truly Clare.
Preside outside the Courthouse
Over the courting couples round your statue,

226

With *bodhráns*, pipes and fiddles round your feet.
For I have seen the young virgins of Ennis
Holding hands with their fellas
On benches round your statue and your plinth,
But your eyes are always shut, thin obdurate man.
Open your eyes, behold your children free
To stay at home, work at home, play at home,
Nights in the Gardens of Clare.

On a good day I wake and hear
The River Fergus at my window
But on a bad day, and the bad days are many,
I wake and see far down below me
The coast of Doolin, black as black can be;
The black, black, black coast of Doolin;
I am falling, falling, falling,
Into the black, black, black coast of Doolin.

The rocks of Doolin are waiting to gnaw me.
The cliffs of Moher are waiting to guzzle me.
The shores of Malbay are waiting to spew me.
My father's ship, the *San Marcos*,
Breaks up on the reefs of Lurga Point
To the caterwauling of the laughter of the Irish,
All that scorn and derision,
All that greed and gluttony,
And the screams and pleas and howls of the souls of the
    drowning Spanish;

O Donal Thornton
                 I want to die
In your arms tonight;
             let me die
In your arms tonight,
              O Donal Thornton.

DONAL   Soledad, you're so far away from home.
Come away with me to Corcomroe and I will
Love you among insects who will protect you –
The Confused, the Burren Green, the Anomalous,
The Pearl-Bordered Fritillary, the Little Blue, the Beautiful
    Brocade.

Come away with me to Corcomroe and with me pray
At the altar of the three-light window;
Was ever a tale so believable, yet so tall,
As the tale of the Universe seen through a three-light
    window?
At the Hub of the great Wheel of Fate,
An infant child seen through a three-light window.

SOLEDAD Our Lady of the Fertile Rock,

DONAL   Have mercy on us.

SOLEDAD Our Lady of the Puzzled Forehead,

DONAL   Have mercy on us.

SOLEDAD Our Lady of the Running Stream,

DONAL   Have mercy on us.

SOLEDAD Our Lady of the Homeless,

DONAL   Have mercy on us.

SOLEDAD Our Lady of the Travelling People,

DONAL   Have mercy on us.

SOLEDAD Our Lady of the Spanish and the Hungarian and the
         Ethiopian and the Palestinian Refugees,

DONAL   Have mercy on us.

SOLEDAD Our Lady of the Northern Irish,

DONAL   Have mercy on us.

SOLEDAD Our Lady of the Southern Irish,

DONAL   Have mercy on us.

SOLEDAD   Our Lady of the Pure Smile,

DONAL   Have mercy on us.

SOLEDAD   Our Lady of the Addicted to Death,

DONAL   Have mercy on us.

SOLEDAD   Our Lady of the Glow of Life,

DONAL   Have mercy on us.

SOLEDAD   Soledad, you're so far away from home.

DONAL   Come away with me to Poulnabrone and I will
          Hold you in my arms, in your skintight
          Blue jeans and your skintight white jumper,
          Like the priest holding up the Eucharist at Mass,
          The skintight white wafer of the Host with blue feet.
          I will put you standing on the capstone
          Of the Portal Dolmen of Poulnabrone
          And you will open your arms wide to the white-hot sun
          So that your breasts will sing to the points of the compass,
          Your breasts will be as tuning forks quivering,
          Your breasts will be voices in the white-hot sun,
          Voices with their nipples audible.
          Your breasts will sing innately to all men of peace and
                goodwill
          And the world will be free.

SOLEDAD   Soledad, you're so far away from home.

DONAL   Come away with me to Corofin and I will hide you
          Under the weir, under the weir,
          In Bankyle House beside Lake Inchiquin,
          There to sleep, wake, walk, read in silence and peace
          In the company of Rose and George and Donough.
          I will tell them you are coming to stay with them,
          Rose and George and Donough;
          Under the weir, under the weir,

In Bankyle House beside Lake Inchiquin.
After the war is over, after we have all died
And have been born again, over and over, born again over
    and over,
There will be a time for loving and a time for smiling.

SOLEDAD Soledad, you're so far away from home.

DONAL Come away with me to Lissycasey and at Fanny O'Dea's
I will pour an egg-flip down your slipper-red throat,
An egg-flip to beat all egg-flips;
Not even my own dear mother could beat
An egg-flip such as Fanny O'Dea can beat.
After egg-flips at Fanny O'Dea's
We will ride on white horses
Across the red islands of Ennis
To the green airport at Shannon,
A frozen jet on runway Number 3,
A trembling hare crouched
To fly you back to your Spanish shore,
The Mountains of your Dread,
And the Coasts of Barcelona;
And the Coasts of Barcelona.

* * *

The One-Armed Crucifixion

after Giacomo Manzù

How many thousands of hours on the shore at Galway,
In the drizzle off the back of the sea,
On the sodden sands,
Did we spend hurling together, father and son?
Pucking the *sliotar*, one to the other,
Hour in, hour out, year in, year out.
How many thousands of times, old man,
Did you strike a high ball for your young son
To crouch, to dart, to leap,
To pluck the ball one-handed out of the climbing air?

Study of a Figure in a Landscape, 1952

after Francis Bacon

– Did your bowels move today?
– Yes, Daddy.
– At what time did your bowels move today?
– At eight o'clock, Daddy.
– Are you sure?
– Yes, Daddy.
– Are you sure that your bowels moved today?
– I am, Daddy.
– Were you sitting down in the long grass?
– I was, Daddy.
– Are you telling me the truth?
– I am, Daddy.
– Are you sure you are not telling a lie?
– I am, Daddy.
– You are sure that your bowels moved today?
– I am, Daddy, but please don't beat me, Daddy.
  Don't be vexed with me, Daddy.
  I am not absolutely sure, Daddy.

– Why are you not absolutely sure?
– I don't know, Daddy.
– What do you mean you don't know?
– I don't know what bowels are, Daddy.
– What do you think bowels are?
– I think bowels are wheels, Daddy,
  Black wheels under my tummy, Daddy.
– Did your black wheels move today?
– They did, Daddy.
– Then your bowels definitely did move today.
– Yes, Daddy.
– You should be proud of yourself.
– Yes, Daddy.
– Are you proud of yourself?
– Yes, Daddy.
– Constipation is the curse of Cain.
– Yes, Daddy.
– You will cut and reap the corn today.
– Yes, Daddy.
– Every day be sure that your bowels move.
– Yes, Daddy.
– If your bowels do not move, you are doomed.
– Yes, Daddy.
– Are you all right?
– No, Daddy.
– What in the name of the Mother of God
  And the dead generations is the matter with you?
– I want to go to the toilet, Daddy.
– Don't just stand there, run for it.
– Yes, Daddy.
– Are you in your starting blocks?
– Yes, Daddy.
– When I count to three, leap from your starting blocks.
– I can't Daddy.
– Can't can't.
– Don't, Daddy, don't, Daddy, don't, Daddy, don't.

Fjord

You were Abraham but you were also Jesus.
In your Jesus suit
You liked to teach for the sake of teaching.
You were a teacher before you were a judge.

You'd descend with a word like *fjord*,
By the light of the standard lamp
On a winter's night in firelight,
Savour it, bless it, deposit it on my tongue.

"*Fjord*" – you'd announce – "is a Norwegian word."
I'd gaze up at your icicle-compacted face
As if you'd invented Norway and the Norwegian language
Especially for me.

You'd confide that we had fjords of our own in Ireland
And the noblest of all our fjords was in County Mayo,
The Killary fjord in the safe waters of whose deep, dark thighs
German submarines had lain sheltering in the war.

Look into your Irish heart, you will find a German U-boat,
A periscope in the rain and a swastika in the sky.
You were no more neutral, Daddy, than Ireland was,
Proud and defiant to boast of the safe fjord.

The Persian Gulf

The skylight is our escape route in the event of fire.

At night after supper we kneel on the floor
Of the dining room and recite the rosary in Irish.
Kneeling with my elbows in a dining-room chair,
My skull ensconced between the two arms of a carver,
I dream of the Persian Gulf and try
To imagine what the skylight would look like
On fire but I can no more visualise it
Than I can visualise the prayers we are saying

233

In a language in which we do not converse
And which is as strange to me as Urdu or Arabic.
Praying in Irish to a skylight on fire is an abstract art.

Abstract Art was in Ireland long before Abstract Art.

As the great Ferris wheel of the rosary
Monotonously revolves on a winter's night
I am borne away on the wings of prayer
And I see our three-storey house going up in flames,
57 Dartmouth Square,
And Daddy in his blue-and-white striped pyjamas,
With the cord tied in a dicky bow over the fly,
Gripping the stepladder
While we clamber up the fire escape to safety.
As we stand on the roof of our burning house
We are speaking Irish to one another as to the language born.

The fire-brigade engines, having charged
Through the city streets blaring their klaxons,
Assemble in the street below to feed up their ladders,
Spool them out to us sliding down the slopes of the rooves.
Daddy stands by a chimneypot, admiring the night sky,
Looking like Danny Kaye in *The Court Jester*
And putting his arms around my shoulders,
With that Connemara *blas* of his he says to me ruefully,
"It is a fine, bright night to be abroad, God save us."

When the first fireman reaches us
And cries to us – "Are you all right?" –
Daddy says to him in Irish: "We don't speak English."
The fire-brigade man, barely visible in smoke,
A pair of horn-rimmed spectacles on his gaunt, lean face,
All black helmet and black gauntlets,
Shrugs his eyebrows and climbs back down the ladder.
The ladders are retracted and the fire engines driven away,
Leaving us to burn to death speaking Irish.

Next morning, except for the crows in the trees
And the ruins of the house sticking up through the waters,
It is all quiet in the Persian Gulf,
A skylight on fire floating upstream.

Crinkle, Near Birr

Daddy and I were lovers
From the beginning, and when I was six
We got married in the church of Crinkle, near Birr.
The *Irish Independent* photographed the wedding.
My mother gave me away.
My sister was best man.
He was forty-two and a TV personality in Yorkshire,
Close to his widowed mother in Mayo,
Always having his photograph taken,
Always grinning and polite and manly and coy and brittle,
Checking the stubs of his cheque books,
Tying up his used cheque books in elastic bands,
Putting money away for a rainy day,
Making gilt-edged investments.
It was in the days before he became a judge.
He compèred boxing fights and women's beauty contests
In an accent that was neither English nor Irish nor American.
It was known as the Athlone accent.
When he spoke of Athlone
Listeners were meant to think
Of a convent in the middle of a dark forest
To which the speaker was chaplain.

We went on our honeymoon
To Galway, the City of the Tribes.
We stayed in the Eglinton Hotel in Salthill.
For breakfast we ate grapefruit segments and toast
And the manager bowed, the waiters goosing around us.
We stood on the Salmon Bridge counting
Squadrons of salmon floating face down in the waters below,
Waiting to go upstream to spawn.

In the afternoons we spawned our own selves in our hotel bedroom
Listening to cricket.
The West Indies were playing the MCC at Lord's.
We lay in bed listening to Rohan Kanhai batting for a double
    century
And Garfield Sobers taking six wickets for forty-five runs.
O Owen of the Birds,

That is what it meant to be Irish and free –
To be father and son in bed together
In a hotel in the City of the Tribes
Listening to cricket on the BBC Radio Third Service.
After dinner we walked on the pier at Spiddal,
Holding hands, watching schools
Of porpoises playing in the apple-light of the western sea.
One night after dinner we drove to Gort,
Where Daddy let his hair down
And we played a game of cricket
In the back garden of another father-and-son couple.
When Daddy bowled, I was his wicketkeeper.
He fancied himself as Ray Lindwall
And I fancied myself as Godfrey Evans –
Godders jack-knifing over bails and stumps.
When we returned to the hotel, we entered
By the fire escape, feeling in a mood to be secretive,
Black iron staircase flicked up against white pebble-dash gable.
Daddy divided the human race
Into those who had fire escapes and spoke Irish
And those who had not got fire escapes and did not speak Irish.
Another night we sat in a kitchen in Furbo
With a schoolteacher hobnobbing in Irish
Exotic as Urdu, all that rain and night at the windowpane.

The marriage lasted five years.
On a summer's night in Newcastle West
After a game of cricket with boys my own age
I came back into the house without my school blazer.
"Where have you left your school blazer
Which you should not have been wearing in the first place?
School blazers are not for wearing.
School blazers cost money."
I had left it on a fence in the field.
When I went to retrieve it, it was lolling out of a cow's mouth,
One arm of it.
Daddy took off his trousers' belt,
Rolled it up in a ball round his fist,
And let fly at me with it.
In a dust storm of tears I glimpsed
His Western movie hero's eyes stare at me.

When I was twelve, I obtained a silent divorce.
Ireland is one of the few civilised countries –
And the only country outside Asia –
In this respect, that while husbands and wives
Can only at best separate,
Children can obtain a silent divorce from their parents.
When I look back at the years of my marriage to Daddy
What I remember most
Are not the beatings-up and the temper tantrums
But the quality of his silence when he was happy.
Walking at evening with him down at the river,
I lay on my back in the waters of his silence,
The silence of a diffident, chivalrous bridegroom,
And he carried me in his two hands home to bed.

Life-Saving

after Francis Bacon

Having served my apprenticeship in tree-climbing in Mayo,
I climbed up onto the roof of our Dublin home
By the banks of the Grand Canal
And knelt down at the skylight over your bedroom,
Feeding my nose into its pane of clear glass.
I could see you but not hear you.
Mother was reclining on her back on the carpet,
Kicking her legs in the air.
You dived between her knees,
Snaked your hands under her back,
Put down your head into her shoulder
And she locked her arms around your neck.
I could see her laughing with her eyes closed.
Not since the night of my twelfth birthday,
When she permitted me to take her
To the film of *War and Peace*
In the Adelphi in Middle Abbey Street,
Henry Fonda as Pierre,
Audrey Hepburn as Natasha,
Had I seen her look so inconsolably delighted – that anarchic smile
Of hers, so characteristic of her clan,

The MacBride clan
Of Antrim and Mayo.
Between the chimneypots
A barge was sliding past.
Back down in the kitchen after tea
Offhandedly, I asked you what you'd been doing.
You replied without looking up from the table,
A chord of peremptory surrender in your voice:
"Your mother was teaching me life-saving."

Ulysses

I am hiding from my father
On the roof of Joyce's Tower
In Sandycove.
He is downstairs in the gloom
Of the Joyce Museum
Exchanging euphemisms with the curator,
The poet Michael Hartnett,
Meteorological euphemisms,
Wet and cold for June.

I am standing at the battlements.
I am eighteen years old.
The battle is whether or not
He will buy a copy of *Ulysses*.
It is a battle about money
But it is a battle also about morality
Or "morals" as it is called.
It began this morning at the breakfast table
When I asked him for twenty-one shillings
To buy a copy of *Ulysses*.
He refused on the grounds that on top
Of it being an outrageous sum of money
Which a poorly paid judge could ill afford,
It was a notoriously immoral book.
Even the most liberal-minded Jesuits
Had condemned *Ulysses*
As being blasphemous as well as pornographic.
My mother jumped around from the kitchen sink:

"Give him the money for the wretched book
And let the pair of you stop this nonsense
For pity's sake.
Will we ever see peace and sense in this house?"
My father stormed out of the kitchen,
The *Irish Independent* under his arm:
"I'll not be party to subsidising that blackguard
Bringing works of blasphemy into this house.
In the year of Our Lord nineteen hundred and sixty-three
I will not be an accessory to blasphemy."

I caught the 46A bus out to Joyce's Tower,
Newly opened as a museum.
The curator offered to share with me
A carafe of vodka left over
From a literary soirée of the night before.
It was the day after Bloomsday.
Monday, 17 June 1963.
We sat in a compatible silence,
Contemplatively, affably,
Until upheaval of gravel
Eradicated reverie.
I rushed to the door and glimpsed
My father at the foot of the iron steps.
I climbed up to the roof, hoping to hide
From him up there in the marine fog,
Foghorns bleating in the bay.

I hear footsteps behind me, I know it is he.
He declares: "I suppose we will have to buy that book.
What did you say the name of it is?"
I tell him that the name of it is *Ulysses*.
I follow him down the staircase and he submits:
"Mr Hartnett, I understand
You stock copies of a book entitled *Ulysses*.
I would like to purchase one copy of same."
"Certainly, Your Lordship, certainly,"
Replies the ever-courteous, Chinese-eyed curator.
When from his wingbacked chair behind his desk
He takes from a drawer
A copy of the jade-jacketed *Ulysses*,

The Bodley Head edition,
My father asks him if he would have brown paper
With which to wrap the green, satanic novel,
Make a parcel out of it.
The curator peers into a wastepaper basket
"Made by the Blind",
As if peering down into a bottomless lift shaft,
Casts a funicular, questing second glance at my father
Before fishing out crumpled bags of brown paper
Which the night before had ferried bottles of vodka.
He lays them out on the desk top
And smoothes them, taking pains
To be obsequiously
Extra punctilious, extra fastidious.
Formally, he hands it over to my father,
As if delivering to some abstract and intractable potentate
A peace gift of a pair of old shoes.
My father pronounces: "Thank you, Mr Hartnett."
The curator, at his most extravagantly unctuous, replies:
"Very glad to be able to oblige you, Your Lordship."

My father departed Joyce's Tower with the book.
The next day when I asked my mother if she'd seen it
She said it was in their bedroom beside my father's bed.
Her bed was beside the window and his bed
Was between her bed and the wall.
There it was, on his bedside table,
Ulysses,
With a bookmarker in it – a fruit-gum wrapper –
At the close of the opening episode.
When a few weeks later
I got to reading *Ulysses* myself
I found it as strange as my father
And as discordant.
It was not until four years later
When a musical friend
Gave me my first lessons
That *Ulysses* began to sing for me
And I began to sing for my father:
Daddy, Daddy,
My little man, I adore you.

Sport

There were not many fields
In which you had hopes for me
But sport was one of them.
On my twenty-first birthday
I was selected to play
For Grangegorman Mental Hospital
In an away game
Against Mullingar Mental Hospital.
I was a patient
In B Wing.
You drove all the way down,
Fifty miles,
To Mullingar to stand
On the sidelines and observe me.

I was fearful I would let down
Not only my team but you.
It was Gaelic football.
I was selected as goalkeeper.
There were big country men
On the Mullingar Mental Hospital team,
Men with gapped teeth, red faces,
Oily, frizzy hair, bushy eyebrows.
Their full forward line
Were over six foot tall
Fifteen stone in weight.
All three of them, I was informed,
Cases of schizophrenia.

There was a rumour
That their centre-half forward
Was an alcoholic solicitor
Who, in a lounge bar misunderstanding,
Had castrated his best friend
But that he had no memory of it.
He had meant well – it was said.
His best friend had had to emigrate
To Nigeria.

To my surprise,
I did not flinch in the goals.
I made three or four spectacular saves,
Diving full stretch to turn
A certain goal around the corner,
Leaping high to tip another certain goal
Over the bar for a point.
It was my knowing
That you were standing on the sideline
That gave me the necessary motivation –
That will to die
That is as essential to sportsmen as to artists.
More than anybody it was you
I wanted to mesmerise, and after the game –
Grangegorman Mental Hospital
Having defeated Mullingar Mental Hospital
By 14 goals and 38 points to 3 goals and 10 points –
Sniffing your approval, you shook hands with me.
"Well played, son."

I may not have been mesmeric
But I had not been mediocre.
In your eyes I had achieved something at last.
On my twenty-first birthday I had played on a winning team
The Grangegorman Mental Hospital team.
Seldom if ever again in your eyes
Was I to rise to these heights.

Apartheid

When after twenty-seven sessions of Electric Convulsive Therapy
I was discharged from hospital in London,
I got the night train from Euston to Holyhead,
Sipping baby gin-and-tonics in my empty carriage,
Savouring the consolation of the passing night,
The invisible emptiness of the universe.
Daddy and Mummy met me at seven-thirty next morning
Off the boat train at Westland Row.

Driving home through the deserted streets of Dublin,
None of us could think of anything to say
Until outside the National Maternity Hospital
Daddy imparted to me that in the afternoon
He and I would be attending the Rugby International
Between Ireland and South Africa.
Our cousin, it seemed, was playing in the front row
Of the scrum for Ireland,
Propping up the scrum for Ireland.

As I sit in the East Stand freezing,
All the men of Ireland with rugs on their laps,
Whiskey flasks in their hip pockets,
I ask Daddy why there are no black men
On the African team.
"Apartheid" – he answers authoritatively – "Apartheid."
He pronounces the word *Apartheid*
With such élan, such expertise,
With such familiarity, such finality,
As if it were a part of nature,
Part of ourselves.

I try to remember what Apartheid is.
I cannot remember what Apartheid is.
Odd to think that only this day last week in London
I was having my twenty-seventh session of Electric Convulsive
    Therapy
While today I am sitting in the East Stand in Dublin
Watching an African team with no black men
Playing an Irish team with all white men,
Daddy's arm around me, his chin jutting out.
If I was a black man, I would play for Africa.

Stellar Manipulator

I

Judge Durcan, you wanted
Your eldest son to be a lawyer.
But wanting always to be
Like the other you, Daddy,

To become your understudy,
I became at the age of twenty-five
Stellar Manipulator
At the London Planetarium.

When I went for the interview
With the Director of the Planetarium,
John Ebdon,
He so much looked
And sounded like you
I had to be careful not
To address him as Daddy.
"I hear that you write
Poetry" – he exclaimed.
I winced. He continued:
Many a night I saw the Pleiads,
rising through the mellow shade,
Glitter like a swarm of fire-flies
tangled in a silver braid.
When I failed to identify
The author, he said
"Tennyson" – and gave me the job.

II

Seven a.m. on a black Sunday morning
In Ladbroke Grove.
The black telephone. Your black voice.
"This is Harrow Road Police Station:
You are requested to act as bailsman."
Down at the station at 7.45 a.m.
The duty officer takes down details.
Status: Married. *Sex*: Male.
Nationality: Irish. *Age*: 25.
Occupation: Stellar Manipulator.
The duty officer focuses his eyes
And asks me to repeat my occupation
That he can note it down correctly.
I say it with deliberation,
Pronouncing solemnly each syllable:
"Stell-ar Man-ip-ul-at-or."

He smiles as you used smile, Daddy,
If ever there was so much as the remotest
Rumour of humour in the universe,
A smidgen of light in the black.

III

Back home in Dublin
In the locker room of the golf club,
When other members of the fourball
Enquire after your eldest son,
Knowing that I am the black
Sheep of the family,
Thinking to get a rise out of you,
"Well, what's he working at now?"
You take your time,
Scrutinising the clay adhering
To the studs of your golf shoes,
Scraping it off with a penknife.
Your rejoinder is indifferent,
Laconic, offhand:
"He's a –" satisfactorily
Flaking off another lump of clay,
"Stellar Manipulator."

Bare Feet

"Be grateful, mind,
That you have shoes on your feet" –
You used warn me, reminding me
That in nineteen hundred and fourteen
You had to walk to school
In your bare feet:
Before daylight in the black, wet cold
Of a Mayo boreen
One and a half miles to National School
In your bare feet.

Shoes were the sole item of drapery
You deemed worthy of mention.
When I was forty-three years old,
In the year of your dying,
And I needed a new pair of shoes
You offered me an old pair of your own shoes,
Stately big black men o' war
With long, thin, twiney black laces.

When I demurred at wearing them
You were scandalised
That I would not step into your shoes.
At the end of your life
As all through your life
I scandalised you.
Should I have stepped into your shoes?
I should have stepped into your shoes.

Whenever I pass a shoe shop I stop
To look in the shop window for you.
I scan the shop window for you.
Whenever I see a man wearing a pair of shoes
And nothing else except a pair of shoes
I know it is you,
Old Bare Feet
From the Ox Mountains.

Once in the Ox Mountains
You were Young Bare Feet,
An Indian tinker boy
With a future flaming ahead of you.
After eighty years of walking
Up and down the world
You became Old Bare Feet,
An Indian elder tinker man
Burned out in Dublin city.
Daddy,
Every street is a tightrope
I see you balancing on
In your bare feet.

The Mayo Accent

Have you ever tuned in to the voice of a Mayoman?
In his mouth the English language is sphagnum moss
Under the bare braceleted feet of a pirate queen:
Syllables are blooms of tentativeness in bog cotton;
Words are bog oak sunk in understatement;
Phrases are bog water in which syllables float
Or in which speakers themselves are found floating face
    upwards
Or downwards;
Conversations are smudges of bogland under cloudy skies.
Speech in Mayo is a turbary function
To be exercised as a turbary right
With turbary responsibilities
And turbary irresponsibilities.
Peat smoke of silence unfurls over turf fires of language.

A man with a Mayo accent is a stag at bay
Upon a bog rock with rabbits round its hooves.
Why then, Daddy, did you shed
The pricey antlers of your Mayo accent
For the tree-felling voice of a harsh judiciary
Whose secret headquarters were in the Home Counties or
    High Germany?
Your son has gone back to Mayo to sleep with the island
    woman
Who talks so much she does not talk at all.
If he does not sleep with her, she will kill him – the pirate
    queen.

Dovecote

The black dog temper of the Durcans
Was notorious in Keelogues and Turlough;
The landlord riding out on his horse
From his saddle by your grandfather clutched,
Dragged to earth.

After your mother gave birth to your father.
On the side of the road
She crawled out of the ditch
To a dovecote in the meadow,
The columbarium of the Big House.
She stared up from his floury, bloody, shut-eyed kittentorso
And saw 12 circles of pigeonholes,
12 pigeonholes in each circle,
144 doves beating their wings.

All the days of your life
You brooded about eviction.
Why were you so angry with life?
Eviction.
Why were you so hard on us all?
Eviction.
Why always did you invoke the name of Michael Davitt?
Eviction.
Why in Straide did you always stop the car?
Eviction.
Why always did you stare at the tree where the house once stood?
Eviction.
Why did you begin every journey an hour early?
Eviction.
Why did you worry about everything always?
Eviction.
Why did you stitch your money into your trousers' belt?
Eviction.
Why did you stash your cash under the mattress?
Eviction.
Why did you hate landlords?
Eviction.
Why did you become a landlord yourself?
Eviction.
Who was the first landlord?
The Lord God in Heaven was the first landlord
And he was a Gentleman Farmer in Mayo.

Today I stand in the same deserted dovecote
– Grey day, black skies –
Staring up at your evicted face about to be cremated,

Staring up at your multifarious faces in their pigeonholes,
All 144 of them,
Their 288 wings beating in vain
The flames of the landlord's ovens.
Evict: Why do priests eat gods?
Evict: Why do gentlemen commit genocide?
Evict: Do doves eat doves? Souls souls?

Micky Donnelly's Hat

I'm in Baku, Micky, in Azerbaijan,
And by God, Micky, I'm in trouble.

Faïf – a small, round, middle-aged Mussulman –
A little barrel of a gentleman the hoops
Of whose years have humbled him –
Is twirling his worry beads.

He's worried because he's got me on his hands.

What he does not surmise
Is that I've got beads –
My father's beads –
My father's wine-dark rosary beads –
In my jeans pocket,
And twined in perspiration
My fingers are around them clenched.

When Daddy slipped on the ice,
I salvaged his rosary beads from the bin,
The black bin beneath the windowsill.
I carry them about with me wherever I go,
Such as now, Micky, in Baku,
A spot of bother in Baku,
Where to the north the Caspian Sea is aflame
With oil derricks – a gallows for every wave –
While to the south, it flows – becalmed, as it appears –
Onto the Iranian shore.

Will the sins of the sons
Be visited on their fathers, Micky?
It is the same
In Baku as in Belfast.

But so long as grown men
Can sit and twirl their worry beads
– Worry beads that were once their fathers' worry beads –
There is a pixie of hope, is there not?
Only today an old lady came hobbling into the local teashop
Enquiring hopefully after her lost pixie;
She cries out between the counter and the door –
"Has anyone seen my pixie?"

Micky, I like it that you wear your own hat at an angle
As I like to think I do mine.
In Baku Airport,
As in Belfast Central,
I pray to my father and I begin to discern
The profile of a smile glow in the ruins of his eyes.
When you're an Azerbaijani in Belfast
You don't stop twirling your worry beads.

Antwerp, 1984

We are keeping silent vigil at the window
Of the train from Amsterdam to Brussels,
Sitting opposite one another,
An agèd judge and his middle-aged son,
Shooting the dykes
Into flashfloods of oblivion
At the bottom of a vertical sky.
We are travelling at speed
Through the suburbs of Antwerp.
I am staring at a poplar tree
Quivering in a November breeze
When I glimpse your face in the window
And you glimpse mine.
In the high-speed window
Our eyes meet, each of us

Yearning for what the other yearns:
To be a tree – that tree.
By the time the message
Arrives in my brain
The train is a half-mile past
The level crossing
Where we glimpsed one another
In the poplar tree.
You elect to break the silence.
"My favourite poem" – you announce –
"Is 'Trees' by Joyce Kilmer."
"My favourite poem" – I reply –
"Is 'The Brook' by Lord Tennyson."
That is all we have to say
To one another.
I look at you
As you are
In your train seat,
Not as you were
A moment ago in the window,
Your own limbs are unleafing
And quivering
With Parkinson's,
All your roots
Heaped up in bundles
On your lap,
The dark floor beneath your feet
Gone, vanished.
You have five years to live.
I gaze up at your treetops
– Your glazed eyes underpainted with moonlight –
And I pledge that when they fell you,
While they will sell you for firewood,
I will give logs of you
To a woodcarver in Sligo,
Michael Quirke of Wine Street,
Butcher turned woodcarver,
Out of which to magic statuettes
Of the gods and goddesses of Ireland,
The Celtic Deities.
I will wash your body

In linseed oil and turpentine.
I will put you in the window
Of his butcher's shop in Wine Street.
I will call you by your proper name,
Mac Dhuarcáin,
Son of the Melancholy One.
As we approach the crossing of the Rhine
No man could look more melancholy
Than you – Melancholy Daddy.
God took out a Stanley knife,
Slashed the canvas of life,
Called it a carving of your face,
Called it you.
As we crawl over the Rhine
I put my hand on your knee,
Your quivering knee,
The pair of us gazing down into the wide river far below.

The Two Little Boys at the Back of the Bus

The two little boys at the back of the bus,
You and I.
Where would we have been
Without my mother?
As well as being my mother
She was your mother also.
All you and I were able for
Was playing rugby football
Or swooping up and down the touchline
Shrieking at one another
To maim or kill our opponents.

We were Jesuit boys,
Sons of peasants
Who played a burgher's game
Which was called Rugby Union,
The ideology of which was to
Enact in the muck and lawn
Of the playing fields of Ballsbridge
A parody of homosexual aggression:
Scrum, hook, tackle, maul.

We thought it right and fitting,
Manly and amusing,
That our clubs were named
After barbarian tribes.
You played for the Senior Vandals,
I played for the Junior Visigoths.
Our life's ambition was to play
For the Malawians
Against the Springboks
In Johannesburg,
Drinking lager,
Putting the boot in,
Taking the boot out.

After the game
And the whooping-it-up
Of male bodies
In the showers,
The boisterous buttocks,
The coy penis,
The Jesuit priest with a box camera
Lurking outside the cubicles,
The ex-missionary
Father A'bandon with an apostrophe.
You and I always got dressed
Ahead of the rest
To bag the back seat first.
We were always, you and I,
The two little boys at the back of the bus,
Going home to Mother.

Safe in the back of the bus
At seventy-two you share your biscuits with me,
Your packet of digestive biscuits,
As we head back down the Stillorgan Road
To Mother.
Mother will meet us at the bus station
And drive us out to the plane
Which she will pilot herself,
A Fokker 50.
When we are safely ensconced

At an altitude of seventeen thousand feet
Turning left at Liverpool for Preston,
She will come back down from the cockpit
And put us both to sleep
With an injection of sodium amytal.
Isn't that what we've always yearned for,
Father and Son,
To be old, wise, male savages in our greatness
Put to sleep by Mother?

Poem Not Beginning with a Line by Pindar

Having photocopied Goya by moonlight, the IRA
Hijacked a minibus on a circular road
In Armagh of the Nightingales,
Tromboned ten Protestant workmen into lining up
Along the footlights of the Armagh hills,
To kick high their legs, look left, look right,
And fed them such real midnight jazz
That not even Goya on a high
Could have improvised a tableau
Of such vaudeville terror, such prismatic carnage,
Bodies yearning over bodies,
Sandwich boxes, Thermos flasks, decks of playing cards.

Next morning at breakfast in the kitchen
I enquire of Daddy his judgment.
The President of the Circuit Court
Of the Republic of Ireland,
Appointed by the party of the Fine Gael,
Scooping porridge into his mouth,
Does not dissemble as he curls his lip,
Does not prevaricate as he gazes through me:
"Teach the Protestants a lesson,"
And, when I fail to reciprocate,
"The law is the law and the law must take its course."

"Teach the Protestants a lesson,"
That's what the man says,

The judge says,
The President of the Circuit Court
Of the Republic of Ireland says.
If you are mystified,
Dear Oxford University Reader in History,
What it reveals are not lacunae
But black holes
In your encyclopaedic knowledge
Of the roots of fascism in Ireland.
The party of the Fine Gael is the party
Of respectability, conformity, legitimacy, pedigree,
Faith, chivalry, property, virility,
The party of Collins, O'Higgins, O'Duffy, Cosgrave,
Great men queuing up at the bride's door.
Walk tall to the altar rail in pinstripe suit and silk tie.
Talk the language of men – *bullshit, boob, cunt, bastard* –
And – *teach the Protestants a lesson.*
The law is the law and the law must take its course.

Geronimo

Although we were estranged lovers
For almost thirty years,
When Daddy knew that he was going to die
He asked that we marry again.
After a reconciliation under a Scots
Pine in Palmerston Park
We remarried in the Church of St Aengus
In Burt, near Pluck.
In the navel of the Grianán of Aileach
We lay side by side on our backs
For the wedding photographs
Taken by a tall thin youth
With tresses of platinum grey hair
In a mauve suit and white sneakers.

We spent a second honeymoon
In the lakes of Sligo,
Putting up at the Ryan
Yeats Country Hotel

In Rosses Point,
A seaside hotel named after a poet
With special rates for families.
Throughout his life
Against all-comers
Daddy had maintained
That the lakes of Sligo
Were more scenic,
More bountiful, more placid,
More inscribed, more hallowed,
More inky, more papery,
More sensual, more ascetic,
More emblematic of what we are
Than the lakes of Killarney.

By the shores of Lough Arrow
In his eightieth year
At Ballindoon in the rain
In a two-light window
Of a roofless Dominican friary
He sat in profile
While I crouched behind a holly tree
Snapping him with my pocket Japanese camera.

By the shores of Lough Arrow
In his eightieth year
Among water-rolled stones with cranesbill
I spread out a tartan rug
For us to sit on and picnic
Listening to lakewater lapping,
Holding each other in one another's arms,
Resting our heads in one another's laps,
Hares springing up out of their own jackets.

For the umpteenth time
I told Daddy the story
Of Patrick Pearse's visit
To Daniel Corkery's house
In Cork City – the weather-slated
House by the Lough of Cork –
How Pearse solemnly informed Corkery

That the Lough's lakewater lapping
Had kept him from sleeping –
"A regrettable inconvenience," coughed Pearse.
Daddy loved to hear me
Tell that story and he'd hoo-hoo-hoo
Like a steam train chugging through Tír na nÓg.
He'd snort, "Tell me it again,"
And I'd tell him it again
And it was part of our liturgy
Of courtship and romance and marriage
That I should leave out bits
So that he could take a turn also
In the storytelling – we were a pair
Of choirboys among the rocks,
Chanting in orgy on a summer's morn
Our girlish devotion to the rain.
In the Corkery story, Daddy's line
Was the name of Corkery's novel
That celebrates the weather-slated house,
The Threshold of Quiet.

By the shores of Lough Arrow
In his eightieth year
At the cairn of Heapstown
While I stood atop the capstone
Daddy lay down in the uncut grass
And curled up like a foetus,
An eighty-year-old foetus.
"What are you doing?" I shouted down at him.
He made a face at me.
"Climbing goalposts," he shouted back up at me.

By the shores of Lough Arrow
In his eightieth year
Among the passage graves of Carrowkeel
In the Bricklieve Hills
He sat down in the bog cotton
And gazing north-west to Knocknarea
And to Deerpark and to Creevykeel
And to Ben Bulben and to Classiebawn
He began to weep in his laughter.

He wrapped his long white hair
Around his shoulders and refused
To utter for the rest of the day.
That night by the light
Of a golden-sepia half-moon
We walked the cliffs at Rosses Point,
Hand in hand among the actual shells.
He cupped my ear in his hands and whispered:
"Geronimo."
"I know," I said, "I know."

By the shores of Lough Arrow
In his eightieth year
In the main street of Ballinafad,
In the only street of Ballinafad,
On the steps of the Castle of the Curlews
He stood, and shaking out his brolly,
"You Curlew, you," he said.
"But for the red perch in the black stream
My life has been nothing, son.
Be good to your mother."

In the six months of white horses
Between our second honeymoon
And his deathdive
Geronimo's lovingkindness to me
Was as magnanimous as it was punctilious.
His last words to me were always,
"Be good to your mother – bring her
Flowers every day – what she likes
Above all is phlox."
As we shook hands and kissed
In the doorway, waiting for the elevator,
He'd add: "Don't be long."
I won't, Geronimo, I won't – be long.

"The Dream in the Peasant's Bent Shoulders"

You are sitting on a chair
Upright, moulded plastic,
At the end of your hospital bed
In the seventy-bed ward.
"Where are my pyjama bottoms?"
You cry at me, with a hoe in your hand,
A small, split cry.
When I fail to answer you, you cry,
"What have they done with my pyjama bottoms?"
"I don't know, Daddy, I don't know."

All I know
Is that you served the State
Unconditionally
For twenty-eight years
And that on this December afternoon in Dublin,
Without providing any reason or explanation,
They have taken away your pyjama bottoms.

Outside on Pearse Street
My mother weeps at the hospital gates.
Such was your loyalty to the State,
Your devotion and fidelity to the State,
You took Mother on one holiday only in twenty-eight years –
A pilgrimage by coach to the home of Mussolini
And Clara Petachi near Lago di Como,
A villa in the hills above Lago di Como.
Did you see in Mum your Clara?
Starlet, child bride, all negligee and tulle.
Loyalty to the State was the star
In the East of your life
And reward by the State.
Instead, they have taken away your pyjama bottoms
Leaving you only with your pyjama tops
And a hoe in your hand.
Your peasant's bent shoulders have ceased their dreaming
As you crouch down before me, a jewel in torment.
Out of willow eyes you stare at me.
"Hold my hand," you whisper.

A blond male doctor struts brusquely past
As we crouch here holding hands in twilight.
"Hold my hand," you whisper.
"I am holding your hand, Daddy," I respond.
But you do not hear me.
Clinging to your hoe
And gripping tightly my hand, you scream:
"Hold my hand."

Cot

We cringed around your bed in the hospital ward.
The matron announced you would die in half an hour.
She spoke as if dictating from a train timetable.
Always in Italy the trains run on time.
I was dispatched to telephone the relations
But visitors to the dying had access only to a payphone.
None of the family had any change.
I had to borrow two tenpenny pieces
From the matron who had scheduled your death.
The first payphone did not work but the second did.
The relations said they would be with us in no time.
When I came scuttling back into the ward
And peered over the shoulders of my brothers and sisters
I saw that the deathbed had become a cot
And that you, Daddy, were a small, agèd infant
Struggling to stay alive in the world.
You were kicking up your legs in the air,
Brandishing your bony white knuckles.
I realised that you were my newborn son.
What kind of a son will you be to me?
Will you be as faithful a son to me
As you have been a father?
As intimate, as funny, as alien?
As furry, as skinny, as flighty?

Old man, infant boy,
As you writhe there
On your backside

In your cot
How helpless you are,
A minuscule helplessness
Heaving with innocence;
A baby dinosaur
With an expiry date.
You begin to bawl.
My mother takes off her black glove
And lays her hand
Across your threadbare skull.
You wave her goodbye,
She who loves you
After one day
And forty-four years.
You go back to sleep,
The black world to rue.
Bonny boys are few.
Don't fret, son,
Don't ever again fret yourself.

Glocca Morra

Dear Daughter – Watching my father die,
As one day you will watch me die,
In the public ward of a centre-city hospital,
Mid-afternoon bustle,
A transistor radio playing two or three beds away,
Paintwork flaking on the wall,
His breath dwindling,
His throat gurgling,
A source disappearing,
Source of all that I am before my eyes disappearing,
Well, watching your own father die slowly in front of you,
Die slowly right under your nose,
Is a bit like sitting in the front row of the concert hall
Watching a maestro performing Tchaikovsky's Grand Piano Sonata.
It's spectacular, so to speak,
But the audience feels helpless.

When Daddy died
I wrung my hands at the foot of his bed
Until a consultant doctor told me to stop it
And to show some respect for the dead.
The old prick.
He had done nothing for Daddy
Except pollute him with pills for twenty years
For fees in guineas.
They threw a sheet over him
And put screens around his bed
But I stood my ground
At the foot of the bed
While the transistor radio,
Like something hidden in a hedgerow,
Went on with its programme –
Rosemary Clooney crooning
"How are Things in Glocca Morra?"

Outside the ward window –
Which was in need of cleaning, I noticed –
The sun was going down in the west over the Phoenix Park
Where Daddy and me
("Daddy and I" – he corrects me –
He was a stickler for grammar),
Where Daddy and I
Played all sorts of games for years,
Football, hurling, cricket, golf, donkey,
Before he got into his Abraham-and-Isaac phase
And I got the boat to England
Before he had time to chop off my head
O Daddy dear –
As we find ourselves alone together for the last time,
Marooned in this centre-city hospital public ward,
I think that there is something consoling – cheerful, even –
About that transistor playing away in the next bed.
The day you bought your first transistor
You took us out for a drive in the car,
The Vauxhall Viva,
Down to a derelict hotel by the sea,
The Glocca Morra,
Roofless, windowless, silent,

And, you used add with a chuckle,
Scandalous.
You dandled it on your knee
And you stated how marvellous a gadget it was,
A portable transistor,
And that you did not have to pay
A licence fee for it,
You chuckled.
A man not much known for chuckling.
The Glocca Morra,
Roofless, windowless, silent and *scandalous.*

Rosemary Clooney –
The tears are lumbering down my cheeks, Dad –
She must be about the same age as you,
Even looks like you.
I bet her handwriting
Is much the same as yours,
You had a lovely hand,
Cursive, flourishing, exuberant, actual.
Whatever things are like in Glocca Morra
I'm sad that we're not going to be together any more.
Dear Daughter – When the time comes
For you to watch me die,
In a public place to watch me
Trickling away from you,
Consider the paintwork on the wall
And check out the music in the next bed.
"How are Things in Glocca Morra?"
Every bit as bad as you might think they are –
Or as good. Or not so bad. Love, Dad.

Mortuary

When you were laid out in the mortuary,
Put on display, mounted and framed,
In an open coffin on trestles,
Before they lidded you,

And we all filed in
For five decades of the Rosary,
Halfway through the "Our Father"
A lady in a fur coat
Flew in the door
– A spurt of hairy-hemmed saliva –
And she stood in front of us,
Right up close beside you,
Belladonna at your nose tip.
I observed the smile on your lips.

After the last "Glory Be
To the Father" had been mumbled
And as we all began
To shuffle out into the night
To climb into the mourners' cars
With our little white hands
In front of our little black suits,
She whispered to me: "Leave me
Alone with your father."

When I turned around in the doorway,
Sideways under the lintel,
To salvage one final glimpse of you,
I saw that she was wearing a blue bikini
Whose brassiere was studded with emeralds.
The smile on your lips was subtle.
You seemed to be saying to her:
"You have unbuttoned your fur coat."
She whispered to you: "My Lord,
For you I have unbuttoned my fur coat.
In all the years to come of oblivion
Never again will I button up my fur coat.
For you my fur coat will remain always open."

Bank Clerk

I

There is no justice in life
But in your court there was justice
And the price of it
Was loneliness —
Loneliness that became a circus legend
In Circuit Court mythology
With your own family tagging along behind
In a caravan painted black on black
With the letters RIP in white.

While you ran the fairest court
In all of Connaught
Your family rested in peace.
For fear of being prejudicial
Or being seen to be prejudicial
You had the exquisite fingers
Of your hyper-sociable nature
Amputated, and locking yourself away
In hotel bedrooms, you declined
To visit even your own relations
In their home across the street
From the courthouse.

When you were made to retire
After twenty-eight years on the bench
— They were afraid that in old age
You might relax into wisdom,
"No Buddhism on the bench," minced
Your national socialist handlers —
You sat out the remaining years
On a bench in your bedroom
In red-eyed loneliness;
The obedient hound
Of your hair lying down
In a coma at your feet.

You were a great judge
Because you were a great clown.
In a wig and gown
You were the biggest act in Connaught.
Not any old wig and gown
But a wig and gown festooned with chains.
In chains from neck to ankle
You felt attired to deliver
The balanced verdict;
And you did.

II

In the treetops of your top-storey apartment
You crouched at your bedroom door
Like a grey squirrel, gnawing at it
Until you had gnawed a loophole in it,
Just as I three miles away across the city
In my bunker with no windows
Like a rat had gnawed a loophole
In my own act.
Once a month with your pension cheque
You took a bus down to the bank,
Just as I once a month
Took a bus to the unisex hairdresser's
To feel a woman's hand upon my skull.

You could have had your cheque
Paid directly into your account
But by having it mailed to you
You had a pretext.
You took a bus down to the bank,
Deliberately forgetting to bring
Your chequebook with you, thereby
Obliging the bank clerk to talk to you,
To confirm your identity, to look up
Your bank account number, to repeat it,
To tap into her computer terminal
And caress your identity, fondle your identity.

You rejoiced to stand at the counter,
Gazing through the hatch at the face of the bank clerk,
Her young shelly face framed by the hatch,
Just as a half-dozen shop fronts down the street
I rejoiced to recline before the looking glass,
Gazing up at the coiffeuse caressing my scalp.
She'd smile at you and your red eyes
Would turn blue and your lips quiver
And your nostrils itch
And you'd make no attempt to be businesslike,
Content to stand there at the well of her face,
Supping smiles from the well of her face,
Chewing the cud at the fence of her spectacles,
Swishing your tail in the face of the customer behind you.

When the priest – like a striptease-show impresario –
Flicked the electric button
To release your coffin onto the rails
That would trundle it into the cremo
– Into the fiery furnace with the dainty pink curtains –
There was a solitary bouquet of loose flowers on the coffin lid,
White freesias
Left there by the bank clerk.
The men in peaked caps were afraid to remove them
When they removed the chrysanthemums and carnations and
    cards.
They were afraid to remove them because they were loose
From your bank clerk,
A solitary bouquet of loose white freesias,
All your haloes, Daddy, wild blooms
On the blacks and the ivories of a grand piano
In the apartment of the unknown woman.

Kierkegaard's Morning Walk in Copenhagen

after Tony O'Malley

Outside the crematorium, listening to men
Being sensible and not talking about their feelings
About Daddy having been a moment ago incinerated
And exchanging informations about the afternoon's rugby fixtures
– "Is it today Blackrock are playing Old Belvedere?" –
And their wives discussing the menu for luncheon
– Mushroom soup, leg of lamb, meringue with chocolate sauce –
Stamping my feet and swinging my arms,
I spot my father in the porch of the crematorium,
Putting on his top hat, waiting for a lift.

He looks so doll-like, vulnerable, cuddly;
Bandy-legged little judge
In green frock coat and black topper,
His head barely measuring up to the stomach
Of the important lady he's chatting to,
Barely measuring up to her navel,
Her gold filigree navel
Inlaid with treacle of ebony.
"Always poking his nose into other men's wives' groins."
Oh the simple malice of the respectability.

With a black Bic biro I scribble a note to him,
Scurry across the tarmacadam and hand it to him:
"A Memento for your Hatband" – I shout to him and he smiles,
Barely measuring up to her navel,
And taking off his top hat he inserts it in his hatband.
It reads in my father-like-son handwriting:
"Purity of heart is to will one thing."

Sitting up in the back of my uncle's Opel Kadett,
I can see Dad still standing in the porch
Of the crematorium, waiting for the man
With the ash bucket to come and take him away.
He is taking on and off his top hat
And taking my note in and out of his hatband,
Holding it up to the light and scrutinising it,
Blushing, the colour of virtue,

Apparently finally putting it back into his hatband.
The ashman slams down his bucket and folds his arms
While Daddy once more yet again takes off his top hat,
Barely measuring up to her navel,
To pluck out of his hatband a by-now familiar tune:
"Purity of heart is to will one thing";
Her gold filigree navel
Inlaid with treacle of ebony.

Chips

I am sitting alone in the window of the Kentucky Grill,
Staring out at O'Connell Street in the night,
Shoving chips into my mouth.
Girls in paper hats are mopping up floors all around me.
Presently they are mopping up my feet.
"Excuse me" – I overhear myself say to them
As I hold up my feet to accommodate their mops,
Shoving a last chip into my mouth.
On the bin at the door it says:
FEED ME.

When Daddy died I gazed upon his chips
– I mean, his features –
While a priest poured a bottle of ketchup over him.
I thought it strange
And I walked out of the hospital into the city of night.

When I was seven and he took me to see
Charlie Chaplin in *City Lights*
In the Regal Rooms,
After the film was over we walked all the way home
From Hawkins Street to Leeson Street
Through streets that were dark and wet and cold and homelier
Than any landscape I was to see again,
Until after your death to Newfoundland I came
To give one quick, brief,
Received-in-boots-of-woolly-warmth-
By-fishermen's-wives
Recital of my verses.

There is no one in my life
Whom I disliked so submissively,
Yet whom I loved so mercilessly,
As you, Daddy. To me
You were at once saint and murderer.
When you raised your right hand
To smash in my face,
I saw the face of the murderer.
When you spoke the name
Of a belovèd townland or parish,
Keelogues or Parke,
I saw the face of a saint.

You were the artist of artists,
Ur of the Chaldees;
Priest of priests,
Melchisedech of the Ox;
Storyteller of storytellers,
Homer of Nephin;
Piper of pipers,
Carolan of the Moy;
Poet of poets,
Raftery of Turlough.
That's it –
I've had my chips.

The Repentant Peter

after Francisco de Goya

Tonight is my forty-fifth birthday –
You are two years dead.
Last thing I do before getting into bed
Is kneel down beside bed
In my Marks & Spencer's women's pyjamas
Which I purchased thinking they were men's pyjamas,
A womanless man on a shopping spree.
Laying my head in my hands on the bed
I give thanks for the gift of life,

For your authorisation of me,
Your retrieval of my future,
An ape seeding himself in the Rift Valley.
I ask for forgiveness for my sins.

First time my wife saw me
Kneel down beside bed
She ate my head off
She was that shocked.
I do it
Because that is what you taught me to do.
I could not
Not do it.
You taught me that like you
I am destitute animal,
Frailer
Than plump lamb under candlelit chestnut,
Frailer
Than mother cat wheezing in cartwheel,
Frailer
Than galaxies of geese,
And that behind all my sanctimonious lechery,
It is all night, with only daylight above it.

Our Father

I was going over to Mummy's place for lunch.
I had said my morning prayers
But I had not expected
My morning prayers materially to alter the day.
Our Father who art in heaven
(Daddy had died two winters ago)
Hallowed be Thy name, Thy kingdom come,
Thy will be done on earth as it is in heaven.

I had decided to catch the Number 13 bus to Palmerston Park
From outside Dáil Éireann in Kildare Street
But at the last moment I changed my mind
And I caught the Number 14 bus to Dartry.
I do not know why I changed my mind.

Possibly it was because the Number 14 came first
Or possibly it was because of the memory
That Daddy, when he was alive, appeared to be perplexed
That I never came home by the Number 14 route.
He seemed to think that I should come home by the Number 14
        route
And that it was a crime against nature
To come home by the Number 13 route.

I sat at the back of the bus on the lower deck
With two bunches of flowers for Mummy in my lap.
When I became aware that the conductor was staring at me
We were stopped outside the National Concert Hall and I thought:
Maybe he likes the look of me.
He commented: "I like your irises."
"What?"
"Your irises – I like your irises."
The conductor swayed above me, a knowing smile in his eyes,
As the double decker lurched around Kelly's Corner –
A landmark of Daddy's
Because on it stood a pub called The Bleeding Horse.
It was the name that attracted him.
He was never inside it in his life.
Every time we drove past The Bleeding Horse
I stared at the blood trickling out of the white mare's withers,
All menstruation and still life.
"I love flowers" – the conductor continued,
Licking the baton of his forefinger –
"My wife says I'm mad and of course I am.
I am mad about flowers.
Lovely irises you have – let me touch them.
I have my own greenhouse – the width of this bus.
My father-in-law built it for me donkey's years ago.
My orchids are in bloom at the moment.
If I'd my way, I'd have nothing but orchids.
All the same a man's got to be pragmatic."
He clung lithely to the vertical rail as the driver
Flew the bus over Portobello Bridge.

"I've aubergines, peppers, tomatoes, lettuce.
The neighbours are keen on my iceberg lettuce.

They're always pestering me also for my courgettes.
Cucumber too – but you have to be cautious with cucumber.
What with the way the males pollinate the females
You've got to be terribly cautious with your stamens.
Cucumbers are very much that way inclined:
Proliferation, proclivities, you never know where you are.
I have to keep all my cacti on the upper shelves."
As we slowed down near Rathmines Town Hall, senior citizens
On Free Travel called out to the conductor to collect fares.
"Do your duty now, Mister, and collect fares."
But he waved to the passengers who were disembarking,
A wave that was at once a valediction and a benediction:
"I am not collecting fares this morning," he confided in me,
"There are times in public transport when it is more auspicious
Not to collect fares and today is an auspicious day.
I adore my greenhouse. It can get so hot inside it.
Anything more than a pair of shorts and I'm scalded.
'Where'd you get your tan?' – the neighbour woman asks me.
'In my greenhouse, where else?' – I answer her back.
A perfect lie.
She wags her finger at my magnolia in the front garden
And she teases me: 'Oh, a cherry blossom
Is good enough for the rest of us but not for the likes of you.
For the likes of you it has to be a *magnolium* no less.
Only a *magnolium* is good enough for the likes of you.'
That's what she calls it – a *magnolium*."

We were whizzing past the pharmacy on Upper Rathmines Road
And the Church of Ireland Teacher Training College
But he wanted to dwell on his magnolia:
"It's not a real word at all, you know, *magnolia*.
There was a Frenchman – Magnol was his name –
From a place called Montpellier. My wife knew a man
From Montpellier – that's how I remember it.
But I do like your irises.
You have to be patient in this game
And it can be so tedious on top of that.
My grapes, for example. Grapes are too excitable.
I have to keep each grape separate from the other.
Time-consuming it is
Keeping all my grapes separate from each other.

273

Each grape has to be totally separate from the next grape
And only a few weeks ago I lost fifty pounds' worth
Of azaleas – wiped out by Jack Frost.
When I'm skedaddling off to the depot I ask the wife
To remember to open the greenhouse window
But if she remembers to open it,
Sure as not she will forget to close it.
You know what wives are like – not to mention husbands.
At the moment, actually, I'm all sweet pea."
I apologised to him as I dismounted at Dartry.
"Sorry, but I have to get out at this stop."
"Don't be sorry – be nice to your irises."

As the bus swerved away from the kerb, I thought:
Amn't I the lucky breadman that I got the Dartry bus
Instead of the Palmerston Park bus,
The Number 14 instead of the Number 13?
The conductor waved to me as the bus picked up speed.
I looked about me on the street to check if anybody was looking.
I blessed myself.
Our Father who art in heaven.
I could feel the conductor's knees brush against my lips
As he ran his fingers through the clay of my hair.

Under the chestnuts and the pine trees and the copper beeches
I walk down the street where Daddy slipped on the ice.
He had lain here until a gas worker had found him
And put him in an ambulance and waved goodbye to him,
A gas worker with a piece of piping in his hand.

I press the bell to Mummy's apartment.
I stare up into the surveillance camera lens.
I am a suspect in an interrogation centre,
A forty-five-year-old amoeba dwindling under a microscope.
When a light bulb flashes and her voice crackles over
The intercom I know she can perceive
The panic in the pupils of her son's eyes.
After lunch – soup, a chop, potatoes and peas –
She says that she does not understand my new book of poems
Which are poems I have composed for my dead father.
"But" – she smiles knowingly – "I like your irises."

CRAZY ABOUT WOMEN (1991)

The Virgin and Child

after Lorenzo Ghiberti

My mother is as much
A virgin at seventy-five
As she was at seventeen;
As much a small
Stream going nowhere;
As much a small
Ocean going everywhere;
Terracotta moon
In pink nightie.

When I visit her
In her apartment
In the solitary suburbs,
I jump up into her arms.
She hugs me, holding me up
With her left hand under my bottom:
"O my curly-headed
Little golden wonder
What has become of you?"

Once a virgin mother
Always a virgin mother.
In my forty-seventh year
My virgin mother cradles me in her arms;
A brief trout of a frown
Jumps up
The brief weir of her face.

Mother most lost;
Mother most found.
Mother most dogged;
Mother most frail.
Mother most peripheral;
Mother most central.

Truth is, son,
You and I as a pair

Are, were, always will be
Out on a limb,
Outcasts in terracotta;
Refugees in clay.

The Separation of the Apostles

after the Styrian School

My name is John – one of the twelve
Gay men selected by Jesus.
I think he selected us because we are gay.
In the era of Aids we would be
The most appropriate ones to communicate his message
Of mercy to the world – the genocidal world.

We have been many years together and some of the gold leaf
Of our halos has flaked off but for all that
Our tenderness for one another has multiplied with the years
And as I dip my jug into the well at the gate
I can feel all my maternal love for the world
Swell in my breast and the prospect of the TV studio
Tonight on the current affairs programme
With the columnist from *The Irish Times* whose speciality's
Haruspicating the entrails of men with feminine souls –
The prospect does not intimidate me as once it used to.
My greatest fear would be to have been born
With the maternal feelings God gave me
But not to have recognised them. How privileged I was
To have had for a father a man who when asked what he thought
Of his eldest son being gay, he declared that he loved me.

The real pain is the pain of separation – that the twelve of us
After living together for so many years in County Mayo
In the Delphi Valley between Leenane and Westport
In what was once a shooting lodge of Lord Sligo's –
That after living together in peace and harmony and affection
We must separate. The fact is that we always knew
We were in the end on our own and that God's trust in us

Was precisely that we would never commit the lie
Of being dependent on one another – yet love one another we do.

In this most genocidal era of all, the era of man's trousers,
Cavalry twills, combats, fatigues
We are men who wore dresses:
Long flowing dresses of all colours and fabrics,
Pinks, scarlets, greens, cottons and woollens.
We wore halos also and in the long winter nights
We'd all fall silent, halos nudging halos,
Making a longdrawnout clang, a brisk clamour.
The secret to the apostolic life is dance
And today is our dance of separation
On disco floors of desert – bare feet arias.

You catch us at the Ball of our Dispersal
Fine tuned with hysteria, grief, despair even,
A moment of besieged delicacy.
The oldest among us, Andrew and Bartholomew,
Are dancing a foxtrot together,
A middle-aged couple at a Sunday afternoon tea dance,
Holding one another up,
Bartholomew being mindful of Andrew's arthritis.
Andrew suffers also from insomnia, poor man.

Young Thaddeus – watching the old pair –
Puts a pilgrim hipflask to his lips and drains it to the dregs.
I like the butterpats in his buttered beard.

Peter and James, slow jiving,
Shake hands as they break bread for the last time:
We two boys together clinging;
We two boys together shaking hands;
"Don't forget to send me a postcard from Berlin."
"I won't – you neither when you get to Paris, Texas."
Matthias looking over his shoulder does not know
Whether he is coming or going, whence or whither,
All fancy hat and cane;
When all is always said and done, always a song and dance man;
A bit of a dandy the way he holds his cane
And he cannot help sniggering as he goes.

Is he looking back at Simon already gone off on his own
Travelling at speed across a creek? Simon was always one
For dashing about – a psalmist on speed someone called him.
He is holding out his cane like a water diviner's rod.
James the Less has hitched his cloak to his cane and appears
About to go hang-gliding over Cong and angelic Philip –
He used to be a schoolteacher in Belfast –
Has already made friends in his new life but all we can glimpse
Are his wings sprouting out from behind a rock,
His red cloak bunched around his cane.

Thomas and Matthew are sharing a last cup of wine:
Little men with such innate good natures
Be it in the handball alley at dusk
Or at first Mass at dawn – such etiquette, such decorum:
Their choreography always a joy – such spiritual logic;
Everything so mercifully poised between them;
The line between life and death so thin;
Constantly in a state of nearly falling over.

Out front of us all on this foreshore where
The river's exaltation loses itself in the sea's desolation
The Master of the Separation of the Apostles
Getting ready to put away his paintbrushes for another night
Leaving behind him gold skies of midnight suns,
The melting, cracking sound of his mother's heart:
Her black purse thrown down on the ground.

The Holy Family with St John

after Francesco Granacci

My oar is dragging and my boat
Is turning almost full circle
To drift sideways onto the family shore.
Although I am a man without a family –
A leaf in driftwood – I revel
In the human family's animal beauty.

Amplitude, ambiguity, affinity;
Horseshoe sandals, frisby halos:
Her young fellow all ebullience with his young playmate
Whose trim penis peers out like a bullfinch from a bough:
Her husband the carpenter, sweetest of men,
And his donkey, conversing with one another;

Putting their heads together, attentive to one another,
Donkey doing his alert best to believe his ears
Having stopped in his hoofprints to take it all in,
What the husband is confiding about his sensational spouse:
Her toes, her knuckles, her eyebrows:
The human family – what it knows.

I row back to Trim. I go into The Judge and Jury.
I drink a long slow black pint with a halo on it,
Feeling crimson with every sip, crimsoner and crimsoner,
Gold in my belly.
Back out there on the river – a pretty emotional picture.
What is it that a donkey sees in a man?

The Veneration of the Eucharist

after Jacob Jordaens

I

I am disappointed when after Mass
As we sit into your red Fiat,
Overloaded with Sunday newspapers,
You remark that at Holy Communion
You observed me standing in line
To receive the Eucharist.

As a vision of fact the Eucharist
Is all that matters to me.
Inarticulate with post-coital grief
If I could tell you – which I cannot –

I would tell you that every moonburst
We have intercourse, you and I,
It is a eucharistic union.
I place my two hands on your thighs,
Hold you up to our sea-strewn skies.

I am the cross you must gladly bear.
You are the cross I must gladly bear.
The children that may or may not
Be shed to us
Will live their lives with flaming hearts,
Will have crosses of their own to gladly bear.

II

I am standing at the counter of the newsagents
Feeling guilty for having bought *The Irish Times*
When I notice in the doorway a lion of mature years
With a young woman sitting sidesaddle
Whom I instantly recognise
But whose name I cannot remember.
She is holding up the Eucharist in a monstrance.
Her white dress is cut low – giving full rein
To the champagne ponies of her breasts,
A sturdy pair of Connemara ponies.
The lion growls, his glazed eyes glaring beyond me.
I shrink back against the counter
Ready to receive the Eucharist
But apprehensive of the lion; to leap into her bosom
And to die forever –
Not to die for a half-day or a day or a week
But to die forever.
The lion nudges me out of the way at the counter.
Chiding me for not remembering her name
She dispenses the host to me on the tip of my tongue:
The Body of Christ.
My hands joined, my eyes closed,
I exit out of the shop backwards.
That's all I have ever wanted to do – to die forever.

The Levite and His Concubine at Gibeah

after Jan Victors

After Paul Durcan left his wife
 – Actually she left him but it is more *recherché* to say
     that he left her –
Would you believe it but he turned up at our villa
With a woman whom we had never heard of before,
Much less met. To *our* villa! The Kerrs of Dundalk!
I, Mrs Kerr, with a windowframe around my neck!
You will not believe it but he actually asked me
To put him up for the night – and his friend –
A slip of a thing, half his age.
I said that I would but in separate bedrooms.
This is a family home – I had to remind him.
I resented having to remind him.

The pair of them proceeded to squat in silence
In the living room for what was left of the evening
So that I could not even switch on the television.
As a consequence I missed *Twin Peaks*.
What got up my nose
Was that she sat on the step of the fireplace
On a cushion from our sofa thrown down by him
With her hands joined around his knees:
Himself sitting in my husband's armchair
As if he owned it – without so much as a "May I?"

She was got up in a loudspoken yellow dress
And those precious little hands of hers around his knees
As if his knees were pillows;
Her face a teatowel of holy innocence
As if margarine would not melt in her tonsils.
I would go so far as to say that it was indelicate –
The way she had her hands joined around his knees.

As soon as I began to yawn, he began to speak:
Holding forth until three o'clock in the a.m.
On what he called his "Theory of Peripeteia" –

A dog's dinner of gibberish about the philosophical significance
Of "not caring being the secret to transforming misfortune".
Finally I stood up and declared "Peripeteia, Goodnight."
I installed the pair of them in separate bedrooms.
I left my own bedroom door open.

I fell asleep about five.
When I knocked him up for breakfast
She answered the door. I was that indignant
That when they came down for breakfast
I gave them porridge – like it or lump it.
I did not utter one word to them
Until they had finished.
Then I took him aside and I let him have it:

Now listen to me Paul Durcan:
You may be a poet and a Levite
But you will not take advantage of me.
Get yourself and your – your – your concubine
Out of my Dundalk villa.
How dare a woman wear a loudspoken yellow dress –
When you set foot in Gibeah next time
Do not ever Durcan my doorstep again.

Know what his response was? To ask me
If he might borrow my Shell Guide and my donkey?
To be rid of him I gave in – more fool I.
He shimmied out the door singing to himself:
"We borrowed the loan of Kerr's big ass
To go to Dundalk with butter . . ."

Know what he did then? He went down to that old peasant
In the lane at the end of the avenue – Kavanagh –
Who goes about the town always with his socks down
Because he used play football for Mucker-Rotterdam:
Kavanagh with that – that ridiculous –
That – that vulgar –
That – that gross
Brass knocker on his front door.

The Riding School

after Karel Dujardin

Dung, cobble, wall, cypress;
Delight in art whose end is peace;
No cold-eyed horseman of the Irish skies
Can compare with me
Leading out the Grey of the Blues.

I in my red blanket
Under the Cave Hill Mountain
Leading out the Grey of the Blues:
The blindness of history in my eyes;
The blindness of history in my hands.

To get up at four every morning
And to lead out the Grey of the Blues;
Delight in art whose end is peace;
Hold his reins with my eyes open;
His dappled hindquarters;
His summer coat;
His knotted mane;
His combed-out tail;
His swanface;
His bullneck;
His spineline;
His tiny, prancing grace-notes.

And I in my red blanket
Under the Cave Hill Mountain
Leading out the Grey of the Blues:
The blindness of history in my eyes;
The blindness of history in my hands.

I take pride in my work;
Delight in art whose end is peace;
The way I lead out a song;
The way I hold the reins of a song in my hands
Between my stubby fingers.

I talk to my song;
My song talks to me.
In the blackest weathers
We have our sunniest hours.
How many early mornings
In black rain I have talked my song
Round and round the pink paddock!

I in my red blanket
Under the Cave Hill Mountain
Leading out the Grey of the Blues:
The blindness of history in my eyes;
The blindness of history in my hands.

My song is nearing the end of its tether;
Lament in art whose end is war;
Opera glasses, helicopters, TV crews;
Our slayings are what's news.
We are taking our curtain call,
Our last encore.
True to our natures
We do not look into the camera lenses
But at one another.
In a gap of oblivion, gone.

I in my red blanket
Under the Cave Hill Mountain
Leading out the Grey of the Blues:
The blindness of history in my eyes;
The blindness of history in my hands.

The Dilettanti

after Cornelius Troost

My boy is playing a lullaby
But I am not at all certain
Who his mother is.
Difficult to sit still and concentrate.

My feeling is that his mother
Was a Haarlem cleaning woman
Who drowned herself in a canal
The Michaelmas before last.

I fancy Susanna was her name.
I think so because when he began to play
I observed the corner of the carpet sit up
And make faces at me and display
A particular charlady's prominent front teeth
Cascading forth her red-blue lips, O God.
I am drumming my fingers,
My paunch in dry dock.

Bishop Robert Clayton and His Wife Katherine

after James Latham

I

My dear children of God, – I am an old cod
But once I was a young cod on the Grand Tour
Delighting and delighted. I held forth on sport
And war, quoting *ad nauseam* from the classics;
Tibullus, Virgil, Archilochos, Propertius.
"He eats, drinks, and sleeps in taste" –
Lord Orrery wrote of me. He did!
I say to you: I, your bishop, incite matrimony
In spite of all the inconvenience it entails.
Which is why you behold me in my portrait gaze
Not upon myself nor upon a *mememto mori*
Nor upon any other specious bauble of *vanitas*
But upon my wife Katherine in her unique chair
With its splat in the shape of a love-heart;
Upon her decolletage
In whose umbrageous rocks divinity dwells,
Dwells the godhead.

I ponder not upon her educated and cultivated mind
– A Donnellan to her knees, I can tell you –
But upon her carnal fault which is her soul.
I hold with Catullus and with Sappho and with Christ.
I hold with intuition of the votive earth
From which I come, to which I will return,
The votive earth which alone adorns my sleeve.
I hold the Gospel in my left hand.
Her thigh in my right hand.
Although first love can never be repeated
I live in faith that she may yet again
Row out my little boat upon her lough.

II

This Xmas morning on our way across to church,
A gravel path of not more than fifty yards
From scullery to sacristy,
Between herbaceous borders,
We succumbed, my dear wife and I, to grimacing
In a sort of embroidery at one another.

III

This Xmas night
I having placed three pillows beneath her back
She will draw back her knees up past her cheeks
Until her knees recline upon her shoulders
So that I can douse her haunches with my tongue,
Install myself inside her,
Until we two are become as one divinity;
One divinity crouched in interlocking stillness on a bough;
The sole sound – the small rowboat of my member
Bobbing on the waters of her lough.
In the Name of the Father, and of the Son, and of the
    Holy Ghost.
Amen.

Joseph Leeson

after Pompeo Batoni

I am a chap
Who dictates his best novels
Standing at the urinal.

Indeed, it ought to be clear from Batoni's portrait of me
That I am a chap of the first water.

In twenty-seven words:
The sort of chap who even while he waits
His turn to go the Gents
In his mother's fur hat
Holds himself in
With verisimilitude, tact, ego.

The Earl of Bellamont

after Joshua Reynolds

I like a man who does not care.
The Earl of Bellamont arrives into the National Gallery
Every other day for luncheon in the restaurant
But he does not merely arrive in – he splashes down,
Unbattening the hatches as he splashes,
Firing off kisses to all and sundry,
To non-entities as well as entities.
The Earl of Bellamont is a man who does not care.

The get-up, the get-out of him.
Created by Sir Sploshua.
He does a line in cloaks and today
It is a pink flesh-toned affair
Noosed at the breast with two lengths of cord
From whose terminals dangle between his thighs
A pair of tassels –

A pair of the most affable, episcopal, ding-dong, sedate,
     steadfastest, one-eyed
Tassels.
The Earl of Bellamont is a man who does not care.

He takes his place in the queue in the restaurant.
While waiting for his lasagne to hot up in the microwave
He leans nonchalantly on his swordstick
Airing his opinions on the state of the art market:
"Every man should apprise himself of his own value.
I cost £550 – that is exactly to the penny
What Henry Doyle paid for me.
You see before you £550 worth of pure Coote."
As he airs he languidly crosses his legs
To give ample recognition not only to his tassels
But to his rosettes:
On each suede slipper a pink rosette.
"Tassels are all" he complains
"And yet rosettes are more."
The Earl of Bellamont is a man who does not care.

Like all regulars in the National Gallery Restaurant
He has his favourite pew and woe betide
You who would purloin it from him – you will be woebegone.
It is the table adjacent to Power's *Fish*.
He keeps his hat on in deference to Power's *Fish*.
When foreign visitors focus their attention
What they behold is a green fish soaring up some marble
In a grove of white feather and plume
While on his lap he cradles his tassels.
Not like others I have seen in the National Gallery
Cradling objects more obnoxious than any tassel –
Be it a tassel of a Coote or a Bulfin.
The Earl of Bellamont is a man who does not care.

After luncheon in the National Gallery Restaurant
We diverge outside at the statue of Shaw:
I to Sybil in the Rutland Memorial Fountain
In drizzle rejoicing in life, literature and art;
He to his tubes in Trinity College
To which he owns a postern gate key.

I have never asked him what exactly
His work is – but I gather
It is in software, not surprisingly.
The Earl of Bellamont is a man who does not care.

Mrs Congreve with Her Children

after Philip Reinagle

Although I am the girl's mother
I have to admit I fear for the lives of her men
When she is a grown gal.

Many is the garden path,
The exotic shrub, she will lead them up
With that squirrel of hers.

Even if ever they catch hold of her squirrel
It will either slip out of their hands
Or nip them in the wrists.

That squirrel of hers will eat a buck's nuts
Until a buck's got no nuts left –
London town littered with bucks with no nuts.

My little boy with his cannon is the soul of predictability
Like my husband up the wall behind me. He will be a proper
    husband.
Good, dull, fire off his cannon at regular intervals.

My other daughter is a worm – a bookworm.
I see no future for her unless she learns to ride a horse
And marries a farmer.

Most likely she will marry a divorced antiquarian
And become his devoted and unhappy wife, silly girl.
I do not really pity her one farthing.

She does not know anything. Thinks this drawing room fell out
    of the sky.
Would not know a carver from a girandole or a hand-knotted
    pile
Or whether her ancestor's portrait was a Kit-Cat or not.

She does not know her carpets – Axminister, Turkish,
Transylvanian, Smyrna, Sparta piles – all the same to her.
What hope is there for a gal who does not know her carpets?

Marguerite in Church

after James Tissot

A franc for them?

The choice is: do I want to rise from the dead?
To live in sin with the right man, Dr Life,
Or to live in virtue with the wrong man, Dr Death?

I will marry Jesus
In spite of the fact that he is an atheist,
That he is twice my age,
That he is dead,
That he is a non-smoker,
That he is a non-drinker,
That he is the father of children,
That he has enemies,
That he is a poet,
That he is insomniac,
That he is half-bald, shortsighted, jowly,
Congealed in candlegrease.

I will marry Jesus
For his intelligence, his wit, his grace, his awkwardness;
For his extraordinary good sense, creative imagination, originality;
For his shyness, his fear, his audacity, his affection;
For his cniptiousness;

For his casual approach to everything;
For his informal ways which have many forms;
For his not being fussy about what clothes he wears
Nor about what time he gets up in the mornings.

In the long evening of my young life
He will tell me stories while I curl up at his feet
With my arms around his knees;
For him, alone, always, I will wear red and black.

Boy Eating Cherries

after Pierre Bonnard

What Granny likes
Is to see a little boy eat up his cherries;
Little boys who eat up their cherries
Become big boys who eat up their cherries.

Man Walking the Stairs

after Chaim Soutine

Odd to overhear that you think I am saying
"Man walking the stars"
When all my life I have been saying
"Man walking the stairs."

Living alone in a semi-detached villa
Between the mountains and the sea
I spend a great deal of time on the stairs.
Halfway up the stairs
I pause at the window overlooking
The entrance to our cul-de-sac,
The lancet window in our gable;
I pause or climb on.

When I get to the top of the stairs
I cannot remember why in the first place
I came up the stairs
But that is in the nature of living alone:
I am neither perplexed nor perturbed.
I go back downstairs and start
All over again, read another page,
Drink another cup of tea, hover
At the kitchen window, hover
At the front window, hover
In the hallway, hover
At the letterbox, hover
Before the looking-glass in the coat rack
That we bought in Christy Bird's for two-and-sixpence.

I know what it is I must do.
I must go back upstairs and search
Under my bed for that book I have mislaid –
The Oxford Dictionary of Quotations.
I am searching for a line from Donne:
"Make my dark poem light."
But I pause again at the gable window
This time to behold pine trees
Clutching at one another in a gale,
Pair of pines reprieved by the developer.

When I conquer the top of the stairs
I fall down the stairs,
All the way down to the foot of the stairs.
Lying at the foot of the stairs
For three days and three nights
I behold bills – gas bills
And telephone bills – final notices –
Swirl through the lips of the letterbox
And the attic trap door at the top of the stairs
Is flying, descending, circling, advancing.
It keeps getting closer to my face.
If they ever find me and I am still alive
They will accuse me of having been drinking,
Of having been at the sherry.

What is wrong with being at the sherry?
Pale dry sherry – her throat, her lips, her eyes.

I could never understand people
At any time but especially people
Advising me I ought to sell my home
Because of the stairs. "What you must do
Is to find yourself a convenient bungalow
And save yourself the stairs."
Like advising a man to swim in a pool with no water.
The whole point of my home
Is the stairs. Can you conceive
Of a life without stairs?

My life is the saga of a life on stairs.

When I was nine with my cousin William
Sliding down bannister rails
To crashland on beaches of linoleum
My father peering over cliffs down stairwells
Already unbuckling his trousers' belt.

From thirteen to seventeen years
I sat on the stairs keeping vigil
With myself and the stair rods
Watching through bannister uprights
My father and mother coming and going.
I could not speak to them
Because when I spoke I stammered.
I clung to the bannisters,
Creature of the stairs.

Marriage at twenty-three and seventeen years
Of hoovering the stairs;
A flight of stairs and a hoover
And I was the sainted spouse.
Upstairs mowing away, I could hear
My wife downstairs whistling away
Scanning the morning paper.

Stairs into stairs.

One stair at a time or
Three stairs at a time or
Four or five stairs at a time
In our forties when she and I
Were to our bedroom racing
In the middle of the day
Barely able to reach it in time,
Slipping, clambering, getting there,
Her arms around my knees,
Or to the bathroom to bathe
Together in the same bath and make
A mess of water on the floor;
A pot of phlox on the window sill
Or a cruet of lambs' tails from the hazel tree.

Days when we were not speaking
Or, truth to tell, days when
I was sulking and she kept out
Of my way, I'd sit all day
On the stairs, my knees tucked up
Under my chin, my elbows
Around my shinbones. I preferred
Sitting on stairs to sitting on chairs,
Sitting on the stairs facing the front door,
Facing south, facing south to the sea,
Remembering the Café Neptune in Batumi.

Man is the inventor of stairs.

How many miles of stairs
Have we walked together?
A great many, yet much less
Than the thousands of miles of stairs
I have walked alone.

I like to look around me on these long
Walks on the stairs;
Redwoods convulsed in gales, Scots pines,
Olive trees, sycamores, my wife's ashes.

Man walking the stairs.
Man doing nothing else

Except walking the stairs.
Man scattering his wife's ashes
Either side of the stairs.
Sower stalking the stairs.

Our only son lived a long
And good life, only to be
Knocked down by a motorcar
On Leeson Street Bridge.
We buried him in the front garden
Along with our two black cats.
I think of him on the stairs –
How he used crawl face forwards
Down the stairs if I promised
To catch him at the foot of the stairs.

I carry my stairs in my arms
Up through the treetops of Provence,
All my treads and all my raisers.
Love is not love that is not courtly;
That's what every woman knows.

Man walking the stairs
Is man treading water.
Our house of water:
Do not open the door.

Odd to overhear that you think I am saying
"Man walking the stars"
When all my life I have been saying
"Man walking the stairs."

Draughts

after Jack B. Yeats

Solids and liquids;
Bodies and souls;
Thread.

Grand Canal Basin:
Belly of water
By a buckle
All held in.

I have got a pain
In my gut:
Your move.

It is all a blue bag – as the Tailor used say.
We have seen Eternity and it is mortal.

In the Tram

after Jack B. Yeats

No one wanted him; he was outcast from life's feast.

– A Painful Case

I am afraid – I confide in my doctor –
After the operation for my duodenal ulcer
That when I am discharged from hospital
I will not be able to cope with the isolation;
That my wife having left me for her brother-in-law
And being myself a middle-aged country man
With a clerical position in the city waterworks
With no close friends or relations or acquaintances
I will have no choice but to prostrate myself
Under a train at Sydney Parade
Or in my overcoat with the velour collar
Go for a late-night swim in the River Dodder
With stones in my pockets.

The doctor – a burly blustering Kerryman –
Plunges his thumbs into his pinstripe waistcoat:
"Self-pity's slurry, I will not allow it, wallower you.
What you must do when you leave hospital
Is learn to ride the trams.

I appreciate that you are an outcast in Dublin
But once you have learned how to ride the trams
You will have penetrated the secret code of city life.
You have no idea the numbers of unattached women
Who use the trams but I have the statistics.
At least 72 per cent of the women riding the trams
Are in want of a man, especially the married women.
But obviously also the unmarried women.
All you have to do is ride lots of trams, lots of them,
And Bob's your uncle, Nan's your aunt,
You will have a woman in no time.

"Personally I recommend the Lucan Route
Under the Phoenix Park Walls, the Knockmaroon Gate,
But what route you choose is a matter for yourself.
For all I know your needs might be best catered for
On the Dun Laoghaire Route.
The South Side is *terra incognita* to me
But that it is *terra firma* my registrars do assure me.
Your difficulty will be in selecting the right woman.
The crux will be cranking up
A *sacra conversazione*, so to speak, with the appropriate lady:
It is likely, I must warn you, that she will be living alone
With her only child – her grown-up daughter."

As I sit bolt upright alone on the tram, a solitary epitome,
I endeavour to imagine what it must be like to be the tram
        driver
Glancing back over his shoulder into the laughing faces of
        three women
Under tinted ventilators
A conspiracy of handbags,
How as a trio they remind him of high tide at Bulloch
        Harbour:
Beyond them, across an empty expanse of ocean
– An empty seat can be an eternity –
The single sail of a solitary gent,
His hat featherless.

Glancing back over his shoulder, the tram driver
Glances a dray,

299

Brakes, and I am tipped up, over and out of my seat.
The three women slide back down along the rexine,
Collapse on top of me in a kerfuffle and for seconds
I am smothered in petticoats – a swansong come true.
I have always had a yen for petticoats.
Their female voices. I could listen to it all day.
Heat and light. I dare not look around.
I feel so cold myself although it is the month of April
And thirty years past puberty.
I would not recognise my own voice if I heard it,
I do not think. It is 1923. I would say
I have about another seventeen years to live
Or seventeen minutes. I am going crazy –
Crazy without women.

Flower Girl, Dublin

after Jack B. Yeats

Afternoons in winter
I sit in Robert Roberts' café
Watching men and women,
Especially women.
I am crazy about women.

Just because I am a man without a woman
Does not mean that I have no interest in women.
In fact, I am preoccupied with fundamentally nothing else.
I read all of Nietzsche when I was seventeen.
Then it was time to grow up.

Would you please hose some of your hot liquid into me?
Mother of five to boy at coffee dispenser.
She must be forty at least but as she sips her grounds –
Her Costa Rican grounds –
As she smacks her lips
Trickling her tongue tip along her lip rim
She is a girl not yet nineteen
Haughty as an Englishwoman in Shanghai.

Red cloche hat, grey wool overcoat,
Black low high-heel shoes.

I see in today's newspaper a black-and-white photograph
Of a woman in a black miniskirt at the opening
Of the Sean McSweeney retrospective last night
(There is a man who can paint – not many can
Since the Great Yeat died in 1957).

But much as that photo causes a stir in me –
An abstract stir in me –
It is as nothing compared to this glimpse of ankle –
Ankle –
Of the mother of five in red cloche hat –
Would you please hose some of your hot liquid into me?

Time to go – home. I dally to loiter
In the doorway of the café eyeing myself
In the shop window opposite, my bowler hat,
My frock coat, my gleaming galoshes.
A flower girl with a single red rose in her hands
Is passing the time of day with the mother of five
Not making any particular pitch to sell.

Timorousness entices me to my right –
But I know, Jack, I know
I should step briskly to my left,
Proffer the single red rose to the mother of five,
Nail my colours to the mast.
Will I or won't I?
And give all my loose change to the flower girl –
All my loose change?

Grief

after Jack B. Yeats

I

I am a man;
All that is human is alien to me.

I insert my penis gun into your mouth and –
As the quaint old mantra has it –
"Blow your brains out."

How I delight to behold
At evening by the campfire on the seashore
After our games of softball
The wild, wild hedgerows'
Fuchsia of your dripping brains:

Oilily –
When I drop my Judaeo-Christian trousers,
Spread out my legs across the Islamic sky,
Drop my droppings on you.

What I admire most about myself,
What I most cherish
In my children's bedrooms
As I lull their cradles,
Is my own ordure.

A man's own ordure
Is the basis of culture;
In the hi-tech of my ordure
Ticks the future of my futurelessness.
My golden locks
Are things of the past.

I am a man;
All that is human is alien to me.

II

I was on the Dublin–Cork train minding my own business
When a not-so-young man opposite me – about the same age
    as myself –
Put down his paper and asked me without a by-your-leave
"What class of occupation are you in yourself?"
To my surprise I answered him:
"I am an art gallery attendant."

I can still hear myself saying it:
"I am an art gallery attendant" –
Has a ring to it.
The beautiful thing was that it shut him up.
We were only pulling out of Kildare
But he did not open his mouth again
The whole way down to Cork.

I am an art gallery attendant
In the National Gallery of Ireland.
I am the man
Who sits under *Grief*
At the head of the Gallery
Watching fleets of feet paddling towards me.
If anyone asks me what *Grief* means
I say I do not know what *Grief* means.
That is the truth. I do not know what *Grief* means.
I do not think anyone knows what *Grief* means.
It is a pretty picture – that is all I know about *Grief*
After having sat under it for twenty-five years
And I think that is all anybody knows about *Grief*.

Another thing that I do not understand
Is people who make a racket with their footwear on the
    parquet.
It never fails to grate on my nerves.
What's in it for a body to wantonly introduce
Noise into a place of worship?
It's like people who say you can accommodate wars
When obviously there is no way you can accommodate wars
Or people who see fit to bite hard-boiled sweets in cinemas.

I suppose it's something inherent in society and the individual,
Crowds and power.
That is what I often think
Sitting here under *Grief*.

People often ask me also the way to the restaurant.
By the time they have finished asking me
They have spotted it and they apologise
For having asked me in the first place.
By this time they have caught a glimpse of *Grief*.
They stop in their tracks. They stare up at it
Like as if they have seen a horse come through the wall.
All of us hanging about in the parade ring at a race meeting.
Nervously, they approach it and at the last moment they make
A dive into the corner to sniff the label.
They canter up and down the length of the picture
Before standing back out again in the middle –
Connections in the middle of the parade ring –
Pleased with themselves to be at the centre of the picture,
Yet anxious to get back outside again and to watch –
Or not to watch, as the case may be – from a safe distance.
Grief. I scratch my chin. They scamper off for their coleslaw.
Punters scoff a lot of coleslaw in the National Gallery of Ireland.

A SNAIL IN MY PRIME (1993)

My Belovèd Compares Herself to a Pint of Stout

When in the heat of the first night of summer
I observe with a whistle of envy
That Jackson has driven out the road for a pint of stout,
She puts her arm around my waist and scolds me:
Am I not your pint of stout? Drink me.
There is nothing except, of course, self-pity
To stop you also having your pint of stout.

Putting self-pity on a leash in the back of the car,
I drive out the road, do a U-turn,
Drive in the hall door, up the spiral staircase,
Into her bedroom. I park at the foot of her bed,
Nonchalantly step out leaving the car unlocked,
Stroll over to the chest of drawers, lean on it,
Circumspectly inspect the backs of my hands,
Modestly request from her a pint of stout.
She turns her back, undresses, pours herself into bed,
Adjusts the pillows, slaps her hand on the coverlet:
Here I am – at the very least
Look at my new cotton nightdress before you shred it
And do not complain that I have not got a head on me.

I look around to see her foaming out of the bedclothes
Not laughing but gazing at me out of four-leggèd eyes.
She says: Close your eyes, put your hands around me.
I am the blackest, coldest pint you will ever drink
So sip me slowly, let me linger on your lips,
Ooze through your teeth, dawdle down your throat,
Before swooping down into your guts.

While you drink me I will deposit my scum
On your rim and when you get to the bottom of me,
No matter how hard you try to drink my dregs –
And being a man, you will, no harm in that –
I will keep bubbling up back at you.
For there is no escaping my aftermath.

Tonight – being the first night of summer –
You may drink as many pints of me as you like.
There are barrels of me in the tap room.
In thin daylight at nightfall,
You will fall asleep drunk on love.
When you wake early in the early morning
You will have a hangover,
All chaste, astringent, aflame with affirmation,
Straining at the bit to get to First Mass
And Holy Communion and work – the good life.

A Spin in the Rain with Seamus Heaney

You had to drive across to Donegal town
To drop off a friend at the Dublin bus
So I said I'd come along for the spin –

A spin in the rain.
Bales of rain
But you did not alter your method of driving,

Which is to sit right down under the steering wheel
And to maintain an upwards-peering posture
Treating the road as part of the sky,

A method which motoring correspondents call
Horizontal-to-the-vertical.
The hills of Donegal put down their heads

As you circled upwards past their solitary farmhouses,
All those agèd couples drenched over firesides,
Who once were courting couples in parked cars.

You parked the car in Donegal town and we walked the shops –
Magee's and The Four Masters Bookshop.
You bought ice-cream cones. I bought women's magazines.

We drove on up through the hills past Mountcharles
And Bruckless and Ardara.
There was a traffic jam in Ardara,

Out of which you extricated yourself
With a jack-knife U-turn on a hairpin bend
With all the bashful panache of a cattle farmer –

A cattle farmer who is not an egotist
But who is a snail of magnanimity,
A verbal source of calm.

Back in the Glenties you parked outside the National School
Through whose silent classrooms we strayed,
Silent with population maps of the world.

Standing with our backs to a deserted table-tennis table
We picked up a pair of table-tennis bats
And, without being particularly conscious of what we were at,

We began to bat the ball one to the other
Until a knock-up was in progress,
Holding our bats in pen grips.

So here we are playing a game of ping-pong
Which is a backdrop to our conversation
While our conversation is a backdrop to our game.

We are talking about our children and you speak
Of the consolation of children when they grow up
To become our most trusted of all companions.

I could listen to you speak along these lines
For the rest of the day and I dare say
You could listen to me also speak along my lines:

I have always thought that ping-pong balls –
Static spheres fleet as thoughts –
Have flight textures similar to souls'.

I note that we are both of us
No mean strikers of the ball and that, although
We have distinct techniques of addressing the table –

Myself standing back and leaping about,
Yourself standing close and scarcely moving –
What chiefly preoccupies us both is spin.

As darkness drops, the rain clears.
I take my leave of you to prepare my soul
For tonight's public recital. Wishing each other well.

Poetry! To be able to look a bullet in the eye,
With a whiff of the bat to return it spinning to drop
Down scarcely over the lapped net; to stand still; to stop.

Faith Healer

to Donal McCann

I

First night of *Faith Healer* at the Abbey Theatre
I walk on water into the bar;
Acquaintances of acquaintances of acquaintances
Pushing me from one to t'other;
Knocking me down on the floor;
Picking me up off the floor
Only again to knock me down on the floor.

My spectacles get knocked off my nose.
When I bend to pick them up off the floor
An accountant shoves me from behind;
An auctioneer shoves me from the front;
A solicitor shoves me from the side;
A gallery owner puts his two arms around me.
When I demur, they cajole me:
Why do you react like an infant child?
Why take yourself so seriously?

II

Not like, but am, an infant child.
What I take so seriously's the play.
Who knows who my mother is?
Who knows who my father is?
Every fallen birch leaf of it.

I want to kneel down under the play;
Under the jagged stars of its stillness;
Under its torrents of chatter
As they freeze before my eyes;
I want to kneel down in my seat
And be prayed over, and pray;
I want to keel over;
I want to lie down with the frost
Before its final surrender,
Before its final sunrise;
I want to be sleet in daylight.

I want to pray at the footlights
Where in the dark night of my grave
I have seen the candle flame
Become an exculpated face
Explaining my fate to me:
A flame in all its facets of flight;
An infant child in a hole in the ground;
A nimbus of ashes in a post hole;
A circle of cows peering down at me.

I want to hear the play confide in me
After the play has ended.
I want to meet my mother and father
On their way home from my grave,
Going home to Kinlochbervie.
I want to rest with the rest
On the Rest on the Flight into Egypt.
I want to eat Rembrandt Bread,
Friel Potato Cake.

III

First night of my grave
I want to stand alone centre stage,
Gaze out into the wings either side of me,
Flies of blood
Which are my wings also,
Webbed wings of my hands,
These hands which are all that I am and you are,
Fingertip to fingertip,
Thumb to opposable thumb.

To be seen for whom I am and you are:
Infant child;
My snail's slime glistening from era to era;
An actor alone in his dressing room;
A playwright in a jam jar;
Acquaintances of acquaintances of acquaintances;
Deposed, somnolent, cruciform.

In the bar of the Abbey, I lie down on the floor
At my own pace;
First-night faces peering down at me,
All fezzes and tassels;
What will you have? What would you like?
Give me some water and let me die a little.

In my watery grave
I mind and do not mind
What you say about me –
I who was born in Kinlochbervie.
To be wholly alive is to be wholly dead.

27 November 1990

The Toll Bridge

to Francis Stuart on his ninetieth birthday

I

The woman in the toll
Down at the Toll Bridge –
Furry creature, big ears, snub nose –
A moose she is –
A moose under a bus –
Is teasing me
For having my meter on with my taxi empty.
I am delivering a book – I advise her –
Northside to southside.

When she enquires the name of the book and I enlighten her,
She states that I will have to pay her a toll on it.
I know she is teasing me but I pay her a toll on it.
I like paying her the toll – paying her any toll –
Having to fling the toll into her empty basket
Or having to lean out of the driver's seat window
And deposit my coin into the palm of her hand.
She reiterates the book's name: "*A Hole in the Head.*"
I reiterate the author's name: "Francis Stuart."

II

It became our passion.
I scoured the bookshops of Dublin City for a copy.
None of them had it. They said that it was "out of print",
That there was "a question mark over Francis Stuart".
She peered down at me from her perch in the toll:
A question mark over Francis Stuart?
Why don't you nick me a copy?
Nick you a copy?
From the party you delivered it to.
If there is a question mark over Francis Stuart
I would like to partake of Francis Stuart;
A man with a question mark over him
Might be a man with ninety question marks over him.

III

The party had an address in Dundrum.
I remembered him because he answered the door
In a seaman's polo-neck navy-blue knitted pullover
Holding in his hands a white rabbit.
I decided to call on him, ask him for a loan of
A Hole in the Head.
I felt ill waiting for him to answer the door;
As it happened, on that particular night, dejected.
But talking to him was like talking to one of the old masters
If you can envisage the old masters as being Japanese
– The red horse at the black well –
– The boy on the mountain –
– The sea in flower –
And I came away from him with bunches of new skates in
    both hands.

When I reported to him our passion he asked me her name.
When I told him I did not know her name
He said that that was how it should always be –
That it was better for a man and a woman
Not to know one another's names;
That it was better for a man and a woman
Never to know one another's names,
The thing in passion being anonymity.
He held out the rabbit to me.
I was afraid, but I took it.
He held my head in his hands –
His hands warm from rabbit fur.
He ran his fingers through my hair
Before sinking a forefinger
Down into the slime of my brain.
He whispered: The hole in your head.
When he bowed his dark head of white hair
I could decipher the profile of the nimbus
Round the hole in his own head:
A full moon on a cloudy night.

He loaned me the book –
On condition that I never gave it back to him.

She, in her turn, when I gave it to her
Made it a condition of our passion
That we would never address one another
By one another's names
And that I would continue to pay her the toll,
Continue always to pay her the toll.

Although our passion continues to grow
And we can do things that we used not be able to do
And what we do now we do better,
I never miss a chance to drive back down along
The Toll Bridge
At night – late at night –
And pay her my toll.
The Toll Bridge
Is our dovecote, our ghetto, our haunt, our suburb, our ark –
Our ark of the north on the south bank of the Liffey.
We chat and she drops my coin on her floor
And she is saying: What does it mean to be a writer?
I jump out of my taxi and climb up into the toll with her
And we get down on the floor on our hands and knees
And search for my coin.
I say to her: To be a writer is to be nothing.
Nothing in my life has vouchsafed me such gold dust
As to get down on my hands and knees on the floor with her
Searching for my coin.

Swapping straws we suck.
She shivers: I will stay in Ringsend.
We leave it at that
But on feast nights –
Storytellings, homecomings, pay packets, new licence plates –
She shudders: I will go back to Berlin.
She swears: Christ, I set eyes on him once.
At the beginning of the film *Wings of Desire* –
Der Himmel über Berlin –
He was standing on top of the broken tower
Of the Gedächtniskirche
In a navy-blue overcoat with wings,

Aged about forty, and a voice said:
"If mankind loses its storyteller
It will lose its childhood."

V

I squint down into the hole in her head.
I stick my tongue into the hole in her head.
I shout out into the hole in her head:
Stop all traffic;
Drop down all the poles of the Toll Bridge.
I lope out into the centre of the plaza at the Toll Bridge –
A snail in my prime –
And, my soul all humility and periphery,
I proclaim to the Republic of Ireland and Ulster,
My cosmos, my ice rink:
Finally, I bequeath to you this painting
Which henceforth will be the only priceless
Painting in our national collection in Merrion Square West.
It is by Francis Bacon
When he was a vagabond in Provence with Vincent Van Gogh
Seeking asylum from mankind
And it has been hanging in a woman poet's bedroom in Berlin
Since the year 1944.
It is Bacon's masterpiece and it is entitled
A Question Mark over Francis Stuart.
As you will observe,
It is Bacon's intaglio of the postmodernist halo.

Shall these bones live?
With a sickle in one hand and a satsuma in the other hand
Francis Stuart is dicing himself into portions
Feeding the birds at the Toll Bridge,
Sparrows on the fenders of Fiestas;
Feeding the leopards at the Toll Bridge,
Strays in the rear mirrors of Fiats;
The poles lift up;
And the horns do not too harshly blow –
Do not too harshly wind up their themes:
Driver, driver; improvise, improvise.

A Hole in the Head is all that I implore;
A Hole in the Head with Charity in Paris.
A Hole in the Head is all that I implore;
A Hole in the Head with Charity in Paris.

29 April 1992

My Daughter Síabhra in Moscow, 19 August 1991

I

Monday lunchtime
At the Edinburgh Book Festival
Meandering the marquees
In Charlotte Square.
Dermot Bolger,
In his hand *The Journey Home*,
Yells down a duckboard-walk:
Gorbachev's gone!

Phone calls to the Irish
Department of Foreign Affairs.
No lines to Moscow.
All afternoon at the tiny
TV in my hotel room
Watching the tanks in Moscow.

Father fretting for his daughter,
Yet pleased she is at the heart of things
Learning Russian. Next morning,
Telegram from Moskva:
THERES BEEN SOME SORT OF COUP DETAT TANKS ON THE STREET
    IM FINE DONT WORRY LOVE SIABHRA

II

We are caught up in a family civil war
When you fly back into Dublin on August 30th.

By virtue of your Bulgakovian midwifery
We manage to induce a truce
Although not until eight months later
When at your prodding
We all get together to attend *The Cherry Orchard*
In a theatre over a maternity hospital.

Thanks to you I get to know
Chekhov's untranslatable word for a human being –
You Nothing you –
And to see Cyril Cusack at eighty-two
Playing the eighty-seven-year-old Nothing.
Dear Daughter – After all that has transpired,
All that I aspire to be is Nothing.
So, at my deathbed, you will smile:
You Nothing you!

Father's Day, 21 June 1992

Just as I was dashing to catch the Dublin–Cork train,
Dashing up and down the stairs, searching my pockets,
She told me that her sister in Cork wanted a loan of the axe;
It was late June and
The buddleia tree in the backyard
Had grown out of control.
The taxi was ticking over outside in the street,
All the neighbours noticing it.
"You mean that you want me to bring her down the axe?"
"Yes, if you wouldn't mind, that is –"
"A simple saw would do the job, surely to God
She could borrow a simple saw."
"She said that she'd like the axe."
"OK. There is a Blue Cabs taxi ticking over outside
And the whole world inspecting it,
I'll bring her down the axe."
The axe – all four-and-a-half feet of it –
Was leaning up against the wall behind the settee –
The fold-up settee that doubles as a bed.
She handed the axe to me just as it was,

As neat as a newborn babe,
All in the bare buff.
You'd think she'd have swaddled it up
In something – if not a blanket, an old newspaper,
But no, not even a token hanky
Tied in a bow round its head.
I decided not to argue the toss. I kissed her goodbye.

The whole long way down to Cork
I felt uneasy. Guilt feelings.
It's a killer, this guilt.
I always feel bad leaving her
But this time it was the worst.
I could see that she was glad
To see me go away for a while,
Glad at the prospect of being
Two weeks on her own,
Two weeks of having the bed to herself,
Two weeks of not having to be pestered
By my coarse advances,
Two weeks of not having to look up from her plate
And behold me eating spaghetti with a knife and fork.
Our daughters are all grown up and gone away.
Once when she was sitting pregnant on the settee
It snapped shut with herself inside it,
But not a bother on her. I nearly died.

As the train slowed down approaching Portarlington
I overheard myself say to the passenger sitting opposite me:
"I am feeling guilty because she does not love me
As much as she used to, can you explain that?"
The passenger's eyes were on the axe on the seat beside me.
"Her sister wants a loan of the axe . . ."
As the train threaded itself into Portarlington
I nodded to the passenger "Cúl an tSúdaire!"
The passenger stood up, lifted down a case from the rack,
Walked out of the coach, but did not get off the train.
For the remainder of the journey, we sat alone,
The axe and I,
All the green fields running away from us,
All our daughters grown up and gone away.

A Cold Wind Blew in from Lake Geneva

Belovèd daughters, I would like to be cremated
Early in the afternoon, 3.30 p.m. at the latest;
A woman to say Psalm 23;
A painter to say a poem from memory;
A poet to hold up a painting;
An architect to improvise a slow air.

Throw a party –
The kind of party that Michael Cullen
Threw in Brighton Vale in April '92,
Or in Henrietta Street in April '90:
A stand-up feast, a round table piled,
Bread and wine, the best of cheeses,
Homemade pâté, olives, cucumbers,
Salami, hams, salads,
Strawberries, pineapples, melons, cream,
Bouquets of irises, daffodils, chrysanthemums,
The window open to the street.
Open all windows, let breezes
Catch napes, necks, breasts,
Cheekbones, earlobes, curtains.
When the poet Rilke died
Someone at that instant opened the bedroom window
And a cold wind blew in from Lake Geneva.

Invite by advertisement,
By word of mouth,
Anyone who felt the slightest
Affection for the deceased.
In my name drink a toast
To Human Nature and Frailty.
Whisper my two logos: *Provincials to the Wall*
And – *Never Conform.*

Later, when it suits –
When you have a weekend to spare –
Take back my ashes to Mayo,
Climb the Reek on a blue day,

Scatter my ashes in the direction of Clew Bay.
Not to worry if a west wind
Blows them back in the opposite direction –
That would be in the nature of things.

If all that is asking too much
Take my ashes out for a walk in Ringsend
Down the Drain;
No more seductive entrance to the world
Than the Drain in Ringsend;
Not even the Champs-Elysées
Quite match the Drain;
Down Pigeon House Road,
Past the Tech,
Past the Toll Bridge,
Down to the Gut;
No more seductive exit from the world
Than the Gut in Ringsend;
Not even the Statue of Liberty
Quite matches the Gut.

Cast me out into the Gut
So that one will never know exactly
Whether my ashes fetched up
In Dodder or Liffey or Grand Canal:
The thing in the end being The Mixture.
PS
If you would rather not,
I mean if all of this strikes you as too, too much,
Put my ashes in a black refuse sack and remember
To put it out on Wednesday morning
Along with the dustbin and the empties –
The golden, golden empties.

A Snail in My Prime

Slug love:
Older than the pyramids
Christ Jesus
I am a snail in my prime.

On the banks of the Boyne on a June night,
I repose under the snail cairn of Newgrange
Watching men go to the moon
While their women give birth to more women.
My snail soul is light-sensitive.
I repose in the central chamber of the passage grave
Inhaling the stillness of the earth
While my daughter daubs slime on my face,
Inserts slime in every crevice of my body,
Between my toes, behind my ears.
Small, plump, sleek thrush on wall-top with snail in beak
Banging it, cracking me open.
Between each embalming, she goes down to the river;
Returns with her hands glistening with snails.
(Oh to hold in my hands my father's walking stick
And to press to my lips its brass ferrule and to lean
On it with his chamois gloves on the handle and to test
The floor with its point – that is the point!)
I have never seen my daughter so congenial
As this evening at the signal of my burial.
I have never heard such laughter on her lips,
Such actual, gratuitous, carefree laughter.
She cries: "Thank you for bringing me to the water."
Under the corbelled roof of her own shell;
In the central chamber of her soul;
In the passage of her root;
At the entrance stone of her eyes;
Behind the kerbstones of her knees;
In the quartz stones of her ears;
In the basin stones of her elbows;
Inside the stone circle of her hair
I listen to her voice echoing in mud millennia:
"Thank you for bringing me to the water."

I like to spend Christmas in Newgrange
Alone with my extended family
In shells all of different stripes and hues
But unisoned in a bequeathal of slime.
At dawn, at the midwinter solstice,
We creep into the corbelled vault
Of the family tomb.
Down in dark
Death is a revealing of light
When a snail inherits the sky,
Inherits his own wavy lines;
When a snail comes full circle
Into the completion of his partial self.
At my life's end, I writhe
For the sun to fatten in the east
And make love to me;
To enter me
At 8.58 a.m.
And to stay inside me
For seventeen minutes,
My eyes out on stalks.
You feel like a spiral
Inside me; you feel
Like three spirals inside me.
After such early morning lovemaking –
I always preferred making love at daybreak –
I spin out my fate
Under my lady's capstone.
The snails of her breasts
Peep out from behind
Their pink petals.
At my life's end in Newgrange
There is light at the end of the tunnel.

Round and round I trundle my bundle of ego,
My nostril tumbril,
My ham pram, my heart cart,
My dreaming shell, my conscious horns,
My spiral of tongue
Unspiralling over the years,
My crops of teeth.

I am a smudge of froth. All I can hear
Is the tiny squeaking in prehistoric forests
Of my antennae being bent until they snap;
The Great Irish Snail in his prime
Coating the cones of Scots pines with his slime,
The orange aura of desire.
I am not a womanizer,
I am a snail.
When it is all over
And my daughters have eaten me,
Cremated me
In earthenware pots
With my stone beads
And there will be from me no more poems,
No more antler, no more horn,
And the last tourist coaches have departed,
Morsels of my antennae will be plucked up
By departing house martins, digested,
Deposited off the shores of Africa
In plankton of the South Seas
To enter into the bloodstream of sea lions . . .
Last night, when we made love up behind our pillows,
A pair of sea lions mated on a sud-strewn rock,
Who moments ago were snails in separate beds,
The River Boyne curled up at our feet,
My tail in your tail, my slime in your slime.

Slug love:
Older than the pyramids
Christ Jesus
I am a snail in my prime.

GIVE ME YOUR HAND (1994)

The Adoration of the Kings

after Jan Gossaert

Jesus Christ is my name.
I was born in Belfast city
But I live in New Zealand,
In the city of Invercargill,
In Southland,
South of Dunedin,
Five miles from Bluff,
Last stop
Before the South Pole.

Back in Belfast
I was known in my time.
Won trophies for table tennis.
My father Joe was a fitter
In the Harland and Wolff shipyard,
A meek, hysterical man
Who always wore red,
Who always saw red;
My mother Mary was a charlady
Who always wore blue,
Always saw blue.

We lived in the gate lodge – one room –
"The Pits" it was called –
Of the ruins of a medieval fortress
In Friendly Street
On the banks of the River Lagan
Right in the city centre,
Five minutes' walk from City Hall.
Every Christmas the politicians used converge on us –
"Everything that crawls must converge."
They'd haul Mother out into the middle of the ruins
And plonking her down there with her latest pot-bellied babe
(There were seventeen of us)
They'd stage this elaborate, operatic photo call
With them all presenting her with gifts,
"Pressies" they'd croon,

Employing the folksy idiom.
Belfast was a dandy place for the folksy idiom.
They'd arrive dressed up in their folksiest clobber:
All turned out in the latest golfing gear.

And when it wasn't politicians
It was paramilitaries
And when it wasn't paramilitaries
It was press.
Press – I think they were the worst
For palaver. Convoluted bullshit.

Father and Mother were so compliant,
Civil, co-operative with these gaudy chancers,
Especially Mother and yet
Mother was imperturbable.
If your intentions were truly evil
You could not get to her or at her.

Mother was comprehensively insignificant
In the scheme of things in Belfast city.
She had no position on or in anything
Nor did she read newspapers
Except the odd tabloid or watch TV
Except for *Coronation Street*
Or go to poetry readings
Except when her friend Edna'd tell her
They were having Charles Bukowski up at Queens
She'd chuckle: a grand wee man, that Bukowski.
He's like my poor wee Joe, that Bukowski.
In the depths of winter and squalor,
Orgy, murder, universal pretentiousness,
Mother was radiance – a candle in water.
She was placid with a global temper.

These guys – the politicians, the paramilitaries, the press –
They'd go on and on and on and on and on at her
With words. That's what I detested
About them so much – the words – always
The words. Worse than guns words are.
But she'd never react, never.
She'd sit there in contemplation of her body.

Father was a horrible worrier – an armpit of *Angst*.
He'd cast up his eyes to the cameraman, screeching:
"If all these people turned up on your doorstep
When your wife was having a baby, how would you feel?
I need to be taken care of, put away for some time."
Father knew that to them she was dirt
And that in fact she was dirt
And that she was the mother of God.
That was my father's attitude to women –
He was the sort of man to whom a woman
By definition is the mother of God.

Every Christmas would be the same old pantomime:
The Three Ugly Brothers, each with his hangers-on,
His backslappers, his blurb writers.
One would get down on his knees
Proffering his hands in prayer at Mother's knee
Giving her newborn babe – all navel and curl –
A chalice of coins to commune with.
He'd have a large invisible placard round his neck:
I am a politician, a paramilitary, a pressman
But I am also a man of prayer.

On Mother's right-hand side
There'd be this bonzo in orange suede boots
Who'd have just clapped on a tiara
So in love with himself
That although he'd be holding a gift
It would be to himself he'd be giving it.
He'd spout – never once looking at Mother.
He'd spout poetry – poetry backwards.
He'd awarded himself prizes for his Backwards Poetry.

Numero 3 was always the silent type,
The man of few words, the laconic bod
Wanting to get it over with,
Thinking ahead to the next appointment,
The ex-commis waiter balancing his gift in one hand,
Fancying his dexterity. He wrote poetry sideways.

Mind, we never minded the neighbours having a good gawk.
One who always stood opposite Father
Had the most beautiful face in Belfast city.
Nor the boys at the back of the church
Nor the dog rooting about in the broken tiles
Nor the other bitch having a piddle.
Nor Father's donkey. He always kept an ass –
An ass was his grip on reality.

Up in the sky the ubiquitous helicopters,
Crews dangling from them – women with wings
Chatting away on their walkie-talkies for all to hear:
"Do you think baby ought to go to bed?"
"Do you think we should put a stop to it?"
Father would be groaning away
"Don't cry for me, Enniskillen."
And he'd say to me:
"Christ, get the hell out of here,
It's a slaughterhouse.
All these politicians, paramilitaries, press.
Butchers the lot of them."

Like most sons
I did not take my father's advice
Until aged thirty-three
I was executed in a football stadium in the suburbs –
Ravenhill Park.

So now I live in New Zealand.
No matter
What my past life may hold
I will never
Go back to Belfast.
Speaking for myself
As Christ the son of Joe and Mary
Let the Kings adore themselves.
Count me out.

Not only do I never want to see
A White Christmas again,
I never want to see any Christmas again.

My own wife here – Mary also –
Maori girl – we live on the *marae* in Island Bay –
She confides in me:
Christ – Christmas is not for you,
Does not agree with you.
She's right.
Christmas is for politicians, paramilitaries, press.
A fairytale to keep butchers happy,
A fairytale to keep the blood flowing –
And the cabbage, the smackers, the tin, the spondulicks, the
    tickle-tickle.

Jesus Christ is my name:
For me Christianity is not on.

1st February 1993

The Presentation in the Temple

after the Master of the Life of the Virgin

I was a middle-aged playwright in London going nowhere
When on a grey Saturday afternoon in January
I wandered into Westminster Cathedral – a home
From home – its black unfinished domes
A source of consolation. In the bosom of Abraham,
I feel, sitting under them, imploring God's mercy,
I who had flown into a rage the previous night in a Battersea pub
Because my poor wife had worn her green frock with a slit in it.

There was a little ceremony in progress in a side-chapel.
Father Simeon, an old Jesuit I've known for years,
Decent skin, camping it up on the altar
But in the most touching way you can imagine.
A young couple presenting to him their baby son,
The manic-depressive husband fishing in his purse for money.
That was the moment of my alteration,
My copping-on to myself, my epiphany.

331

Bareheaded in the background with my hat in my hands
I says to myself: Enough of all this old self-pity.
Enough of groaning under the weight of the world
Like them two little black lads under the altar.
I've got as pretty a pair of feet as any male playwright
In Great Britain and Ireland – time I made use of them.
Flaunt what you have – as the girl said.
(From Tasmania, she was. Hobart. Sue.)

Look at Simeon – the care with which
He's holding up that child – the effort of affection he's putting
Into the whole simple little mundane transaction.
Sexy is not a word you'd properly associate with Simeon
But today it's the only word, the right word, the procreative word.
Just look at that bit of ankle he's showing.
From knee to spine he's all ankle.
That's what living in the here and now does for you.

Enough of living in the past – all stabbings and drunkenness,
Father and son, brother and brother, prophet and prophet,
Old hat.
From this day on – this grey January afternoon
I am going to take in my hands
The child of the future
And my tuning fork will be his spiky halo.
I'll have two plays running simultaneously in the West End

And me and Father Simeon will take a holiday in Spain
On the proceeds – why not?
It's a matter of hands but it's also a matter of feet.
Look down at your own feet and think for a moment:
Think of all the men you know who have women's feet.
Next time you are walking down the Charing Cross Road
Look up at my name in red neon lights:
My *nom de plume* – "The Master of the Life of the Virgin".

The Arnolfini Marriage

after Jan Van Eyck

We are the Arnolfinis.
Do not think you may invade
Our privacy because you may not.

We are standing to our portrait,
The most erotic portrait ever made,
Because we have faith in the artist

To do justice to the plurality,
Fertility, domesticity, barefootedness
Of a man and a woman saying "we":

To do justice to our bed
As being our most necessary furniture;
To do justice to our life as a reflection.

Our brains spill out upon the floor
And the terrier at our feet sniffs
The minutiae of our magnitude.

The most relaxing word in our vocabulary is "we".
Imagine being able to say "we".
Most people are in no position to say "we".

Are you? Who eat alone? Sleep alone?
And at dawn cycle to work
With an Alsatian shepherd dog tied to your handlebars?

We will pause now for the Angelus.
Here you have it:
The two halves of the coconut.

The Death of Actaeon

after Titian

I am slumped on my horse
In the woods of my own self
Watching Actaeon die
In Ladbroke Grove;
Actaeon, my closest friend,
England's finest painter.
His wife Diana, tall, fair,
With her bow but no bowstring,
Is striding in for the kill.
Her torrent of anger at her side.
Her skies of resentment at her back,
Her ground of bitterness at her feet.

Actaeon had his heart
Set on Diana from the start.
When he chanced to meet her
Bathing naked in the river,
Naked at its source,
She demanded from him intercourse.
Such was her delight
She invited him that same night
To make a home with her
And her four Alsatians.
Overnight he became
The most celebrated painter in London town,
Exhibiting annually in New York and Berlin.
Actaeon could do no wrong
Because Diana was his song.

After ten years of matrimony
On her thirtieth birthday
She threw him out of the matrimonial home:
Enough of being your song.
Actaeon went to live in a bar
On the corner of Ladbroke Grove
And Westbourne Park Road.

He never painted again.
He grew minusculer and minusculer,
He lost weight and height,
Until he became by day
A stag at bay,
A glass of whisky in his cloven hand,
A haunted sizzle in his eyes.
Even the four dogs felt pity for him
Caressing him in his throes.

It is chamber music to his young wife
To watch Actaeon die.
She feels reborn in the light of his dying.
His dying casts a new light over everything,
Has given her something to live for.
A flaming feminist
She strides down Ladbroke Grove
Past clumps of narcissi.
Gutters in spate.
Amber lamplight of streetlamps
Lighting up her crimson negligee.
She strides out with her right breast exposed,
Her nipple erect.
She strides out Ladbroke Grove
To the Television Centre in Shepherd's Bush
To present her own arts show on TV –
A documentary on the life and work
Of the greatest English painter of our time,
The Actaeon Trilogy.

At the moment of transmission
Actaeon is standing at the bar
Being held up by hangers-on
As he swallows his own tongue.
There is nothing anyone can do for Actaeon
Because Actaeon adores the woman
Who is killing him. Actaeon
Will not hear a word against his goddess;
He adores his woman because she is killing him.
He croaks: Give me your hand.
The film expires in scarlet and gold

335

With Actaeon crawling on his hands and knees
Slurping brandy from her hand.
The art world's comet
Chokes in his own vomit.

Samson and Delilah I

after Andrea Mantegna

I

Pity about Samson.
I love him.

But let me be not sentimental.
He got what he wanted –

Got to die in my arms,
Making love to me.

What every Samson yearns for –
To die in his Delilah's arms.

A man can have
One hangover too many.

My poor old ram
Expiring in my clutches.

The nape of his neck.
I'd know that nape anywhere.

Only the waters of life can save him –
Of the next life.

II

On my milking stool
Under the grape tree

I am a cellist
Playing my man.

My knees wide apart,
A furore of stillness.

A red sky at night
Is a shepherd's delight.

Black stars
In a red night.

When I am done playing
My little man

I hold him over the trough
While he gulps his gulp.

A woman's task is to learn her man
The reality of the Resurrection.

Pity about men
All the time pining to die.

Cardinal Richelieu

after Philippe de Champaigne

Mother, I do appreciate how chuffed
You must be that your son is a cardinal
But it is a hard old station staying off the drink.

You in your turn must appreciate
That what takes precedence in my life
Is not you or wine but my red biretta.

Life now is all a matter of biretta.
I have got to think biretta, sleep biretta, eat biretta.
No more booze. Biretta biretta.

Life is a cruel rota of checks and balances.
Of suppressing the shakes. Of mints and lozenges.
Of learning to hold on to one's biretta.

I take lessons every morning.
Eighteen holes before breakfast.
Drinking golfers call me "The Dry Biretta".

Mother, you above all should understand
If I so much as once drop my biretta
All my knickers will seize up,

My palaces of knickers,
My lace girdles, my frilly panties,
My starched collars, all my taffeta.

Mother, you above all know without censure
What a ponce I am – the way I comb
My hair back over my skullcap

In a quiff – quite against the rules –
And my sneer. A seventeenth-century Teddy boy.
All that concupiscence tethered to etiquette.

For you alone, Mother, I unhitch my *capa magna*,
Don my biretta, dance you out on to the patio poolside.
Draw a gold curtain over our relationship.

I'm all right, Ma, I'm only manic.

The Rokeby Venus

after Diego Velázquez

I lie on my bed
In the raw watching videos.

Soap after soap,
Weeping my eyes out.

On a Yorkshire moor
A kicked-over heap of tears.

Is that not what a woman is –
A kicked-over heap of tears?

Pity.
Pity about men.

Mr and Mrs Andrews

after Thomas Gainsborough

Tweet-tweet-tweet-tweet-tweet-tweet-tweet.
Twitter-twitter-twitter-twitter-twitter-twitter-twitter.
Boo-boo-boo-boo-boo-boo-boo
He is sulking because he wants his din-dins.

Fanning myself in the Suffolk desert
I mince round a corner of horizon
And there midst all that silly sand
Is a wrought-iron garden seat
Peeking out of old oak tree,
Stooks, sheepies, poppy
And, choreographed on seat,
Oneself.

The sort of dream out of which stuff is made.
Oneself
In most à la modish blue frock,
Pink high-heel slippers,
Floppy hat,
And, lounging up against rail of seat
Like a skimpy stag against its scratching post,
One's very own chap,
A spaniel in his parts
Sniffing,
Taking time off from his economics lectures
Or his ballet classes or whatever.

Bobsie Andrews and Me:
We two drips together dripping.
I murder him
With his own gun.
The nice thing is that the neighbours
Think it an accident.

I think my feeling was that I did not really want
To have to share the landscape.
It is a rather fetching landscape
In spite of all the suffocation
And I think I will rather enjoy it on my own
For the next fifty years
And not spoil it with children and inheritance
And all that sort of thing.
Fetch.

Exhibition of a Rhinoceros in Venice

after Pietro Longhi

I remember winter afternoons in strip clubs in Soho
In the company of witty lawyers
And thinking that I had known much more engrossing times
And that was when I was a teenage girl in Venice
And Mother used drag me along to the women's club –
The Jane Austen Reading Club in a disused church
Where they kept a rhinoceros on exhibition in the sanctuary.
Mother and her accomplices used saunter about the pews
In masks, tricorn hats, fans.
At first I thought the fans were for dispelling smells
But later I realised they were for something else,
Something to do with sudden heat.

Nowadays whenever I find myself alone in a lift
With a rhinoceros
I have no need of fans, masks, hats.
To be a woman alone with a rhinoceros in a lift
Is to feel quite – quite ludicrous.
I enjoy it enormously.

I enjoy it enormously.
Too often nowadays in these rancorous
Politically correct times
I find myself alone in a lift
Without a rhinoceros.

The Painter's Daughters Chasing a Butterfly

after Thomas Gainsborough

Little sister and I – there is a year between us –
Although we are different as chalk and cheese
We are the closest of friends and my deepest fear
Is of something happening to her. I have dreams
Of her being shredded in car crashes on black ice
Or of her mistaking cockroach powder for Parmesan cheese.

In the dream of life she and I
Are a pair of butterflies.
I am holding her hand as in her wilfulness
– She makes Eve Defying look like Eve Demurring –
She chases every single butterfly she ever sees.

Although we both detest Fisticuffs
(Dad loves it!)
Our favourite motto is Muhammad Ali's
"Float like a butterfly, sting like a bee,
Rumble, man, rumble."
Little sister and I
Love to rumble in the woods,
Meet small, dark, bright-voiced, uncouth boys,
Thistles under butterflies.

Our mother and father are also butterflies
Separated but inseparable.
Thistles incompatible.
We are closest to Mum but Dad is daft about us
And we are fond of him provided
That he does not overdo the torch.

That is Dad's problem – the torch.
This Yuletide – Noël! Noël! –
We received a letter from him in Sudbury
(We dwell in London with Mum)
Specifying what he wants from Santa Claus:

A head-torch!
He writes: I am getting on in years
And when I lose my way in the woods at night
On my way home from Gentle Annie's
I would like to be able to consult my bible –
That is to say, my ordnance survey map, my dears –
By the light of a decent flame in my forehead
Like any other sinner on this godforsaken, blasted earth.

He says we can purchase the head-torch in any odd shop in
    London.
We reckon that he owns at least five thousand torches,
The majority of them hand-torches,
But also backside-torches, navel-torches, groin-torches.
I am an artist – is his great excuse –
I am not afraid to live by the light of my own darkness.
The only time he ever comes to London
Is when there is a Lucien Freud exhibition.
Fathers like to beam torches in their daughters' faces,
Especially in their eldest daughters' faces.

Darlingest Dad, – We will be down on Boxing Day
Or at least at the very latest
By the Feast of the Epiphany
Provided you promise not to overdo it with the head-torch.
We will chase lots and lots and lots of butterfly
With you, you silly old butterfly you.
Meg is going to bring her new white dress
And I will be in gold – as usual. Pigs of love. Mary.

General Sir Banastre Tarleton

after Joshua Reynolds

I wanted my son to play for England,
To play at out-half for England,
And he did – against France in Twickenham.
On a typical Saturday afternoon in February,
Dull, overcast,
All of fifty years ago.
He rode up for the game that day
On a red Hunter, black plumed hat,
Skintight breeches, hunting jacket,
He was that on fire about it all.

In my wheelchair on the seafront at Brighton
Gazing out across the sea to France
I can see him out there in the grey field,
His drowned red hair flowing behind him,
In the very act and combination of kicking
The drop goal from play that won the game
For England and Northampton:
In the very act of preparing to kick
He bends ever so slightly
To pull up his sock and tie up his garter
And he has his two hands on his thighs
And as he steals a quick glance at his scrum half
He inhales, exhales, the smoky February air.
As the ball zips into his hands
(He had a superb pair of hands – the boy,
The safest hands in the UK – they used say)
He does not even trouble to look up at the French posts,
He stares down at the oval ball in his hands
– The prey, the sacred prey –
And drop kicks it into the sky between the posts.

In after years, of course, they tried,
As is the current fashion in Great Britain and Ireland,
To take his name and character from him
When he died last year from Aids.

343

But his wife stood by him, always did.
Decent girl, always was.
They say he was gay. Oh
He was gay all right, my boy, he was gay all right.
Dear brave sweet tender genial Banastre.

I am bloody awful lonely here in Brighton
On the seafront in my wheelchair
In the front lines of old age,
The great guns booming across the Channel
From France as they have always done
And always will. War is in the nature of life
Like love. The two things go together.
You cannot have love without war *and*
– *And* I say (this is what
Those buggers in the tabloids as well as in the quality
Press, suppress) – you cannot have war without love.

Dear dear Banastre! The old woman
On fire in the wheelchair beside me is a she-bear
And I – as she says – am a little old monkey
With silver hair and my private parts
Are bits of gold – tarnished gold.
I lean over and insert my little finger in her garter.
Bloody awful lonely here in Brighton, son.
Bloody awful lonely here in Paradise, sir.
Goodnight, General.
Goodnight, Father.

A Cornfield with Cypresses

after Vincent Van Gogh

Let me make no bones about *A Cornfield with Cypresses* –
Make clear straightaway who I am.
I am the painter's mother.
I am old, frail, quivering on my pins,
My trees almost leafless
Being stripped into senility.

344

But I have still got enough leaves to be able to see
My son's picture for what it is –
The serenest canvas I have ever seen.
(That's saying something
Because my son painted a great many
Serene canvases.)

So why am I so hot under the bra?
(Yes, the bra, I still wear bras
For old times' sake. I am old-fashioned.)
I am sore and vexed because the art historian says
That Vincent's *A Cornfield with Cypresses*
Is evidence of an unbalanced mind.
Poppycock.
Oh I am sure that the art historian
Is a nice little man somewhere
In the lobes of Hampstead
Tending his own poppies, tending his own cocks.
But I do wish that he would look at my son's picture.
Is that too much to ask?
That the art historian might – might – might – might – might
Look at the picture?

I am Vincent's mother
Come to heal the wounds of art history
So smile a little and let me touch you
And as you gaze into the cornfield
You will find yourself
At the heart of the megalotropolis of London
Sitting still and being calm and seeing
In the skies – as my son saw in the skies –
The soul of tiger.
If you look long enough you might even hear a fieldmouse
Piping: Nought sad about death.

Portrait of Greta Moll

after Henri Matisse

Yea my red panther,
My black and green cat,
In her blue cage
In the Jardins des Plantes
Will she meet me tonight
After work?
Come to a movie with me?
Teach me how to live?

My mouth states it all – states of mouth.
Lips that would not kiss you at the point of a pistol
If they chose not to;
Lips that would kiss you into the grave
If they lipped your lips;
Lips that are as self-sufficient as worms,
Yet as reliant as jam;
Lips attuned to society;
Lips addicted to solitude;
Lips with arms.

I am a working woman –
A very different kettle of fish
To that Madame Moitessier in the next room.
Regardez-moi! Moi!
Done up to the gills in her finery.
She's not a fish. Not even a kettle.
She's a doll
For middle-aged men to play Balthus with.

I am a working woman.
It is not merely for decorum
That I have my sleeves rolled up,
My hair tied up;
That I wear a serviceable blouse;
That I fit into a tight skirt,
My tummy no matter.

346

I am a working woman
With a studio of my own,
A room with a stove.
When I come home
In the evening I fling
My things on the floor,
Put on Nina Simone,
Curl up on the wall
With my man and
If he's a good boy,
Tall, thin, tender,
Teach him a thing or two,
Theology, ecumenics, Hebrew,
Oh yes, and be taught
By him too –
Currency relations, monetary union,
John Maynard Keynes, Adam Smith.

As I recline on the edge of the motorway
After midnight with my head
The wrong side of the yellow margin
On the hard shoulder,
A pint bottle of vodka in my tummy,
I am not troubled by men
In their toy cars racing past
Who might or might not behead me.
I put my right hand in my left hand
And adjusting my hips
Gaze almond-eyed at the stars
Reading their Arabic from right to left,
Orion, the Plough, the Pleiades,
Feeling self-contained.
I am dear – dear to myself –
Dear Greta Moll.

Leisure

after Boris Anrep

I

Scared as I am of a Tom on the wall
I would be infinitely more scared
Of a Wystan on the wall.
Hug a shady wet nun!

II

I love lying up in Loch Ness
The whole day long
Doing nothing,
Just scrutinising my wife's breasts,
Pondering the 2.30 at Ayr.

III

Questions and answers.
Funny things.
If there were answers
There would be no questions.
How could there be?
$E = mc^2$.

IV

Einstein, is it the case with the world
That the Loch Ness Monster, my wife and I
Are all one and the same person?
Not to mention my father?

V

In the bosom of the monster
Lying facedown on a balustrade overlooking Ness
I who carry the century in my slippers.

Much painting to be done, much sculpting,
Much sitting down in the Regency armchair,
Much getting to know the corner of Einstein's Field.

VI

All shall be well
And all manner of thing shall be well
When leisure is the basis of culture
And the novelist wakes up without her husband
Nagging at her to scratch his back or console his coccyx
And the education adds up:
In the name of the mother, the daughter, and the Holy Spirit.

The Mantelpiece

after Edouard Vuillard

Staring into the marble, I stray into it
Exploring its pores, its veins, its stains, its moles.
A block of marble on legs of marble.
Is it a memorial? An altar?
Am I going to die?
Where is she? Will she ever come back?
Who is she? What is her name?
What kind of a woman
Would have an altar for a mantelpiece?
Would rescue a down-and-out at her gate
And put him to sleep in her own bed?

When she does come back in the late afternoon
She does not speak except to exclaim
"It's May!"
She puts a glass vase of Queen Anne's lace
And daisies on the mantelpiece,
A single poppy, a bramble blossom,
Medicine bottles with labels
Prescribing for me when and how to take them.
She reiterates "It's May!"

As if she herself is the month of May.
She gives me a book entitled *Howard's End.*
How does she know that my name is Howard?
She erects a clothes horse
Draping it with white cotton nighties.
I put out a finger with which to trace the marble
But trace her instead – trace her cheekbone.
Is your mantelpiece an altar?
She smiles: Are you my spring lamb?
I am.

That was five and a half years ago.
The world that is the case is everything and new.
O my drowned spring lamb!
O my wild, wild mantelpiece!

A GOOSE IN THE FROST (1995)

to Seamus Heaney in Stockholm, December 1995

In the goose house at night the geese
Scour the walls where the walls meet the floors
For the darkest wainscot; nothing less
Than the darkest wainscot – the darkest deepdown wainscot – will
  do.
Darkness is all. Geese go by the light.

Out of the Caspian Sea the sun is ladder-rattling west
Over the Caucasus, daubing the highlands
Of Armenia with undercoat;
Pebbledashing the Crimea;
Twirling its paintbrush in the fog on the Black Sea;

Dragging its horsehair across the Mediterranean;
Gonging the Aegean; xylophoning the Carpathians;
Trumpeting the Alpes Maritimes in a livid lather.
As shepherds in the Pyrenees – Magi of Transhumance –
Are plucking at the earlobes of their snoozing spouses –

Encore du jour in which to be articulate,
To be rhetorical about sheep's udders,
Wool, and the first *cafés au lait* of the day
Are being brewed in Toulouse and Tarbes –
In the dead silence of first light in Derry

Geese are waking up keening with desire.
The goose house is a cloister
Teeming with tantalising women
Drifting about in the darkness.
Darkness is all. Geese go by the light.

The droppings of ten thousand antecedents
Are the satiny mattress upon which bubble
Spools of goosely desire:
Stirrings in Derry in 1995
Procreate a thirtieth-century Armenian goose.

353

They are shuffling their feathers to order;
Bump to the goose house door to queue up
For the light – to queue up and to peel off
At the altar rail of the half-door when the bolt
Is yanked back; goose, gander, gosling –

In that order – file out, turn right,
Trundle down aisle between nettle stalks of Childhood;
Straight on out under the arch of Adolescence;
Left along the gauntlet to the weeping willow of Adulthood;
Right through the wrought-iron garden gate

Into the Front Garden of Infancy.
What are we? Vehicles of memory,
Long memory, capacious with curiosity;
Queue-maestros in file swaying along skylines;
Males oozing at our orifices with hegemony;

Airbuses zigzagging across ocean floors.
Grass. At last. First, light; secondly, grass.
A passion for grass. But this daybreak –
Frost. White host
Focusing out of gold monstrance of sunrise.

God with his mother's milk in a spiky halo.
Am I in the correct crèche? The correct oratory?
Whatever I had made allowance for,
I had not made allowance for this.
What kind of oasis is an oasis with no grass?

What is this nuptial froth that the priests call frost?
This pabulum that weighs so ponderously
On the souls of snowdrops?
Oh, and indeed, and aye, I make a wee bit of a fuss;
A wee bit of a rumpus.

I throb, shudder, squawk; flap
My wings; stump about my spouse;
Gossip to my goslings but almost
Instantly slide out of my kneeler
To roost in God's semen,

The eucharistic seed.
I sink down deep into frost
With my fury in my breast;
Rock with exuberance in it;
I who never lusted after frost

Nor had beak know-how of frost;
Who navigated only for grass –
Smooth-stalked grass geese dream of –
See myself at sea in the frost;
A goose in the frost

The day the earth stands still:
A goose is a flying saucer beached
In a white field circled by Magi;
A goose – to look you in the eye –
Squints slant.

The end of poetry is innocence:
A child in the sun;
One who knows how to take his time.
My project is to be placid which I am.
Wherefore I disintegrate with rectitude in the rising sun.

Fore and aft in frost
I peer out over the prow of my soul;
Focus my prehistoric eyes;
Dip my beak in particulars;
Suck crystals; daydream

A goose I knew,
The goldenest goose in goosedom,
Who asphyxiated of loneliness
In a basement room
In St Stephen's Green;

Who is interred
In a common grave
In Glasnevin
Under lager cans, used condoms;
Who is gesticulating to me

From the shore like a goose girl
With his dog-collar round her wrist
Waving to the conscience-chasmed priest
Upon the waters of Goldengrove,
A neck in a punt.

He in the treetops, a drowned man spinning,
Beholds her green eyes bloom;
A goose girl in her fourteenth year
Be the snowdrop of Elysium;
Let my ego die.

Harry, Deirdre, John, Christiane
Feeding crumbs to the geese;
Circling the soul of Father Hopkins;
The star-struck loneliness of man.
Afternoon tea in the Shelbourne.

Goose girl – goodbye,
Teach me to see.
How to sow my vow.
How to die.
How to say Goodbye

With a smile on my beak.
How not to cry
As with gauche élan
Wolves circle my soul.
Darkness is all. Geese go by the light.

Hotel Wales, Madison Avenue, New York/
La Louveterie, Puyvert, Vaucluse

CHRISTMAS DAY (1996)

from *Christmas Day*

[· · ·]

The skin on my face
Is beige and my hair is grey
From woman-hunger.
For days the phone
Does not ring and then
When it does and I run
To snatch it up
The shy, reticent voice
Of a woman in the South Island,
New Zealand, whispers
"I'd like to knit you a woolly hat
But I don't know
What is between those ears of yours."
To live alone
Is not to know
One day from the next:
Letting myself in
And out of the house;
Tramping the streets
With my skull on my neck
And with my hand in my pocket
Twiddling my house key.
Christmas is the Feast of St Loneliness.
I streetwalk at night
Looking in the windows
Of other people's houses
Assessing their Christmas decorations,
Marking them out of ten.
This Christmas I have spotted
In the front window of a three-storey
Town house in Percy Place
A little Christmas tree
Adorned only
With electric candles.
I give it eight out of ten.
What amazes me this Christmas

Is all the menorahs.
Menorahs are all the craze.
Every second window in Ringsend
Has a menorah. Oh, Sharon,
Your menorah is only gorgeous.
Don't be talking, Deborah.

[· · ·]

Frank is proud of himself.
I am proud of Frank.
He has not only prepared the feast
But he has set the table.
The set table
Which is the city of God
According to Manuel Bandeira
In Santa Teresa,
Rio de Janeiro.
Napkins
& skyscrapers.
Condiments
& flyovers.
Frank says grace:
"He hath showed thee, O man,
What is good;
And what does the Lord require of thee
But to do justly, and to love mercy,
And to walk humbly with thy God."
In the middle of the table
Centre-stage
Perches a miniature Christmas Tree –
Plastic –
With a candle inside it.
In silence we stare at it –
At the minuscule flame of candlelight flickering
With all around it the black lacy tide foaming in –
Our four eyes peering at the embryo of flame
As well as at each last penultimate wave breaking –
All these peregrinations and perambulations of peripheries.
Frank whispers: "Where is my cigarette lighter?"
With a cigarette – Silk Cut

(He is trying to stay off
The Benson & Hedges)
Dangling from the corner of his mouth
He dotes on all this food and plenty
Which he – and he alone –
Has put on the table.
He proclaims: "Lash into it."

We run around the table,
Flap our wings, get down
Into low chairs. Our Adam's apples
Chug into port. Two turkeys
Sitting down to Christmas Dinner
In excitement, yet grief,
Mindful of our case histories –
The Turkey Sheds
That so many of our contemporaries
Did not survive.
Two-faced padlocks.
In wet twilight
All those thousands of pink gobs
Black with fright.

[· · ·]

"Tea or coffee, Mr D?"
"I'm all right, Frank."
"For the love of Scobie, Paul,
Will you stop being so polite –
It does not become you.
The horriblest git in Ireland
Is that murderous little archimatect,
Carleton O'Flaherty.
We are agreed on that.
That baldy little satyr
From Mulhuddart, ensconced
In his solar pad in Shrewsbury Road
With his two Doberman Pinschers
And his five wives
Who all went to Mount Anville.
We all went to Mount Anville

You can hear them screeching
From the rooftops of Shrewsbury Road.
We all went to Mount Anville
And took a degree in sociology
In UCD.
You could do with a little
Murder in your soul, Paul.
Now, you can have any kind
Of coffee your intestines crave:
Maxwell House Instantaneous
Or Bewley's Groundswoman –
I do a mischievous
Blend of slinky Costa Rica
And husky French Roast –
Or you can have chaste Barry's Tea
Or Early Grey
Or Tardy Breakfast
Or even Breaking Orange Pekoe
Or Twig Smithereens."
"I'll have a cup of hot water."
"By the hokey, Mr D,
You are an exotic creature."
When I fish out from my breast pocket
A teabag of herbal –
Rose Hip –
And slip it
Into the cup of hot water
Frank raises his eyebrows
Higher than I have seen
Anyone's eyebrows ever go –
So high I begin to see
His eyebrows scuttling about
The wainscotting of his scalp
Between his forehead and hairline.
When I scoop out the teabag
And drop it in the ashtray –
An Eiffel Tower ashtray from Paris –
He snatches it and holds it up
To the light like a mad cat
With a mouse by the tail,
His eyes all teeth a-glittery;

Swinging my teabag
By its limp G-string;
"What have we got here?"
After a brief, hot struggle
With my anger and shame,
My whining *amour propre*,
I see that he is not a catatonic cat
But a fifty-year-old child
Luxuriating in astoundment –
He has never before in his life seen
A herbal tea-drinking male of the species.
"Rose Hip – you don't tell me!"
He murmurs over and over
Like Lord Tennyson making love
To his chambermaid:
"Rose Hip – you don't tell me!"

[· · ·]

GREETINGS TO OUR FRIENDS IN BRAZIL (1999)

Greetings to Our Friends in Brazil

I

On the Friday night before the last Sunday in September
I got a phone call from Father Patrick O'Brien, CC, in
    Kilmeena, Co Mayo
Inviting me to drive over to his house on Sunday afternoon
And watch the All Ireland Football Final on television,
Mayo against Kerry.
He told me that he had to say the eleven o'clock Mass in
    Kilmeena
But that after Mass he would be free for the day:
We could drive into Westport, have lunch at the Asgard on the
    Quay,
Drive back to his house in time to watch the match.

His invitation solved the problem of the weekend.
I was staying thirty miles away in Dugort on Achill Island
In a cottage with no television – an ex-soldier's outpost
On the side of a mountain – a German soldier
Who had fought on both fronts.
Like everyone else in Mayo and Kerry
I was keen to see the match. On the Saturday night
After answering a pile of letters –
After slicing the top off the pile –
I went to my bed an expectant, contented man –
Army surplus bed, cast-iron frame, wire springs.
Tomorrow would be a day of affection as well as of rest:
An authentic Sabbath;
No politics;
No jealousy or rivalry;
Lunch and conversation with a compatible man
And – in the Asgard on Westport Quay!
I'd never been in the Asgard before!
And then the centrepiece of the day, the highlight of the year,
    the big match.
Watching it in the comfort of the fireside of Father O'Brien's
    study.
Coasting sleepwards I got to thinking –

If I manage to get up at any kind of reasonably early hour
    tomorrow
I might also catch beforehand the eleven o'clock Mass.

II

As I drove up the hill to Kilmeena parish church – the holy
    mountain
Of Croagh Patrick asleep on its back on the skyline in blue
    pencil outline –
God on his back asleep under a haycock –
Early-morning elders out on the golf links at Carraholly –
Their seminaked wives in sunglasses in patio chairs –
All the Susannahs of Fahy –
The bell was tolling three minutes to eleven.
I jumped out of the car, not even bothering to lock it.
Not even bothering to roll up the driver's window.
I felt like a man without a care in the world.

I was surprised by the atmosphere in the chapel:
Devout but without
The normal social hypocrisies of Sunday church attendance.
Country people engrossed in the present tense:
Stallion with mare; mare with foal;
Cocks on the verges of fantasies;
All the hens in their pews cackling "Shhsh-shhsh";
Ultra-orthodox guinea hens negatively not shrieking;
Geese in their grey greatness;
The future not a chimera but a possibility;
The past not a millstone but a life raft.
All of us being toasted by electric fires high up on the walls:
All of us gazing altarwards at the stained-glass window of
    Mother and Child –
The Gold Madonna of Mayo.

The bell tolls again, the congregation stands up,
Enter the tiny procession
Of three altar boys in white surplices
Being shepherded by the celebrant in green-and-red chasuble.
The stocky quiet man I had known for twenty years
In that instant became a prophet of the Lord.

He shed his years and spoke in a strong voice –
A young, lifeboat coxswain's voice
Reeking of daring;
Every inflection, every gesture
Effected a rescue of innocence:
Not so much as an iota of unctuousness
Or melodrama or power-tripping or patronage
Or Uncle Tomming or craw-thumping or Musha, God Help
    Us.

III

It was the Twenty-Sixth Sunday in Ordinary Time.
A small boy read from The Book of Numbers:
How the spirit came down on two men who missed Mass –
Eldad and Medad. "Me Dad" the little boy pronounced it.
"If only the whole people of the Lord were prophets,
And the Lord gave his Spirit to them all."
A small girl read from the letter of St James:
A message for the well-off;
"On earth you have had a life of comfort and luxury;
In the time of slaughter you went on eating to your heart's
    content.
It was you who condemned the innocent and killed them:
They offered you no resistance."

Father O'Brien waded to the lectern.
In the cadences of the shoulders
Of the dead fishermen of the islands of Mayo –
The drowned kings of the roads of Clew Bay –
He read out his sermon:
The sheepdogs of his words pricking their ears
To the pitch of his soul's whistling;
Slow, easy-going, rope-narrow cadences
Humping on their broad, gleaming shoulders
Hundreds of little children with big, wide eyes;
The sprightly and the handicapped;
Every time I looked up at Father O'Brien
He seemed to be getting younger by the paragraph.
He looked like a drowning man who had no fear of
    drowning;

His enthusiasm tipping its red forelock to nobody;
The cliff-high, forest-roaring, tiger-snarling sea
Of rip currents cowered under his words.

He spoke of his friend who had died in a plane crash, John
 Feeney:
Of how when John Feeney had been editor of *The Irish Catholic*
His editorials had so displeased the Archbishop of Dublin –
His Grace John Charles McQuaid –
Feeney plagiarised the letter of St James for his next editorial;
St James would be an imprimatur
That would not only suffice but impress;
Copied it verbatim but without quotation marks.
The Archbishop of Dublin slashed a red marker pen through
 the entire editorial.
James – Father O'Brien told us – is the leading editorial of
 Christianity.

IV

We had a good, honest lunch in the Asgard sitting up at the bar:
Chowder, plaice, chips, whiskey, ginger ale, coffee.
Invoking old friends; Tony O'Malley, Brendan Kennelly, John
 Moriarty.
We got back to his house in good time for the preliminaries:
The teams one by one tumbling out onto the park –
Young bulls in their groiny primes
Charging out the tunnel into the arena of their fate.
Bouncing up and down in the silky greensward.
Trying out their tails; bucking their butts.
Draining their nostrils; tossing their horns.
Spitting. Sniffing. Swearing.
Revving. Jiving. Cartwheeling.
The teams getting their photographs taken;
The parade, the mime-singing of the national anthem.
Father O'Brien lit a turf fire and brought in a tray of coffee;
The four walls of his study decorated
With photographs and postcards and prints
And paintings with antiquely wrought cobwebs on their frames,
And the blinds drawn, and the television working.

Getting good television pictures, we turned down the
     volume –
The diligent Ger Canning churning out clichés –
And, marrying radio sound to television picture,
We tuned in to the radio commentary
By the cordial Kerry maestro Mícheál Ó Muircheartaig.
"We send greetings to you all from Djakarta down to
     Crossmolina
And the ball goes to Kenneth Mortimer having a great game
     for Mayo
He has a brother doing research work on the Porcupine Bank
But now it goes to Killian Burns of Kerry
The best accordion-playing cornerback in football today.
We hope you're on the astra if you're in outer space.
On my watch it says two minutes and fifty-three seconds left
     but
We haven't had time to send greetings to our friends in Brazil
Proinnsias O Murchu and Rugierio da Costa e Silva."

We watched our native Mayo get defeated yet again,
Commiserated with each other.
A few last parting words about Steiner's *Errata*,
George Steiner's autobiography
Which Father O'Brien had read on the Westport train on
     Wednesday.
Father O'Brien whispered: "He's very good on Israel."
I blurted: "Can you recommend a commentary on the Bible?"
Father O'Brien put his finger to his lips and ran upstairs
And came running back downstairs with a disintegrating
     tome:
"If it is any use to you, you can borrow my Jerome."
He walked me to my car in the grave-digging rain,
Clouds with broad black brushes
Smearing the white vellum of the sky,
Gales brewing their hysterias.
Wishing each other well for the winter months ahead.
Counselling one another with tears and smiles.
Encouraging one another.
See you again next summer.
We embraced goodbye.

On the Siberian, Saharan, Gobi drive back to Achill Island
I stopped at Burrishoole to give a lift
To a small, middle-aged woman standing alone
On the edge of the road in the grieving storm.
She looked like a bat at nightfall in a doorway
Under the lintel hovering
"In darkness and secrecy and loneliness."
Her arranged lift had fallen through.
She said: Do you mind if I smoke?
I said: I don't mind at all.
Actually, I minded fearfully:
Cigarette smoke nauseates me in the gut.
She was smoking Sweet Afton
The name of which I have to admit I do savour.
She also had been watching the match but to my consternation
Far from being dejected she was cheerful –
Cheerful for having watched it. We discussed players.
She furling and unfurling her green-and-red scarf;
Fondling her green-and-red flag in her lap.
We agreed Kenneth Mortimer had a powerful game.
The sensitive subject of Liam MacHale had barely been
      broached
Before the rain teemed so hard I could not see out the wind-
      screen –
My wipers flailing in ecstatic futility –
And I had to stop the car in the middle of a red bog that looked
As if it were turning white in the storm.
She put a hand on my shoulder and a little finger on my cheek.
She smiled: I hope you don't mind me saying so
But you have got a bushy left eyebrow and there seems
To be a baby spider caught up in the fibres.

I said: Thank you.
She said: I hope you don't mind me saying so but you look quite
      depressed.
I said: I take Seroxat.
She said: Never mind the Seroxat.
I said: Do I look that bad?
She said: Look at me!

I said: I'm looking at you.
She announced: I'm destitute!
She smiled the wry grimace of an angel in Los Angeles
Who's been around in the western world for a long time:
A smile as accustomed to a fireside chair
As to a hard wooden bench against the wall;
A smile only the tippy-toes of whose feet
Are apparent at the end of the couch;
A smile with which you cannot tell
Whether the smiler is laughing or crying;
A smile bent double in January woods
In long, blue, denim skirt,
White blouse, black stockings,
Black patent leather shoes,
Long, black overcoat,
Picking posies of snowdrops
For brave, nameless women in mortal combat with cancer;
For brave, nameless men in mortal combat with cancer.

I drove on and she didn't speak again for the rest of the journey.
At the bend in the road outside Achill Sound she asked to get
    out.
Glancing up at the sky, she remarked: Himself is at home –
I have a whole family to feed and to clothe.
I said: Boys or girls? She said: Seven girls and two boys.
I dug thumb and forefinger into my breast pocket
And fished out a note.
Hovering in the shelter of a small oak with rhododendrons she
    said:
Goodbye. God bless – I said. God bless you – she said.
For the remaining nine miles I held on to the driving wheel
As if it were the microphone on the bridge of a ship going down;
Going over the tops of the crests of the blanket bogs;
Navigating Bunnacurry, Gowlawaum, Bogach Bawn;
Muttering as if my life depended on it:
Greetings to our friends in Brazil.

VI

Landed in the German soldier's cottage
On the side of the big mountain

373

Between the mountain stream and the roadside fuchsia
I light a turf fire and sit on the sofa
With my hands joined across my stomach.
On the last Sunday in September
For the first time in years
I feel no craving:
Not for food not for drink not for anything.
Not for grapes.
Not for newspaper not for book.
Not for radio not for television not for telephone.
I hear the tempest o'er the mountains and the seas.
I hear the silence of the spheres.
I see two hundred million pairs of shut eyes
Of two hundred million sleeping faces
Behind two hundred million windows in the warring night.
Only the dead are not homeless.
Each to their layers of skins.
Each to caravans on hard edges.
Each to their pigeonhole in the dovecote.
Each to their breeze-block in the estate.
Each to their liftshaft in the tower block.
Each to their cardboard in the doorway.
Each to their roost in the ashram.
Each to their cabin on the mountain.
I hear sheep baa-baaing to sheep on the mountainside:
Genocide, genocide.
I hear ravens diving the peaks:
Ethnic cleansing, ethnic cleansing.
I hear tied-up terriers barking:
Thoughtlessness, thoughtlessness.
I hear Father O'Brien at my side at my ear:
His exegesis of the word *mercy* –
Its Aramaic etymology;
"Mercy is by definition exclusively divine.
Mercy is a divine, not a human term."
I feel ready to go to bed.
Let me pray:
Greetings to our friends in Brazil.

25 October 1997

Recife Children's Project, 10 June 1995

Crèche Nossa Senhora Dos Remedios
Inaugurada Com Missa Solene Por
Dom Helder Camara
No Dia 22 De Outubro De 1978

On a Saturday afternoon in Recife, humid, grey,
An aimiable Englishman, Eddie Edmundson,
A linguist whose father was a clogger in Clitheroe –
"An eddy of semantic scruples," he was later to say –
Drove me out into the suburbs and shantytowns
To visit Father Frank Murphy, Holy Ghost missionary,
Founder of the Recife Children's Project:
A seventy-year-old County Wexford priest
Who has organised a school for the children of mothers
Who have no choice but to work on the streets
Selling their bodies for shelter and food.
Father Murphy was proud of his *crèche* –
That's what he calls it, his *crèche* –
But mostly what he wanted to talk about was poetry.

In the dying day darkening by the edges
Of a concrete pond of black, red-headed swans
In virgin jungle in north-west Recife
That agèd, placid Wexfordman lifted his sore head
Skywards past coconut trees, quoting
In all its meticulous intricacy,
"Rage for Order" by Derek Mahon.
When he had done, giving the thumbs-up sign,
He put his hand on my shoulder:
"This is what we do in Brazil."
Driving back into the *centro* of Recife
Past "scorched gable ends and burnt-out buses"
We drove in silence until I declared
"We have spent this afternoon with Che Guevara."
Eddie the Englishman said: "Yes . . .
Yes, I know exactly what you mean, you are right."

Father Frank Murphy, founder of the Recife Children's Project,
Thirty years working in the streets of Recife,
For whom poetry is reality, reality poetry,
Who does not carry a gun,
Who does not prattle about politics or religion,
Whose sign is the thumbs-up sign of Brazil,
Who puts his hand on your shoulder saying
"This is what we do in Brazil."
Che? Frank!
No icon he –
Revolutionary hero of the twentieth century.

Self-Portrait '95

Paul Durcan would try the patience of the Queen of Tonga.
When he was in Copacabana he was homesick for
    Annaghmakerrig;
When he got back to Annaghmakerrig
He was homesick for Copacabana.

The Last Shuttle to Rio

to Patrick Early

It's been a bad day in São Paulo.

Paulistas have a saying –
"Life is a game of the hips"
But today my hips have had a bad game.
My knees have been up to the mark
But my hips have been pathetic.

Standing up at the counter of the café
In the airport at Congonhas,
Stirring my coffee with my right hand,
Holding my mobile phone in my left hand,
I am whispering to my publisher;

Whispering in low, steadfast, tightlipped whines
"Why were my books not there?"
"Where were my books?"
"Why was Ivan Kerr in Belo Horizonte
When he was supposed to be in São Paulo?"

Through the condensed perspiration of my hysterical whispers
I discern a small, lean, nine-year-old black boy
With a shoebox on his shoulder pointing down at my shoes.
Yet another intrusion in a day of multiple intrusions.
I bounce my skull angrily: *Sim, sim, sim.*
Hopping the ball of my skull off the tiled floor of my anger.

I resume berating my publisher
Immediately erasing from my mind
The shoeshine boy kneeling at my feet
Until I feel a tapping at my knee.
"What do you want now?"
He wants my left foot.
He's done with my right.

I glimpse the frills of his jet-black hair.
Perfect frills –
Perfectly formed pasta frills.
What a shine he is giving me!
For the first time today
I feel a pang of well-being.

All the while he is polishing me
He is watching me
With hot, scooped eyes staring up
Out of his yellow T-shirt
Inscribed PACIFIC WAVES.
I am no longer abusing
My hurting publisher.
The shoeshine boy is sprinting.
He is putting his right arm into it.
Putting everything into his right arm.
Putting everything into his rag.

He leaps to his feet.
He has finished. He squashes
A coke tin in his small fist.
I beg my publisher's forgiveness.
I hang up,
Clipping my mobile
Back on to my hip.
I thank him for giving me
Such a brilliant shine.
I say: "*Obrigado.*"
He replies with a shy shrug:
"*De nada.*"

My God, you have made
My day in São Paulo
And you have the audacity
To reply "*De nada*".

With your shoebox on your shoulder
You repeat with unconditional candour
"*De nada*"
Gazing up unblinking into my eyes.

I stutter: "What is your name?"
Out of your mouth-womb
Leaps your divine name:
"Einstein! Einstein João Luis Soares!"

Samambaia

Living in the clouds in Brazil
Or living in the clouds in Ireland
Is vast of a vastness –

Fern
Behind whose face paint
My Indian eyes blink.

Night is day:
Nothing stays the same.
Everything changes.

Sunlight is rain:
Nothing should stay the same.
Everything should change.

If you love her
You will never
Take her for granted

Nor will you think twice
If the choice
Is between love and fame.

I, Elizabeth,
Do take you, Lota,
For my lawful, wedded cloud.

The Geography of Elizabeth Bishop

There is a life before birth
On earth – oh yes, on earth –
And it is called Brazil.
Call it paradise, if you will.

Reared in New England, Nova Scotia,
I was orphaned in childhood.
Despite the fastidiousness of aunts
I could know myself only as an alien –
An authority of courtesy –
Until aged forty on a voyage round Cape Horn
I stepped off in Rio, stayed, discovered
My mind in Brazil. Became again an *infanta*!
A thinking monkey's *compañero*!
Fed, cuddled, above all needed.
In the treetops of Samambaia
I made a treehouse;

In Ouro Prêto I made a nest
In a niche in a cliff in a valley
Of nineteen golden churches.

At forty I discovered that my voice –
That cuckoo hymen of mine, mine, mine –
Was a Darwinian tissue:
That in God's *cinéma vérité*
I was an authentic *bocadinho*.

Back in Boston, a late-middle-aged lady,
I became again an orphan,
Put on orphan uniform,
Endured the timetable of the orphanage –
All these invigilators sliding
In and out their Venetian blinds
With not a baby elephant in sight
Nor chimp nor toucan nor parakeet.
I stilled the pain with alcohol
And with self-pity – in spite
Of which, death waxed merciful.

There is a life before birth
On earth – oh yes, on earth –
And it is called Brazil.
Call it paradise, if you will.

The Daring Middle-Aged Man on the Flying Trapeze

to Munira Mutran

The sort of travel I'm into nowadays in São Paulo
Is going to bed early with my wife,
Staying in bed late in the mornings with my wife.
However, when I heard that on June 16
In Finnegans Pub in São Paulo
A Japanese actor would be declaiming in Portuguese
Extracts from *Ulysses*
My wife persuaded me to fly with her to Dublin.

380

I remonstrated with her: "Dublin? *Fly* with you?"
She insisted: "Dublin is a gas,
Dirty, ordinary, transcendental city – just like São Paulo!"

We stayed in the YWCA in Sandymount –
Radcliffe Hall in St John's Road:
£13 per person sharing for a chalet
In the rose garden behind the Hall.
I liked the Hall because it was beside
Not only the Martello Tower on Sandymount Strand
But the Church of Ireland in St John's Road
Which is so C of E
It makes the Roman Catholic Church
On the far side of Sandymount Village –
The Star of the Sea –
Appear Low – so very Low!
Myself, I am Brazilian Armenian Orthodox.
(Last year I had some of my ashes buried in Armenia
After my left leg was amputated below the knee
Following an accident during Carnaval –
A loose nut on my trapeze.)

I liked Radcliffe Hall most of all for the rose garden:
Kingsize, queensize double beds of roses;
Red roses, white roses, yellow roses.
At midnight – 9 p.m. São Paulo time –
We sat out in the rose garden under a Howth moon
Listening to motor traffic – the Japanese actor
Declaiming *Ulysses* in Portuguese
In Finnegans Pub in São Paulo –
The rose petals staggering off their stems.

I sat with my hands on my knees
(I have still got my *two* knees)
Thinking how simple a thing peace is
In spite of man's addiction to war.
Although I am a middle-aged man on one leg,
When my wife asked –
Will you walk me along Sandymount Strand –
Actually, what she said was
"Let's check out the modality of the visible" –

I said "Yes" and I saw her –
I saw her quite simply, clearly, wholly –
Skip down the strand ahead of me,
Her meagre, white blouse billowing,
Her brown shoulders gleaming.
I thought:
James Joyce is the only man in the world who comprehends
    women;
Who comprehends that a woman can never be adumbrated,
Properly praised
Except by a Japanese actor
In Finnegans Pub in São Paulo
Declaiming extracts from *Ulysses*.

Jack Lynch

to Mike Murphy

Jack Lynch is an accountant in Rio.
Born in São Paulo in 1939
Of a first generation Brazilian, middle-class father from Ballinasloe
Who was devoured by a mulatta working-class goddess.
His father had him christened Jack because he liked the black
    look of him.
If he hadn't liked the black look of him he'd have called him
    Claude.
(His father divided up the human race into Jacks and Claudes.)
Jack made his home in Rio thirty-odd years ago.

Nothing happens in Rio that Jack Lynch doesn't know about.
Yesterday I sat with him in a cardboard shack
In a shantytown in Rio and listened to him
Tell the wide-eyed chisellers about his own daughter
Jumping off the top of Corcovado.
(His daughter is a champion hang-glider.)
He shakes his head, holding back the tears:
"I can't say I'm not proud of her."
The slum kids offer him handfuls of grime
Crying out to him – tell us it again.

Today it's the same story.
Only this time we're on the patio
Of the private members' bar
At the Golf Clube 10 kilometres west of Rio
Gazing up at yet another Sugarloaf Mountain
With yet another shantytown adhering to its precipices
And from whose peak his daughter
Has jumped off in her hang-glider.
Back in Rio at twilight walking the Red Beach
Under the Sugarloaf Mountain at Urca
Just when I think there's nothing more
He can tell me about his hang-gliding daughter
He points a finger up at a cliff-rim –
His daughter has been known to ride a motorbike
Along the edge of the cliff.

Jack, what do you mean –
"Along the edge of the cliff"?
He explains about a two-foot wide rim.
Anyway . . . that's another thing his daughter does:
She rides motorbikes along narrow spaces
On the tops of things – cliffs, roofs, parapets.
It's not just that Jack Lynch lives on another planet:
It's that Jack Lynch is himself another planet.
Jack Lynch is a Brazilian who lives in Brazil.
The slum kids offer him handfuls of grime
Crying out to him – tell us it again.

The Chicago Waterstone's

I'm your girlfriend from the past
And I'm always thinking of you.

When you're revisiting her city
On your twenty-two-city reading tour to promote
Your latest, barcoded,
Extracted-with-great lethargy
Volume which your ingenious publicists advertise as
"The most accessible poetry

Since Mallarmé"
She leaves a message at your hotel,
The Chicago Ramada.
With your mouth in your heart
You make haste to phone her
Only to get her answer machine:
Her voice is throatier, darker,
More intimate, yet more formal than before.
She commands you to leave a message after the tone.

Next day you meet her in the restaurant
Of the Art Institute of Chicago
And after you have ejaculated –
Excessively as always –
Over Caillebotte's
Rainy Day, Paris
She tells you how marvellous you look –
That you haven't changed in ten years
In spite of your grey hair and bifocal lenses.
For five seconds you believe her.
She drops names like a rabbit on a rampage:
"Saw Simmons last week in NY. How's Carson?"
She condescends to refer to your new book
As if you were a neurotic travelling salesman
Which in fact of course is what you are.
She simply yearns to know about its title
A Snail in My Prime:
"I simply yearn to know
Why did you call it
A Snail in My Prime?
Does it allude to an artwork?
Perhaps a *hommage* to Matisse?"
She yodels: "It resonates with allusion."
She enquires about the reading tonight
In the Chicago Waterstone's.
Brandishing her eyelashes
And pulling down tight
Her Greenpeace T-shirt
Over her Anti-Global Warming breasts
She enthuses: "I will be there."

But when you're getting up to go
And you're kissing her on both cheeks
Just a little bit too fervently
She confides that she's not a hundred per cent sure
If she can actually make it tonight
"Because of a priority engagement
And you know what priority engagements are like,
I guess."

I do. I guess I do.
In the Spring of 1985
When I was the Robert Frost Fellow
In Franconia, New Hampshire
And she was my Monitor
And I was sitting out on the porch
Doing my best to do nothing
As prescribed by the master,
The Old Silkworm Frost,
Scanning Mount Lafayette,
The Notch beyond the maples,
The Dragon in the Fog,
She whispered acoustically
Like an Arabist
Deciphering the Koran
"You have such – such
Goddamn-turquoise eyes"
And as I blushed like a baboon –
Like a baboon's bottom –
Gravely she enquired
"May I comb your ponytail?"
And while I dilly-dallied
She plopped her anchor
Into my shallow waters,
Her chic, little, five-clawed, Tiffany's grapnel.

At the reading in the Chicago Waterstone's
There is not a sign of her.
You scan the empty chairs.
Every time the door behind you opens
You glance around. It dawns
On you what she had in mind

385

And there is nothing you can do but wince,
Wince through the reading,
Wince back to the hotel,
Sit up in bed late into the night wincing;
Draining your bladder;
The Chicago Waterstone's;
Draining your bladder;
The Robert Frost Silk Farm;
Draining your bladder;
At the airport in the morning wince;
At O'Hare wince;
Wince & wince & wince & wince & wince & wince;
Wincing all the way back to Shannon;
Wincing in Shannon in the dark before the dawn;
Wincing into Dublin in the rain at 7.30 a.m.;
Wincing in the long-term car park;
Wincing all the way back the road to Slane
To the home of your 1995 girlfriend
Who looks up from her book *Wild Swans*
And says "Oh – it's you."

I'm your girlfriend from the past
And I'm always thinking of you.

Remote Control

In the summer of '97 I lost my remote control
And it ruined my summer and all belonging to me.

I reported to the woman at the counter of Multichannel.
She looked so severe I was slow to speak to her.
I stammered: "I have – I have lost my remote control."

She, all her bones like fish undulating underwater,
Her eyes swooping like kites,
Her breasts kicking up dust under her blue blouse,

She replied: "I can find you a remote control."
I said: "But it's lashing rain outside."
She flung up the counter hatch and strode out in a red pelmet
    mini,

All thirty-odd years of her, with a striped golfing umbrella.
She strode out into the streets of Drogheda
Where the River Boyne had already burst its banks.

She strode across the flooded street – the mud
Flecking her white legs with black sequins,
Her high heels pricking the puddles.

She jumped into a white '97 Seat Ibiza and signalled
For me to jump in beside her.
She drove up the town and into the Lourdes Hospital.

"There is a man up here with a remote control like yours
But he doesn't need it anymore."
She flew into the hospital under the feathers of her stripes.

Back down at the counter of Multichannel
I signed a receipt for the dead man's remote control.
I asked her: "Was it cancer?"

"Yes" – she sighed – "it was cancer, cancer of the bowel.
Cancer is all over the shop.
I think you will have more luck with his remote control."

I have had a lot more luck with his remote control.
Dr Patrick Nugent says he's never seen me looking so well:
"What any man needs is a good woman and buckets of
        television."

Yes, and the way it is now on bright, warm, September mornings
Before even I get out of bed the television
In the corner of my bedroom is beseeching to be switched on

Especially on Saturday mornings at 9 a.m.;
Channel 4's morning racing preview;
John McCririck in Big Top form: tick-tack; good going.

A good woman is a Jewish jeweller.
Beyond words are good women
Bejewelling telephone lines.

Never before has it felt so good to be alive
Thanks to the woman at the counter of Multichannel;
Her politics, her technique, her take it-or-leave-it audacity.

In the autumn of '97 I was gifted another man's remote control
And it made my autumn, and all belonging to me.

Dirty Day Derry

When I ask the young widow for a cylinder of gas
She laughs: "Have you chained up your empty?"
She loves to be able to say that to me.
"Have you chained up your empty?"

As outside in the street in the storm
In which people are crouching to keep on their feet
And umbrellas are lying dead in the gutter
Turned inside out –

Although the young widow's heart lies a-bleeding,
She folds her arms under her bust and peers out
The window over the stacked cornflakes laughing at me –
An older man chaining up his empty.

I know all about boys and girls:
About gas, about chains, about empties.

Island Musician Going Home

after Veronica Bolay

Driving home alone the bog road at night in the rain
Leaving the village behind me, its harbour lights
Pegging down the marquee of the sea,
I am half sunk by the stone of my heart.

Mile after mile of bog road in the night in the rain,
Not a single dwelling on the mountain either side of the road,

Not knowing when a mountain sheep will light up under my
     wheels,
My audience all couples canoodling behind in the village.

But when I drive up to the maroon-painted five-barred gate
And I switch off my lights, and I climb out of my car,
And I can see nothing, and I can hear nothing,
I see again that home is the skirl of silence.

I kiss the darkness, and all loneliness abandons me.
A life without a wife is nothing to boast about
But that's music. I walk back up the road
Kissing the darkness; and a small mouth of cold gold

In the clouds is becoming aware of its soul.

Thistles

I

Middle-aged lovers –
Gossips brand us.
We blush.
How I wish
We could have had children of our own!

Instead the field outside our bedroom window
Is a roofless crèche of thistles:
A homeless thistle for every child we might have had;
A tattoo of embryos
Whose fingernails have never been cut.

As we grow older
We make love more easily –
Polythenely, polythenely –
Throwing caution to the nitpickers at the gates
And to the crawthumpers in their charabancs.
I teach you Chinese boxing.
You teach me Thai.
You arm wrestle me and, as always, win.

Kicking up clouds of thistledown,
Washed up on our pillows,
Circled round
By seven or eight vases of sweet pea,
We glimpse the winds reap
The practical consequences of our spirit combat –
The prickly, theoretical ghosts of our might-have-been
    children.

II

Lopes
Our hardy neighbour
Old Farmer God
With ashplant stick
Slashing the skulls off our thistles.
In the wake of his wellington boots
Transports of headless urchins
Skulk in our field
With their tiny, green, boney fists twined
In polythene bouquets
In front of their big, bloated, empty bellies
Beseeching us for a life we cannot give to them.

III

Dearest, when you catch me by surprise tonight
At a corner of twilight;
When you step out from behind a screen of dusk
Between bathroom and bedroom;
When between window shutter and wardrobe mirror
You take the pins out of your hair;
When at your dressing table
You pluck out your spikey earrings;
When on top of your chest of drawers
You lay out your amethyst rings;
When on your floor
You throw down your keys
And step out of your skirt,
Your wrap-around skirt;
When from the hook on the back of the door

You hoist on one hand
Your white silk nightdress;
While our ghost progeny hold their breath;
I am going to ask you to dance with me
Upside down on the Ceiling of Old Age –
On the Floor of First Infancy.

IV

When Old Farmer God asks me
"Do you not know
That thistles are an offence?"
I am going to stand on my head
And wreath my feet around your neck
And wait for your fingers to nip
Down my shinbones into my thighs
And there will be a silence
In which we will hear only
Ourselves crying out one another's names
And the actual grinding of the original sugar cane
And the juice spewing down the chute
And a rush of thistledown accumulating
To percolate out down across the field
And the clatter of its seed seeding itself,
All that genetic *tohu-bohu*,
All that pedigree *ruaille buaille*,
All that metaphysical *brouhaha*.

We will go down into sleep –
Be it in war or peace –
To a sitting-down-from-hunger ovation
From our might-have-been children:
Their keen-eyed, gratuituous, omniscient, exhausted applause.

October Break (Lovers)

I

She and I are sitting out in the conservatory
Of the Renvyle House Hotel in Connemara,
Recommended to me by John McGahern,
On a bright October afternoon, rain
Milking down on the glass roof.
After the waitress has brought us out
A tray of coffee and scones and jam,
Laid it down on the glasstopped wickerwork table,
She sits back down into her wickerwork chair with her book,
A large volume in a red dustjacket
With a reproduction of Klimt's *The Kiss*:
The World Treasury of Love Stories
Selected and Introduced by Lucy Rosenthal
With a Foreword by Clifton Fadiman.

II

I sit back in my wickerwork chair and stare up
At the redistribution of raindrops on the glass roof,
At her two eyes redistributing the words of love stories.
For seven years I have been her lover.
For seven years visiting her in her home.
For seven years coming and going.

III

Wandering around Ireland at the height of summer
I visited John McGahern and his wife Madeline
In their County Leitrim home
On the shores of Laura Lake.
He told me about the American woman
Who had fallen in love and bought a home.
He took me in his car and drove up the side of a mountain,
The Iron Mountain.
On top of the mountain he got out,

Leapt across a stream
Loose with yellow loosestrife,
Disappeared off into a clump of trees,
High sycamores round a litter of stones.
He declared: "Well, now, isn't this a grand place!"

IV

She closes her book and smiles and I say
"Do you mind me asking you a question?"
And she says "Not at all" and I say
"Is it possible for a lover to have a home?"
And she says "Unfortunately not" and I say "Why?"
And she says "We don't have children of our own"
And I say "What does that mean?"
And she says "Home is where children are"
And she smiles and I smile and we stare
In silence at the glass walls all around us
Beseiged by precipitation
And I estimate that over the last seven years
She and I must have made love one or two
Thousand times and where have all *those* children gone?
Where have all those *raindrops* run off to?
Where is *their* home?
Our home?
I enquire: "Is it a good book?"
She exclaims: "It is the ideal book":
The World Treasury of Love Stories
Selected and Introduced by Lucy Rosenthal
With a Foreword by Clifton Fadiman.

Man Circling His Woman's Sundial

On a July evening in my fifty-second year –
My woman has gone to Greece on a cruise
With the Women's Democratic Association –
I drink a bottle of white wine and I get
To feeling better about the world and I put

393

A CD into the CD player and I sit
In the front room of her farmhouse
On the couch with its back to the window –
The trim, hard couch she got newly upholstered
After I'd retrieved it from my first wife's skip –
My first wife acquired it twenty-five years ago
From the Booles who were dumping it –
The Booles later also split up –
Is there a marriage in Ireland
That has not split up? –
Is Joe Lee in Cork
The only man in Ireland
Still in the married state?
Still saying "I do"? –
I recline with my right arm idling
Along the rim of the back, listening
To Tom Waits – "Innocent When You Dream" –
And the sunlight is sliding in the window
And all the years that have gone past –
That I had thought were dispersed for ever –
Are regrouping down in the glens of the carpet
Like the clans of the MacGregors
And it is the case that nothing that I have done –
Not the least thing, good or bad, is expiring;
Everything is alive, gilt-edged, piping.

In the big mirror over the white marble mantelpiece
I can see the reflection of her sundial on the lawn.
Halfway down the bottle of white wine I get a brainwave:
I will phone the parish priest and ask him
If when I die he would kindly arrange
For my ashes to be buried under my woman's sundial.
I pick up the phone and I dial the parish priest's number.
He whispers: "Is this the drink talking, Paul?"
"No, Father, it is me – the real me."
He is sympathetic, solicitous, soulful – sisterly even.
Bishop Smith, he insists, will be supportive.
When men are sisterly, there is truth in the valley.

I gaze out the window at her garden
On which she has worked all her life and I see

My woman's reflection in the window.
Possessive, yes; aloof, even – but so what?
With her silver goose-topped walking stick
She is at peace with Greece.

After two thousand acts of love,
Hurt, negligence, thoughtlessness,
We still bear affection for one another.
Tonight everything is coming together –
Coming together and falling apart,
Falling apart and coming together –
Delphinium, iris, opium poppy, mullein,
Seagull rose, yellow loosestrife, sumac;
I am two hours behind her;
She is two hours ahead of me;
My woman in Greece pole-vaulting at nightfall
The cracks between the flagstones of Doric temples.

Next morning I wake with a shock to recall
That I phoned the parish priest and said what I said.
Maybe it is time to give up the wine
Or – at my age – to stick to the herbal tea.
Yet when I walk out into her garden
And walk around her sundial and finger it,
Decipher it, stand by it, go by it,
I rejoice that I asked him to bury my ashes under it
For this is what more than anything else in the world
I want – to rest in peace under my woman's sundial.
Life is a deathwish – an open secret
To share and rejoice in and not to be ashamed of.
Only then will my woman wholly appreciate me –
In the finale of my corruption –
Wholly comprehend the body she has lain with
Two thousand times in the dark in the magnolia white bedroom.

I turn and behold again in the drawing-room window
My woman smiling in at me –
My tiny-footed broad-shouldered Chinese
Feudal swordswoman smiling down at me.
I am dead – wonderfully dead – and I am gazing up
Into her all-merciful eyes.

The Only Isaiah Berlin of the Western World

The first adult book I read was by Isaiah Berlin
When I was fourteen;
On my mother's ticket for Switzer's Lending Library
In Grafton Street
I borrowed *Karl Marx* by Isaiah Berlin.
It was the author's name more than the title
That seduced me.
Karl Marx was taboo-illicit
But Isaiah Berlin was omnipotent-prophetic.

Omnipotent-prophetic
With in my arms Isaiah Berlin
I cycled home
With no hands on the handlebars
To 57 Dartmouth Square
On the banks of the Grand Canal
Knowing in the backs of my legs
I was cycling into the Russia of my fate;
A motorcycle escort of the years
All around me at the bridge
In a thirty-strong ring of outriders;
Into the Russia of my tiny fate
To knock knees with Isaiah Berlin
On the banks of the Fontanka.

It was October in Leningrad –
Golden canalbanks, true love, mortality;
Armenian women, Afghan colonels;
Diarrhoea, herbal tea.
Isaiah Berlin took me under his wing:
Skipping sessions
We patrolled the canals conferring, conferring;
We patrolled the summer gardens conferring, conferring;
Pushkin, Gogol, Turgenev, Herzen.
By banks of red primula candelabra
He stooped tall and taught me:
"No end can justify the means.
The evilest murder is the political murder."

I glanced down through mottled, veined freckles
Into the big, broad hands of his enthusiasm.
I said: "Poetry is pure research." He clapped hands and sang.
I said: "I am a Protestant Tinker!" He bassooned:
    "Double odium!"

On Apothecary Street
He bent down and picked up a leaf –
A lime-tree leaf, I think it was –
And he handed it to me
As if it was the most precious, rarest, yellow rose in the world;
The yellow rose
Which is the flower of friendship.

I knew then that my soul
Was a young girl who was born
And should never die –
A princess, proud, unhappy, unappeasable –
And that is how I have lived my life;
Either floating in my own immortality
Or getting punched in the eyes
By a bewhiskered auctioneer
Who fears and loathes me
Because I write poetry and love love;
Who derides me
"Nobody could live with the likes of you."

Isaiah Berlins don't grow on trees
And now I have lost him,
I have lost him surely –
The only Isaiah Berlin of the Western World.

17 November 1997

Karamazov in Ringsend

In our redbrick terrace – a cul-de-sac in Ringsend –
Everybody parks their car tight to the kerb.
Not least the poet Durcan. Watch him
As he drives up and slides backwards
Into his space in front of his front door
Which hasn't seen a lick of paint in thirteen years,
All cracks, blisters, stains, smears.
Sometimes he spends up to ten minutes
Parking – getting tight to the kerb,
Slotting into his sacrosanct parenthesis of five-and-a-half metres.

Next door to him – three houses down –
Resides the politician Mary Banotti.
The way she parks her car
Demonstrates not only the difference
Between the solemn poet and the carefree politician
But the difference between a man and a woman.
She drives up at speed and she leaps out
Almost before she has stopped, leaving her car
At least six inches from the kerb,
Sometimes even more than a whole twelve inches,
Her front wheels locked to outward and away.

When the pair of them have disappeared
In behind their separate doors
And the small, sprightly, bedenimed figure
Of Karamazov in Ringsend
Materialises out of snow
Searching for his Mokroe
It is Mary Banotti's door and keyhole
That he presses against, lends an ear to,
Before whirling around and hullabalooing like a blue-flamed
      house alarm:
Whip up the horses, Andrei, and drive up with a dash!

Behind the man poet's door he can hear only the groans of the
      drowned;
Behind the woman politician's door he can hear only the
      laughter of the saved.

Notes Towards a Necessary Suicide

The practical consequences of loneliness and depression –
Apart from a tendency to contemplate suicide at awkward
    moments –
Meeting an acquaintance on the street and having to rock
Back on my heels in affability –
Are taking an age to do the washing up
Or taking another age to make the bed
Or, in both cases, winding up by doing neither
Or, as was the case this morning,
In a tactic to buck the rut,
Driving over to Sandymount Strand,
Only to find myself unable to get out of the car.

I sit up in the driving seat
Trying to keep sitting upright,
Trying not to put my head in my hands,
Trying to concentrate on Dublin Bay's gallops of white horses.
I drive back to my den, fretful
I might not be able to make it
From car door to house door,
I climb up the stair – climb and climb and climb
And climb and climb
And climb and climb and climb –
And get into bed in my clothes
And pulverise the ceiling
With making-eyes blinks
Before pulling down a pillow over my head
And listening to the booming of my own sobbing.

Ad infinitum I think of Virginia Woolf and I know
That sooner or later I will have to go down to the river:
The Dodder at night where it flows past Lansdowne Rugby
    Ground
And join my father and his brothers down among the
    umbrellas and fridges,
The hoops and the horseshoes.
I have always been affiliated to umbrellas and fridges,
Hoops and horseshoes.

I think of buckets of champagne and rain bucketing down.
Not perish but relish the prospect of suicide
In the rain with ice-cold champagne.

"In Ringsend Park this morning the body was discovered
Of the middle-aged, minor-major poet Paul Durcan
In black suit, white shirt, bow tie
Under a tree in the rain with piles
Of empty champagne bottles all around him,
Greeting cards, faxes, bouquets.
His amused colleagues did not express astonishment;
All were agreed that he was,
In the words of Brian Ryan, playwright,
'A serious man for the weddings.'"

Paddy Dwyer

Vona, how I envy Paddy Dwyer!

Paddy Dwyer has his own
Shoe shop in Drogheda –
Paddy Dwyer's of Shop Street.
If I'd known what I was about
When I set out to be a poet
Up the road from Edgeworthstown
I'd have walked for ten years
In the footsteps of Paddy Dwyer.
I'd have served my time
Not in the literary pubs of Dublin
And London but in a shoe shop
In Dusseldorf or Nîmes
And in the course of time
Set up shop in a country town
With upstairs my books and my
CD radio cassette recorder.

I'd have wanted to be
A great lyric, rhyming poet
Up there with Yeats and Keats,

With Pushkin and Baudelaire.
Therefore I'd have emulated Paddy Dwyer
And sold quality shoes at affordable prices:
Bally, Nike and K.
I'd have worked out front in my shop
With my sleeves rolled up selling shoes;
Welcoming customers, making customers
Feel unique, equal, wanted.
Like you, Vona, and your husband Conor
I'd have wanted you to feel
Like myself about feet –
That feet have hill-top cities
In their Italies called toes;
That feet are of the first water;
That feet are different;
That feet are serious;
That no two pairs of feet are the same;
That feet are vulnerable;
That feet can get gangrene;
That feet have minds of their own;
That knees are peacocks
That stoop in their tails;
That shoes are tiaras;
That I am king of my shop;
That every customer is an infant Christ
Before whom I must kneel down and adore;
Caress his feet on a footstool;
Tie up his laces.

I'd have courted a country girl
From the heart of Meath –
From Yellow Furze –
With a heart of gold like Roslyn
Who works in the Peter Mark hairdressing salon
In Drogheda town centre.
I'd have concentrated on affection and business –
The business of affection –
And on the horticulture of shoes.

I'd have let the poetry look after itself
In my home above the shop;

401

Late at night in the a.m.
In the cage of my patience;
My portable typewriter on the kitchen table,
My wife asleep in the next room;
The spine of Michael Hartnett
Looking sideways at me
From the top shelf of the dresser;
The ghost of Nano Reid
Luminous over the kitchen sink;
I'd have cultivated
Only those brands of poems
That demand cultivation.

Having got to know other men's feet
After my own
Maybe I'd have had the compassion
To write for my townsman
The song of his soul
And still like Paddy Dwyer
Opened a second shop across the street
Selling ladies' shoes.
Stiller and stiller.
I'd have had to get to know ladies' feet;
Without presumption or arrogance known
Myself the equal of Owen and Shearer,
Ronaldo and Dunga.

Instead at fifty-two here I am
Not only without a home
But without a shoe shop of my own;
With only a shoestring to my name.
What hope have I of writing a poem
Without a shoe shop of my own?
Not to mention a home?
I look into the busy, chuffed face of Paddy Dwyer,
Affable, ruddy, watery, crackling,
Those hectic, steely eyes
Dreaming dreams, seeing visions
Of Leeds United
As he shoehorns my feet
Into a pair of Ks —

Black leather slip-ons –
And ask myself am I likely
Ever to write poems
As well-made, yet casual?
As light, yet durable?
Shall I ever be quite the poet on fire
As is the shoe-shop man Paddy Dwyer?

Vona, how I envy Paddy Dwyer!

Cissy Young's

to Rosa Alice Branco

That first year in Cork city – '71/'72 –
I spent the afternoons from four to six
Sitting alone sipping pints of Smithwicks
In a public house on the Bandon Road,
Cissy Young's,
Reading Bishop Berkeley's *A Treatise*
Concerning the Principles of Human Knowledge.
I, ex-footballer, ex-hurler, ex-high-jumper,
Branded by the dominant males
Of the Irish tribe "a hippy",
Rejoiced in the eighteenth-century
Metaphysical atmosphere of Cissy Young's.
I sat in the private lounge,
As distinct from the public bar,
Because the private lounge was nearly always empty.
Men in the public bar saluted me
Through the hatch.
Cissy Young's, all formica, banquette,
More anonymous, cosier by far
Than any salty, arty Kinsale bar.

That year in Cissy Young's reading Berkeley
Was a foundation year in my life as a writer
And, if I may meekly, profoundly trumpet,
My life as the virtuoso university teacher

I never became:
An attacking player on Berkeley's dream team.
Cissy Young's on the Bandon Road
Was my University of the Bermudas
Where I learnt the basics of my trade:
Learnt to think the hard way;
Learnt how to head the ball one way, looking the other way;
Learnt the relationship between soul and body;
Learnt to communicate through the hatch;
Learnt how to introduce Libyan storytellers to Cork insurance
    officials;
Learnt that reality is poetry, poetry reality;
Learnt the way of all things;
Learnt the existence of God –
That at five in the afternoon
On the Bandon Road in Cork city in Ireland
In the empty, private lounge of Cissy Young's
"To be is to be perceived."

Tea-Drinking with the Gods

The telephone rings and I squeeze open my eyes.
My publisher tells me that he has sold the rights
To all the poetry I have ever written
For one hundred and seventy three pounds
And fifty pence. My belovèd beside me in bed
With her back turned to me tells me
She plans to spend Christmas with her son.
Driving out the gate I catch my tail light
On the gate post and hear a short, sharp crunch.
In the newsagents when I stammer Good Morning
The newsagent does not hear me.
In the post office the postmistress
Insists that there is no mail for me.
My mother when I visit her for lunch
Scolds me that I do not eat enough.
When I decline her Ambrosia rice pudding
She casts up her eyes to heaven.

At 7 p.m. I arrive at the National Gallery
To give a poetry reading
From my book *Crazy about Women*.
I stand up in front of three hundred people
And recite for an hour and fifteen minutes
Wondering if I will ever get to the end.
My mind is on other things.
In today's newspaper the British government states
That its private stance is the same as its public stance.
Halfway through the reading a man in the audience
Stands up, walks up to the microphone
And whispers into my ear: "Where is the toilet?"
He walks out of the hall and two poems later
Walks back in with two bottles of whiskey.
At the end of the reading there are waves of applause.
People milling around me with books
To be autographed. One middle-aged couple
Trying to come forward, reluctant, reticent,
The husband pressing a carrier bag into my hand
Explaining: "My wife made this for you."

I walk home alone in dark, wet, cold,
Past the palings of Merrion Square,
Black silent spear-carriers;
Down the canyon of Mount Street,
Down along the Grand Canal,
Past Kitty O'Shea's,
Past the empty gasholders
Down along South Lotts Road,
Through the deserted streets of Ringsend and Irishtown.
When I get in the door and switch on the light
The light does not come on. Another bulb gone
And I forgot to get spare bulbs
And I bet the battery in the torch is dead.

But the battery is not dead. The battery is alive.
By the light of the torch
I investigate the contents of the carrier bag,
A creased post office carrier bag.
Between tissue
Reposes a tea-cosy,

A patchwork tea-cosy
With in red thread
Three words stitched:
CRAZY ABOUT PAUL.
I stand alone in the dark
Staring up at the street lamp
Through the dust-iced fanlight
Before tramping up to bed.
Between the sheets,
My spout sticking out.
Cosy, cosily, cosiness.
Wholly alive, wholly dead.

Ashplant, New Year's Eve, 1996

Year in, year out, I tramp Sandymount Strand.
Is there no one to talk to in Ireland?

We Believe in Hurling

to Mícheál Ó Súilleabháin

I have such a craving for thee, O Donal Óg,
Because you praise my days with hurling deeds;
When you make leaps with your back to the goals
Plucking high balls out of teeming skies
To hurl them low between the posts;
Deeds alone are certain good.

3.15 p.m. Sunday afternoon
In the bar of the Slievemore Hotel
On the side of the flapping mountain
Pegged down in cloud.
Red-eyed with grief, perched
On a high stool at the bar,
I am staring up into a blank screen.

Will nobody switch it on –
The TV up there on its black bracket?
Have I come out in vain
In the gale and the rain?
Do none of you here believe
In the All Ireland Hurling Final
Between Tipperary and Clare?

If I ask – if I ask
The man behind the bar
To switch on the television
Will he? My scepticism
Stutters: He'll – he'll not.
He smiles a barman's Japanese smile.
Pictures alight on the screen

Like birds on the bough.
The woods of Croke Park are alive!
The hurlers of Tipperary and Clare
Are warming up in the goals.
Like young fillies at Ascot
At the starting gate prancing;
All halters, all helmets.

For seventy deluged minutes
I do not budge from my stool.
I roost on my stool
Making faces at the screen;
Big faces, little faces
At each orbit-of-the-earth trajectory of the ball;
Catch, cut, hook, puck, double, solo, hop.

These are the boys who were born
To sweeten and delight;
To bejewel and beautify.
I laugh, I gasp, I frown.
At the final whistle
I jump down to my feet,
Hug myself.

I stride over to the TV.
I stand under its black bracket
Gazing up at the Great Loughnane
Being interrogated after the game.
Tears alight in my eyes
As I listen to him rhapsodise
That it was the game that won the game.

He cries: "The game of hurling
Is pure poetry.
Pure inspiration. Pure technique.
Hurling won the game today,
Not Tipperary, not Clare.
Today we saw the greatest game
Of hurling we will ever see."

I stride out of the bar
Into the gale and the rain
I hasten off up into the mountain
Bareheaded, open-necked
Into the fuchsia, into the montbretia;
Into the stick-boss solitudes:
As free as a man can ever be.

Hurling is the father of freedom.
When Jamesie O'Connor with a minute to go
At full tilt in the middle of the park
Pointed for Clare
Spacemen on *Mir* saw Planet Earth
Fly up out of its tree.
The hurler strikes, and man is free.

I have such a craving for thee, O Donal Óg,
Because you praise my days with hurling deeds;
When you make leaps with your back to the goals
Plucking high balls out of teeming skies
To hurl them low between the posts;
Deeds alone are certain good.

14 September 1997

Surely My God is Kavanagh

to John McHugh

A horse and cab drives up to the Grand Canal
At Baggot Street Bridge. Out scramble
Five foxes – five scented young ladies –
Over from Liverpool for a weekend in Dublin
Barking to pose for photographs on the seat
Alongside the bronze poet Kavanagh.

The first blonde sits beside Kavanagh
With her hand on his knee, well above his knee;
The second blonde stands behind Kavanagh
With her hand on his head,
Her false nails plucking his eyebrows;
The third blonde sits the other side of Kavanagh
With her cheek against his cheek,
Giving him a long, full kiss on the lips;
The two redheads stand sentinel smirking
Either side of the tableau.

The second blonde murmurs to Kavanagh:
"What do you like, honey?"
Kavanagh reflects: "Women with fivers."
Second blonde: "This is my fourth time in Ibiza."
Kavanagh: "Are there any locals in Ibiza?"
"All the time – Ibiza is full of Scousers."

The five ladies ride off into the sun at noon
Low in the sky of a November day,
Heading for the Rowley Mile –
Leeson Street, Merrion Row.
Along the towpath stroll
A couple in their thirties
With baby in pram and a six-year-old
Fair-haired, blue-eyed, curly-headed boy
Whom they hail as Sebastian
Shrieking at the height of his bent:
"May I sit on his knee?

May I sit on his foot?
May I climb up his leg?
May I stand on his tummy?"

The little boy plays with the bronze poet
Until mum and dad – more mum than dad –
Coax him away and a courting couple
Stroll up and she unsheathes a camera – an Olympus –
And asks her man to sit beside the poet
But her man is shy and he tiptoes behind the seat
To cringe bashfully behind the poet.
She remonstrates with him and he yields
And crawls back around and slides down
Into the seat with embarrassment
Scratching the back of his neck,
Glancing up at the poet beside him
To ask for permission:
"Nobody sitting here, is there?"

The bronze poet seated with arms folded
Shakes his head and smiles
That infinitely baffled, infinitely affectionate,
Other-galaxy smile of his
And resumes talking to himself:
"I am fulfilled because the canal is fulfilled."
Across the canal on the opposite bank
Over the heads of three swans and half-a-hundred ducks
On a seat erected by Dublin Tourism
Old locals delight to watch the goings-on,
Observe that the bronze poet is an honoured soul,
Catch his soliloquy on the soul-caressing breeze:
"A tourist attraction! Well, you don't tell me!"

Surely my God is Kavanagh!
Who is content with feeding praise to the good.
While other poets my comic light resent
The spirit that is Kavanagh caresses my soul.

23 November 1997

On First Hearing News of Patrick Kavanagh

October 1960, Gonzaga College, Dublin:
"Boys" – Father Joseph Veale, SJ, joins
Together in a steeple his long, cloistral fingers –
Our teacher whom we'd trust with our lives –
Our tall, dark, enigmatic man in whom
Are spliced in a thrilling, glamorous mix
Gravity and levity –
"Boys – thank you, Paul, yes, open the window –
You all know my distrust of the word 'phoney';
Well, I don't like saying it but poetry
Or, I should say, what passes
For modern poetry is phoney
Or strikes me as phoney. In our country only
Patrick Kavanagh strikes me as genuine
And in America William Carlos Williams
Whose 'Flowers by the Sea' you will remember
I chalked up on the blackboard in April.
Yeats for all his indubitable mastery of rhetoric
Strikes me as nailed down to a trick.
Alas, you will hear, if you have not already heard,
People make unkind, cruel even,
Cuts about Patrick Kavanagh;
I have heard an urbane, honourable senator state:
'Patrick Kavanagh is an absolute lunatic.'
When I protested the senator added:
'Patrick Kavanagh would talk to anything.'

"Myself, I have seen with my own eyes
Patrick Kavanagh conversing with trees
On Waterloo Road.
As I walked past, I thought to myself:
There is a man in touch with reality.
Poetry, I believe, when it is not phoney,
Is – like Milton – the figure of reality.
What I thought the trees were saying to Patrick Kavanagh was:
'Come Dance with Kitty Stobling'
Which, as it happens, is the name
Of Patrick Kavanagh's most recent volume

Published by Longmans in London.
But boys – please take note –
It was not a one-way conversation.
Patrick Kavanagh was talking to the trees –
Yes, he was – in down-to-earth, matter-of-fact, everyday tones;
But the trees also were talking to Patrick Kavanagh
In similar vein – in down-to-earth, matter-of-fact, everyday tones.
Now, let us resume *Paradise Lost.*"

Waterloo Road

On Waterloo Road on an August day
I met Patrick Kavanagh in his garden flat.
After I rang the bell there was a long pause –
To open . . . or not to open –
Before I identified two sad, wise, humourous eyes
In black horn
Peering out at me through the spyhole window high up in the
        door.

Patrick Kavanagh led me up the long hall
To the living room at the back looking out on the garden.
He sat down in an ocean-going armchair of a past era
With dozens of anthologies of American poetry
In stacks round about his shoeless feet on the floor.
He blinked up into the skies behind me:
"The American anthology is great for the kickstart."
We sat in silence – two deferential elephants.
He the old cobbler at the term of his days;
I the young apprentice in my first pregnancy.
"The apprenticeship," he declared eagerly, sitting out forward
"The apprenticeship, you know, is twenty years."

It was a golden day on Waterloo Road –
Blue skies, shirt sleeves, bicycles, miniskirts –
As we strolled down to the Waterloo House
Past Michael Kane's big window for a lunchtime drink.
There was an anticyclone over Ireland.
At the construction site on the corner of Waterloo Road

That was to become the office block of the Yellow Pages
Patrick Kavanagh halted with his hands on his hips
Gazing up at the meteoric men in yellow hats
Walking tightropes smoking fags.
From them to me he switched gaze solemnly.
Divining the mystery of the universe, he announced:
"Men at Work!" He tossed his head back. "Men at Work!"

That day Patrick Kavanagh had a wedding to go to
In the Shangri-La Hotel on the hill of Dalkey.
Through the armies of the sun we rode a taxi
Like Lenny Bruce and Billy the Kid
In a chariot along the shore of Dublin Bay.
Although I was homeless, jobless, futureless,
I felt wholly safe in Patrick Kavanagh's company.
I uttered: "Today is such a golden day
It reminds me of days I stayed in the monastery –
The Trappist Monastery at Mount Melleray."

Consternation in the back of the taxi.
Patrick Kavanagh groaned:
"On a summer's day like today
Don't be thinking about monasteries.
On a summer's day like today
You should be thinking about beautiful women."
When in the lobby of the Shangri-La
The head waiter spotted us
He took us for a pair of winos,
Made to throw us out,
Only for the bridegroom to rescue us.
Patrick Kavanagh was the guest of honour.

Humming snatches of "On Raglan Road"
Patrick Kavanagh sat down on a couch behind me –
"For that I'll vouch on any couch" –
While I, sitting up at the bar, found
Myself beside a beautiful woman
With long red hair, green eyes, freckles.
Nessa O'Neill was her name and she invited me
To go for a swim with her at the bottom of the garden.
The Shangri-La backed on to the Irish Sea.

There was an Indian Summer that year in Ireland
And in October she and I set up home in London.
We lived together sixteen years,
Rearing two golden girls.

On Waterloo Road on the first of August I met her first and knew
That her red hair would weave a snare that I would never rue;
I embraced the danger, I sailed along in the enchanted cab
And I rowed my oar by the star of Patrick Kavanagh.

Patrick Kavanagh at Tarry Flynn, *the Abbey Theatre, 1967*

Where the devil did I put me cap?
Every night at eight o'clock on the dot
I take a taxi from the Bailey public house
Soberly sozzled, never noxiously stocious,
North across the Liffey to the Abbey Theatre
Where my *Tarry Flynn* has been playing for over a year –
Playing to full houses. In the back seat of the taxi
I join hands on my belly, incline my head to my left,
Incline my head to my right, gazing out the windows,
Giving the passers-by my salute and my blessing.
In my time I have known presidents and archbishops
But did any of them know this kind of suzerainty?
I am a suzerain honoured in my sulky streets
Playing to full houses for over a year.
Ye can't say it often enough, can ye?
Playing to full houses for over a year!

As I gaze out the taxi windows at the middling-to-good faces
Of the ordinary, decent heroes and heroines of my parish
Hurrying home in the rain under lamplight
Clutching string-tied barm bracks in force-nine gales
I observe them bowing to me and they are beseeching me:
Paddy Paddy Paddy Paddy Paddy
Come on in home into the Fifth Estate of Suburbia.

While the box office count my share of the day's takings –
The author's sacred ten per cent –
I sit in the back stalls watching young Donal McCann
Playing me as I was when I was twenty-three –
The same age then as he is now
And I, like an ould, black, shaggy tomcat
In my sack of sixty-two years, am lifted up dripping
Into the gods of ecstasy – not the frenzy of power,
Not the hysteria of possession,
But the freedom of the audience.
We are all members of the audience,
If we only knew it.

Young McCann grew up in the suburbs of Dublin,
Yet he catches me better
Than I could catch myself;
He has gutted me of that sickly sentiment
That has been the bane of my bastardly days;
Gutted me of begobbery; boggery; bardery.
Instead he has caught the universal thing –
The purgatorial boy under his mother's wing.

Thanks to young McCann
For the first time in my life
I have a daily income
And am in debt to no man!
Oh how skippily he treads those boards!
Skippily as I did trod those fields!
Sticking his big toe
Into a little mystery!

In a minute I will collect my ten per cent cut.
At the end of my life kyboshed in the back stalls
My baby soul is bobbing in death's waves rearing to go!
Where the devil did I put me cap?

The King of Cats

to Francis Stuart on his 95th Birthday

Francis – on a Friday evening in Dundrum
At the curtain of the twentieth century –
Dares me to be a child again:
"Imagine being Dostoyevsky . . ."
(*Pause*) "Or a gnat." Lucky me
To be sitting in the company of a dead man.

How many years ago is it since you died?
You have always been a cat but since your death
A before-only-sniffed-at flexibility buzzes your fuzz
Entitling you to enlighten me in the evolution of flight –
To give me a gnat's-eye glimpse of the cosmos
And of Russian fiction – the last word in death.

Over twenty golden years
We have spent hundreds of hours in silence
Confronting one another in your shadowy living room
Over coffee and cheese
From five to seven
On the lookout for words.

I visit you at rush hour.
Rush hour! – you exclaim
Pawing the phrase
Before dousing it in laughter:
That skimming, cormorant chuckle
Halfway between a revelation and a peep.
Goodbye, Francis – see you soon.
See you soon, Paul – you cry out.

In my car at your gate I perch in the dark
Under the orange streetlight a gnat in an Astra
Facing downhill to the Great Wall of China –
Your local corner takeaway – and the Scots pines
High above the Central Mental Hospital kremlin walls.
I can hear a spade undressing clay

Or is it the blackbird in your snowdrops –
The blackbird you announced to me when I came –
"The first blackbird of spring"?
I switch on the ignition – glance
Back over at the switched-on porch light of your home.
Yet again I have visited your tomb and found it empty.

The Stoning of Francis Stuart

It was a dark, cold day,
Empty, windy, wet,
The day of the stoning
Of Francis Stuart.

January the sixth,
Nineteen ninety-eight,
Eleven a.m.
Stoning Old River Man.

It was a St Patrick's Day
Parade kind of day;
The police erected
Crowd control barriers.

Thanks to friends
Of enemies, we had seats
At a fifth-floor window
Of a Temple Bar weekly.

Down below us
Fleet Street
Was empty and silent
But for the Stoning Catwalk.

Motorcycle cops
Accelerating, stopping;
Blue sirens of police cars
Whirling, swirling.

When Francis Stuart
Was led out
He looked more than
His ninety-five years.

He had been on the run
In the Wicklow mountains;
Blackthorn to blackthorn;
Nursing home to nursing home.

But although he was carried,
Or half-carried out,
When he came to his spot
He stood upright, unaided.

In a pair of new, yellow underpants
He cut a spinsterish figure:
Potbelly billowing out
Over spindly legs;

Wispy white hair
Strewn like aftermath
Over bone-structure in which
Bobbed a shrivelled, black penis;

Jolly journalist next me
Whispered in Anglo-Irishese:
"Would fetch a pretty penny
At auction – Stuart's dicky."

Round the Stoning Plinth
The chief critics of Ireland
Stood in a line,
Each with an arty stone.

As for the stoning itself
It was oddly boring;
It was hard to maintain
One's concentration.

It was like being
At a matinee,
Or at a bullfight –
Deadly but dull.

One's eyes straying.
There was a microphone
Stapled to Stuart's ear
But he screamed nothing.

Some thought they could hear
The old man humming
The Edith Piaf song:
Je ne regrette rien.

He staggered and fell,
Half stood up and crawled;
Waved his hands in the air,
Vomited. Shat.

I found myself staring
At the faces of the critics
As each of them took
Their turn to stone him.

The chief critics,
As chief critics will,
Put little effort
Into their stoning.

The chief critics
Were half-hearted,
Quarter-hearted,
In their stoning;

Devoid of dexterity.
The chief critics
Missed the target,
Blushed guiltily.

The chief-chief critics
Wore homespun balaclavas;
With clenched mittens
Warming their groins with their stones.

The chief-chief critics
Aimed for the head;
Principally pranging
The frontal lobes.

Finally, it came
To the turn of the paramount
Chief-chief critic of Ireland:
A tall, dark, young man

With a wedge moustache
On the upper lip
Of his elf-beak,
Like a fast bowler

With a Cork arm,
A Cork accent,
A Cork wrist-action,
A Cork frenzy,

He took a long
Run up before
Letting fly a rasper,
Scoring a bull's eye:

Knocking out Stuart's middle stump;
A yorker between the eyes;
Boring a small pink hole
In the nonagenarian reprobate's forehead.

The buttons of his underpants flew off
Exposing ancient buttocks
Which from behind looked
Like a girl model's face:

A pair of cheeks
In a looking glass;
Mandolin-shaped;
Pale, smooth;

Carol's bottom
In profile
Styled, cleaved
By Brian of London.

He toppled off the plinth.
It was fun
Watching him
Cartwheeling backwards.

After he'd been quite stoned to death
There was the ritual kicking.
The critics of Ireland queued up
To give Stuart a kick each.

Tedious too but curious.
One middle-aged leatherclad female skinhead
Made a bags of kicking in Stuart's head.
Instead she kicked out his Adam's apple.

Meek, strident cries of
"Old bollox" and
"Old fart"
Squeaked in the wind.

Bits of Stuart in puddles . . .
Polite applause
Trickled out of the crowd
Up along Fleet Street

Into the front office
Of the Temple Bar weekly,
Up the stairs and into
The editor's office.

An assistant editor –
In the middle of an editorial
Conference on men's fashions –
Franked his pad with a spit;

Picked his nose,
Stared at his fellow editors
Watching him nose-picking,
Ticked his spit with his red biro.

I am considering it;
I am not a nitwit;
A minute – while I deposit
My mucus under my armpit.

My Marks & Sparks mucus;
Microwave mucus.
Our line is clean on it;
Stuart is a shit.

After Stuart's corpse
Was humped away
To be dumped
In an unmarked grave

Under a chip-shop wall
Between the Central
Mental Hospital
And the Luas light railway line

The chief critics
Of a totally united Ireland
Held hands in a daisy-chain
Under Oscar Wilde's statue

While a bonfire was made
Of Stuart's books;
Although none of them
Had ever read Stuart's books

It was felt that etiquette demanded
Stuart's books be burned;
At the sight of *A Hole in the Head*
And *Memorial*,

The High Consistory,
Redemption, Pillar of Cloud,
Things to Remember,
We Have Kept the Faith

And, of course, most of all
Black List, Section H
All going up in flames
The critics' souls were warmed.

As Stuart's last book burned
The chat was not of Stuart
But of next week's dinner
To honour Salman Rushdie.

'Twas a noble idee
To beg The Beestie
To do a head of Rushdie:
'Twas a noble idee!

'Tis a gladsome orgy
Of bad faith I'll organise;
Stuart's great granddaughter
With smackeroons I'll flatterise.

Taxis were finger-snapped
For Malahide and Churchtown;
The consciences of the playboys
Of the nation rode home

To their sub-suburban estates;
Before fornication hour
To watch themselves on the nine o'clock news
Stoning to death Francis Stuart.

"Good evening, here is the news:
In Dublin this afternoon
Despite heavy rain and gale-force winds
The ninety-five-year-old writer,

Francis Stuart, was stoned to death
By his critics.
Reports afterward indicated
That it was an average stoning.

In Mullingar prices
For cattle and pigs dropped
By point three of a euro;
The Euro Bank is not to issue a statement."

Making myself comfy
Between sheets and pillows
I svent to svleep sviling:
Stones skimming into Stuart's puss

Is such a satisfying image.
We forgot to drown Stuart's cat –
Black Minnaloushe.
That was remiss of us.

"Alone, important and wise"
Yeats used call Stuart's cat
That sat always in Stuart's lap;
"Alone, important and wise."

Dancing with Brian Friel

to Brian Friel on his 70th birthday

Quarter-way down the wrought-iron staircase
Of Waterstone's bookshop in Dublin
I see down below me bottom left
At the Irish Drama counter

Brian Friel browsing.
I must not say hallo.
Man at Browse: Do Not Disturb.

I have not seen him for twenty years.
Real Inishowen man!
At seventy, how quick he looks!
In a danced-in, linen, creamy, summer suit,
Blue shirt open at the neck, white T-shirt,
On-shore-leave sailor dancing the bookshops!
Tracking the steps of Gene Kelly, Fred Astaire,
Shuffling sideways the shelves,
Tapping exits, entrances.

My little bull of Affection begins to bellow
And without ado
Crashes through my thicket of Etiquette.
In the *Galateo* of '99
Monsignore Paolo della Casa falls at the first!

We exchange smoke signals of Recognition,
Torches of Greetings.
So much to talk about in seven-and-a-half minutes!
The courage of Donal McCann and what
Really it means
To be a man of faith. My God! My God!
The "Elegy for Iris" by John Bayley
In last week's *New Yorker*.
I say: "Wasn't it very touching?"
"Oh it was," Brian Friel smiles,
A sunny surmise
Lapping the steep, black cliff-face of his brow
"But I wonder if it might not have been
A wee bit *too* touching?"
"Oh Brian!"
We laugh and laugh and laugh. And laugh and laugh.
He adds gravely "Some good things here"
Lifting up from the counter and brandishing
A copy of *The Yellow Book* by Derek Mahon.

He has to hurry off to meet a Mr Colgan
To discuss a new translation of *Uncle Vanya*.
I clutch in my hands a novel by Haruki Murakami,
The Wind-up Bird Chronicle.
I say: "Everyone in Belfast's reading Haruki Murakami."
He says: "Are they? Haruki Murakami?"
What a relief to meet a northerner
Who not only has not read Haruki Murakami
But who has never heard of Haruki Murakami!
I say: "They are also all reading Banana Yoshimoto."
He cries: "Look, Paul, this Mr Colgan is waiting for me."

He leaves me in the hands of a Mrs Sweeney,
A woman sailing-friend from County Donegal with
Her own white teeth, her own golden hair, her own blue eyes.
I turn to the Waterstone's man Cormac Kinsella and implore him:
"After meeting Brian Friel every twenty years
I always feel like dancing!"
Cormac Kinsella obliges as Cormac Kinsella always obliges:
"Dance away!"
I look Mrs Sweeney in the eye.
She blinks and I take her in my arms
And we begin to waltz around Waterstone's bookshop,
In and out the New Fiction shelves,
Poetry and Irish Biography.

On the Waterstone's 1920s wind-up gramophone
With His Master's Voice brass horn
Cormac Kinsella puts on a 78 of "The Blue Danube"
And I shout into Mrs Sweeney's ear:
"Is Brian Friel a grasshopper?"
"No, he is not a grasshopper.
You *scallywag* you.
Don't you know yet?
Brian Friel's a dragonfly!
And with all due respect to your parvenu feet
He's the only man in Ireland who knows how to dance."

Dancing with Brian Friel!
Who lives in that part of the South of Ireland
Which is more northerly than the North;

Who lives far away up in the South –
In the South that's far north of the North;
In County Donegal;
On the Inishowen Peninsula;
Who knows every millimetre of the road between Muff and Aught:
The North Road to the Deep South
By Brian Friel.

Life begins at seventy!
The all-clear of death
Being sounded far out to sea
Beyond Tory and beyond
On a single key of black ivory with one blind young lady's pink
    little finger.

At the Funeral Mass in Tang and the Burial Afterwards in Shrule of Dr Hugh M. Drummond

I dream of my death
As a young girl dreams of her wedding –
The most important day of my life.

I

1.15 p.m. in the cafeteria at Dublin airport
Trying to prise open a pre-packaged overpriced ham sandwich
On Thursday February the fifth and realising
That most things are beyond me.

II

A week today at this very minute
February the twelfth
Instead of seeing off my daughter Síabhra flying to London
To meet up with your son Blaise
I am standing on the banks of the River Inny
Attending your funeral Mass in Tang
And the burial afterwards in Shrule.

427

Dr Hugh M. Drummond
In no sense could it be said that I knew you;
Yet this I know – that you were a good man
Because only a man who is good
Could have lived and worked in Liverpool
All the years of his life
To wind up in Tang and Shrule
In a house with a garden,
In a grave under a tree
On a hill overlooking a river.

I am consoled by the beating down of clay on your coffin;
The downpour of clods and spadefuls;
By the hand in the trouser pocket of the officiating priest
Giving out the rosary
While holding in the other hand the banner
MAY OUR LIVES BE ROOTED IN LOVE.

III

Back in the house – your home –
Thronged with mourners drinking and eating
My last glimpse is a glimpse
Of your son Blaise with my daughter
In the half-dark of a doorway,
A potted oak tree in his hands.

I walk away, revisit your fresh,
Filled-in, heaped-up grave;
Find you standing at the edge.
You point upstream
To a patch of sunlight on dark water
And you cry out:
"That's my son Blaise in his 'yacht'."

IV

Yes yes yes dear dead Dr Drummond!

In the deserted village of paradise
You stand like your own grave-digger
With your chin on the handle of your spade watching
Your son Blaise lighting up the darkness
Of the earthly world far down below;
May our lives be rooted in love
Of the earthly world far down below;
"Thou hast given him his heart's delight."

I dream of my death
As a young girl dreams of her wedding –
The most important day of my life.

Mother in April

i. m. Iris O'Neill

The little cherry tree of my life
By cancer's pinking shears
Shorn of its surface,
Its tidal blossom,
Its soul-silk.

After the service in Gilnahirk
Presbyterian Church,
After the Minister has uttered,
Good John McVeigh,
Vouched for me,
He will take down his saw,
Lop off my boughs
So that my singing-by-the-sea daughter
Will have firewood for the shores of winter.

Dearest – now that I am cut down –
Cut down – not gone –
I will keep you warm.
Bury your head in the heat of my death;
At my soul's knees glowing
I will keep you warm.

The Bloomsday Murders, 16 June 1997

> – A nation? says Bloom. A nation is the
> same people living in the same place.
> *Ulysses*, Bodley Head edition, 1960, p.489

Not even you, Gerry Adams, deserve to be murdered:
You whose friends at noon murdered my two young men,
David Johnston and John Graham;
You who in the afternoon came on TV
In a bookshop on Bloomsday signing books,
Sporting a trendy union shirt.
(We vain authors do not wear collars and ties.)

Instead of the bleeding corpses of David and John
We were treated to you gazing up into camera
In bewilderment fibbing like a spoilt child:
"Their deaths diminish us all."
You with your paterfamilias beard,
Your Fidel Castro street-cred,
Your Parnell martyr-gaze,
Your Lincoln gravitas.
O Gerry Adams, you're a wicked boy.

Only on Sunday evening in sunlight
I met David and John up the park
Patrolling the young mums with prams.
"Going to write a poem about us, Paul?"
How they laughed! How they saluted!
How they turned their backs! Their silver spines!

Had I known it, would I have told them?
That for next Sunday's newspaper I'd compose a poem
How you, Gerry Adams, not caring to see,
Saw two angels in their silver spines shot.

I am a citizen of the nation of Ireland –
The same people living in the same place.
I hope the Protestants never leave our shores.

I am a Jew and my name is Bloom
You, Gerry Adams, do not sign books in my name.
May God forgive me – lock, stock, and barrel.

Rainy Day Doorway, Poyntzpass, 6 March 1998

A conversation from under two cars: Philip Allen and Damien Trainor

PHILIP: Did you hear the news?
DAMIEN: I did.
PHILIP: Water on the moon!
DAMIEN: I'm going. Are you going?
PHILIP: Funny hearing the news when you're dead.
DAMIEN: I'd prefer to hear it alive.
PHILIP: So would I.
DAMIEN: Do you think they'll give us our lives back?
PHILIP: Not at all. Do you?
DAMIEN: Not at all. What'll we do?
PHILIP: Let's stay talking under our cars.
DAMIEN: Dammit, you're right. Let's stay talking under our cars.
PHILIP: If only people believed in cars the way we do.
DAMIEN: Och, people do when they're let.
PHILIP: Are you right there, my dark Damien, next Tuesday for
          an old glass on the moon?
DAMIEN: I am right there, my fair Philip, next Tuesday for an
          old glass on the moon.

North and South

At Ireland's extremities –
Malin Head in the North,
Mizen Head in the South –
Two identical notices:
PRIVATE KEEP OUT

The identical islander
At the end of his identical tether:
Dune grass, starved sheep, barbed wire;
Whitewashed, womanless cottage.
PRIVATE KEEP OUT

431

Politics

> In our time the destiny of man presents
> its meaning in political terms.
> THOMAS MANN

At the bottle bank in the shopping centre car park
I was slotting wine bottles into the green tank
When I saw what I thought was a human leg
Clad in trouser and boot, protruding
From under the far end of the tank.
I peered round the tank and saw
That the leg belonged to a face I recognised
Although I had not set eyes on him
For at least seventeen years.

It was the Associate Professor of Modern Irish History.
He was sitting upright on the ground
Between the tank and the hedge.
He had a white enamel toothmug in his hand
Into which he was emptying a litre can of Guinness.
There was froth on his lips and he had not shaved
For a week or two, sporting a fine, white stubble.

"Down and Out in Dublin and Paris"
He announced before I had time
To reach for words myself
"But" – he added, an erudite smile in each eye –
"Who's complaining?
I'm not!"

While I lurked above him foostering,
Shifting from one foot to the other,
He adjusted to a more
Comfortable sitting position,
Crossing his legs,
A Lord of the Animals position,
And – not taking his eyes off me –
Took out of his breast pocket his pipe

And in between swallows
Lit up scrupulously, painstakingly.

It was embarrassingly obvious that I puzzled him
As if somehow I seemed out of place.
Compassionately he stared up at me
Out of black horn-rimmed spectacles
Brushing back a forelock of his mane of grey hair.
In my jerkin and jeans I felt so commonplace
Whilst he looked so distinguished sitting down there
At 11.30 a.m. in the morning in between showers.

He delivered himself of a second pronouncement:
"The boot now is definitely on the other foot."
I stared at his grand pair of laced black boots,
His crumpled pinstripe suit, his polka-dot bow tie.
He remarked: "Not a bad car park?"
I assented and when I could think of nothing else to say
He declared: "Recycling is catching on.
Young people like yourself are beginning
To take recycling seriously."
He sighed snotfully.

He took another deep, long, puff from the pipe
And a scoop of his stout
And folded his arms and nodded his head.
I saw satisfaction steaming out of him.
But not only satisfaction – something else also,
Something you might call tranquillity.
Or rectitude.
"The truth" he added
"The truth is that we should never have left the Commonwealth."

He sat up straight, looked me in the eye more steadily
With that medley of deference and defiance
That an elder in the palaeolithic would deploy
Looking down the lens of a TV camera.
And I – I in my Nike white trainers
And my Nike white baseball cap –
I felt even more commonplace.

Later, on my way back from the pharmacy,
With my little, white, pocket carrier bags
Of sleeping pills and antidepressants,
My Tranxene 7.5 and my Seroxat 20,
And my newspapers under my arms,
The *Guardian* and *The Irish Times*,
Worrying about war and war's alarms,
About Irish and Northern Irish and English politics,
I spotted him at the checkout in the supermarket,
A box of Kellogg's Special K cradled in his arms,
The teenage checkout girl listening to him rapt
To the fury of the tight, small queue behind him.
He is chatting her up!
Jail would not be half good enough for him!
Dirty old man!
Sodden sodden sodden sodden sodden!
Look at his brains! His purple brains!
Soufflé all wormy with lechery!
"Do you know you're a really pretty young woman?
You and I must try out the disco in The Hunter's Moon
Across the street from Dardis & Dunn Seeds.
Have you ever looked into Dardis & Dunn Seeds?
Compared to the 1916 Crucifixion up the road
Dardis & Dunn Seeds is appealing.
Yes. Well. You know.
The truth is that we should never have left the Commonwealth."

56 Ken Saro-Wiwa Park

Having heard this morning's news of the hanging of Ken
    Saro-Wiwa
With eight comrades in the state prison in Port Harcourt
I drove immediately to the Nigerian Embassy at 56 Leeson
    Park, Dublin 6.
I expected to find the embassy cordoned off by police,
The gates locked, the curtains drawn and, in my confusion and
    shock,
The Nigerian flag to be flying at half-mast.

Instead, the gates were open, the curtains were open,
And there was not one single Irish policeman in sight.
There was no one nor nothing to be seen in Leeson Park
Except in the gutter a black, bloody ooze of leaves.
There were only gyrating crimson leaves on quartz, granite
    steps;
Ogoni bannerettes gyrating in wind and rain on stone.

As I stood alone in the gutter, ankle-deep in the crimson ooze,
Gazing up at the squeaky-clean sash window
I began to realise I could discern a face in that glassy black
    limbo –
A bejewelled, black face fanning itself with a white shell fan –
Her Excellency the Ambassador gazing back out the window
    lasciviously
At the sedate, autumnal tranquillity of this leafy Dublin city
    suburban morning.

How nice to be in Ireland this slightly irritating morning.
How nice to be in Leeson Park with gravel paths, palinged lawns.
How residential, opulent, decorous Leeson Park is.
How nice the Irish are this slightly irritating morning.
Look me in the eye, Madam Ambassador.
Listen to the renaming of Leeson Park.
Because of your murdering hate
Leeson Park can never again be Leeson Park.
I am now standing, you are now sitting
In Ken Saro-Wiwa Park.
Madam Ambassador, get out your new headed fax paper:

    Her Excellency Mrs N. U. O. Wadibia-Anyanwu,
    Embassy of the Federal Republic of Nigeria,
    56 Ken Saro-Wiwa Park,
    Dublin 6.

11 November 1995

Mohangi's Island

Me and Mohangi were sitting over a pot of tea
In the lobby of the Hilton in Mogadishu.
Mohangi said to me: How are things in Tír na nÓg?
I said to Mohangi: Things ain't good in Tír na nÓg.
Mohangi said: What do you mean – things ain't good in Tír na
    nÓg?
I said: The young are getting old in Tír na nÓg.
Mohangi said: I'm going into islands.
I said: Glad to hear you're going into islands, Mohangi.
Mohangi said: There's an island north of Europe.
I said: An island north of Europe? Sounds cool.
Mohangi said: If I buy, will you manage?
I said: What's in it for me, Mohangi?
Mohangi said: Grass, seaweed, treebark.
I said: But, Mohangi, you know that what I like best to do in
    life is to judge – to do lots and lots and lots of judging.
Mohangi said: Oh – there'll be a whole lot of judging going on.
I said: Oh, Mohangi, I would like to judge and judge and
    judge – and judge and judge and judge and – judge
    and judge and judge and judge and judge and judge
    and judge and judge and judge and judge and judge
    and judge.
Mohangi said: You could judge till the cows come home.
I said: And drop live cows out of airplanes?
Mohangi said: And drop live cows out of airplanes.
I said: We have lift off, Mohangi.
Mohangi said: Take her up, Durcan, take her up.

All my best friends are dying in Mohangi's Island,
All sitting at home in their houses dying.
But I – I am flying low over Mohangi's Island
Dropping cows on my best friends' houses.

Travel Anguish

A stranger in Belfast,
Alone in the universe,
I am a child astride my mother's shoulder.

In the arrivals hall of David Ben Gurion Airport in Tel Aviv
A little old man in a flaming temper
Is leaping up and down at the hatch of the carousel
Exhorting his baggage to appear.

Despite the solicitous, fraternal warnings of baggage handlers
And of fellow travellers including myself –
(The nerve of me!
I who am always frantic about my baggage!)
The little old man plunges his fingers into the flames –
Into the swaying black drapes of the baggage ovens,
Snatching at bags.

But then when the little old man attempts to climb into the
    baggage oven
A youthful rabbi with babe in arms
Who is gazing into the calm, azure eyes of his own smiling wife
Hands over the infant to his wife
And puts his two arms around the little old man, in a loving
    lock.

The baby howls but when the little old man's *attaché case* materialises
And he lifts it up, hugging it, embracing it, feeding it,
The baby smiles and we all stand around and watch
The little old man skip about with his *attaché* case in his arms,
His newborn babe delivered at last from the flames
In the midst of all these multitudes and signs.

Under the night sky outside the arrivals hall
Confronted by mobs stacked behind a high wire fence,
Millions of screaming faces in the night clinging to the wire.
I try to turn back but the little old man prods me forward,
Roaring into my ear: "The important thing is to get out."

Outside the wire,
On the perimeter of the screaming crowd,
He urinates into the grass,
Patriarchal piss.
He is all overcoat lapels,
Giving his breast to the universe,
Repeating his message to me:
"The important thing is to get out."

Pointing me in the direction of the Jerusalem bus,
And buttoning up his fly,
He puts his two hands up to his star-shaped lapels,
And twirling his two wrists round his breasts,
Lays his head on his left shoulder, and sideways bows to me.
I take my leave of him, bold for my journey.

A stranger in the Holy Land,
Alone in the universe,
I am a child astride my mother's shoulder.

* * *

Omagh

1. From the Omagh Quartermaster: Memo to GHQ, 16.08.98

Gerry, *a chara*, I am vexed with you.
I have every right to be vexed with you.
I am referring to your "unequivocal condemnation".
Lucky for you, you did not go any further.
I was *terrified* – always a man for the pun – *terrified*
You might sound off about the "sanctity of life"
Or that you might start apologising for the past
And say something really stupid like "I'm sorry."
What is the matter with you, Gerry?
When I did the very same thing in Jerusalem
(Those two overcrowded buses, d'ye nae remember?)
There was not an *ochón* out of you.
You're a terrible man when it comes to the truth about terror.
You and your boys need to cop yourselves on.
We were in it with the ANC, and Hamas
From the start, and we are not copping out now.
What I would like to know is:
Are you seriously proposing that Omagh
Is a different kettle of fish to Canary Wharf?
By the way, remember the name of the Paki
We topped at Canary? For the life of me, I cannot.
(In my next seminar in Libya on terror –
Remember singing "Kevin Barry" in Irish in the Colonel's tent? –
I must remember to tell the Libos
That massacring people is bad for the memory.
The more you kill, the less you remember.)

Okay, it was a balls-up in Omagh.
But in the past we've had many balls-ups
And we learnt long ago not to be crybabies
And to blame it always on the Brits and their agents,
Their stooges and stool pigeons.
The republican family is a family –
Not a bloody orphanage.
We've been in terror for thirty years, Gerry.
Or are you telling me that you're an ex-terrorist?

There is no such thing as an ex-terrorist
And well you, above all, know it.
Terror is terror that has no end.

Here we are, Gerry. What about the next Omagh?
And the next Canary Wharf?
What about all the Omaghs down the road?
For every Good Friday
There has to be a Feast of the Assumption.
A terrible beauty
Was never, is never, and never will be born.
Come on, pop the propaganda and face up
To all the Omaghs and Canarys of the future.
Terror is terror that has no end.

Tell you what.
You stick to the word games – to all the palaver,
All the mantras: "The politics of the next atrocity."
"The atrocity of the last politics," etc., etc.,
(By the way, congratulations on "dissident republican" –
A grand wee contradiction in terms.
How about a bit of "progressing pacifism"
Or "moving pacifism forward"?)
Enjoy the rest of your holidays.
In spite of everything we still need boys like yourself
Who can sing in Irish and influence people.
Leave the real talking to us – we
Who are the real *óglaigh*, Beir bua. The Quartermaster.

2. *Le Monde*

In tomorrow's *Le Monde* there was a reprint of Robespierre's essay
"On the Theory and Function of Terror in History".

3. *First Litany*

Omagh
Omagh
Carrickmore
Buncrana
Buncrana
Buncrana

Madrid
Madrid
Drumquin
Beragh
Aughadarra
Aughadarra
Aughadarra
Aughadarra
Beragh
Omagh
Omagh
Gortaclare
Omagh
Omagh
Newtownsaville
Omagh
Omagh
Carrickmore
Omagh
Omagh
Omagh
Omagh
Omagh
Omagh
Omagh

4. Second Litany

Breda Devine
Julie Hughes
Brenda Logue
James Barker
Oran Doherty
Sean McLaughlin
Fernando Blasco
Rocio Abad
Philomena Skelton
Esther Gibson
Avril Monaghan
Maura Monaghan
Unborn twin baby Monaghan

Unborn twin baby Monaghan
Mary Grimes
Geraldine Breslin
Anne McCombe
Veda Short
Aidan Gallagher
Elizabeth Rush
Jolene Marlow
Samantha McFarland
Lorraine Wilson
Gareth Conway
Alan Radford
Fred White
Brian White
Brian McCrory
Olive Hawkes
Deborah Anne Cartwright
Sean McGrath

5. *Third Litany*

Aged twenty months
Aged twenty-one years
Aged seventeen years
Aged twelve years
Aged eight years
Aged twelve years
Aged twelve years
Aged twenty-four years
Aged thirty-nine years
Aged thirty-six years
Aged thirty years
Aged eighteen months
Aged minus one month
Aged minus one month
Aged sixty-five years
Aged thirty-five years
Aged forty-eight years
Aged forty-six years
Aged twenty-one years
Aged fifty-seven years

Aged seventeen years
Aged seventeen years
Aged fifteen years
Aged eighteen years
Aged sixteen years
Aged sixty years
Aged twenty-seven years
Aged fifty-four years
Aged sixty years
Aged twenty years
Aged sixty-one years

6. After the Remembrance is Over

Seven days and seven nights
And twenty minutes after the massacre
It is half past the hour of three o'clock
On Saturday afternoon in the town of Omagh.
The Act of Remembrance is over.
What are we to do now,
O People of Sion?
O People of Tyrone
Where will I go?
To the hills?
To Ben's Bar?
Back to my room?
I ask you.
What? Where? With whom?

7. Efforts of Conversation

What do you make of Omagh?
Roma?
No, Omagh?
Oh, OMAGH!

8. Sunday the Twenty-third of August

Blinking in Omagh.

9. *What Ben Says*

Do not talk to me of "death
Giving birth to life".
Do not talk to me
Of "post-trauma management".
Do not talk to me.

10. *Ben Again*

If you want to give me something –
Really give me something real –
Give me the allegiance of your silence.
Man to man, Ben to Ben:
Never to have to speak again.

11. *Tall Ships*

Towards the end of the twentieth century,
Four days after the Omagh Massacre,
While the funerals were steaming
The Three Rivers of Omagh
To and from the Black Bog,
The Tall Ships Race berthed in Dublin:
Mir of St Petersburg,
Libertad of the Armada Argentina,
Sir Winston Churchill of the United Kingdom.
Old Dublin men, old Dublin women cried:
The happiest civic event of the century!
On cobblestones, a million children shone.

12. *Letter to Ben, 22 August 1998*

There is no such thing
As eternity.
There is no such thing
As the "eternal reciprocity of tears".
In Omagh of the Blackbirds
Nonreciprocal are the tears
Of a murdered daughter's father.
In this summer of rain, my closest grief

444

Lies in Tyrone dust. There is no man
Who would not murder his brother.
So, in history, the ridge becomes deserted now and then:
Right now, just you and me, Ben, and the species.

13. The Wednesday after the Wednesday after the Saturday

I stand in my doorway in the sun at noon.
Paul Francis Durcan at home in Ringsend.
The Wednesday after the Wednesday after the Saturday.
Wednesday. Bin collection day –
Until this week. Last week
I received a notice from Dublin Corporation
Cleaning Division, 66/71 Marrowbone Lane:
"As from next week your weekly Collection will take place on
      a Tuesday.
Any inconvenience this change may cause is regretted."

Standing in my doorway wondering if the post has come.
My doctor posted my prescription for antidepressants
And sleeping pills three days ago.
The avenue is empty, pink under blue skies.
A '97 red Volkswagen Polo drives in –
My friendly neighbour Bernie. I notice
Four black plastic bulging refuse sacks
Most neatly stacked under her windowsill.
I ask her if she got post today.
"Oh yes I did, Paul, he came early today."
I attempt to conceal my bowel-puncturing anxiety.
I ask her if she received the Corporation notice.
"Oh Lord I did but I forgot all about it.
Jim will kill me!
Oh well, it's not the end of the world."

I go back inside my den and phone
The local postal delivery office.
No sign there of my missing precription.
A quiet-voiced, slowly spoken man murmurs:
"These things happen, unfortunately."
I put the phone down and place
My two hands flat on the desk.

445

Calm down, Paul, calm down.
Listen to the broad hum of the city.
Dublin is a broad city and you are part of it.
How lucky you are to be part of it.
As lucky as the people of Lisbon
Are to be part of Lisbon.
Pray *to*, as well as *for*,
The people of Omagh.
You who have water, gas, electricity,
The kindest of neighbours.
You who are sated with tranquillity,
Brimming with sufficiency.
Books, paper, pens.
Fruit, bread, milk.
Pray *for*, *to*, the people of Omagh.
Omagh have mercy on me.

14. The Last Post

No, I cannot forgive you.
For the extinction of the moans –
Unborn, born –
Of children's cries in Omagh,
Of wives' cries in Omagh,
Of husbands' cries in Omagh,
Of students' cries in Omagh,
Of the cries of single women in Omagh,
Of the cries of single men in Omagh,
I cannot forgive you.

* * *

Real Inishowen Girl

to Dr Aubrey Bourke

I'll be ten in September.
She's real Inishowen girl.

When I go out playing with Tessa,
Chasing, leaping after her
Across ditches, dung,
I'm in stitches keeping up with her.
I always get stung.

I'll be ten in September.
She's real Inishowen girl.

She pretends to get cross
When I get stung
But she likes the chance to be boss.
She snags clumps of docks,
She scours my flesh.

I'll be ten in September.
She's real Inishowen girl.

I like her when she's cross with me.
Secretly she's proud of me,
Proud of my stings.
Her eyes are ice lollipops.
Her freckles are biscuits.

I'll be ten in September.
She's real Inishowen girl.

Her favourite game is "Souls-and-Bodies".
She hides behind the Carndonagh Cross.
All I see of her is her arms
And the palms of her hands.
The rest of her is all Cross.

I'll be ten in September.
She's real Inishowen girl.

Concealed in the Cross, she cries
"I'm dead, catch me."
All I can see of her is her soul.
I know the outside of her soul
Like the palm of my hand.

I'll be ten in September.
She's real Inishowen girl.

When I die, I know
I will go to heaven or hell.
But how can I go to heaven
When I am already in heaven?
Tessa O'Donnell is heaven.

I'll be ten in September.
She's real Inishowen girl.

Meeting the President, *31 August 1995*

I

Driving up to the Phoenix Park
For a meeting with the President
On the last day of August
My father – eight years dead –
Steals my place;
Shoulders me aside;
Playfully, crudely.

I do not try to stop him
But even if I did try to stop him
It would make no difference.
As I get older, my dead father gets younger.
My hands on the driving wheel are my father's hands.
My shoulders in the driving seat are my father's shoulders.

II

I get out of bed. I shave with soap and water.
I go back to bed with my breakfast tray –
A pot of tea with no milk or sugar.
I get back out of bed at 9 a.m., go downstairs
To my daughter. "Do I look respectable?"
She – cross-legged on the couch with the Koran –
She is a week back from Marrakesh –
Reassures me that I look respectable.
Black shirt, green jacket, black slacks, black shoes.
I take a sideways glance at myself in the mirror,
Behold my father's face peering out at me,
Eyebrow antler-hairs curling down into his eyes,
Jawbone flecked with ice.
He steps out the door of my one-up and one-down,
Switches off the car alarm – two blank beeps,
Lowers himself down into the driving seat, performs a U-turn
In the redbrick cul-de-sac, turns out onto the Pigeon House Road.
He drives slowly upriver to the Phoenix Park.

III

Riding upriver across the city of Dublin
Is for my father the most sensual of rides.
Every street name is an enigma of consolation.
It is a straight line from Ringsend to the Phoenix Park,
Only the street name changing itself every half-mile:
Ringsend Road, Pearse Street, College Street, Westmoreland Street;
Aston Quay, Wood Quay, Usher's Island, Parkgate Street.
He takes each fence in his stride;
One hand on the reins,
The other hand between his thighs.

At the Phoenix Park gates
He checks his watch. 10.05.
He stops at the Wellington Monument, gets out.
"The Duke of Wellington was Irish,"
He used muse to us children. "Trim!"
Clasping the obelisk to his breast, kissing the plinth,
He gazes upon all these flights of steps

449

To which as a Judge of the Circuit Court
He is dedicating his life,
All these myriads of treads and raisers.
At 10.12 he drives off again and takes a right turn
In between the Polo Grounds and the Zoological Gardens
Arriving at the east gate of Áras an Uachtaráin
At 10.16. It is all locked up, no sign of life.
Surprised by himself, he does not panic.
At the west gate he gets out of the car,
Peers through more locked gates. A young garda
Opens the door of the gate lodge, scratches the back of his head
Under his peaked cap, calls out Good Morning.
My father is in his element:
This all appears to be happening in the middle of Dublin city;
Musically it is all happening to the tune of County Mayo.
My father says: What part of the country are you from?
The garda says: I'm not from County Mayo.
My father says: What do you mean by that?
The garda smiles: Every garda in Ireland is from Mayo – except me.

IV

My father drives up the avenue under oak and beech.
An army officer is standing bareheaded in the doorway
Waiting to escort him.
"Commandant Lester Costelloe.
The President will be with you in six minutes.
She will come in through the door by the window.
She will sit down at the end of the couch.
She will invite you to sit down on the chair beside her."

The President speaks to me about Aids –
The ungraspable magnitude of the scale of Aids.
"In the hospital in Lusaka in Zambia
35 per cent of the mothers will die of Aids."

V

The army officer tells the President that her time is up.
The Bosnia-Herzegovina group is waiting to meet her.
My father picks his own way down the steps,
Alone again in the universe.

He stops the car under a chestnut tree bristling
With growths of conkers – olive sputniks –
Opens up the boot, starts to undress.
I try to stop him but he is without fear or shame.

No rhyme nor reason why he should change his clothes.
Perhaps he is changing his clothes
Because he thinks the President is changing her clothes?
Who knows? It is the way he likes to do things
As, forty years ago, outside the town of Ballina
He used stop at Attymas and change his clothes;
As I myself when I am playing
Like to change my clothes.

Under the chestnut trees in the Phoenix Park
At 11.17 on the last day of August
I look around and stare at my father –
A red deer standing sideways to the car.
I drive out through the Castleknock gate
And stop at Myo's pub in Castleknock village.
I walk in and ask for a cup of coffee.
The barman says without looking up from his business
"And how are the red deer this morning
On the last day of August?"

IV

Women with mops and buckets are washing down the pub.
The barman picks his way across the wet, gleaming floor,
Puts down his tray on my table. He stands over me
Rubbing the back of my neck, stroking my nose,
Feeding my thick, wet, steaming, dribbling lips
With crisps and peanuts.
I click my hooves on the floor.
Through shut lips he mutters, "Not to worry."
Doing my best not to bleat or bellow
I ask him his name.
He takes a deep breath:
"Nijinsky when I am alive," he confides,
Skimming a tabletop with his teatowel
"Nijinsky when I am alive."

451

VI

"So you met the President!"
Mother roars when I get home.
Why is Mother always roaring?
If only Mother would stop roaring.
If only John, Bill, Gerry, Ian, David would stop roaring.
If only everybody in the world would stop roaring.
What use is a minute's silence? No use.
Let gales peter out into massed snowdrops.
If only the world would be quiet and watch it.

The Mary Robinson Years

The just shall flourish like the palm tree
Psalm 91:13

I

In November 1990 Mary Robinson lit a candle in her window
For all the exiles of the Irish diaspora.
Seven years later Mary threw her farewell party
In the Copacabana Palace Hotel
On the seafront in Rio – a gem of art deco;
Her husband Nick being an architectural historian
Has a professional interest in art deco
And in any case that's where Mary happened to be
And she thought it would be an agreeable idea
If we all flew out to Rio to join her –
Bride and Luke and Barbara and Enda and Ann and all the gang.

It was a fireworks night in Rio.
All the men as well all the ladies
Came in smart, casual attire.
The best of champagne, wine, rum.
Motivated conversation
Bejewelled with serious
Humour of the right kind.
Fernando Henrique
Attended with Ruthie.

That the party had helicoptered
Over Corcovado –
The Statue of Christ the King
Far below us on its hill top
Overseeing Rio and the sea –
Ignited theological controversy
A propos liberation theology;
The nexus, if any,
Between inequality
And the Ascension into Heaven;
What Leonardo Boff called
"The aerodynamics of injustice".
Amidst the rocks of his own laughter
The curly, grey, apostle-like Boff cried out:
"Bearded in my own den –
Danton amongst the Robespierres!"

The only other jarring note
Was that although
I was seated opposite Mary
I could not get a word in.
In fact, I could not
Make eye contact with Mary.
If I didn't know Mary
I might have thought
She was snubbing me.
But then suddenly at the end
She caught my eye:
"Black eye, Paul?"
I blushed puce.
"No, no, no, no –"
I cried, rubbing the red
Bruise under my right eye –
"That's my birthmark.
Keeps getting me into deep water!"

II

It was a palmy night
Outside the Copacabana Palace Hotel.
The most stunning woman I have ever set eyes on in my life –

Six foot tall, mulatta, red hair down to her hips –
Stepped right up to me,
Whipped up her T-shirt
To show me her incredible breasts,
Whipped it down again.

She said: "Don't faint, darling.
I'm a transvestite and
You won't believe this but
I'm from Tipperary."
I said: "Oh!
Whereabouts in Tipperary
Are you from?"
"Killenaule" – she smiled – "Killenaule."
I said: "What are you doing in Copacabana?"
"My night off" – she smiled – "my night off!
I'm an NGO relief aid worker.
Faith and good works and all that.
The Gospel according to Saint Matthew."
She added: "What are you doing here?"
I said: "I'm a friend of Mary Robinson's."
She said: "Oh you're not!
Only a friend?"

She turned her smouldering spine on me
And strode off into the night of Rio,
The gigantic, ocean waves of the South Atlantic
Breaking in rainbows of fireworks behind her.
It was midnight, September 1, 1997 –
High time to get down on my knees
And to light a candle in the sand,
Cupping a flame in my hand.

Only a friend
Cupping a flame in my hand.

CRIES OF AN IRISH CAVEMAN (*2001*)

Give Him Bondi

Gerard enquires: "Is there anything you'd like to do
On your last day in Sydney?"
I reply: "I'd like to go to Bondi Beach."
Too cautious to confess:
I'd like to swim at Bondi Beach.
Cautious not for fear of drowning in the sea
(I have been swimming since aged seven –
I've never thought of myself drowning –
Unseen, only other people drown)
But for fear of drowning in my own mortification –
An off-white northman in a sea of bronze loin-clothed men
With their bronze loin-clothed women.

As I step down onto the quartz sand of Bondi
I have to step around a young, topless virgin
Lying flat out on her back, eyes shut,
Each breast strewn askew her chest
Like a cone of cream gimleted with a currant
In a shock of its own slack:
Primeval Still Life awaiting the two Chardins,
Teilhard, Jean-Baptiste.

Will she one day
At the age of twenty-two
Not knowing she is not alone
With her infant twins in her arms
Commit suicide
On the newly carpeted staircase
Of her showcase home?
Please God open her closed eyes.

In our black slacks and long-sleeved white shirts
Gerard and I tip-toe up and down Bondi Beach
Like two corkscrewed, avid seminarians
On a day trip to the seaside.
Only that I, in a spasm of morning optimism,
Instead of underpants donned swimming briefs.
I feel – Gerard must also feel –

Estranged from our surroundings;
Teetering loners
Amid flocks of lovers,
Boys and girls
Skating precipices of surf.

In wistful exuberance resuscitating lives
Of priests, nuns, writers we have known –
Solvitur ambulando –
We promenade for an hour before
Gerard cries: "It's nearly time to go."
I am booked to recite to the pupils of his old school –
Robert Hughes's old school, too –
And Mick Scott's and Charlie Fraser's –
St Ignatius's at Riverview in North Sydney.
I gasp: "To hell with it – this is idiocy:
To be standing here at Bondi, not swimming."

I yank down my trousers to expose black briefs –
Too brief, really –
Body-Glory briefs –
And Gerard coughs, smiles, splutters:
"Well played, old chap –
Swim between the flags."
He'll stand guard over my little cache of manhood:
My wristwatch – my twentieth-century tag;
My white shirt folded in a sandwich;
My black slacks curled up in a chaste ball;
My black nylon socks twinned back to back;
My black leather slip-ons with fake gold studs.

I tumble out into the shallows where maybe twenty-five
Youths and maidens gay frolic
And I chin-dive and become a boy again –
A curly-headed blue-eyed fourteen year old
Leaping and whooping in the surf,
Romping into the rollers,
Somersaulting into the dumpers,
A surf-flirt in my element,
In the spray of the foliage of the sea.
Gerard patrols on the fringes of the foam

With his pants rolled up, snapping me
With a disposable Instamatic I've handed him.

I essay a breaststroke, but desist –
Being unfit, overweight, dead-beat.
Yesterday I flew in from Ayers Rock;
The day before alone in the low 30s
Humping five litres of water,
I trekked five miles in the Olgas.
Again I strike out, this time with an overarm
But after six or seven strokes flail up against
A barrage of exhaustion.
I spin over self-cossetingly on my spine,
My pudgy vertebrae,
And float, watching my toes:
Inspecting my toes
Strutting their stuff
On a catwalk of silver faucets,
Toenails pared and gleaming,
Their parings littering
A hotel bathroom floor
In the Northern Territory;
All ten toes of mine present and correct,
Pristine, pink, erect, perky,
Bouncing on a trampoline
Such is the buoyancy of Bondi.

This is my Theory of Floating
Which has served me well,
My Theory of Daydreaming.
If one may speak well of oneself
I may say I have not craved
Conquest or complacency
But exclusively
The existence of existence,
The survival of survival,
The dreaming of the day.
I did not climb Ayers Rock,
Not out of an excess of virtue
But out of a modicum of attention
To the signposts of the local people:

Please do not climb our sacred mountain.
It would have been a sin
Against the genetics
Of all the chromosomes of ethics
To have climbed Ayers Rock.

To float is to be on the whale's back.
Gurgling to myself:
There she blows!
Only three weeks ago
In the company of Mary Clare Power
And Nicholas Shakespeare
On a motorboat off Fraser Island
In Queensland
From fifty yards away
I saw two humpback whales
Steeplechasing the waves, courting;
Rising up, cresting, plunging;
Flaunting their tattooed tails.
Toe-gazing, I go on chatting to myself:
Amn't I a humpback too?
Mother shrieking at me: "Straighten up
Or you'll get curvature of the spine
And you'll be a humpback!"
She meant the Hunchback of Notre Dame.
Guy de Maupassant
Was *her* mother's idol.
Why did *my* mother eat me?
Her mother minded me.
In my prime I could scoff
Back in one gulp
15,000 gallons of salt water
While continuing to speak
Ten to the dozen
About anything under the sun.
Never mind, this day is Elysium!
Alone to own and range
The bush of the sea.
How fortunate I am
Who in spite of all my loss and failure –
All my defeats quadrupling daily –

460

I find myself here floating at Bondi Beach –
A little, pale saffron, five-and-a-half dollar boomerang
In a black penis-purse.
I flip over my gaze upon the hard blue sky.

But I must not keep Gerard waiting.
Time to swim ashore, go on
With life's obligation.
I flip over on my belly to swim
To see that I am twice as far out
As I should be! Pulled out to sea
While floating! Out of sight
Of the flags! But I'm an old hand
At swimming. Didn't Uncle Mick
Teach all of us to swim
At the age of seven
Off the famine pier
At Enniscrone of the Seaweed Baths?
Out of our depth
On the deep, steep steps
And not, not, not
To be afraid?
By God he did!
I strike out for home.
Only to find myself swimming backwards!
Christ O Lord the sea
Is kidnapping me!
Like that man in the back lane
When I was nine
On my way home from school!
He asked me to climb over a wall
With him and I did. No!
I decline to believe it! No!
            I go
Into denial!
            Stop, sea, stop!
Into hysteria!
            Stop it, stop it!
O save me, save me!
            No! No!
O God, O God!

461

O save me, save me.
Of what use be these now –
All thy litanies of ejaculations?
All these cries aeons ago
Airbrushed into extinction.

Pounding forwards I am surging backwards.
Instead of me catching the waves,
The waves are dumping me backwards!
I who presume myself a porpoise
With fifty years of Floating Theory
Chalked up on my flippers
Am now a mouse being toyed with
By the tom-cat of the sea!
In this drifting micromoment
The stopwatch stops:
I behold my death eyeball me
Like a sadistic schoolmaster
Cornering me at the blackboard.

I wave, but no one sees me
And, as I wave, I begin to sink.
I'm being eaten alive.
Save me, O Christ, save me!
Your what? Your own death?
Your own end? Your own oblivion?
Death by drowning?
        The fury of it!
The remorseless deep closing o'er your head!
Alone, alone, all, all alone!
Within seconds, to be but a swab –
A trace in water –
That scarcely decipherable but tell-tale trace
In the sea after a substance has sunk.
Fear frying your bones.
I thought I had known fear –
Oceans of fear – but I had not:
Not until now
This micromoment of 100-carat fear;
My body incapable of coping
But my psyche clear with fear

Not muddled or mesmerised,
But clarifed – a seer
Of the final second, seeing
The sea about to snatch,
Suck, swallow me.

The sea! Oh, the sea!
That stunning, wholly together She –
The one with her Mountain Passes
In all the right places.
You've flirted with her all your life
Having it both ways as always;
Your wife your mistress not your wife;
Your mistress your wife not your mistress;
Solitude your company;
Being mortal claiming immortality;
Every single time without exception
That the air hostess models the life jacket
You insouciantly ignore her,
Flaunting yourself a superior stoic
Who plumbs the secret of the voyage.
Voyager your voyage about to end
Faster than an airliner plummeting
How goes your voyaging?

Why are you standing in water
Out of your depth dying?
Far from your own bed?
Naught now between your legs
But disdainful water?
Being buried alive?
Dying, Durcan, dying
In your own standing?
Hanging on by one hand
From the sky's yardarm
About to plop
Down into Davy Jones's locker?
Where be your swashbuckling now?
Your hip-hop-hip mating?
Your waistcoated machismo?
Where be all your cheek-to-cheek glowing?

Your eyebrow-to-eyebrow acrobatics?
Where be all your toe-to-toe conniving?
You are being struck down,
Having glowed, having connived.
Neither being seen nor being heard
But tomorrow in a scrap of newscasting
On ABC:
"Irish poet trapped in rips,
Washed up between the Heads
Of Sydney Harbour."

Ocean – compleat ocean – clenches me
In its JCB claws,
Hissing at me that this time there'll be no pause
And my brains gape down upon my own terror.
In the vice of drowning I know
I have no power, my fate
Decided, all I can
Be said to be doing is lingering;
Out of my depth, flailing
Legs, arms, caterwauling
In my kitty
And meekly screaming – I am lingering;
Fresh blows the breeze from off the bow;
My Irish boy, where lingerest thou?
This fling in which you're lingering
Will last but seconds and after
You will be but a thing
Flung against the automatic sliding doors
Of the sea's casino.
My father and mother
Each a wowser
Resenting one another,
Resented me
Because I was a bother.
How so much better
It would have been
Not to have given birth
To such a bother.
All presumption walloped o'er the horizon,
All my naïveté, all my toxic pride,

All my vanity, all my conceit.
There is nothing I can do – I realise –
Except shout, bawl, cry, whimper.
In the cot of the sea,
On the rails of the waves
I bang my little knuckles.
The sea seethes:
Paul Durcan, you are
The epitome of futility.

I cry out "Help! Help!"
But no one hears me.
A cry? I –
Did I ever reply
To a cry?
A cry of a tiny, frail Scotsman
In a damp basement bedsit
In Buckingham Palace Road
Choking on his own loneliness?
Aye! A cry!
Nobody hears me, the dead man!
I cry out again with all my ego.
The about-to-be-overtaken sprinter
At the finishing line,
Lunging one last futile fingertipslength.
The ocean is the mighty woman
You have hunted all your life.
But now that she has got you
In the palm of her hand –
In her thimble of no reprieve! –
You are crying out "Help!"
She is moulding her knuckles around you.
You are her prey.
This is the yarn you will not live to spin,
The blackest yarn,
A groundswell is spinning out your life
At once slowly, speedily –
A groundswell no longer a cliché
But a mother of death!
You are a puppet out of your depth
And your legs are diced dancers

Dangling from deadwood,
Thrashing in their throes
Out of sight slipping.
The sea is a headless goddess
All flesh sans eyes sans mouth.
Paul Durcan, this is one lady
Through whose eyes and mouth,
Through whose free looks
You will not talk your way.

HELP!
My teensy-weensy voicette fetches
Over the uncut surf and the sealed ocean
To two young men who shout back –
Their seal heads bobbing a quarter-mile off –
Something like "Hold on! Hold on!"
And blubbering I pant for breath
As my head slides beneath the waves,
My shoulders caving in,
My paunch of guts dragging me down,
My kidneys wincing,
My crimson ankles skipping,
My snow-white fetlocks like faulty pistons
Halting for the last time.

I can hear myself sobbing "O God, O God!"
Floating downwards with every surge;
Hurtling upwards with every heave.
"O Christ, I don't want to die!
After all that church-going and hymn-singing
This is not the only life I know
But it's the only life I want!
I WANT TO LIVE!"
They clutch me round the neck
And flail and thrash to lug me shorewards.
A third joins them – an off-duty lifeguard
Called Brian who happens to be doing
A stint of training – but the breaking rollers
At each crash uppercut me.
Each other roller clubs me on the head.
Not once of course, but again again

Clubbing, clubbing, clubbing,
Such stuffing as is in me goes limp.
My rescuers scream: "Keep your lips tight shut!"
As each wave crashes I writhe for consciousness –
A newborn baby pawing air;
My lungs spewing up bladders of salt water –
The rash smart sloggering brine.
Wrenching me they fling me shorewards –
These three fierce young men –
Until they lash me to a surfboard
And sail me in facedown the final furlong,
The final rumble strips of foam,
Racing the shoreline, beaching me,
Dumping me on wet sand bereft of ocean,
Raising me up by the armpits, hauling me.
On my hands and knees
In amber froth
I crawl the final metre.
On the keel of an upturned boat I sat down
And wept and shivered and stretched to vomit.
Sat retching there like a shredded parsnip,
The cowering genius of the shore.
Another Bondi casualty bent forlorn
Upon the tourist shingles
Of New South Wales.

When I am able to look up
My three midwives have gone
Whose names I do not know,
Only Brian. The two together
Were English boys. They waddled off
Into the anonymity of selflessness –
"All part of the lifesaver's ethos"
It is explained to me weeks later by
The North Bondi Surf Life-Saving Club.
Drowning and trying to wave
And not being seen
But being heard in the nick of time.
On the instructions of Brian,
With Gerard's help,
I present myself

At the Bondi Medical Centre,
34 Campbell Parade.
A young Chinese doctor who cannot help
In spite of his instinctive etiquette
Smirking at my ludicrous appearance –
Trouserless in a green blazer –
Applies a stethoscope to my spine
And chimes: "Sir, you're fine."
Dr C. Chin.
35 Australian dollars.
Cash payment.

Gerard drives me to St Ignatius's school
Where for half-an-hour
I play the serious fool
To waves of applause.
That night I do not dare to sleep
But keep on the bedside light
Listening to my own breathing,
The possum in the wainscotting.
Instead of being a cold cod
On a slab in Sydney morgue
I am a warm fish in bed –
How can this be?
What sort of justice is this?
The crab of luck?

May I when I get home,
If I get home,
Chatter less cant
Especially when it comes
To life and death
Or to other people's lives;
May I be
Less glib, less cocky;
May I be
Never righteous.
If I conclude
I ever have the right
To call Ayers Rock "Uluru"
May I be

Not smug about it –
Remember I'm only a white man.
May I take to heart
What the Aboriginal people
Of Brisbane, Alice Springs, Canberra,
Said and did not say to me.
May I never romanticise
The lives of Aboriginal people.
May I never write trite
Codswallop about indigenousness;
May I begin to listen.
May I decipher next time
Silences under gum trees:
"Give him Bondi!"

Don't think I will swim
Again in any sea.
Doubt if I will walk
Again by any sea.
But if I do –
If ever again I should have
The cheek to walk
The strand at Keel
In Achill Island –
To walk those three
Skies-in-the-sands miles
By those riding-stable half-doors
Of the Sheik of Inishturk,
With their herds of white horses
Leaning out at me fuming –
I will make that long walk
In nausea as well as awe:
The wings of the butterflies in my stomach
Weighed down by salt for evermore.

Next day I board a Boeing 747
From Sydney to Bangkok
Not caring – glancing over
My shoulder on the tarmac
At Mascot, not caring.
Not caring about anything.

Not about Egypt.
Not about Mayo.
Not about Ireland.
Not even longing for home.
Not even longing for home.
Praying once for all
I am gutted of ego;
That I have at last learnt
The necessity of being nothing,
The *XYZ* of being nobody.
In so far as I care
May I care nothing for myself,
Care everything for you –
Young mother of two
In the next seat;
A boy and a girl.
Thumbs in their mouths,
Helplessly asleep.
Back in Dublin
One person in whom
I can confide: Colm,
In that brusque,
Anti-sentimental,
Staccato-magnanimous,
Shooting-self-pity-in-the-eye
Tongue of his whispers
On the telephone at noon:
"I swam in Rottnest
Off the coast of Perth,
Nearly lost my . . .
The sea is different in Australia, Paul,
A different pull."

A year later
I cannot sleep
For thinking of Bondi;
Nightly re-enactment
Of being eaten alive
Under bottomless ceilings,
Pillows sprinting above me,
The bedroom window

Declining to open,
A schoolyard of faces
Pressing their noses
Against double-glazed glass
Waving at me
Hail or Farewell? –
I cannot know.
I am come into deep waters
Where the floods overflow me.

* * *

On Giving a Poetry Recital to an Empty Hall

to Theo Dorgan

The engagement was to recite for one hour
At the Ballyfree Community Arts Festival,
And I did, and I gave it my all
To the empty hall.

The empty chairs gazed up at me in awe.
I caught the eye of a chair in the third row
And it would not let go,
Toying with my plight.
A redheaded, dumpy chair on the edge that never once smiled,
And the more droll my poem, the more it pouted.

When I had done, the Chairman of the Committee
Before even the non-applause had died down
Scrambled up onto the podium.
He spoke with brusque authority
And at length
About the significance of poetry in the new millennium
And how it is always so much more congenial
To have a small audience or, better still,
No audience at all.
He sighed piously, "It's more intimate."
And he blew his nose and he shrieked:
Go raibh míle maith agaibh go léir –
To you all a thousand thank you's!
He turned to me and he winked and he muttered:
"That's the last poetry recital we'll have in this town."

Auntie Gerry's Favourite Married Nephew Seamus

After dropping his eldest boy back to boarding school
Seamus was driving home to Athlone with another man
When he came upon a woman hitching a lift.
He lifted her and the next thing –

She offered him sex. In the car!
Seamus was shell-shocked.
It's a miracle he didn't crash.
He was very embarrassed!
In front of the other man!
But as I said to him on the phone –
In a crisis he always phones me –
Wasn't he lucky that he wasn't alone?
That he had the other man with him?

Homage to Tracey Emin

I

Apart from being a unique work of art
What appals me about Tracey Emin's bedroom
Is how similar it is to my own bedroom –
Same white sheets the colour of stagnant dishwater –
Same worndown, wornout, scruffy slippers,
Punched out pill sachets, underwear, price tags –
U-W Bra White 32C £31.00 –
One unopened bottle of *Orangina*
And in blue neon in the ceiling
The legend as in my own bedroom
Every Part Of Me's Bleeding
And I drink much of the night
And I stay in bed in the morning.

Tracey Emin is a seaside of fresh air.
Tracey Emin is the T. S. Eliot *de nos jours*.
Tracey Emin on Margate Sands can connect nothing with
    nothing.
Inside every fluid human
A small girl is frozen
In the wings waiting to walk on
To ask the sixty-thousand dollar question
At the Cardinal's Ball:
Where does the holy water come from?

II

That autumn the winds came and blew the leaves off the trees
And there were leaves stuck to the windscreens of the cars
And I saw that the lines on my face were pleasant places
And I took the first flight out of Gatwick
To go find my father on the shores of Cyprus.

Father, will you swim with me in the high seas?
Will we jump together?

Tracey, Tracey, hold on tight

7 December 1999

Donal

to Geraldine Berney

In the heaven-haven
Of Our Lady's Hospice
In your native Harold's Cross
Around your deathbed
Men henpecked like mothers.

Sebastian Barry at the foot
Of your bed explaining
Like an army chaplain's wife
The procedure of dying;
Bob Quinn like a granny
Groaning "I never thought –
I never thought –";
John Cronin like a midwife
Interpreting, adjudicating
Every inhalation, every tremor;
Jimmy Berney at your elbow
Like a sage aunt
Concentrating on prayer;
Brendan Sherry like a seamstress
Fermenting in the wall
With pins between his lips.

Old-fashioned Donal!
Old-fashioned to the end!
How you courted death!
With such grace!
With such ardour!
With such deadpan panache!

Once she gave you her hand
How gallantly you courted her;
Yet on the day of your death –
Death who was your bride
Became your daughter;
All that Saturday in mid-July
Death came chugging up the aisle on your arm,
Up the Grand Canal,
Like a barge from Athy
Along the black hairs of your wrist
Past whistling waterhens
And at 10.57 p.m. you gave her away!

In that helter-skelter relay
Of baton-change handover
You looked so composed!
Hand over hand.
From your high white pillows
You were gazing down
Into her freckled red face.
How proud you were of her!
You closed your eyes.

Donal macushla,
My dark Donal,
Father of the bride,
The day you died
You gave her away
With such style
That the Chairperson
Of the Crafts Council
Of Ireland
Waved his arm
Above his head
Like Jim Larkin

In O'Connell Street –
Your favourite sculpture –
Because he could find
No words to describe
What he felt
About Donal McCann.
He stammered:
"Such a – such a –
Stylish man!"

Seconds after you died –
Your birthpangs audible
Outside in the corridors –
All of us men-mothers –
All of us hen-men –
Your pals, your cronies –
Ran out into the streets
Onto the airwaves.

For all of the next week
Like pigtailed Hasidim at the Wailing Wall
We proclaimed your birth to the Nation.
On the steps of the Temple
Sat the Nation's Cantors –
David Hanly, Eamon Dunphy –
The stones of their microphones
On chains around their necks –
Solemnly chanting your birth,
"A saviour has been born to us and . . ."

Even the brats of the Nation
Got in on the act,
Myers & Co,
Spoilt brats preaching to us
About the sins of Donal McCann,
Making us grin with their
Larks of pomposity,
Their pranks of hypocrisy,
Although once or twice
As they upstaged one another –
How you detested upstaging! –
Little did they know

How close they were
To earning a clip on the ear
From Master McCann.

O you who taught me,
Dead Donal,
The truth of the art
Of the tragicomedy of Christianity –
The fact of the Resurrection,
The logic of the Crucifixion –
Have mercy on Myers and me.
At the end of the Comedy
Are we all about to be?

Baptism, communion,
Confirmation, marriage,
Ordination, extreme unction –
Not omitting confession! –
All seven sacraments
Going hell-for-leather
Pell-mell up-hill
Like the *peleton*
In the umbrageous sun –
Ten down,
Three across –
You with your hands
On your knees at the TV
Roaring at them.
At all of us,
To keep our heads down,
To keep our eyes
On the words,
Cycling into the sun,
Into the business of no one;
Into the mud on the peak
Of Alpe d'Huez, to die
Or to nearly die
On the side of the road,
Who knows?
God knows.

O Dearest Donal!
Dead Donal!
Piece of my heart!
Immortal clown!
Black and white
In technicolour!
A smile is general
All over Ireland.

The 24,000 Islands of Stockholm

How you do pontificate
About the politics
Of Stockholm –
About how too sedate,
Too predictable
Are the politics of Stockholm;
How the politics of Stockholm
Are like the citizens of Stockholm,
Too rational, too clinical.

On, on, you sermonise
About the Swedish Academy;
How the waters are awash
With bobbing condoms.
I doubt – but keep
The thought to myself –
That condoms "bob",
Whatever their content
Or lack of content.

Have you nothing to say
About the islands –
The 24,000 islands of Stockholm?
Nothing?
About even, say, a single skerry?
A rock, a pine, a hut?
Nothing?

Not even about one of them?
One of the 24,000
Islands of Stockholm?
Nothing about skimming
With forefinger and thumb
Water-rolled slivers
Of infant granite?
Nothing about how oaks
Can conceive in crevices
On a rock in the Baltic?
Nothing about why
A man and a woman
Might choose to be sparse
On an island in Stockholm?
Nothing about how the Bergman
Question posed by the Garden
Of Eden is whether a human
Can handle leisure or not?
About the origin of deprivation?
About whether or not
The Goth has got it right
In the islands of Stockholm –
In the 24,000
Islands of Stockholm?

29 August 1999

The Bunnacurry Scurry

O Deirdre, meet Deirdre
    Of the sleet-on-the-mountainpeaks smile,
    Sumps-of-streams eyes,
    Bog cotton in your hair
    With your Harry,
Like you I'm in a hurry –
    In a delicate hurry –
To do the Bunnacurry Scurry.

Once, before time began,
　　　When we were in our teens,
It was the Dooagh Rock,
　　　The Innishbiggle Skiffle,
　　　The Dookinella March,
　　　The Crumpaun Jig,
　　　The Dooniver Hornpipe,
　　　The Saula Hucklebuck,
　　　The Valley Waltz,
But now in May ninety-nine,
　　　In the primes of our lives,
It is the Bunnacurry Scurry.

I meet Phil in the Caravanserai –
　　　Phil McHugh that's married to Peadar –
Peadar the TV repair man who loves TV sets so
　　　much, says Vi (approaching ninety but doing
　　　fifty-five), that he holds on to sets for days and weeks
　　　and months and years and eras and centuries –
I'm on my way back from Teddy Lavelle's –
Teddy that's married to Margaret –
From not getting the one *Independent on Sunday*
　　　that did not come in
When everything else came in including the *Observer*
　　　and *The News of the World*
Just as yesterday the one *Guardian on Saturday*
　　　did not come in.
Phil gives me the last *Sunday Times* on Achill Island,
　　　with its Hieronymus Bosch cover of the
　　　　　postmodern, glittering
　　　snake's belly of hackette Terry Keane
　　　　　masticating wads of sterling
　　　notes whilst vomiting up her lover's guts.
Quare stuff to be gawking at after ten o'clock Mass.

Once, before time began,
　　　When we were in our teens,
It was the Dooagh Rock,
　　　The Innishbiggle Skiffle,
　　　The Dookinella March,
　　　The Crumpaun Jig,

The Dooniver Hornpipe,
    The Saula Hucklebuck,
    The Valley Waltz,
    The Cabin Fever,
But now in May ninety-nine,
    In the primes of our lives,
It is the Bunnacurry Scurry.

When I come to Achill on holiday or sabbatical
It is not of course for a holiday or sabbatical.
I come to do a year's work in a week.
I come to dress in green and blue,
Browns, yellows, greys.
I come to do the Bunnacurry Scurry.
Midmornings I do not go down –
Much as I crave conversations of affection –
To Mary Hoban's garden on the mountain,
Or to Mikey O'Malley's post office at Keel
Or to Maeve Calvey's diner for breakfast
Or to Alice's P.O. in Dugort
Or to P. J.'s Seal Caves on the strand,
Stopping in the ditch with delight to let
Ann Fuchs in her yellow Volks wheel past;
Instead I scurry around the bog to the back
    of the mountain and back –
The Bunnacurry Scurry.

Once, before time began,
    When we were in our teens,
It was the Dooagh Rock,
    The Innishbiggle Skiffle,
    The Dookinella March,
    The Crumpaun Jig,
    The Dooniver Hornpipe,
    The Saula Hucklebuck,
    The Valley Waltz,
    The Cabin Fever,
    The Sound Jive,
But now in May ninety-nine,
    In the primes of our lives,
It is the Bunnacurry Scurry.

Is the mist down for the day?
Will it lift in an hour?
Have you noticed in the last twenty minutes
A brightening in the sky –
A slight, slight brightening
Of the sky over Blacksod?
Will you go Newport or Ballycroy
On the road home to Toome?

Once, before time began,
   When we were in our teens,
It was the Dooagh Rock,
   The Innishbiggle Skiffle,
   The Dookinella March,
   The Crumpaun Jig,
   The Dooniver Hornpipe,
   The Saula Hucklebuck,
   The Valley Waltz,
   The Cabin Fever,
   The Sound Jive,
   The Dugort Foxtrot,
But now in May ninety-nine,
   In the primes of our lives,
It is the Bunnacurry Scurry.

23 May 1999

New Year's Eve, 1999

Thank Ophelia that's all over –
Eileen Dubh, Greta Garbo –
One thousand years of teens!
But will our twenties
Be any wonderfuller?
Up the cul-de-sac behind every disco,
Creeps & fiends?

O tomorrow let's be warm
Who today are cool.

It's 3001 I pine for:
The treeline of fiction;
Children of the New Forest;
Our Lady of the Fertile Rock;
You and I –
A pilot and a doctor
Of the fertile ice.

O tomorrow let's be warm
Who today are cool.

What a cheesy scene
Adolescence has been!
The Black Plague when I was thirteen,
Wars of Religion at sixteen,
Famine at eighteen,
Aids when I was nineteen,
Cromwell, Hitler in between.

O tomorrow let's be warm
Who today are cool.

Countdown to 11.27,
Nuzzle noses at 11.38,
Fire off our retro-rockets at 11.49,
Up into our goosepimples at 11.53,
Zapping in the Eye of Midnight
A space shuttle docking – spraying soft slow sticky
        stuff o'er all the beanbags and the screens!
Another small-screen step for kinderkind!

O tomorrow let's be warm
Who today are cool.

Charles Brady's Irish Painter

Camouflaged under a willow tree in Rossnaree,
   Solo in a coracle conceived for three,
Blinking up out from under her black beret,
   Camille Souter – war refugee.

Murphy's Farewell

I

– Oh Mike, don't be mad at me!
– Paul, I am about to don my shades and go back down through economy
class to the driving range in the tail of the plane – in the *tail* of the plane
– and under no circumstances do I want to be intruded upon, and if the
Fasten Your Seat Belt sign comes on I'll fasten my own *portable* seat belt and
keep on driving and driving – my Christy O'Connor swing, once unfurled,
it just keeps on swinging and swinging and swinging – no matter what
the turbulence I'll keep on driving and driving, finding my range and
finding my range and all the time thinking of dear old middle-aged
Cardinal O Fiaich of belovèd memory on the 3 p.m. Aer Lingus flight
back from Rome on 10 October 1982 in thunder and lightning over the
Pyrenees and he *strap-hanging* in the aisle with a cigarette *Carrolls No 1*
making yellow manure of the fingers of his right hand – his *right* hand!
– and he chatting about ecumenism and architecture to Peter Pearson
who is a Quaker – Peter Pearson is a *great* Quaker – and all the life-loving
Aer Lingus hostesses too in awe of His Eminence to say, "Your Eminence,
it is considered not right and fitting to strap-hang at 36,000 feet in an
electrical storm with a lighted cigarette in your hand," because, you see,
Paul, when all is shrugged off or not shrugged off, it's a long way to
Orlando, Florida, it's a long long way to Orlando, Florida, it's an awful
long long way to Orlando, Florida, and never did I cast the first stone
nor indeed never did affable, courteous, convivial Cardinal O'Fiaich –
had I not become a broadcaster I would quite likely have been a Cardinal.
Cardinal Murphy of Orlando, Florida, bugger the begrudgers.

The Laughter Existentialist – that was he.
A serious man for the laughter.
If you canoe'd far enough into the crocodile glades of his glee
You came upon a silent, neglected jetty.

From Kierkegaard to the Marx Brothers and Chaplin
Via Jack Cruise and Laurel and Hardy;
From Maureen Potter to Albert Camus –
Is it possible to laugh on the neglected jetty

Of the world? Is it possible to be polite
In an evil place? To be courteous
In an evil time? To be politely drastic
And simultaneously enthusiastic?

In his Mike-in-the-Box way he was a dead serious man
Up to his neck in the sands of Carnival!
Who will know about all that sunken gold of affection
Until long after the Friday night of Murphy's Farewell?

Until long after the Friday night of Murphy's Farewell.

19 May 2000

The Death of the Mother of the Dalai Lama

to Dr Patrick Nugent

Sitting up in bed, waiting to die –
Root-and-branch pain –
Brooklyn Bridge
Seems to me to be swaying
Inside its plain black frame.

My son, my dutiful son,
Brought it back from New York
After he visited the United Nations.
Hung it himself on the wall
At the foot of my bed.

My son, my thoughtful son,
He remembered to come
Armed with hammer and nail
In his shoulder bag,
Asked me which wall.

At the foot of the bed, I said.
After he'd gone I asked
My sister to take down
Everything else in the room.
Leave me alone with Brooklyn Bridge –

Brooklyn Bridge which
Seems to me to be swaying
Inside its black frame.
Bumble bee in Milky Way.
My son, my dutiful, my thoughtful, my good-as-gold son.

Night-Elegy for Thérèse Cronin

The living pray to the living to recognise difference

Thérèse, black though the day be –
Blackest of January –
Grand Canal in flood –
Darkness at noon –
Raining cats and dogs
On ducks and drakes –
Drenched reeds and supermarket trolleys
Emerge thriving on your glamorous beauty.

At Huband Bridge under a silver birch,
My collar turned up, my cap pulled down,
Like Tony on the road to Moscow,
Feeling like I think you must feel
In your death – coming into your own
Into the heart of the heartless world.

Under the redbrick wall

Not of the Kremlin
But of Sun Microsystems Ireland,
One lone black waterhen
With green legs – green legs, Thérèse! –
And red-and-yellow beak!

Past Baggot Street Bridge
Swirling out of the West
I pass P. K. on his seat
Stopping out in the rain,
Bareheaded, with the hat beside him
For company, a pair of swans
Crossing the bar of his gaze.

Calm cob, calm pen
Not for the first time nor for the last,
Stopping out in the rain, Thérèse,
Stopping out in the rain.

7 January 1999

In Memoriam Sister Mary Magdalena, Martyr (1910–99)

I was born in Westport, County Mayo,
At the start of the blackest century;
Christened Una, third daughter
Of Joseph and Eileen MacBride.
I saw my father taken hostage
By the Black and Tans,
Sunbathed on the rocks of Murrisk,
Played tennis with bank clerks
In the 1920's, spoke French,
Bicycled free in France,
Became a nun of the Holy Faith,
From the North Wall
Sailed for Trinidad in the 1940s
To become a schoolteacher in Couva.

Only thirty-seven years of age
I made my home in Trinidad,

Loved the people as they loved me.
In Trinidad I could be myself;
Could be the girl I always was,
The soul of the party, the Irish nun
Who could not stop laughing;
Could be a friend to Thee
In spite of a jealous bourgeoisie;
Permitted to revisit Ireland
Every five or six years
To see my mother for a day.
Forty years bicycled by
Until too wiped out
To support myself in Trinidad
I was brought back to the mother house
In Dublin in Glasnevin
On Tolka's northern banks.
There, as I knew I would be,
I was arrested by Alzheimer,
But not before I took the gospel chance –
My scriptural prerogative –
To speak from the dock
To the community in the convent chapel:

"I want you to hang me up in the chapel tonight
Head down by the ankles crossed
Christ O Jesus
And cut me open and drain off my blood
And brim up all the chaste enamel buckets
And tiptoe out onto the banks of Tolka
And empty the buckets out into the stars –
Out into the black river of stars –
The believable stars of the night sky.
I want you to stand on Glasnevin hill,
Dearest Sisters of the Holy Faith,
While my blood floods off into the stars –
The Bloody Way:
In which I see
My life and death rhyme
Across the night of time."

* * *

Early Christian Ireland Wedding Cry

I

And now that these two earthlings have been by the poet-priest
  blessed
I will be able to telephone Sarah and burst out
"May I speak to your *husband*?"
Or to telephone Mark and burst out
"May I speak to your *wife*?"
How knees-on-the-full-moon I will feel to bawl
Such interstellar language: *Husband, wife* –
Vocabulary as prehistoric as a tree.
Children – to see the world – climb the treetops of matrimony.
It was for matrimony that we earthlings espoused language;
Husband, wife. Eureka!
The waters of reality are spousal – Gerard Manley Archimedes.
Be it man-made canal or ice age mountain stream,
Water is hand-over-hand, pooled magnanimity.

II

Mark Joyce, Sarah Durcan, we thank you
For shepherding us all to this far, secret, idyllic niche;
Nephin, Lough Conn, Rake Street, Enniscoe.

By marrying each other, you are marrying us
To the marriage place – to the mountain
And to the lake; to the street and to the house.

Long after this afternoon is mustard ashes,
Our eyes will remain upon the mountain,
Sipping insights from our primary sources:

All our childhoods – all those eras:
All those epochs of contemplation when it was nothing
To spend all day on the lakeshore gazing upon the waters;

The unfathomable ticking of one's own heart;
The inscrutable parades of waves;
The unimaginable bottom of the lake.

All those rain curtains of Sunday afternoons
Driving up to Enniscoe House to see what it looked like
And to glean what could be gleaned from the prospect.

All those six-month summers gazing upon the mountain,
Robed in her grey blueness over Conn;
Taliswoman of our fortune and our fate;

Deferring to her for our stimulation and our aim.
Waiting for her to wash herself in a dawn sky
Her man assembles their abode of grass and rain.

III

Marriage is the sunrise of contemplation
In which two creatures compose themselves
Inside the catastrophe of war.
Each is the other's cloak and asylum.
In the last of the light they cleave to one another
On the barbed-wire shore.
Back to back in the weeping and warring night
One sleeps while the other tracks
The cracks upon the moon-stacked windowpane;
The other sleeps and the one awakes
To track a snail shadowing the moon
On that polar hike across the cracked glass.
You are the meaning of my life
And I of yours – the piscina in the niche.

IV

On Midsummer's Day when this chapel was being built,
A housepainter from Lahardaun cried from his ladder:
"Raise high the roofbeams, carpenter!
On Midsummer's Day a hundred years from now
A Durcan will step into this chapel to marry a Joyce!
The tabernacle will needs be inserted in the wall!
Needs be rakes of candlestick racks!
These Joyces and these Durcans – in their communions,
They are fierce people for the lighting of candles!
Needs be also the outside freshly whitewashed
For these two will also be painters!
Members of the craft as well as of the wedding!
We will need burial grounds around the chapel

Because these two will also be philosophers
Who ponder mortality –
How mortality is the mother of integrity."

V

All things come in twos – which is why
Marriage is the paradigm of science.
The code of all physics and all chemistry is marriage;
The figure of all energy is two.
Caspar the Cat, I dive round the villages of Mayo –
Hollymount, Roundfort, Turlough, Straide –
Doff my Castlebar hat with its white cockade,
Lean upon my Westport stick with its brass ferrule,
And twinkling at the gate of the scythed hayfield
At the top of Rake Street
I wait for thee, my love, to take my arm
And be my spouse for now and evermore.
One by one we enter the aisle of Rake Street
In order to exit it as two.

VI

By the waters of Conn, under the eye of Nephin,
We sit down and kneel and laugh and pray.
Cloud systems that began their lives in Labrador
Empty their waters on Nephin's peaks;
Mountain streams charge down the mountainside
Past the two-light east window, the lake
Brims, turns over on its sleeping side,
Yawns, smiles, frowns, goes on
Dreaming its 600 million-year-old dream –
This is where the Durcans and the Joyces hail from:
Our dreamspace, the County of Mayo!
We – the wedding guests – die out of the frame
Leaving Mark and Sarah alone in the storm,
Secure in the fleece of the sheep of the yew tree,
Their foreheads thumbed by the asylum-seeker Christ
Who stowed away into earthlingland to secrete compassion;
Leaving them in peace – together, each to each –
Let us now praise these waters and the mountain:
The sleeping woman with her waking man.

21 June 2000

* * *

Cries of an Irish Caveman

I

Every day on the off-chance –
On the ten million-to-one chance –
You might knock on my door
I organise my cave and make my bed.

II

In my bed alone at night I press
My face down deep
Into the cold, white, Egyptian
Cotton pillow of your soul.

III

My arms are empty all for the want of thee:
A pair of arms on the rampage in a crypt.

IV

With whom do you shower?
Do you complete the circle?

V

You who dared me love define:
Love is to see the story in a line.

VI

I drive past your villa on a whim:
Hoping you are out, hoping you are in.

VII

An interloper forceps your name up out of chat:
I stifle a bawl.

VIII

But most of all I miss your laugh:
Your haughtiness's hot bath.

IX

What am I doing standing on no legs outside your gate?
Gargling, only gargling.

X

When in a restaurant behind Victoria railway station
Your name is spoken, my stomach lets drop its plates.

XI

Last night in Hammersmith the barman saw you with Greg.
So that's who it is! Greg!

XII

I am sitting alone in my cave on Friday afternoon.
You have gone to bed for the weekend with your new man.

XIII

I am rocking in the bay of your rejection.
Becalmed in the nirvana of my defeat.

XIV

Beethoven fell out of his podium in love with Teresa.
Arrarra.

XV

All the hot day long your bladderwrack detonates salt water.
All the cold night long my berries bleed.

XVI

I think of you and he lounging in The Rose and Goat:
The suction of your lipstick, he clearing his throat.

XVII

On my answer machine I hear you say "See you in the next
   century."
I stoop into the wrecking ball of the future.

XVIII

I fly over to London and search Hammersmith for you.
Not a trace of you in the hot sardine guts of the pubs.

XIX

You know I know you know the choreography of my humiliation:
My flesh spancelled, my soul bellowing.

XX

A practical woman like you cannot bear to hear
That ejaculation of terror – "I love you".

XXI

What is it? Above all, your voice!
Your voice with its gloved hands!

XXII

I see his head upon your pillow.
I snatch at my nail scissors.

XXIII

I believe that you will come back to me
Although I know you will not.

XXIV

After your social phone call, I brushed my hair with toothpaste.
And there was peace on the sofa.

XXV

I stare across the flooded river at your villa:
I am a Russian at the Finish of Love.

XXVI

Ethics are the co-ordinates of aesthetics:
How to live with the living, how to die with the dead.

XXVII

There is no more peaceful way to spend
    a brutal winter in the north
Than every afternoon at the cave door alone drawing you,
    colouring you in.

XXVIII

Driving through Oola I glare at the derelict petrol pump;
Why are you not standing there filling up your tank?

XXIX

In the hotels of the world I ask always for a double bed:
To turn over on my side and caress your abstract head.

XXX

That a man does not bleed does not mean a man cheats:
A man also has problems with sheets.

XXXI

The scene of the accident is awfuller than the actual accident:
Incinerated intimacy, charred seats.

XXXII

Two months since you left a message on my answer machine:
I play it back every day – Cita's Theme!

XXXIII

The odd time it rings I clutch at the phone:
It's not you, and I cut myself down.

XXXIV

In sleet I slink out to the supermarket.
Checkout girls; heads down; no eye contact.

XXXV

From pub to pub in Hammersmith:
Tossing the poleaxe after the chainsaw.

XXXVI

Muttering to my bookspines on the shelves of my cave:
Will they also one day walk out on me?

XXXVII

Drawing on my walls keeps me sane:
With my fingers, smudges of green.

XXXVIII

I have two TVs in my cave
But I only watch them four hours a day.
I crouch – an amputee –
And tweezer my eyebrows or the walls.
I am scratching the surface:
A cow, a woman, a bucket.

XXXIX

If my end is to be whooping it up in the Alzheimer's disco
It'll be for you I'll be whooping – the lady that's known as Cita.

The Lamb in the Oven

Unreal jealous I am of the lamb
In the Aga – in the bottom
Left-hand oven, a black lamb
On the brink of extinction,
Less than a day old, having
Its existence retrieved by you, Lady
Of the First Snowdrops and the Last Daffodils.

All day you kneel by the Aga
Resuscitating a lamb in a cardboard box,
Feeding it through a straw and
The teat of a baby's milk bottle;
Its own mother – a muddied ewe,
Marooned by a snowstorm –
Cannot feed her own lamb.

At the kitchen window my charcoal jowls
Peeping in, grinding their molars;
Unable to comprehend that feminine
Equals maternal and that you in your rancid,
Brown cords are of all women the most feminine;
Your girl's face on your forty-odd-years-old neck.
At the windowpane of jealousy I woo you, Lady
Of the First Snowdrops and the Last Daffodils.

Torn in Two

That twenty-two page love letter in which
I slopped out my heart to you,
Comparing you, my mountain woman,
With a gold hoard secreted in loughwater
Under a thorn tree in Rear Cross –
How I waited day after day for a reply,
Week after week, month after month.
When after seven months a reply came
I did not recognise your hand on the envelope
But inside there it was, my letter,

My twenty-two page love letter, all of it,
Which you had torn in two.

I get up every day torn in two.
I trudge over to the minimart torn in two.
I buy my sliced pan torn in two.
I buy my low-fat milk torn in two.
I traipse back home torn in two.
I crouch in front of the TV torn in two.
I gobble my microwave dinner torn in two.
I kneel down at my bed torn in two.
I whisper my bedtime prayers torn in two.
I clamber into bed torn in two.
But I cannot go to sleep torn in two.
I read about the Taliban torn in two.
I spend the night on my back torn in two.
I get up every day torn in two.
Have I no hope of being one with you?
I am a bright man torn in two.

My Bride of Aherlow

Oh was it that in my black book sack
I carried too many years?
And that the hairs of my head were grey
And gelled in too many tears?
That in the cave pools of my eyes
There were no goldfish to arouse?
That down the arches of my eyes
Streeled ivy of brows?
O marry me now in my grave, my grave,
My Bride of Aherlow!

Or was it that in my black book sack
There were no seeds to be seen?
Or only such seeds as were too scarce
To sow in a pink tureen?
That for every bead of silver seed
There were too many sheaths of dust?

Or blacker than dust or polythene
An odour of things unseen?
O marry me now in my grave, my grave,
My Bride of Aherlow!

Or was it that in my black book sack
I carried near nothing at all?
Not even food for the table,
Nor drink for the long black haul?
Was it that all I could claim my own
Was the road and the sky and the night?
That my ears were pricked and my nostrils dilated
To a premonition of fright?
O marry me now in my grave, my grave,
My Bride of Aherlow.

Or was it in fact that the actual sack –
The actual Mayo black book sack –
Had nothing in it at all?
That when you delved down dark and deep,
Laughingly hopefully down dark deep,
There was Mars-like nothing there;
Nothing that God or woman could save
Or knead up a thorny stair?
O marry me now in my grave, my grave,
My Bride of Aherlow.

Bovinity

It's not something you're born with,
Like a mouth or an eye.
It's something you detect and cultivate –
It's something you divine –
Bovinity!
Ignoring the crack of her whip,
Flicking my tail.

I am a middle of the road cow.

I like to sit down in the middle of the road,
Curl up and up, before and behind,
Wind my tail around and around myself,
And, accumulating all my flesh and all my soul,
Watch the world go by:
Watch the traffic slowing down and circling round me;
Or turn my head away to browse in the horizon.
I have only one preoccupation in existence and that is
    affection.
In the middle of the road all day
On affection I ruminate.

Cowlady – who stole my love away
In the twilight of time –
Blow your horn or flash your lights
But I am staying in the middle of the road
Where I belong. You go and join
The club of logic, on the left or right.
Bovinity!
Raising one hoof, tendering it
Out over the precipice of the cliff,
Drawing the air, all
500 feet of air
Above the sea below,
Withdrawing it.
Bovinity!

It's not something you're born with,
Like a mouth or an eye.
It's something you detect and cultivate –
It's something you divine –
Bovinity!
Ignoring the crack of her whip,
Flicking my tail.

1999

THE ART OF LIFE (2004)

The Man with a Bit of Jizz in Him

My husband is a man –
With a bit of jizz in him.
On Monday night in Sligo I said to him:
"Let's go someplace for a week
Before the winter is on top of us."
He said: "Where would you like to go?"
I said: "Down south – West Cork or Kerry."
He said: "Too much hassle."
I said: "Where would you like to go?"
He said: "Dublin Airport early tomorrow morning.
I'll drive halfway, you drive halfway."
We caught the Aer Lingus Dublin–Nice direct flight:
180 euro return.
Driving to Dublin he phoned his niece in Hertz.
He said: "I want a car in Nice."
Hertz gave us a brand-new Peugeot.
Only thirty miles on the clock.
(If you're over forty-five, they give you a big car.
If you're a young fellow, they give you a small car
That you can go and crash.)
There's only two ways out of Nice Airport –
West or East: simple.
At the first filling station he stopped
And asked the way to St-Paul-de-Vence.
"St-Paul-de-Vence? Exit 48
And do not come on to the motorway again
Until you want to go back to Ireland."
An hour later I was lying on a duvet
In a three-star hotel in St-Paul-de-Vence.
It was spotless. Spotless!
I was that pleased with him I shook his hand
And pulled him in under the duvet with me.
An attractive middle-aged housewife I may be *but* –
There is nothing to beat a man with a bit of jizz in him.

Golden Island Shopping Centre

After tortellini in The Olive Grove on the quays
I drive over to the adjacent shopping centre,
Golden Island Shopping Centre,
Around whose acres of car park
I drive in circles for quarter of an hour
Before finding a slot in a space painted yellow:
GOLDEN ISLAND EXPECTANT MOTHERS

Two hours later I stumble from Tesco
With high-altitude sickness;
Dazed, exhausted, apprehensive, breathless;
In worse condition than
Many a climber on the South Col of Everest.
Such mobs of shoppers on a Sunday afternoon,
Such powerlessness.

Loading up the boot of my car
I perceive through a white mist
A small, bejowled, red-headed, middle-aged lady in black
Standing in front of my car
With a Jack Russell terrier in a muzzle.
She is writing down my registration number.

I enquire: "What are you doing?"
She snaps: "You can see perfectly well what I am doing."
I ask: "Why are you writing down my registration number?"
From under the visor of her black baseball cap
She barks: "You have no right
To park your car in the space reserved for
GOLDEN ISLAND EXPECTANT MOTHERS."

I rumble in an avalanche of offended dignity:
"How dare you!
I *am* a Golden Island Expectant Mother!
I am a fifty-eight-years old male of the species
And I have been expecting for nineteen years.
Only last week I had a scan.
Despite you and your terrier

Ireland remains my native land –
My Golden Island –
And I will park where I can.
So go soap your jowls in the jacuzzis of Malaga:
I *am* a Golden Island Expectant Mother!"

A Robin in Autumn Chatting at Dawn

Late in the afternoon at the top of the lane
On my way back from a hop to the cliff
I came upon a human – a male – at the gable
Across the lane from the bridge over the mountain stream.
He was middle-aged, overweight, weary, anxious.
Quite like myself.

I uttered nothing and kept *my* head down,
He uttered nothing and kept *his* head down.
Rain clouds split open like rice bags.
He stared at me as if I could shelter him,
As if I *should* shelter him. He dashed himself
Against the whitewashed, dry-stone wall under the sycamore
And stared at me as if the doomsday had arrived.
If I could have, I would have put a wing around him;
A forlorn, middle-aged man in his Day-Glo green anorak.

While he lurked there in the midnight of the tree
I poked about in the ruts of the lane
Amusing myself, which I do when I can.
The harder the rain teemed, the more revived I felt.
I turned up autumn leaves, gutting their undersides
Of their last midges.

The only real dampener was the human
Feeling sorry for himself and glancing at me
As much as to say: "Poor robin!"
Why are humans so patronising of robins?
They don't mean to be, of course, but they are.
When the storm showed not a sign of abating
He began to slink back up the hill to the cottage

I stood erect inspecting his plump rump,
His downcast neck. After he'd departed
I swooped into the nearest fuchsia, preened,
Had a quick perch, a good chirp.

Middle age for any creature is a problematic plummet
But why do humans have to be so crestfallen about it?
With my hands behind my back and my best breast out,
My telescope folded up in my wings, my tricorn gleaming,
I emerge on the bridge of my fuchsia, whistling:
All hands on deck! Hy Brasil, ho!

The Far Side of the Island

Driving over the mountain to the far side of the island
I am brooding neither on what lies ahead of me
Nor on what lies behind me. Up here
On top of the mountain, in the palm of its plateau,
I am being contained by its wrist and its fingertips.

The middle of the journey is what is at stake –
Those twenty-five miles or so of in-betweenness
In which marrow of mortality hardens
In the bones of the nomad. From finite end
To finite end, the orthopaedics of mortality.

Up here on the plateau above the clouds,
Peering down on the clouds in the valleys,
There are no fences, only moorlands
With wildflowers as far as the eye can see;
The earth's unconscious in its own pathology.

Yet when I arrive at the far side of the island
And peer down at the village on the rocks below,
The Atlantic Ocean rearing raw white knuckles,
Although I am globally sad I am locally glad
To be about to drive down that corkscrew road.

Climbing down the tree-line, past the first cottage,
Past the second cottage, behind every door
A neighbour. It is the company of his kind
Man was born for. Could I have known,
Had I not chanced the far side of the island?

Achill Island Man

On Achill Island when I wake in the morning
I find myself in the Amusements Arcade of my own body
And I am standing up against the pinball machine
And I insert 20 cents and I give it a kick
And I watch all the small pink balls of pain
Tripping on lights all over my body.
Oh! No!
Toes! Knees! Elbows! Shoulder-blades!
Everywhere I look, small pink balls of pain
And I mind not to rub my neck. Anyways,
I come out of the arcade and I blink
And despite all the weather
In my body every place I look
I do have to smile at all those lights
Going on and off. It's amazing, I think,
It's amazing I'm still alive. Oh, man!
No, I never watch television!
I might have colon cancer. I might not.
I might have lumbago or sciatica.
I might have gallstones. I might have ulcers.
I might have diverticulitis!
I might have auricular fibrillation!
I might have diabetes!
As a matter of fact, I do have diabetes,
But with the pills it's all the one.
Will I bother having a haircut?
I will bother having a haircut
And I will get a lift home
In time for the five o'clock removal of my neighbour
Who was seventy-one – she had a year on me –

And who was a very quiet woman, but as good a woman as
        you'd find in all of Achill Island
And after that I will have three pints in The Crossroads Inn –
Maybe four –
And after that I will go home and have my dinner
And after dinner I will go to bed and begin
The whole story all over again – isn't that it?

Ireland 2002

Do you ever take a holiday abroad?
No, we always go to America.

HEADLINES

At 8.40 a.m. on the morning of Sunday, 7 September 2003 on an island
in Upper Lough Erne, County Fermanagh, Northern Ireland, an elderly
couple, Mr and Mrs John James Reihill, stepped out of their farmhouse
where the Reihill family have lived and farmed for generations and walked
down the path through the fir trees and the hydrangeas to the shore in
whose reeds their small rowing boat nestled, stepped in and set off across
the waters of the lough to attend 9 a.m. Mass on the mainland in the
Holy Cross Church in Lisnaskea. In Jerusalem the Israeli Prime Minister
Ariel Sharon threatened to assassinate the Palestinian leader Yasser Arafat
who the day before had compelled his own Prime Minister, Mahmoud
Abbas, to resign. In Baghdad the US Defense Secretary Mr Donald
Rumsfeld, who was due to address US troops in Tikrit, had to cancel
his address for fear of being heckled by his troops. In Belfast, Mr Gerry
Adams reiterated his "firm view" that in the light of the discovery of
the remains of Mrs Jean McConville in Shelling Beach and next week's
excavation of a Monaghan bog for the remains of Mr Columba McVeigh,
and in order that these excavations may bring "closure" to grieving
families, it would be better for all concerned not to speak in public any
further about the missing bodies of innocent people murdered thirty
years ago by the IRA. In Dublin on radio, television and in the news-
papers, serious discussions were conducted on the merits of rival TV
chat shows. Mrs Reihill sat in the bow of the rowing boat in her brown

Sunday dress, black low-heeled shoes, long green overcoat and white leather handbag with gold chain. Mr Reihill sat in the corner of the stern and switched on the ignition of the outboard engine. The small craft lifted its bow in the air and, as Mr Reihill sat low in the water, Mrs Reihill gazed down at her husband in his black corduroy cap, his black bespoke suit, his laced-up size eleven black shoes and his ankle-length black-belted leather greatcoat. He seemed to smile through his bespectacled beard, but neither of them spoke. A sentinel heron watched from a stone and five swans sailed in procession past them. At Mass in Lisnaskea they heard the priest read from the Gospel of St Mark, 7: 31–37, where Jesus makes a deaf-and-dumb man hear and speak. Jesus said to the man: "Ephphatha," that is, "Be opened." After Mass and after chatting for three quarters of an hour with Mass-goers, Mr and Mrs John James Reihill visited the newsagents where, tomorrow being their wedding anniversary, each, without the other knowing, purchased a wedding anniversary card before making the return journey across the waters of the lough to their island home. Their sheepdog Bonny lay smiling on the wooden jetty. Pacing up behind his wife through the fir trees and the hydrangeas with his hands clasped behind his back Mr Reihill announced slowly and magniloquently to Mrs Reihill: "John James Reihill needs a cup of tea before he goes any further."

The Celtic Tiger

I

I am an unmarried mother –
Tomorrow is my twenty-second birthday –
And I am waiting for the Number 3 bus
From the power station
To bring my five-year-old son Jack to the clinic.
I was reared in the orphanage.
I loved it in the orphanage.
The nuns were cool,
Especially Sister Louise.
She was my best friend.
She was awesome.
But one day when I was sixteen

I was told to go downstairs
To the parlour beside the hall door.
There was a man and a woman.
They smiled: "We are your parents
And we've come to take you home."
I cried tears and I begged
Sister Louise to keep me
And Sister Louise cried tears,
But I was taken away.
That same day my parents
Sold me to a man called Kirwan –
They didn't tell me his Christian name –
Kirwan is all they kept calling him –
Kirwan! Kirwan!
That night Kirwan raped me.
He was like a looney. His mickey
Had bits of potato on it.
He kept it up all night.
Roaring, moaning, beating me.
Nine months later I had my lovely little boy, Jack.

II

I am my parents' youngest daughter
And they are so proud of me
For all kinds of reasons,
But principally because I earn
300, 000 euro a year
As a corporate solicitor in Dublin
And I am only thirty-one.
They are so proud of my lifestyle.
I own three houses and I buy
Two or three new outfits a week
And I holiday in the Seychelles
And I am always in a relationship.
I am never not in a relationship.
My parents really are so proud of me.
Children? No way!

Asylum Seeker

Hurtling along the road from Castlebar to Westport
In my filthy, two-door, bottle-green Opel Astra,
The last stage of the drive from Dublin,
Five miles out from Westport I catch my first glimpse of
    Croagh Patrick,
The mountain of my birth,
Being stark gently,
Bluely-greyly.

Croagh Patrick, the Reek –
Ararat of Armenia –
Let no Turk try to still my feet –
O Westport in the Light of Asia Minor –
The mountain whose long hands are steepled in prayer,
Whose ten fingers are twinned at their tips
Posing the question
To which no man of salt knows the answer.

My head drops onto the driving wheel,
My accelerator sobs,
For I am almost home. Here
Only is where I can call "home"
Under the Westport skyline
Where I know I can seek asylum;
Where seven thousand years ago
When sea wrestled sky
Noah also did seek asylum.

Here is where I can drop
Dead in the sub-zero dawn outside
Any man's front door and not
Be rolled over and kicked into the gutter.
Here is where the young curate will bless
My old man's baby corpse
And a pass-the-hat-round will get me
A cubby-hole in the clay in Aughawall cemetery
Under the MacBride cairn
Under the holy mountain of my birth –
Croagh Patrick on the Westport skyline.

Tonight at twilight
I land into Westport from Dublin,
Into a huddle of snowdrops under a scarf of crows
In the schoolyard of the bare treetops
At playtime, bedtime,
Cawing, cackling, chasing, circling,
And one yellow crocus under an agèd lime,
And green schools of daffodils
About to wake up into their fate of gold
Three days before Ash Wednesday.
I fling up into the darkening sky
The pancakes of my soul
And jump into the arms of my fleeting god-daughter
As she steps up into a white minibus to transport her to her
    bower.

The Westport Ethiopian

Last Saturday the 28th of February 2004
At the Connacht Junior & Senior Indoor Championships
In the indoor tartan and banked track in Nenagh, Co Tipperary
In the Girls' Under 13s' 600 metres
I saw an eleven-year-old Ethiopian girl
Running in the green-and-red top
Of the Westport Athletic Club:
Maria Caterina Walassie.
Only it seemed to me that she was not really running,
She was making music with her gazelle legs
And the track was the stave, all crotchets and semi-quavers,
Along which, sight-reading, she was striding out
In grace-notes of lopes and bounds.
She won by about fifty-five metres,
But it did not look like winning
So much as chanting
In the old, slow, formal, Ethiopian way.
It was a kind of long-legged chanting –
Chanting the chorus of an ancient tribal chant
Of the lands of her forefathers:
"Over the mountains and far away
In the city of the wise king."

The Beautiful Game

Sunday afternoon in August, sunny, warm,
Watching TV – the beautiful game
Being played with professional ugliness,
Manchester United versus Aston Villa.
My floor littered with the customary Sabbath garbage:
Newspapers, newspapers, more newspapers.

Such a tender knock on the door, I wonder –
Did I imagine it?
I unlock it and see before me
A handsome, middle-aged woman
In dull gold tank-top, dull gold slacks.
I have never seen her before in my life.

I peer out at her over my reading specs,
Not knowing what to say to her,
Saying "Yes?"
She does not speak, but returns
My perplexed, anxious gaze.
She says: "Nessa."

"Oh Nessa!"
We'd been married for fifteen years
A long time ago.
I switch off the TV,
Interrupting
The beautiful game.

"I am on my way back to Cork."
Twenty minutes later she resumes her journey,
Driving away in her blue machine.
I do not switch back on the TV.
I have had more than enough,
For one afternoon, of the beautiful game.

The Wisdom of Ex-Wives

When on the phone to my ex-wife
I admitted I was lonely,
She said: "Why don't you play golf
If you're feeling lonely?"

I said: "With whom would I play?"
She said: "Can't you play on your own?"
That's the sort of thing ex-wives say:
"Can't you play on your own?"

I hooted down the phone:
"Playing on your own is an *oxymoron!*"
I wanted to change the subject and to say goodbye,
And to stand up and cry.

The 2003 World Snooker Championship

Don't lecture me about lint on the baize –
I am ninety-six years of age.

What an old woman like me needs
More than a meal or medicine
Or a life sentence in a nursing home
Is seventeen days in front of the television
In my own home
Watching the World Snooker Championship
In the Crucible in Sheffield.
Although I like rugby,
I am a snooker fanatic.

Don't lecture me about lint on the baize –
I am ninety-six years of age.

I am frail and cranky
And I have a pain in my neck
That would make Humpty Dumpty

Grateful to fall off his wall,
But at a crucial moment in the Crucible
I sizzle with satisfaction
At the spectacle of a young man's bottom
As he bends down low over the green baize
To pot the black –
A superbly turned-out young man's trim bottom,
The left cheek of which is streamlined
With shoe heel and collar bone
When he lifts his left leg to spread-eagle it
Like a pedigree cocker spaniel
Along the kerb of the table.

Don't lecture me about lint on the baize –
I am ninety-six years of age.

And when that young man hails
From Ranelagh, Dublin 6,
And when his name is Ken
I am as much a believer in the Resurrection
As the Pope in Rome.
If there is a heaven –
One must not say so
But I doubt it –
Heaven would be the Triangle at night
Of snooker tables lit by floodlights
Under the whites of whose eyes
Thousands upon thousands
Of trim-bottomed young men
Would be chalking their cues
Before focussing their perfect pelvises
On the white cue ball,
The red and the black,
And on all the coloured balls –
All the coloured balls.

Don't lecture me about lint on the baize –
I am ninety-six years of age.

Michael Hartnett, the Poet King

The poet went to his hotel room and sitting on the edge of the
    bed wished he were dead.
"O God," he said, "I have had enough. Take my life; I am no
    better than my ancestors."
Then he lay down and went to sleep.
But his soul stayed awake and said, "Get up and eat."
He rummaged in his carrier bag and found a doughnut and a
    bottle of still water.
He ate and drank and then lay down again.
But his soul said to him a second time, "Get up and eat, or you
    will not be able to give the poetry reading tonight."
So he got up and ate and drank, and made a cup of tea with a
    teabag, and strengthened by that food he went on giving
    poetry readings for forty years until he reached the hospital
    where he gladly, not sadly, died.
Forty years ago he would have been glad to know that forty
    years later he would gladly, not sadly, die.

The 12 O'Clock Mass, Roundstone, County Galway, 28 July 2002

On Sunday the 28th of July 2002 –
The summer it rained almost every day –
In rain we strolled down the road
To the church on the hill overlooking the sea.
I had been told to expect "a fast Mass".
Twenty minutes. A piece of information
Which disconcerted me.

Out onto the altar hurried
A short, plump priest in middle age
With a horn of silver hair,
In green chasuble billowing
Like a poncho or a caftan over
White surplice and a pair
Of Reeboks – mammoth trainers.

516

He whizzed along,
Saying the readings himself as well as the Gospel;
Yet he spoke with conviction and with clarity;
His every action an action
Of what looked like effortless concentration;
Like Tiger Woods on top of his form.
His brief homily concluded with a solemn request.

To the congregation he gravely announced:
"I want each of you to pray for a special intention,
A very special intention.
I want each of you – in the sanctity of your own souls –
To pray that, in the All-Ireland
Championship hurling quarter-final this afternoon in Croke
    Park,
Clare will beat Galway."

The congregation splashed into laughter
And the church became a church of effortless prayer.
He whizzed through the Consecration
As if the Consecration was something
That occurs at every moment of the day and night;
As if betrayal and the overcoming of betrayal
Were an every-minute occurrence.

As if the Consecration was the "now"
In the "now" of the Hail Mary prayer:
"Pray for us *now* and at the hour of our death."
At the Sign of Peace he again went sombre
As he instructed the congregation:
"I want each of you to turn around and say to each other:
'You are beautiful.'"

The congregation was flabbergasted, but everyone fluttered
And swung around and uttered that extraordinary phrase:
"You are beautiful."
I shook hands with at least five strangers,
Two men and three women, to each of them saying:
"You are beautiful." And they to me:
"You are beautiful."

At the end of Mass, exactly twenty-one minutes,
The priest advised: "Go now and enjoy yourselves
For that is what God made you to do –
To go out there and enjoy yourselves
And to pray that, in the All-Ireland
Championship hurling quarter-final between Clare and Galway
In Croke Park, Clare will win."

After Mass, the rain had drained away
Into a tide of sunlight on which we sailed out
To St Macdara's Island and dipped our sails –
Both of us smiling, radiant sinners.
In a game of pure delight, Clare beat Galway by one point:
Clare 1 goal and 17 points, Galway 19 points.
"Pray for us *now* and at the hour of our death."

Rosie Joyce

I

That was that Sunday afternoon in May
When a hot sun pushed through the clouds
And you were born!

I was driving the two hundred miles from west to east,
The sky blue-and-white china in the fields
In impromptu picnics of tartan rugs;

When neither words nor I
Could have known that you had been named already
And that your name was Rosie –

Rosie Joyce! May you some day in May
Fifty-six years from today be as lucky
As I was when you were born that Sunday:

To drive such side-roads, such main roads, such ramps, such
    roundabouts,
To cross such bridges, to by-pass such villages, such towns
As I did on your Incarnation Day.

By-passing Swinford – Croagh Patrick in my rear-view mirror –
My mobile phone rang and, stopping on the hard edge of
    P. Flynn's highway,
I heard Mark your father say:

"A baby girl was born at 3.33 p.m.
Weighing 7 and a 1/2 lbs in Holles Street.
Tough work, all well."

II

That Sunday in May before daybreak
Night had pushed up through the slopes of Achill
Yellow forefingers of Arum Lily – the first of the year;

Down at the Sound the first rhododendrons
Purpling the golden camps of whins;
The first hawthorns powdering white the mainland;

The first yellow irises flagging roadside streams;
Quills of bog-cotton skimming the bogs;
Burrishoole cemetery shin-deep in forget-me-nots;

The first sea pinks speckling the seashore;
Cliffs of London Pride, groves of bluebell,
First fuchsia, Queen Anne's Lace, primrose.

I drove the Old Turlough Road, past Walter Durcan's Farm,
Umbrella'd in the joined handwriting of its ash trees;
I drove Tulsk, Kilmainham, the Grand Canal.

Never before had I felt so fortunate
To be driving back into Dublin city;
Each canal bridge an old pewter brooch.

I rode the waters and the roads of Ireland,
Rosie, to be with you, seashell at my ear!
How I laughed when I cradled you in my hand.

Only at Tarmonbarry did I slow down,
As in my father's Ford Anglia half a century ago
He slowed down also, as across the River Shannon

We crashed, rattled, bounced on a Bailey bridge;
Daddy relishing his role as Moses,
Enunciating the name of the Great Divide

Between the East and the West!
We are the people of the West,
Our fate to go East.

No such thing, Rosie, as a Uniform Ireland
And please God there never will be;
There is only the River Shannon and all her sister rivers

And all her brother mountains and their family prospects.
There are higher powers than politics
And these we call wildflowers or, geologically, people.

Rosie Joyce – that Sunday in May
Not alone did you make my day, my week, my year
To the prescription of Jonathan Philbin Bowman –

Daymaker!
Daymaker!
Daymaker!

Popping out of my daughter, your mother –
Changing the expressions on the faces all around you –
All of them looking like blue hills in a heat haze –

But you saved my life. For three years
I had been subsisting in the slums of despair,
Unable to distinguish one day from the next.

III

On the return journey from Dublin to Mayo
In Charlestown on Main Street
I meet John Normanly, organic farmer from Curry.

He is driving home to his wife Caroline
From a Mountbellew meeting of the Western Development
    Commission
Of Dillon House in Ballaghadereen.

He crouches in his car, I waver in the street,
As we exchange lullabies of expectancy;
We wet our foreheads in John Moriarty's autobiography.

The following Sunday is the Feast of the Ascension
Of Our Lord into Heaven:
Thank You, O Lord, for the Descent of Rosie onto Earth.

* * *

The Art of Life

A young French family's meanderings
On the cobblestones between the wings
Of the Uffizi Gallery in Florence,
Between the lines of pavement artists
Marketing watercolours of the Ponte Vecchio
Or instant portraiture,
Converge on, circle, halt,
Hover at the stall announcing
Caricatura 10 euro.

In a card-table chair, a man in black
With silver highlights in his black hair,
Black wraparound Ray–Ban sunglasses,
Long nose hooked over thick-lipped mouth,
Laconically dragging on a cigarette,
Legs crossed at the knees.
Slouching in inscrutability
He could be a casual wife-beater
Or a safe, devoted father.

The yellow-shirted ten-year-old son
Clamours to have his caricature done.
Papa hesitates (as papas do),
But Maman immediately acquiesces.
When the question is her unique son
A mother will always trumpet
Where a father fears to coo.
Yet not even she on her decisive feet
Foresees the repercussions.

The appallingly blank cartridge paper –
The white suspense of nothing happening –
The forensic silence of calculation –
The first probings of the scalpel-nibbed pen –
The first smudges of the charcoal –
The awakening of the laid-back artist –
The emergence of a hairline
Decipherable as her unique son –
The unbelievable rebirth of his laughing soul.

The portrait done, the artist allows
A smile to kindle the clouds of his face.
He holds up the portrait for all to see.
Passers-by cluster round the happy birth.
High in the east wing of the Uffizi
The head of a curator peers out of a window.
Papa looks over at his wife and blushes,
Just as he did ten years ago
In the maternity hospital in Nancy.

And she – *Mama* – *Mère* – *Maman* –
She is bashfuller than Mary
In a triptych of the Annunciation
And prouder by a nostril's gauntlet –
Her newborn son alighting on earth
Under the noses of Giotto and Dante.
She lets out a snorted scream,
The scones and jam of her being
Hot on the stones of Tuscany.

Aldeburgh October Storm

At noon at reception in the small, sedate, family-run Wentworth
    Hotel in Aldeburgh
Such are the numbers of guests trooping in the door in gusts and
    windfalls
I find I can neither check in or check out, but instead shelter in a
    corner
Watching the jostling and cries and stumbles and embraces and
    handshakes and pecks and ejaculations.
"There are two parties commencing simultaneously" – the
    landlord tells me,
His pinstripe shirtsleeves rolled up, his silk yellow tie unfurling
    over his left shoulder:
"In the conservatory the christening party of the first son of the
    Briggs-Palmers, Jonny,
Named after the English international rugby outhalf, Jonny
    Wilkinson
And in the library Lady Stevenson-Ellis's ninetieth birthday party,

Lady Florence Stevenson-Ellis of Grundisburgh."
"All the guests have got mixed up in the foyer
And what with the bedlam and the wild wet balmy gale blowing
    in every time the door opens,
The wheelchairs are winding up at the christening party, while
The baby-buggies are shooting around Lady Stevenson-Ellis's
    ankles
And there's not a thing she can do about it, but she doesn't
    mind –
She survived the Normandy landings and she still has not got
    Parkinson's" –
Shouts General Fairley-Duff, himself shaking all over,
To which General McMillan-Thorpe shouts:
"Is there anyone here who has not got Parkinson's?"
Where have I seen all this before?
Ah yes – at Becher's Brook first time round, all sixty-seven horses
Taking off together, leaping together, landing together, falling
    together, getting up together.
Who ever said the English nation is dead? Or that the English
    nation has lost its soul?
"Preponderance of leaf in sunlight in storm – is what I say.
In the face of grief we put our best foot forward, crimson and
    gold in the face of grief.
Hey-ho, trample my shingle, but if it isn't Ingrid Eason over there,
Knew her when she was a Wren, one of the Easons of Dublin,
    newsagents.
Well, what does it matter so long as it pays the mortgage off, a net
    earner,
And, don't look but that's Edwin de Vere Todd, lovely bloke, used
    work for me, utterly useless, totally amoral, King's Lynn;
Only this morning I was feeling doggone abysmal, Jack, – oh God
    I do want to sit down, upholstery or wicker, Jack? –
But I said to myself: come on, old boy, get out your best hounds-
    tooth
And your best twill and take down your blackthorn stick and
So here I am, a large G and T in hand, and still not sure whether
    I'm at the Briggs-Palmer christening
Or at Lady Stevenson-Ellis's ninetieth. By Jove, *some* day, isn't it,
    some rain, but warm rain, eh?
Seagulls all over the shop, seagulls as big as frankfurters on stilts,
    big as frigging Viking longships.

524

See the lifeboat beetling out this morning?
And the North Sea behaving more like the darned Atlantic than
  the North Sea?
Some bloody Norwegian trawler no doubt.
How is it, tell me, it's always us that's rescuing them, eh?
Anyway cheers, and let's hope young Briggs-Palmer is half the
  man Lady Stevenson-Ellis has been –
Well, you know what I mean! Come on, old girl, don't be an old
  stick in the mud!
We'll all beat this Parkinson's, if I've any say in the matter,
Suffolk is the best place in the world – at least I think it is,
Even if life is all Dutch to us lot, and Aldeburgh's the peach in
  the orchard,
Yesterday I had to step over a chap in Neptune Alley, what
Are drunkards coming to at all these days, I says to myself,
Another large G and T there, my good man, and a smear of that
  black caviar on a cheese-stick wouldn't be a bad idea,
Excuse me ma'am, we English, you know, we may be down on
  our luck, but we do bring a bit of malarkey into this old black
  kip of a world, don't we?
Madam, I do beg your pardon."

The Old Man and the Conference

The third morning of the conference,
The Warsaw World Social Studies Conference,
Sitting down at a vacant table
To wallow in a silent, solitary breakfast,
I saw a small, old man
Heading for my table and heard him say
"May I join you?"
I smiled "Yes, of course."
But popping a slice of kiwi fruit into my mouth
I cursed him.
He asked me if I would mind clarifying for him
A remark in my lecture of the previous day
Comparing the Catholic Church in Ireland in the 1950s
To the Communist Party in Poland in the 1950s.
"Scrambled egg," he laughed, pointing down at his plate.
Accelerating backwards into the cul-de-sac of his enthusiasm

I was so surprised by his eyes –
Their youthfulness under his tiny, bald head –
I almost crashed into the lamp-post of his innocence.
At that instant I noticed a small silver brooch
In the left lapel of his blue blazer
Comprising two italicised letters – *AK*.
AK! I am sitting opposite a man who fought
In the Warsaw Uprising in 1944
When the *AK* – the Home Army of the Polish Government in exile –
Rose up against the Nazis, but were destroyed,
While on the far bank of the River Vistula
The Soviet Army – the Red Liberator –
Sat back, not lifting a rifle to help.
The old man with the child's eyes –
A man with no ego –
Tells me that all he remembers of the Warsaw Uprising
Is one day near the end when fighting in a house
On the ground floor or the basement,
He cannot remember which,
Amid gunfire and shelling,
He looked up and saw dangling from a bannister
A woman's leg. He looks over at me
Across a plate of scrambled egg and a bowl of kiwi fruit
And he looks up at the ceiling and I look up with him:
"A woman's leg in a nylon stocking and, I think,
Yes, I am sure, a shoe."
He was taken prisoner by the Nazis and taken to Germany.
After the war he spent two years in New York
Doing a thesis in Fordham University.
He wanted to remain in New York, but returned to Poland
Because he was an only child and he feared also
The other repercussions on his father and mother.
His thesis was entitled "The Early Novels of Ernest Hemingway".

Tarnowo Podgorne

6.30 a.m. in a roadhouse in Tarnowo Podgorne
About halfway between Warsaw and Berlin,
Lining up at the counter, a man and woman ask me

"Are you from Dublin? So are we.
What are you doing in Tarnowo Podgorne?
A poetry reading, is it?"
Marian is wearing a blue Dublin Fire Brigade shirt.
Rory is wearing a blue City of New York Fire Brigade shirt.
"We've got a transit van packed with stuff
For children in the Belorussian orphanages.
The sort of things we take for granted in Dublin –
Women's sanitaries, soap dispensers, Sudo cream –
Things you'd never think of –
And a transport incubator that we got from Holles Street.
Good luck with your poetry reading in Tarnowo Podgorne –
We're hoping to make it to Minsk tonight."

A Poet in Poland

to Anthony Cronin

On Tuesday the 21st of October 2003
In a sixth-storey classroom in a university in central Poland
A poet born in 1925 in the south-east of Ireland
Circles to his feet, stands at the bar
Before the crammed-into-a-tin-can faces of students sitting,
    crouching, squatting, standing,
Their medieval iconic faces hieratic, open-eyed,
And he shakes out his years – seventy-eight years – from his
    eyebrows and shoulders,
A swan shaking out the water from his neck-fleece and
    wing-feathers
And opening his mouth, he closes his mouth.
Is he smiling or weeping?

A poet who has tramped here by way of four airports and two
    railway stations
In Ireland, England, Poland,
Under a tall-stemmed angle-poise lamp
He holds up his book in his hands three inches from his eyes;
He begins to read aloud in an elegiac, laconic, heraldic voice.
Between stanzas I glance up at him

And I catch a glimpse of the holy mountain of his head –
The Mont Sainte-Victoire of his head.
A bare, conical head; a tree; a blackboard.
The engrossment of the students is echoing his voice;
Closer and closer they are leaning forwards and they also
Have become part of the quartz cone of his holy head
As pilgrims they ascend all together with satchel and scrip.

From far off across the wide river Pripyat – from across the
  smoking fires of the Pripyat marshes,
Whence all our Slav mothers and our Slav fathers came –
In the night sky I see a ziggurat of head-torches
Spiralling upwards around and around his cranium
And we are all alpinists as well as pilgrims of his cranium
And we are not deterred by altitude sickness
From going on with him to the summit of his poem
Up above the death-zone at 29,000 feet
And as he utters the last lines of his poem –
A poem entitled "The End of the Modern World" –
We are all perched on the peak of his bare head – only
I am standing the far side of passport control and he
He is swaying into it, his torso and legs going one way,
His head going another way, his bottle-glass spectacles askew,
But he has passport in hand and he is slouching through
The towers of Poznan and Warsaw
Silent, astonishing and new.

Raftery in Tokyo

Suicidal in Tokyo,
A crow on a telegraph pole
Raucous with self-pity,
Ah, ah, ah – I squawk.

From County Mayo to Greater Tokyo
Men with failing eyesight go
Serenading that crazy innocence
They see because they know.

On the Road to the Airport, Northern Hokkaido

The most terrible person I ever met was my father.
Only my mother was occasionally not terrible.
Terrible terrible
Was my father;
Terribler than Mao.
But now in my middle age
On the road to the airport –
Serious snow –
I do not need to know,
I do not need to meet
Any more of the terrible people.
So, father, father,
Stand clear of my stuttering propellers,
Stand clear of my blistered feet,
Stand clear of my ring-less fingers,
Stand clear of my red eyes.

Checkout Girl

A week back in Ireland from Japan,
But I cannot stop bowing.
Only ten minutes ago in the supermarket
I bowed to the checkout girl
With the red cheeks and the limp.

I bowed from the waist to her
And she blushed and I think
When she limps home this afternoon,
Collecting her toddler from the crèche,
It may be with an extra spring in her limp.

Facing Extinction

to Masazumi Toraiwa

When I rounded the corner into Anne Street
And I was confronted by a man squatting in a doorway
I got a shock and I flinched.
For the face I saw was the same face
I saw in the shaving mirror this morning.
Dropping my ludicrous lucre into his beaker
I squeaked: "Are you all right?"
He announced: "I think I'm going to be all right."
And he proffered me a smile, looking me straight in the eye.

I crossed over into Chatham Street
And I slipped into The Great Outdoors
Where I purchased a pair of walking shoes –
Brasher Hillmasters –
Having been instructed last week in northern Hokkaido
By a samurai-ninja protector of bears –
Brown bears facing extinction –
That the time was nigh
For me to face the truth about my fellow creatures.

On my way back along Anne Street
There was a different man in the same doorway
Looking more doomed than the first man –
More doomed to extinction –
His head bowed as if in meditation on death.
Dropping my ludicrous lucre into his beaker
I squeaked: "Are you all right?"
He announced: "I'm fine – how are you?"
And he proffered me a smile, looking me straight in the eye.

In my cave on the edge of the city
A woman on the telephone mocks me:
"You were always a bear"
As if I *should/could* have been somebody else.
Peering again into my shaving mirror
At my bear's eyes, my bear's mouth,
I am surprised by how upbeat, yet melancholy, I look:
In the autumn of my days I am looking forward
To hibernation, facing extinction.

THE LAUGHTER OF MOTHERS *(2007)*

The Story of Ireland

The single most crucial factor in twentieth-century Irish history
    was golf.
Had it not been for golf, the country would have relapsed into
    barbarism.
When the going got bad, men put their heads down and played
    golf.
In a crisis a man put on his golf gloves.
On Sunday mornings good men went to the golf course instead
    of to church.
The bank manager arranged to meet the bank robber on the
    golf course.
When a marriage looked like going on the rocks
A husband and wife started playing golf in their home.
While the husband did putting practice in the bathroom
The wife practised her swing in the drawing room.
In bed the wife would say to her husband:
"Imagine you're playing an approach shot with a number seven
    iron."
Later she'd add:
"Imagine you're putting for the match."
And finally:
"I'll pretend I didn't see you miss your putt."
Or simply:
"I'll give you your putt."
Golf brought back civilisation to Ireland in the twentieth century
So that in the twenty-first century even Sinn Féin started playing
    golf
As well as going into buying and selling
Golf courses in Kazakhstan and Siberia, and most recently
    China.
It is reported by the Belfast News Agency WEDGE
That 27 per cent of Chinese golf courses are owned by Sinn
    Féin.
Sinn Féin's showpiece
Is the Mao Golf and Country Club in Shanghai,
Which worldwide is second only
To the Roman Catholic Church's operation
On the West Coast of Ireland –

The Pope John Paul II Golf and Country Club in Galway Bay
On the site of what used be the city of Galway
And for the building and development of which the city was
    demolished
In 2005 and, courtesy of Allied Irish Banks,
Transferred to Pittsville, Pennsylvania.
The *craic* is said to be gosh-darned okay in Pittsville.

Mrs Barrington-Stuart's Version of What Happened

Mr Barrington-Stuart and I were driving west from Dublin
To spend our annual holiday in Renvyle.
We stopped at Lough Owel to picnic
As we always stop at Lough Owel to picnic.
For fifty-five years we have always stopped at Lough Owel.
We spread out our Foxford rug at the top of the bank
In the same place we have always spread out our Foxford rug.
There we were, sitting erect on our Foxford rug,
Having our picnic lunch in silence,
Enjoying Lough Owel and the islands,
Our cucumber sandwiches and our flask of tea,
When Mr Barrington-Stuart turned over on his side
Like he does in bed in the middle of the night
And, before I could take another bite of my sandwich,
He had begun rolling down the bank.
He rolled all the way down the bank into the lake
And, before I could stand up, he had passed away.
You can imagine how surprised I was.
Nobody would believe me in Renvyle.

In the Shopping Spree on the Last Sunday before Christmas

Spotting, whilst I reversed into a tight parking space,
A traveller woman in a doorway assessing me,
I realised she was about to pounce on me.
Dutifully, as it seemed, she was about to pounce on me,
Stocky tanned lady with jet-black hair in a ponytail.

As I sidled away from my car, double-locking it with the remote,
She stepped out in front of me barring the way
And before I could say anything, she declaimed
In the voice of an old-world actor-manager playing the female
    lead:
"Don't worry, sir, I'm not going to beg from you,
I only want to tell you a story,
Because I can see you have a face on you.
None of these people will even look at me!"
She declaimed, gesticulating at the passers-by.
"I only want to tell you, sir,
That I am a human being
And that my daughter here also beside me
Is a human being,
A poor, little thrawneen of a godforsaken human being.
They don't consider us as human beings
But we are human beings, sir. I need seventy euro
To get the boat to England. My husband
Is after beating me up, no word of a lie."
Knowing I had a ten-euro note in my breast pocket
I fished it out and put it in her hand.
She shut her eyes and pursed her lips
And she shouted "The Lord have mercy on you, sir!
But how am I to get to England?
How am I to cross over the bitter sea?"
Whereupon I fished out another ten-euro note
And handed it to her. Her outrage
And grief intensified as she continued shouting:
"I have eleven stitches in the back of my head
On account of my husband, he broke a bottle across it,
And my daughter has four stitches in the back of *her* head.
I wish to holy God I had never got married!
Sir, I know you have a fifty-euro note in your pocket,
If you give it to me, I'll do overtime praying for you."
How did she know I had a fifty-euro note
In my pocket? Is she psychic?
I handed it to her, stammering
"W-what is your name and w-where are you from?"
She answered me proudly: "I am Mamie Thornton and
    I am from Galway
And my daughter is Tina

535

And she has eaten nothing for near on three weeks
And I'll say a prayer for you to the Holy Mother of God if
You give me that other fifty-euro note in your pocket."
I shouted back at her, "But Mamie, Mamie –
I don't have another fifty-euro note!"
"But I have to get the boat to England!" she shouted.
I began to hurry away, but she hurried with me:
"I can see, sir, you have time for people.
Most people have no time for people.
I know that because I'm from Galway.
Now give me two hundred euro and I will pray
For a month to Our Lady of Fatima for you."
"Please Mamie," I begged her, "please Mamie –
I don't have two hundred euro to give you!"
"Oh but you do, sir," she whispered. "Oh but you do, sir."
Bestowing on me a wounded, reserved look of contemptuous
     compassion,
She turned her back on me and waddled off
And her teenage daughter clinging to her arm started to laugh
And to stare at me as if I was some new class of a settled madman
She had never set eyes on before.
In the winter sunlight under blue skies
In the shopping spree on the last Sunday before Christmas
I stood rooted to the footpath looking after them, lost in
     admiration.

Death on Strand Road

Passers-by stop to try and help the dying man
As he lies flat on his back in the yellow box
Of the On the Run filling station on Strand Road,
A *few* passers-by but not *all* passers-by.
Some do not notice, some are in too much of a hurry
To pay for their petrol or to purchase their newspapers,
Their take-away coffee, their sausage rolls,
To stop to help a man in his death-throes
At half-eleven in the morning on a Thursday in November,
His face changing colour by the second
From grey to red to purple to black

Like a lost sheepdog on its back having nightmares.
He is stretched out beside his silver Ford Focus five-door Estate
In which ninety seconds ago he had been cruising along
Strand Road, admiring the seascape
When his heart blew up. He pulled in
To the filling station, got out, fell down
At the door signed FIRE EXIT! KEEP CLEAR.
The few passers-by who do have time to stop
Do everything they can to resuscitate the dying man:
Three American policemen on holiday in Ireland
Jumping out of a hired Toyota Space Wagon,
Giving him the kiss of life, pounding his chest;
Trying to keep him alive, if he is still alive,
Until the ambulance and fire brigade swoop up,
Scoop him up, rush him away
Down along Strand Road to St Vincent's Hospital,
The tide out, a man in red on the black sands
With a bucket and spade, digging for worms.
The polite young manager of On the Run
In his smart brown-and-yellow uniform
Stands with a clipboard taking names of witnesses,
A young mother in boots pushing a baby buggy trots off
With a muffin in a paper bag bearing the logo
On the Run – A Fresh Call Every Time.
The silver Ford Focus five-door Estate
Stands out-of-focus, abandoned, forlorn, empty,
A blue Ordnance Survey Dublin Street Atlas lying open on the
     front passenger seat
Like another lost sheepdog, pleading, beseeching, inquiring
"Where is Tritonville Road?" or
"Am I an actor in a play?" or
"Do you believe in reincarnation?"
Before being obscured from view, blacked out
By a convoy of artics crashing past to the East Link Toll
     Bridge.
On a trolley in A&E in St Vincent's Hospital
Lies a man's lifeless corpse which but eleven minutes ago
Was a living body on four wheels cruising along Strand Road,
Much of a mild winter's day ahead of him,
Six weeks to Christmas. The polite young manager
Of On the Run blurts out: "The Lord have mercy on his soul."

Lecarrow Harbour

That the smooth blue-and-white lake
Flew into a tantrum;
That we, a small family
In a hired launch, an Emerald Star
Four-berther, a young father and mother
With two small girls, all of a sudden
Were battling for our lives on a summer's day:
These are the headlines that rear tears in my eyes
As this afternoon twenty-one years later
I revisit the harbour that saved our lives;
The name of which none of us could ever forget
In spite of all the lives we would live
And all the roads that would scatter us:
Lecarrow Harbour.

Caught out in the middle of Lough Ree
In a whiplash maelstrom of wind and rain
With nothing between ourselves and the rocks
But a loose fixed compass and a torn wet map
On which we could see, or thought
We could see, north north-west, an inlet
Named Blackbrink Bay
Into which a canal had been cut
For a mile and a half inland
To Lecarrow Harbour.

Our two children in lifejackets crouched in the cabin
As their mother took the wheel
And their father stood at her side
Grappling to relate compass to map,
Trying to chart a course –
Trying to call it out and be heard –
Between St John's Bay and the Black Islands.
They could see nothing but the black waves
Rearing white heads over the bow;
They could hear only the winds
Gusting to gales

And their two parents shouting
And their own voices yelling
And they both felt too petrified to feel afraid.

God clicked the camera of Life and Death
And through its aperture we wriggled
Into Blackbrink Bay; the gale
In the reeds a lullaby to our escape
From the gale on the lake tearing up
The scrolls of the waters.
Along the slim canal we inched
For a mile and a half, each of us
Quivering in our knowledge of death.
Under slow, hilly fields of sheep
We chugged into the world's end,
A stone-clad pen with capstans
And wide steps: Lecarrow Harbour.

Whatever number of days we stayed
In Lecarrow Harbour, to us
It was a lifetime – a lifetime
Of playing hide-and-go seek in the young limes,
A lifetime of sanctuary,
A lifetime of sitting still on the jetty wall
Watching two small girls, curly sisters
Squawking as they paddled around
In the jollyboat among ducks and drakes
Whilst up in the grass in the birch trees
Shelves of chicks sat in their half-dozens.

This afternoon in Lecarrow Harbour
A lone woman sailor in a rickety skiff
Is hanging out tea towels to dry
From a multi-branched clothes hanger
Swaying from a birch-branch.
Ducks and drakes patrol the waters,
Their multitudinous young
In flocks up on the banks.
My elder daughter is expecting next month,
Her younger sister the month after,
Their mother secure in her Cork city nest

With her caretaker man.
In the silence I say prayers
Of thanksgiving and praise
For my daughters and their husbands
And the sane woman of Cork
Before driving off into yet another storm
Lurching in from the north-west,
Beating up black clouds
Low on the hills of Roscommon.

Achill Island Girl

I was born in Murphysboro, Illinois, in 1990,
My parents' eldest daughter.
They christened me Saoirse,
Which is the Irish word for *Liberty*.
It's the best thing they did,
Christening me Saoirse.
There are lots of things I like doing and being,
But best of all is to hear a voice
Calling me by the name my parents christened me,
Someone, anyone, calling out my name across the bridge
Or repeating my name into a mobile,
Saoirse, Saoirse.
My name is a war cry for peace.
But when at band practice in the community hall
The pipe major starts chanting my name high above the
    pipes
My eyes fill with cliffs
And the one hundred-and-sixteen freckles on my cheeks
    begin to swim
Off the edge of my face
And I want to run to my mother and throw my arms around
    her neck,
My father sitting at the head of the table reading from a
    history book to her.

A View of the Bridge

I was standing at the window of my shoe shop at eleven o'clock in
    the morning
Admiring the baskets of flowers on the lamp-posts that we'd hung
    up the previous week
And wondering if I'd bother buying a national newspaper across
    the river in McGreevy's –
What's the point in buying a national newspaper? Maybe I should
    be thinking
About buying a copy of the *International Herald Tribune* if it's in –
When who do I see coming over the bridge, the three-arched
    bridge in the centre of our town,
But Seamus Heaney and John McGahern, our two world-famous
    authors, strolling slowly,
Strolling *very* slowly, fresh as daisies, arm in arm at eleven o'clock in
    the morning.
Fresh as daisies, yet men of an older vintage than me.
I couldn't believe it. It was about four years ago. I ran back into the
    shop
And fetched out the great ledger that we've had for a hundred-and-
    two years and a fountain pen
And I went to rush out the door only for my guardian angel to
    grab me by the scruff of the neck.
"Woa boy, woa, boy, woa, woa!" my guardian angel neighed into my ear
As I gawked out the door at the two world-famous authors as they stood
At the end of the bridge on my side of the river glancing over at
    my shoe shop –
Or seeming to, for they were engrossed in their conversation.
They looked like two sheep farmers after coming out of Sunday Mass,
In their Sunday half-best, black slacks, black slip-ons, tweed jackets,
    open-neck white shirts,
Not so much striking a bargain between themselves as analysing
A grander bargain having been struck somewhere else that they had
    witnessed.
For the love of God, I muttered to myself, it's not every day or
    every week
Or every year or every hundred years that you'd see two world-
    famous authors
Walking the streets of a small town in the west of Ireland and yet –

What right have I to interrupt their morning, their morning
    stroll,
Their conversation, their sacred conversation? "Holy God,"
I roared at myself, "but you have no right to do such a thing!"
I put down the great ledger of 1903 on the counter
And folded my arms and crossed my legs and immediately
I felt an indescribable surge of surprise and good fortune and
    common sense
As I watched them turn around under a high basket of fresh
    flowers and walk off down along the river into the trees.
In our small town we may be behind the times in lots of ways,
    but we're no huxters like some I won't name in big cities
    not far away, isn't life gas?

The Waterford Relays

to Mark Quinn

Running the relay at twelve
Is not half so good an idea
As running the relay at sixty-two.
It's not only that at sixty-two
I drop the baton,
Which is normal,
But that I arrive at the handover without the baton,
Having forgotten to start with the baton in the first place,
Which is even more normal.
Nobody knows who I am
On whom even the clouds shine.

Little Girl Watering on the Sands

Little girl watering on the sands
Twinkles as she grips her hem,
Spreads wide her legs,
Peers down at the splash she has made,
Frowns as she analyses

542

Quickly drying sands:
Surface texture
Of the enigma of what disappears.

For her the passing of water
Is not a euphemism;
What she has performed is comparable
To what Moses performed in the desert;
Yet, water having darted from the rock
Transpires to be seepage:
Her demeanour melancholy
At mortality of divinity.

At the Grave of My Aunt Sara Mary, Turlough, County Mayo

At the grave of my aunt Sara Mary the family
Have inserted a cuckoo clock in the headstone
Under the names of my grandfather and grandmother.
There was no space on the headstone for Sara Mary's name,
So her name was incised on the rear of the headstone
Under the statue of the Virgin Mary, the hem
Of the Virgin's cloak grazing Sara Mary's name.
I falter in front of her grave attempting to pray to her
In spite of her name being on the rear of the headstone
And not realising that the clock is active.
The clock chimes and from behind shut, louvred doors
Out hops a cuckoo – only it is not a cuckoo,
It is a tiny wooden painted statuette of my spinster aunt
Flapping her blue woolly arms and bowing up and down,
Calling out her favourite vocable: "'Ospital! 'Ospital!",
("Life is an 'ospital," she used cry to us children
In her spasm-smiling voice),
Her benignant bosom kicking up under a blue cardigan,
Her red face beaming, her waist-length grey hair
Piled high in a nest on her head.
Just as in life, teeming with anticipation,
Throbbing with expectation, tears of laughter
Brimming her eyes, she used welcome us children home
To the home of our ancestors.

It is five in the afternoon on the 22nd of June –
"'Ospital! 'Ospital! 'Ospital! 'Ospital! 'Ospital!" –
She hops back in and the doors slam shut.
I climb the graveyard to the round tower
And the roofless church with the medieval carving
Over the lintel of a boy Christ with spiked hair,
Splayed hands, splayed knees,
A hand-towel for a loincloth, jiving the Crucifixion
On midsummer's night at sunrise.

My aunt's life was also a crucifixion,
Which she danced with an abandon no one else
In the family could equal. They all motored off
To the cities and the towns to lead professional lives
Of privilege and luxury, property and holiday,
While she stayed at home to run the public house
With oil lamps and water from the well,
Turkeys and hens in the yard, turf from the bog,
And to keep the faith in the parish of Parke,
In the one-street village of Turlough, County Mayo.

In 1949 she gave me the run of the tap room
At five years of age
With a dessert spoon to scoop up porter
From the enamel white tray under the hooped barrel to savour
The life-giving black draught with the foamy cream bubbles.
In 1952 she got red roaring mad with me
For singing "A Nation Once Again" in the open counter leaf
And as she gave me a roasting
Her sunny red face blackened with grief.
"I don't want to hear that nonsense in this house!"
(In 1923 the IRA had put her father up against the wall;
You could still see the bullet holes in the gable.)

At the foot of her grave, down below in the valley,
The French windows of the library door of the landlord's house,
Before whose four blue-grey cut limestone steps
Her father's father stood in line
With all the other tenant farmers of Turlough
To doff his cap and pay his rent –
His rent to breathe the air and cultivate a patch

By grace of the lords FitzGerald of Turlough –
The landlord's agent bestowing a liquid smile
Upon the dry, crisp, lined pages of the ledger rent book,
Until one day her grandfather cursed the landlord to his face,
The landlord evicted him and her father was born
On the side of the road under hawthorn and sycamore;
The landlord's house today a public museum and the glinting
    library windows
Are silver-cuffed, dreamy attendants in livery at her sleeping feet.

Amidst the vintage of her laughter and her porter,
Of her anger and her litanies to the Virgin Mary
I learned to talk with the dead and to love life.
The two yew trees at the gate to the graveyard
She planted with authority fifty years ago:
The two yews sentinel to the daylight moon
Either side of the gate;
Two virginal daughters in bottle-green homespun;
Her identical twins grown to eighteen feet tall;
The only sound the odd footstep of my own.

Paralysed, bed-ridden in her room in a nursing home,
A crenellated Victorian Gothic mansion in a bog,
She commanded me to climb up on a straight-backed chair
And, stretching out my hand across the top of the wardrobe,
Hunt for a brown paper bag and place it on her bedspread
And open it. In a nest of pristine white tissue paper, gleaming,
Two dozen silver teaspoons.
"You're not to tell the Judge I gave them to you!"
(The Judge was my father, her brother.)

On the morning she died two heroes of the IRA,
September 16th, 1974,
Separately arriving at the houses of two judges in Belfast,
Shot them both dead in front of their daughters
As they were eating their breakfasts, cornflakes and sugar,
So that old daily Ireland might be a nation once again;
All that pure pedigree, miller's fraulein, racial opining.

I lie down in the grass beside my aunt Sara Mary's grave
In the dying sun for a nap
And gaze out of the oriel windows of time

Down at her far below in the estuary of eternity
Tinkling in a breeze from the south west
And heaving herself starboard into her doom,
The prow of her pride anchored by her prickly humility.

O generous woman to whom no mean man dare tell lies
Or squeal rats' cries,
For you there are only big open changing skies.
She bustles out of the rear base of her headstone
Calling out the password of the Resurrection:
"'Ospital! 'Ospital! 'Ospital! 'Ospital! 'Ospital!"

Kneeling at the Last Wave

to Jarlath Cunnane

Up there on the stony shore of the North West Passage
you might unearth tears in a man's eyes;
you might unearth even a grimace of compassion;
even the undertone of a premonition of affection.

Seafarer, these are my bones
and here is lichen on my skull:
crimson-scabbed, beige-intaglio'd lichen on my skull.
The different shall inherit the earth, if there are any different left.

Badgers

to Veronica Bolay

At dawn they came in, flying low,
Fighter bombers, grey with black stripes.
Mother crawled on her hands and knees
Through streams and forests.

The operations manager of the mobile phone company,
Requesting his chauffeur to stop the Mercedes

On the back-road on the south slopes
Of the mountain, uncapped his binoculars
To peer across the sheep-flecked valley
At the whitewashed cottage with the red galvanise roof.
By the gold face of his Rolex wristwatch
It was 8 a.m. on a summer's morning
And, as before, there was turf smoke faltering
From the squat chimney.
He remembered, as before he had remembered,
The first time he had visited,
How the woman of the house had offered him tea
And she had asked him:
"Would you like herbal tea or green tea?"
And he had laughed with her, a thing
He had never done with a woman before.
Laughed with a woman!
He had answered: "I'll have normal tea"
And how she had laughed
And how finally he had offered her a half-million euro
And she had said no, no to a half-million euro,
And again he had laughed with her.
To laugh with a woman, at least that was something!
He had said: "I am sorry to badger you"
And she had said: "Oh but I like to be badgered by you"
And she had stepped out of her low-heeled shoes
And surged in her bare feet to the grass-fringed edge
Of the flag of the sill-stone
And his polished laced shoes had rippled a reflection
Of his hurried face.
Putting the caps back on his binoculars,
Requesting the chauffeur to drive on,
Leaning on the elbow-rest in the back seat,
Pawing the knees of his pinstripe suit,
He asked himself what a badger looked like.
Unseen to him, under her cottage on the mountain,
She sat on a rock, her toes clawing wet grass.

At dawn they came in, flying low,
Fighter bombers, grey with black stripes.
Mother crawled on her hands and knees
Through streams and forests.

Women of Athens

Down and out in Athens in the dying sun
I learn where to hang out and not to hang out.
I pass much of the day in Cathedral Square
Pacing up and down under the plane trees,
Gazing up at the clock tower, sitting
On a bench next another white-haired vagrant
With a pair of pliers in his hands,
Mooching in and out of the cathedral
Whose crimson-curtained west door is always wide open:
The Cathedral of the Annunciation of the Virgin Mary.
Loitering at the back of the cathedral in Athens
I am appalled by the explicit devotion of the women of Athens.
Of all ages and classes they come and go
Singly or in couples or in families.
The more chic the woman –
Is there a woman in Athens who is not chic?
In Athens there are no women in tracksuits –
The more chic the woman, the sleeker, the foxier,
The more devout she is,
The more openly, extravagantly, unashamedly devout she is.
She lights her candle and she stands in front of her icon,
Kissing it, thrice making the sign of the Cross, from her waist
      bowing.
In hip-clenching blue jeans, low-cut skin-tight black blouse,
High-heeled lime-green boots up to her knees,
Long, damp, curly hair running down her breasts,
She surrenders herself with abandon to her icon.
I am appalled, never having witnessed
Such flagrant devotion in my native land;
Ireland, reputedly a religious country,
But which now I realise is not a religious country;
In Ireland nobody surrenders
And churches are but memorials to death.
Here in the Cathedral of Athens at twilight in autumn
How can I be a part of flagrant devotion to the gods?
A voice says: But you are a part of it now
In the wall of your complaining, in the ground of your beseeching.
Come down, Paul, from your perch of pride,

Come down off the Areopagus Hill
And like the women of Athens become a free spirit
Before the iconostasis blazing.
Let nobody again ever tell you
That you are not a free man, especially when
Down and out in Athens in the dying sun.

Greek Woman of High Standing

She wears black always, always black,
Black blouses, black skirts
That cling and do not cling
To her limbs in the sun-wind.
Smitten by her
In the porch in Athens,
The caryatid second from the left,
I had not known such mental passion
Transfigured by the physical;
Such feminine intensity
Articulated in intellectual forms.
Her long black hair when she let it down
Flowed down her spine-delta
To converge and diverge in the small of her back.
She stood alone with her arms by her sides,
A caryatid carrying the world on her head.
There was no book she had not read,
Only Proust had been delayed for a rainy day,
That type of rainy day that never really comes to Athens
Except in monsoon-downpours, typhoon-floods.
O Caryatid, did you carry me, too, on your head
In the beginning of time?
And all these handsome, glorious boys standing
Around us suffering from manic depression –
Did you carry each one of them too?
The weight of the weight of the world?
Did you, while walking in the market place,
Soak up the sweat of Socrates on your forehead?
Osmosis? Telepathy?
She said: "My theme is loyalty

In a world of betrayal."
I cried to her: "You must come to bed with me!"
The groin-centred male,
At my feet a sleeping dog of Athens,
The spitting image of my dead father,
That sallow-faced visage.
I meet a caryatid and I think of bed!
She cried: "That is out of the question!
I have a house to support,
A vision of reality to be installed on the plate of my head!"
Greek woman of high standing,
She is a column of support in a crumbling world-order,
The apotheosis of femininity.

Epistemology

If there is nobody to share the world with,
There is no world.

The Moment of Return

Life and death would never be the same
After that morning in the square outside the cathedral in Athens
On "No Day" – the anniversary
Of the day the Greeks said "No" to Mussolini –
And the armed forces were all lined up in platoons in the
    square,
The Douanier Rousseau panoply, peaked caps with gold plumes,
White gauntlets, white cinctures, red braid, brass buttons,
Epaulettes, stripes, medals, motorbike cops in vulture-postures,
Bandsmen writhing in tubas, policemen in cordons dragging on
    fags –
Dainty sailors with bayonets on their shoulders,
Tourists, prostitutes, clergy, locals,
Stretch limos decanting government ministers and their wives,
When he chanced to glance up at the steps and he saw standing
    above him

A young uniformed policewoman in a blue mini-skirt,
Black nylon stockings, black stiletto high-heeled shoes with
    pointy toecaps.
She was standing sentinel on the south side of the square, near
    the west door,
On the top step, with her back to him, her small, soft hands
    folded
Under her bottom, clutching gloves, white gloves.
All the staircases of his life, all the treads and raisers came
    back to him,
Those years when after long hauls to Brazil and New Zealand
    and Japan and Australia and Canada,
Finally after all the longing for home he made it back home
And he put his bag down on the floor of the kitchen
And she took his hand and led him lazily up the stairs
To her bedroom and gradually pushed him onto the foot of
    her bed,
And began to undress him, and he her, until neither of them
    knew
Which was the sea and which was the skiff as they crested the
    waves,
Sheets and pillows and quilts cascading above them
As they approached the headland, the sacred headland,
Each lost in the roofless temples of the other's hands,
And memory and oblivion were one. The young policewoman
    high on her heels
Shifted from ankle to ankle, tilting on her stilts,
And he knew that no matter how close to death he might be,
He would want first and last the moment of return, the union
    of Greece and the soul, of the hereafter with the preamble,
    the blank white cartridge paper of incessant surrender.

Walking with Professor Dillon in the Old Agora in Athens

After what seemed like hours in the noonday heat, fatigue,
    perspiration,
Exasperation with one another for no good reason,
Having strayed up and down the old market place in Athens,
Pottered, toppled, paced, crawled

To and fro its alleys, olive groves, stone arcades
And clambered up a hill to the Temple of Hephaistos
Where under the frieze Professor Dillon remarked
Of woman-throttling man-beasts:
"Wine did not agree with centaurs – centaurs
Got rambunctious on wine . . ."
We spotted what appeared to be the only bench in the Agora,
In the shade of a clump of cypresses, facing east,
The sun high in the western corner of the southern quadrant.
Capturing the only bench
We fell to talking about *Reise-Angst*,
That species of anxiety unique to travellers:
Why it is that some of us feel compelled to arrive at airports
Or railway stations with an hour or more to spare.
We talked of Estonia, the Irish language, his father Myles Dillon,
Of stamp collecting in the 1950s,
Of Archilochus of Paros, poet of love and war,
Of Yannis Ritsos of Crow Street, Athens, of Desmond O'Grady
Of Paros also, Alexandria and Kinsale, of Michael Hartnett
Of Foley Street, Dublin, of whom, paraphrasing E. M. Forster
On Constantine Cavafy, Professor Dillon remarked:
"He stood at a slight angle to the universe."
He remarked also on the great age that Socrates lived to
Who walked these self-same paths all those centuries ago,
That man of barefoot reasonableness.
Our conversation was significant for its gradual flow,
Its ease and silences, without tension or attention-seeking.
Suddenly I heard myself exclaim: "Look, John!"
And he looked and there not five metres from his toecaps
A tortoise had emerged from under a cypress
To commence its navigation across the footpath to the other side.
We watched in silence, face-making in admiration
But also in thanksgiving that we had been blessed
By an order of being outside ourselves,
That we had been ennobled by the company of a tortoise
And its lifestyle. Pausing at many intervals,
The tortoise, an empress in procession,
Conferred on each of us original virtue, that first permission,
That license to live which we so infrequently obtain.
The tortoise stopped and seemed to utter:
"Dillon, John, Regius Professor of Greek:

You are indeed the magnificent scholar that they say you are;
Durcan, Paul, visiting poet: after all these multifarious years
You are entitled indeed to call yourself a poet."
The tortoise trundled into undergrowth and vanished;
With a lightness in our feet, although drained and famished,
We retraced our steps across the old Agora of Athens.
The terrors of the day ahead seemed to lose some of their ferocity,
Obstacles seemed surmountable, the difficult almost desirable.

* * *

Par for the Course

While the American and British armies were landing on the
    beaches of Normandy
And de Valera was keeping Churchill, Roosevelt and Hitler at bay
And Hyde was counting in Gaelic the raindrops on the
    windowpanes in the Phoenix Park,
Sheila was a twenty-eight-year-old bride blossoming in pregnancy,
In her fifth month, her rains drenching all the paddocks and
    boreens of her body,
Anticipating with fearful delight the birth of her first child.
Her consultant gynaecologist, Dr Burke-Wykeham of Fitzwilliam
    Square –
Known as "Wee-Wee" to all the ladies of Dublin
On account of his diminutive size, scarcely five feet tall –
Was reckoned not only one of the best in the business
But also one of Dublin's most eligible bachelors
For his double vents, his large lapels,
His silk handkerchiefs, his bow-ties,
His bouffant silver hair and his annual income,
Estimated at fifty thousand pounds sterling a year.
A room was booked in the Stella Maris nursing home
And when the night came, a windy October night,
At first Dr Burke-Wykeham was nowhere to be found.
The nun in charge tittered to Sheila's husband:
"Wee-Wee is fond of a wee drop, you know."
Her husband was livid, but he could say nothing
Because Wee-Wee was a power in the land;
As well as having played rugby union for Ireland,
He was on first-name terms with government ministers
Whose wives he knew better than they did themselves;
Of all their lineaments and configurations
He was their accountant and statistician.
In the nick of time Wee-Wee showed up
But such was the trembling of his hands
At the moment of delivery he let slip the forceps
With the result that the face of the newborn infant
Was red as a squashed tomato. The young mother
Expressed her dismay, but Wee-Wee brushed aside her fears,
Informing her that it was par for the course, that

He would put the baby's face in ice for a day or two
And all would be right as rain. Mother and son
Left the Stella Maris with the boy sporting
A permanent red eye – a botched delivery –
And this red eye he carried with him for the rest of his life.
"It's only a birthmark," Wee-Wee assured his mother.
The bewildered mother had no choice but to take up that refrain,
Which she repeated to all comers for the next fifty-eight years:
"It's only a birthmark."

The MacBride Dynasty

What young mother is not a vengeful goddess
Spitting dynastic as well as motherly pride?
In 1949 in the black Ford Anglia,
Now that I had become a walking, talking little boy,
Mummy drove me out to visit my grand-aunt Maud Gonne
In Roebuck House in the countryside near Dublin,
To show off to the servant of the Queen
The latest addition to the extended family.
Although the eighty-year-old Cathleen Ni Houlihan had taken
      to her bed
She was keen as ever to receive admirers,
Especially the children of the family.
Only the previous week the actor MacLiammóir
Had been kneeling at her bedside reciting Yeats to her,
His hand on his heart, clutching a red rose.
Cousin Séan and his wife Kid led the way up the stairs,
Séan opening the door and announcing my mother.
Mummy lifted me up in her arms as she approached the bed
And Maud leaned forward, sticking out her claws
To embrace me, her lizards of eyes darting about
In the rubble of the ruins of her beautiful face.
Terrified, I recoiled from her embrace
And, fleeing her bedroom, ran down the stairs
Out onto the wrought-iron balcony
Until Séan caught up with me and quieted me
And took me for a walk in the walled orchard.
Mummy was a little but not totally mortified:

She had never liked Maud Gonne because of Maud's
Betrayal of her husband, Mummy's Uncle John,
Major John, most ordinary of men, most
Humorous, courageous of soldiers,
The pride of our family,
Whose memory always brought laughter
To my grandmother Eileen's lips. "John,"
She used cry, "John was such a gay man."
Mummy set great store by loyalty; loyalty
In Mummy's eyes was the cardinal virtue.
Maud Gonne was a disloyal wife
And, therefore, not worthy of Mummy's love.
For dynastic reasons we would tolerate Maud,
But we would always see through her.

Major John MacBride's Early Morning Breakfast

At 3.37 a.m. in the dark
Major John MacBride was cut down by firing squad.
For Mummy life would never be quite life
And there would never be breakfast in bed.

Treasure Island

On his sixth birthday, October 16th, 1950,
His mother took him to see his first film.
If she had promised him only a bus ride
Into the city centre
He would have been frantic with expectation,
But not only did she take him on a bus ride
Into the city centre – the Number 11
Into Nelson's Pillar, just she and he alone
In the front seat together on the upstairs deck –
But on disembarking in O'Connell Street
She took him by the hand and steered him
Up the steps of the Metropole Cinema.
This new, until-now forbidden world of cinema

Was a second extension of his mother's bedroom
(The first extension being the parish chapel):
The red carpets, the gilded mirrors,
The brass stair-rods, the swing-doors within swing-doors,
Veil upon veil of a temple
Proceeding to an inner sanctum, the plush
Tip-up seats, the hush when the lights dimmed,
The girl acolyte strapped to her tray
Of tubs of ice cream and beakers with straws,
Floor-to-ceiling wine-red curtains being parted
To reveal the forbidden silver screen, and he
Seated beside his mother in the public dark,
Safe in the abyss, gazing up
At the soft black rain of her hair,
Her mouth glistening with plum-red lipstick,
Her white pearl necklace, her white pearl earrings.
What could be more vista-rich for a six-year-old boy
Than to be seated in cinema darkness at his first film
With his young mother, his first sweetheart?
Larger-than-life pictures on the screen
Filled him with freedom, longing, dread:
When horses appeared on the crest of a hill,
Galloping cross-country to the port of Bristol,
He ducked his head in his seat for fear
Of being trampled to death by their onrushing hooves.
Long John Silver made a grand entrance
As the buccaneer to beat all buccaneers,
Parrot on shoulder,
With a glass of rum and a gleaming eye,
And his unshaven, bristling black chin
And his one leg and his West Country piratical voice and
A small boy on his sixth birthday gripped tight his mother's hand.
The first film of his life she had chosen
To bring him to was *Treasure Island*
Starring Robert Newton as Long John Silver,
Denis O'Dea as Dr Livesey
And Spike Milligan as Ben Gunn.
In his cinema seat he became Jim Hawkins
Sitting in secret at the bottom of the barrel,
Overhearing things a boy should never overhear.
For the first time he understood

557

That the price of knowledge is death.
When they emerged out of the film
As out of a book of the Old Testament,
Day had changed into night and it was raining;
All of Dublin was black water and city lights
And his mother queued for a Number 11 bus.
They sailed home aboard the *Hispaniola*
To the coal fire and the brass tongs,
By which they lolled until he fell asleep.
As surely as God created heaven and earth
Thenceforth, aged six years, his life,
In all its people and in all its places,
Would be a *Treasure Island*
A tropic idyll forever under threat,
A geography revealed to him by his mother,
Sweet Sheila MacBride, who had married John Durcan,
One of the black, red-roaring, fighting Durcans of Mayo.

Philadelphia, Here I Come

When her husband the judge had their nineteen-year-old son
In the Spring of 1964
Committed to St John of God mental hospital
She was not consoled, but she was helpless.
The judge said that the doctor knew best
And what the judge said was law:
"All this calling himself an athlete is an escape;
All this running is malingering;
The doctor says he has schizophrenia
And, therefore, he *has* schizophrenia."
After he had done six months a release date was set
And to celebrate his release she booked seats
For herself and her son for a new play
At the Gaiety, *Philadelphia, Here I Come.*
Mother and son had a rare night out in the freedom
Of the grand circle of the packed Gaiety Theatre
But neither of them afterwards spoke about it.
Each was fearful the other might criticise and spoil it.
On the bus home they basked in one another's satisfaction,

Their cheeks glowing in reticent aftertaste.
The play was about a young Irishman, Gar O'Donnell,
Who was emigrating to Philadelphia
On account of his inexplicable estrangement from his father,
A quandary familiar to the nineteen-year-old boy
Tasting freedom after six months incarceration in a mental
hospital
In the company of sedated, rebellious priests committed by
bishops.
He identified, as critics say, with the emigrant,
But although he could see that his mother was enjoying the
play
He did not understand that she too identified with the
emigrant,
Only more vigorously than he did.
The playwright, a new name, Brian Friel,
Had two actors, not one, playing Gar O'Donnell,
Gar Public and Gar Private,
And the ex-mental hospital patient's mother Sheila
Immediately saw onstage her own kitchen table:
At one end Sheila Public and at the other end Sheila Private,
And on either side facing one another
Husband and son bickering, skulking, carping, scowling.
Sheila Public sat in helpless silence
Enduring the pair of them, interjecting
The odd futile, conciliatory phrase;
Sheila Private sat in manic hilarity
By turns mocking and scolding the pair of them,
The two males in her life whom she loved,
Yet who caused her almost nothing but grief.
Schizophrenia, here I come!
Philadelphia, how are you!
For unlike the emigrant in Brian Friel's play
A forty-nine-year-old mother in Dublin in 1964
Had not a slave-girl's chance in Egypt of emigrating anywhere.
Ahead of her another forty years in Dublin
Listening to the same old argument, the same old incestuous
nightmare.

The Wrong Box

When her son – not for the first time having wound up
In a hostel for homeless boys in London – was committed
To a mental hospital, and when from a social worker she
    learned
That he had been incarcerated in the leucotomy ward,
Her husband did not want to know about it – but she did;
Alone she took the plane to Heathrow, Easter 1966,
Booked into the Regent's Palace Hotel in Piccadilly,
Succeeded in obtaining a Day Pass for her son,
Met him on a bench in Leicester Square, asked him:
"Would you like to come to a film with me?"
"Which one?" he asked. "You decide," she replied.
"*The Wrong Box*," he said, which was the big hit of the day,
Knowing nothing about it except that it starred all
Of his favourite comedians: Tony Hancock, Peter Cook,
Dudley Moore, John Le Mesurier, Peter Sellers.
They got up from the bench under a leafing maple,
In sunlight of reconciliation crossed Leicester Square
To the Odeon where they sat in the empty dark for three hours
Watching *The Wrong Box* which, whatever else it was, was the
    wrong film.
Possibly also it was the worst British comedy film ever made.
When they came out of *The Wrong Box* the sun had gone in,
The wind was chilly, her eyes blurred with tears
As she kissed him goodbye, he running for the Epsom train
Back to the mental hospital, she going down into the Under-
    ground
To take the Piccadilly Line to Heathrow – "in the opposite
Direction to Cockfosters", her husband had warned her –
Her husband always had a great sense of direction –
"The judge has a great sense of orientation" –
To catch the Aer Lingus Viscount flight back to Dublin
And the curt "How was he – what did you do with him?"
"We went to a film" – "What was it called?' –
"He has got terribly thin, it was called *The Wrong Box*."

The Gallows Tree

Your father was an old-fashioned man,
A man of reams of words or no words at all.
It was always either a feast or a famine.
You couldn't shut him up or
You couldn't get a word out of him.
The day he proposed to me in 1942
I thought he'd never come to the point,
But that was what made him interesting.
He was always dawdling, your father,
While he was talking, always digressing,
Turning down side-roads of a conversation,
Stopping in a gateway he had not noticed before.
We'd been driving around Mayo all day
Revisiting the old haunts and he was talking
Ten to the dozen about Michael Davitt
And the Land League, how that blackthorn bush
On the side of the road was where Michael Davitt
Was born, and that Michael Davitt
More than Daniel O'Connell or Charles Stewart Parnell
Was the man who really set Ireland free
And finally we stopped in Castlebar
And we walked up to the Mall
And it was a lovely evening, but a bit chilly
Because the sun was going down and he started
Into George Robert FitzGerald again,
George Robert FitzGerald of Turlough
And what an extraordinary buck he was,
Chaining his father to a bear and being
A devotee of the Hell Fire Club in Dublin
And winning every duel he fought
And how he was sentenced to hang
And how right here on the Mall in Castlebar
On the gallows tree the rope broke
And how George Robert FitzGerald
Lost his notorious temper for the last time
And upbraided the hangman for not knowing his job
And how George Robert told the hangman
He'd teach him a lesson

And George Robert in a towering rage
Hanged himself on the gallows tree in front of the mob
And your father turned around and said to me:
"Sheila, there's something I want to ask you,
I've been wanting to ask you for a long time,
Will you marry me?" And I said, "Yes"
And he said, "O Sheila, my own"
And he started to cry.
Your father was an old-fashioned man.

Daughters of the Civil War

How could we have known, we who were the daughters of the
    Civil War,
That before we were young women we would be old women?
That we would not have time to climb the mountain
Before the cold fog of marriage leg-ironed each one of us.
How could we have known, girls on the virgin seashore,
That by the end of the Thirties our lives would be over
And that although some of us, such as I in my silk girdle,
Would survive into our eighty-eighth year
For most of us life would be over
By 1942 and the Battle of Stalingrad,
The year I got engaged to be married?
How could we have known that as well as Collins and Childers
There were other murdered men who had shaped our lives
And how a woman is no more impregnable than a seashore
And for no shallow reason picks the wrong man?
There was Niall and Nevin and yet I chose John
And if the reel could be rewound back to its source
There again would be Niall and Nevin, but again I'd choose
    John.
A woman has to choose the man who is wrong
Over and over again
As if she were fast asleep,
Otherwise how would she know she was the same woman?
How would she know the names of the men who'd been slain
In her childhood in the Civil War when she had been fast
    asleep?

Little Old Lady

Mummy shrank as she grew older.
After Daddy died, she became so small
She began to look like a little girl
And, after a period of grief,
To disport like a little girl – the little girl
In the photograph album of 1927
Making hay in Mayo, raking, tossing it,
In the summer before her twelfth birthday.
At seventy-three she beat her way out of the lethargy
Of old age and she began to hop about
Not only the apartment but the city streets,
Beginning conversations with strangers at bus stops
And hanging out in the new space-age shopping centres.
From a sports shop catalogue she purchased
A steel-and-rope trapeze, which she installed
In a niche over the kitchen door.
"It's compact," she confided one lunchtime.
"It folds up and folds down like a dream."
After I'd washed up and dried the dishes
She demonstrated it and teasingly
Tried to persuade me to buy one for myself.
On the morning of her eightieth birthday,
When I'd brought her a gift of a bucket of begonia,
To my chagrin she showed only
A perfunctory interest in my begonia,
Which I had gone to some trouble to purchase.
Instead she stood on the seat of her trapeze
Mocking me as she swung to and fro,
Her little white tennis skirt fluttering
Above her matchstick knees. She cackled:
"Now what do you think of your little old lady?
Do you think she is surplus to requirements?
Well, don't think I'm fishing for compliments."

Golden Mothers Driving West

The inevitable call came from the Alzheimer's nursing home.
Mummy had been sitting there in an armchair for two years
In a top-storey room with two other agèd ladies,
Deborah O'Donoghue and Maureen Timoney.
The call was to say that between 3 and 5 a.m.
The three of them had gone missing from the room.
At first it was thought that all three had slipped
Out the window, ajar in the hot, humid night.
But, no, there were no torsos in the flowerbed.
It transpired that a car had also gone missing.
Was it thinkable they had commandeered a car?
At five in the afternoon the police called
To say that a Polish youth in a car wash in Kinnegad
Had washed and hot-waxed a car for three ladies,
All of whom were wearing golden dressing gowns –
Standard issue golden dressing gowns
Worn by all the inmates of the Alzheimer's nursing home.
Why he remembered them was that he was struck
By the fact that all three ladies were laughing
For the ten minutes it took him to wash the car.
"I am surprised," he stated, "by laughter."
At 9 p.m. the car was sighted in Tarmonbarry
On the Roscommon side of the River Shannon,
Parked at the jetty of the Emerald Star marina.
At 9.30 p.m. a female German child was taken
To the police station at Longford by her stepfather.
The eleven-year-old had earlier told her stepfather
In the cabin of their hired six-berth river cruiser
That she had seen three ladies jump from the bridge.
Her stepfather had assumed his stepdaughter imagined it
As she was, he told police, "a day-dreamer born".
The girl repeated her story to the police:
How three small, thin, agèd ladies with white hair
Had, all at once, together, jumped from the bridge,
Their dressing gowns flying behind them in the breeze.
What colours were the dressing gowns? she was asked.
"They are wearing gold," she replied.
Wreathed on the weir downstream from the bridge

564

Police sub-aqua divers retrieved the three bodies,
One of whom, of course, was my own emaciated mother,
Whose fingerprints were later found on the wheel of the car.
She had been driving west, west to Westport,
Westport on the west coast of Ireland
In the County of Mayo,
Where she had grown up with her mother and sisters
In the War of Independence and the Civil War,
Driving west to Streamstown three miles outside Westport,
Where on afternoons in September in 1920,
Ignoring the roadblocks and the assassinations,
They used walk down Sunnyside by the sea's edge,
The curlews and the oystercatchers,
The upturned black currachs drying out on the stones,
And picnic on the machair grass above the seaweed,
Under the chestnut trees turning autumn gold
And the fuchsia bleeding like troupes of crimson-tutu'd
    ballerinas in the black hedgerows.
Standing over my mother's carcass in the morgue,
A sheep's skull on a slab,
A girl in her birth-gown blown across the sand,
I shut my eyes:
Thank you, O golden mother,
For giving me a life,
A spear of rain.
After a long life searching for a little boy who lives down the
    lane
You never found him, but you never gave up;
In your afterlife nightie
You are pirouetting expectantly for the last time.

My Mother's Secret

Like all women of her generation
My mother had a secret,
Which was that as a young woman
In Paris in the 1930s
She had played the oboe,
But that when she came home

On the eve of war and got married
She put away her oboe
And never played it again.
Only *she* had the key
To the locked drawer
In the dressing table
In the marital bedroom.
Did she in her last years
In her show-stopping loneliness,
Distracted, disorientated,
At night in the mausoleum of her flat
In the red-brick apartment block,
Unlock the drawer,
Take out the silver oboe
From its satin couch
And put it to her lips
And, kiss of kisses,
Shock of shocks,
Horn of horn,
Blow on it?
Did Mrs Balbirnie in the next flat
Hear sounds in the night?
After she died
And her grown-up children
Had divided up
Her personal effects,
I trekked to the edge of the cliff
Above her childhood home
On the west coast of Europe
And holding out my two hands
I presented her silver oboe
As a parent presenting
A newborn baby
To the priest at the altar
Before letting go of it
To watch it plummet
Down into the opening-up beaks of the rocks.

Notes

"Nights in the Gardens of Clare" is the text of an oratorio by Mícheál Ó Súilleabháin performed by the Harmony Row Choir at the Ennis Arts Festival, 22 June 1988 on the occasion of the 400th anniversary of the Spanish Armada.

"The Centre of the Universe" is part of the text of *The Paul Durcan Suite* by Bill Whelan, performed by the London Chamber Orchestra at the National Concert Hall, Dublin, 5 December 1988.

Crazy about Women is the title of the book published simultaneously with the exhibition "Crazy about Women" in the National Gallery of Ireland, 1991.

Give Me Your Hand is the title of the book published simultaneously with the exhibition "Give Me Your Hand" in the National Gallery, London, 1994.

Glossary of Irish Words

A chara: My friend.

Ach, níl aon tinteán mar do thinteán féin: There's no place like home.

An Trá Bhán, an Trá Bhán, / Cá bhfuil m'athair, cá bhfuil mo mháthair?: The White Strand, the White Strand / Where is my father, where is my mother?

Áras an Uachtaráin: The official residence of the President of Ireland.

Blas: Accent, pronunciation.

Bodhrán: Irish tambourine.

Buachaillín: Little boy.

Craic: High-spirited entertainment.

Crannóg: A man-made island on a lake.

Cúl an tSúdaire: The Irish name (meaning Tanner's Corner) of Portarlington, a town in County Laois near the boundary with County Offaly in the midlands of Ireland.

Dáil Éireann: The lower house of the Irish Parliament.

Dún Chaoin: The Irish name (meaning Caon's Fort) of a village in the West Kerry Gaeltacht (Irish-speaking area) at the western tip of the Dingle peninsula.

Fódhla: Ancient name for Ireland.

Garda Síochána: The police force of the Republic of Ireland.

Giolla gan ceann: Headless boy.

Ketchel: Pet name for a cat.

Leithreas: Lavatory.

Macushla: Term of endearment: my dear, my darling.

Mhic: Son.

Mun: Slang for money (not of Gaelic derivation).

Ná Caith Tobac: No smoking.

Ochón: Cry of lamentation.

Óglaigh, Beir bua: The rebels of 1916 were the Volunteers (*Óglaigh*) *na hEireann*. The Provisional IRA of the 1970s hijacked the term to describe themselves. *Beir bua*: Win the victory. (The whole phrase remains a favourite Provisional IRA salutation.)

Poitín: Illicit Irish alcoholic beverage.

Príomh Breitheamh, Uachtarán: Slán: Chief Justice, President: Farewell.

Ruaille buaille: Uproar; confusion; a free-for-all.

Scoraíocht: Visiting neighbours for festive gossip.

Slán agus Beannacht: Farewell, and bless you.

Sliotar: The ball used in hurling.

Taibhdhearc na Gaillimhe: The Galway Theatre, the first Irish-language theatre in Ireland, founded in 1928.

Tír na nÓg: The Land of Youth (Elysium).

Index of Titles

Index of First Lines

579

Passers-by stop to try and help the dying man, 536
Paul Durcan would try the patience of the Queen of Tonga, 376
Peace, 213
Pity about Samson, 336
Playing croquet with Fionnuala on the Alpine Lawn, 63
Please stay in the family, Clovis, 15
Poets, is not this solitary man's own uniquely, 22
Polycarp has quit the priesthood, 32
Pushing my trolley about in the supermarket, 197

Quarter-way down the wrought-iron staircase, 424

Running the relay at twelve, 542

Sally, I was happy with *you*, 91
Scared as I am of a Tom on the wall, 348
She and I are sitting out in the conservatory, 392
"She came home, my Lord, and smashed in the television, 29
She is the kind of person, 144
She rat-tat-tatted on the glass-paned door of our flat-roofed suburban home, 13
She thinks he's a strange, old, lonely, poor creature, 54
She took one oar and I took the other, 28
She wears black always, always black, 549
Sitting up in bed, waiting to die, 485
6.30 a.m. in a roadhouse in Tarnowo Podgorne, 526
Solids and liquids, 297
Spotting, whilst I reversed into a tight parking space, 534

Staring into the marble, I stray into it, 349
Suicidal in Tokyo, 528
Sunday afternoon in August, sunny, warm, 513

"Take a right turn at the Sputnik Cinema", 191
Ted Rice was that abnormal creature – a normal man, 73
Thank Ophelia that's all over, 482
That first year in Cork city – '71/'72, 403
That spring in Dublin, 168
That the smooth blue-and-white lake, 538
That twenty-two page love letter in which, 497
That was that Sunday afternoon in May, 518
The answer to your question is that I am not your mother, 185
The black dog temper of the Durcans, 247
The British Army barracks in Crossmaglen, 156
The Butterfly Collector of Corofin, 59
The day that Father died, 91
The day the Ayatollah Ruhollah Khomeini died, 207
The doctor said to me: Your father needs a *new* head, 61
The drover's path slopes round between the bog-edge, 34
The engagement was to recite for one hour, 472
The first adult book I read was by Isaiah Berlin, 396
The inevitable call came from the Alzheimer's nursing home, 564
The light in the window went out last night, 83
The little cherry tree of my life, 429

584